HARRY BRIDGES

HARRY BRIDGES

*The Rise and Fall of Radical Labor
in the United States*

CHARLES P. LARROWE

LAWRENCE HILL and CO.
New York   Westport

To Peter Millhouse

Copyright © 1972 Lawrence Hill & Co. Publishers, Inc.
All rights reserved
ISBN clothbound edition: 0–88208–000–8
ISBN paperback edition: 0–88208–001–6
Library of Congress catalogue card number: 72–78321

FIRST EDITION NOVEMBER 1972

Manufactured in the United States of America

1 2 3 4 5 6 7 8 9 10 11 12

Foreword

The idea of writing about Harry Bridges first occurred to me in the mid-fifties. I was finishing a book about longshoring, and one day I said excitedly to my wife, "You know, as soon as I get this done, I'm going to start in on one about Bridges." Happily, she knew me better than I knew myself. "Wait at least five years," she cautioned. "You're so impressed with the guy right now you couldn't do an honest book about him."

For once, I took her advice. In fact, I did even better. I waited six years, so it was 1961 when I wrote Bridges to tell him of my intention and to ask if he would cooperate. He didn't answer, nor did he answer a follow-up letter I sent him a few weeks later.

His staff at union headquarters (the union is the West Coast International Longshoremen's and Warehousemen's Union), by contrast, could scarcely have been more encouraging. "Come on out," they urged me. (I was living in Michigan.) "You'll have access to all the stuff in the records except Harry's personal files. And don't be put off by his negative attitude. He won't interfere with what you're doing and, anyway, he'll come around in time."

They were wrong. He didn't interfere, but he never came around. In 1962, the staff let me use an empty office just off the rooms where the records are kept, and I worked there for a year. Union headquarters is in a small building, and I saw a fair amount of

Bridges. Before long, we were on a first-name, casually friendly basis, but the one time I managed to corner him for a talk about the book he made it clear he was against my doing it.

It seemed reasonable enough to me that he would be. For twenty-five years, the FBI and a pride of private and other government sleuths had been following him around, keeping a record of everything he said and did. I could understand that the thought of my prying into his affairs must have been repulsive. Most of what had been written about him, moreover, had been unsympathetic, much of it unfair.

"For you to do the book right," he told me, his feet up on the corner of his old wooden desk (when he moved them off, I noticed that over the years they'd worn a groove there), "I'd have to let you sit here in this office for six months, watching me operate and asking me questions when I have time.

"And," he said emphatically, "I'm not going to do that!"

I decided to go ahead, anyway.

When the manuscript was finished and several persons friendly to him had read it and pronounced it balanced but on the whole sympathetic, I decided to send a copy to Bridges. He'd said he didn't want me to. "Look," he had told me, "if I read it and correct mistakes and make suggestions, that'll make it an authorized biography. I sure as hell don't want that!"

His reaction to what I'd written took me by surprise, nevertheless. Looking back, I realize it shouldn't have. As Marx once said in a comment on the fugitive quality of history, we can no more accept at face value an era's view of itself than we can a man's opinion of his own character.

"I have gone over the manuscript," Bridges wrote me a week after he got it.

> I don't feel like discussing it with you; on the other hand, if I just pass it over and say nothing, you and other people could assume that I accepted or agreed with what the manuscript contains. I certainly don't. Not by a long shot, and I will give you my reasons.
>
> The book as written just bears out my first reaction to what you asked me to do some years ago—and that was to cooperate with you in writing a book about me and the union. I didn't think then that either the union or myself would get fair treatment, and the book sure vindicates my judgment.

I would say it is hardly more than a series of distortions, half-truths, and, in many cases, outright lies.

I waited several weeks before replying. Then I wrote him that while I was deeply sorry his reaction was so negative, I had re-read the book after getting his letter, and I still thought of it as balanced and as presenting him and the union in a favorable light. I reminded him that I had told him when I was starting out that I was prepared to spend whatever time was necessary to run down every lead, interview everyone who could add to the story, search through archives and Presidential libraries.

"I appeal to you," I concluded, "if you have in mind specific half-truths, distortions, lies, or mistakes, to send them to me so that I can substitute truth for error. I hasten to assure you that a note at the front of the book will make it unmistakably clear to the reader that you in no way or at any time endorsed the book, that consistently, over those nine years, you opposed my doing it."

He never replied.

But as I think back over all the people who helped me with this book, the one who jumps immediately to mind, paradoxically, is Bridges himself. Many of the people I talked to are so devoted to him and to what he has stood for that if he had passed the word not to cooperate with me, many doors would have been closed in my face. Despite his opposition, he never did so.

Staff members at union headquarters who were especially helpful—without exception, everyone who worked there made me feel welcome—were Linc Fairley, then the union's research director; the late Anne Rand, who for many years was the union's librarian; her successor, Margery Canright; Bill Glazier, who was for a long time Bridges's administrative assistant; Morris Watson, founder and editor for two decades of the union's newspaper; Sid Roger, who succeeded him; and Henry Schmidt, who was with Bridges from the earliest days of the union.

The late Paul St. Sure, who headed the employers' association from the 1950s until his death in the late sixties, was very generous in his cooperation with me, as was Sam Kagel, the industry's permanent arbitrator. Aubrey Grossman, one of the San Francisco attorneys who defended Bridges in his early trials, spent many hours patiently guiding me through the legal labyrinths of political trials. Walter Lambert and Conrad Edises gave me valuable help, especially when I was groping for a key to events on the West Coast waterfront in the early 1930s. Andy Knipp, a rank-and-filer who works on the docks in San Pedro, was almost embarrassingly helpful, as was the late Lou Krainock, who, in the early sixties, was organizing farm workers under a modest subsidy from the longshoremen's and teamsters' unions. I owe a special debt to Otto Hagel, who prowled about the Bay Area waterfront with me and endlessly discussed the book as it developed. I am grateful, too, to Sam Darcy, who in the early thirties headed the Communist Party in San Francisco, for the long talks I had with him and for reading the manuscript.

When I was gathering material in Hawaii, Dave Thompson, educational director for the ILWU in the Islands, was tireless in his assistance and encouragement. He read chapter eight and made many helpful suggestions, most of which I gratefully incorporated. Priscilla Shishido, the union's librarian in Honolulu, and Ah Quon McElrath, its social worker, were most helpful. Eddie Tangen, one of the union's international representatives in Hawaii, let me tag along with him when he went from island to island settling grievances, negotiating contracts, meeting with employers. John Arisumi and Takumi Akama, local union officers on Maui and Kauai, dropped everything to arrange interviews for me and to show me the union in action on their islands.

Shelley Mark, a friend from my graduate school days, was head of Hawaii's Economic Development Bureau when I was there, and arranged introductions to a large number of employers and government people I wanted to see. George Won, a former student of mine, is on the sociology faculty at the University of Hawaii and put in many hours with me, talking with fellow sociologists and others about the union's impact on Hawaii. Phil Mayer, theatre critic on the *Honolulu Bulletin,* gave me some off-beat insights into the union's place in the Islands. Bill Norwood, who was then Governor Burns's administrative assistant, generously shared with me his fund (he had been a reporter for years) of Hawaiian social and political lore. Governor Burns, himself, let me take up much of two afternoons while he answered my questions with arresting candor. Later, after he had read a draft of chapter eight, we had another long talk. He kept the draft, and a month later sent it along with a batch of most useful criticisms and corrections.

Librarians, as they always are, were enormously helpful. Margaret Brickett, at the U.S. Department of Labor, deserves special thanks, and librarians at the National Archives and the Roosevelt

FOREWORD ix

and Truman Libraries could not have done more. I am deeply grateful, too, to several of my colleagues—Chuck Craypo, Herbert Kisch and Harold Reinholds in particular—for reading parts of the manuscript, and for sticking with me over the years, somehow managing to show interest when I brought up the subject again and again and again.

Anyone who has written a book knows how important the attitude of secretaries who type the manuscript can be to the author's morale. I was extraordinarily lucky to work with nine very capable and unfailingly encouraging people (a lot of secretaries come and go in nine years): Karen Groce, Jan Kolles, Betty Kronemeyer, Lois Lee, Jean Moeller, Ruth Monroe, Rita Moore, Carolyn Schmidt, and Ellen Wagner.

The Rabinowitz Foundation made it possible for me to spend a fourteen-month sabbatical working in San Francisco and, later, five weeks in Hawaii.

I have saved for the last two people whose help has been especially valuable. Nora Shapiro worked long and patiently with me on style, content, and organization; and Larry Hill read and re-read the manuscript in the several stages it passed through, always with a mixture of valuable criticism and encouragement. Would that every author should have such good fortune in his publisher.

My determination to go ahead was reinforced by the judgment of my son, Peter, who read parts of the manuscript from time to time. He assured me it was going to be a good book.

C. P. Larrowe
East Lansing, Michigan

Contents

HARRY BRIDGES

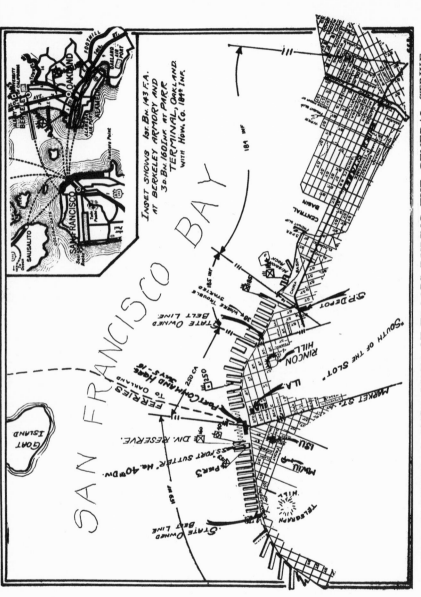

SKETCH SHOWING DISPOSITION OF TROOPS DURING THE GENERAL STRIKE

In addition to the dispositions shown here, a command of Infantry and Field Artillery was stationed at the Port of Stockton.

Up From Down Under

Who is Harry Bridges? Harry Bridges is a British agent, sent here to disrupt the American merchant marine.
A SAN FRANCISCO SHIPOWNER, IN 1934.

"THE TROUBLE WITH YOU," Harry Bridges once told one of his staff, "is you don't have a working-class background."

"Why damn you, Harry," the staff member retorted. "I'll match my working-class background against yours anytime. My old man was a printer all his life. And what was yours? A goddamn realtor."

Bridges may share the classic trade unionist's distrust of the intellectual, but his own childhood in Melbourne, Australia, could scarcely have been more solidly middle–class. His father actually was a realtor and the family was well off. His Irish Catholic mother had been brought to Australia by her parents and the six Bridges children, of whom Harry was the oldest, were also raised in the Church although their father was a Protestant. Harry had a parochial school education and was an altar boy for four years.

When Harry finished high school at fourteen, his father sent him out to collect rents, assuming that his first-born son would enter the family business. It was a painful experience for Harry. Some of the tenants were poor, and young Bridges thought it was cruel to take rent money from them. Then he found a way out. He collected rent from tenants who could pay and loaned money to those who couldn't. Meanwhile, he tried to explain to his father that a realtor's life wasn't for him. Before long, his father gave in, taking Bridges's younger brother into the firm.

Harry's second job, clerking in a Melbourne stationery store, was as dull as rent–collecting had been distasteful. He had trouble keeping his mind on his work, too, for he was reading the adventure stories of Jack London, whose *Sea Wolf* called him to the sea. Another London book, *The Iron Heel*, confirmed the anti–capitalist outlook that characterized him in later life.

His desire for a life of adventure was reinforced by talks with his uncle Renton, a Labor Party official who lived nearby and with whom Bridges spent much of his time. Renton Bridges was a glamorous figure. He had sailed before the mast, panned for gold, dived for pearls, and foot–slogged in South Africa as a volunteer in the Boer War. He told his nephew that when he realized what a dirty war it was, he and some of his comrades threw down their rifles and came home.

When Bridges was fifteen, his father helped him get a job on a small sailing ship that ran between Melbourne and Tasmania. Some of Bridges's shipmates were Wobblies, and they enthralled him with their stories of strikes and job actions, their talk of one big union for everyone, and their IWW MOTTO: "An injury to one is an injury to all." Much of what they had to say reinforced what his uncle had told Harry, but he learned even more from his own experience.

His first two years at sea were a cram-course in working class philosophy and tactics. He had only been sailing for a few weeks when he went on strike in support of another union, and before the year was out he was caught up in a general strike. It was an unforgettable experience for a boy barely a month past his sixteenth birthday.

Forty years later, Bridges told Bill Glazier, a union executive about his experiences:

> I was just a young kid, but I can still remember it. We piled off the ships in Melbourne for a stop-work meeting on the front. There were two or three thousand men gathered there and the meeting was lit up by torches. The whole country was shut down and even the electricity had been turned off.
>
> The newspapers and the respectable labor leaders were all screaming that the strike was an IWW plot to sabotage the war effort, but the rank–and–file was all for supporting the railwaymen since the principle of unionism was involved. "One out, all out," that was our slogan.
>
> Well, we listened to the speeches, then we all took torches and marched two or three miles to an army post on the outskirts of Melbourne where they were assembling troops to use against the strikers. They put up soap boxes right in the middle of the post

and striking longshoremen, sailors and railwaymen got up and explained to the lads in uniform that the strike was for the principle of unionism. Well we convinced the troops or maybe we scared the authorities so much they didn't dare use the soldiers. Anyway, it was a successful demonstration.

That was my first big strike—1917. Renegade Australian Labor Party officials were in power then. And the labor politicians broke the strike with a company union and used farmers, school boys and university students as scabs. Then they screened all of the returning workers for "IWW tendencies." That was what they were after in those days.

Twice Bridges was shipwrecked in the heavy storms his father had thought would discourage him from following the sea, for Bass Strait, between Australia and Tasmania, is notoriously rough. Between trips he went home to his family. He became a hero to his younger brother and his sisters, who listened, enthralled, to his sea stories, but his mother's distress over the dangers of his new life and his father's disapproval of his new ideas and new friends gradually made his visits home less and less attractive. "During the war, when I was 17, I went to sea," he has said.

I was a good religious boy and I didn't know a thing. From some of the things I saw and learned about I decided that religion wasn't much like what Christ taught, and when I got home and talked about it my mother and aunt covered up their ears and said "Don't dare say such things." I was just asking about them.

Well, I took a trip that gave me a look at India and another at Suez, and what I saw there didn't seem to line up with what my father had told me about the dear old British. Then I got "home" and saw London. It was the filthiest, most unhealthy place I ever had seen. And the people in the slums were worse than the natives in India and Port Said—dirty, nasty, no good. So this, I say, is British democracy. Why, back in Australia everybody had enough to eat, everybody had a decent place to live, for years we'd had a labor government and workmen's compensation and old-age pensions and everything of that sort. So I kept traveling around, and the more I saw the more I knew that there was something wrong with the system.

Bridges had been sailing on Australian ships for four years when, on April 13, 1920, his ship put in at San Francisco. He came down the gangplank with his sea bag and his mandolin, paid the $10 head tax required of immigrants in those days, and became a resident of the United States. A week after his arrival, he transferred his membership from the Australian Seamen's Union to the AFL Sailors' Union of the Pacific. For the next year, he worked in the easygoing pattern familiar to seamen, shipping out on one ship after another, with layovers on the beach between trips.

Then came the 1921 seamen's strike in which the sailors' union was destroyed, and Bridges's first encounter with the American Legion, which over the years made his deportation back to Australia one of its major projects. "My experience with them," he has said, "runs back as far as my entire experience in this country: the 1921 seamen's strike in New Orleans, when the employers advertised for strikebreakers and they said 'Legion men preferred.'"

It was the 1921 strike, too, which led him into a brief encounter with the Industrial Workers of the World, which the government was to hold against him twenty years later. He mentioned it to Theodore Dreiser when the writer interviewed him in 1940 for a magazine story.

"Were you working as a longshoreman?" Dreiser asked.

"No, I was a sailor."

"Yet you joined the IWW. But why did you join it?"

"It was right after the sailors' strike in 1921—I saw how the A.F. of L. sold out the strike and that's why I joined. I believed in unions for the working man. As I told you, I had been to England and I didn't like what I had seen—the way the mass had been beaten down—made spineless . . . ."

The IWW, in its way, was as much a disappointment for Bridges as the AFL had been. When he had first heard about the Wobblies from his Australian shipmates, he had been favorably impressed with their tactic of shutting down the job without advance notice as a way of getting the boss to see their point of view. He was a member only a few months when he decided the Wobblies were hopelessly impractical.

"When I found out what the aims and purposes of the IWW were," he said in his 1939 deportation hearing,

I got out fast. Their aims are syndicalistic, I think. They are more or less an anarchist group. In other words, they prate and carry on under a program of extreme rank–and–file–ism, and all they succeed in doing is creating a lot of general disruption and bog-

ging down the advance of labor generally under a cloak or a
guise of democracy.

We believe in strikes, and we believe in direct action under the
proper circumstances and at the proper time when it is the best
thing to do. But there comes a time that you can go a little too
far with direct action. The IWW philosophy was never to sign an
agreement, for example; never to arbitrate; never to mediate;
never to consolidate. . . . They gained many improvements and
benefits for the people they represent, but they are absolutely opposed to any type of political action.

After the strike, Bridges was on the beach for a few weeks, waiting for a ship, so he filed for his first citizenship papers. Then, one
day in February, 1922, after he'd been at sea for a year, he decided
he wanted a change from the sea. He headed south for a few
months, first to the northeast coast of South America, then up
through Central America and Mexico. He was there in the middle
of the Obregon reform administration, and what he saw and experienced in Mexico impressed him.

"Mexico thrilled me," he told Dreiser.

Whether the people had little or nothing they seemed better
suited to the world in which they lived—not as miserable or
beaten or hopeless as the poor people in England . . . .

Seamen, for example, had the best protection and wages in the
world. Also shore workers. For instance, in case of a strike, the
government barricaded the plant—that is, put a group of soldiers
around it to see that it didn't operate. Then the workers, employers and representatives of the government sat down together
and arbitrated until the dispute was settled. The employers
weren't allowed to use strikebreakers either, and if it was a just
grievance the employees had, they won, of course.

But nowhere else in the world had I ever seen that before and
it struck me as a forceful social mechanism that might be employed anywhere by governments, as between the strong and the
weak anywhere . . . .

"Not only that, but there were other laws, too—the laws relating
to the oil fields—because part of the work in the oil field was dangerous and the protection of their workers was stringent. I went as
a rigger, but part of my work was hauling rigs and part explosives.
Being a helper I rode around in a truck that packed explosives—a

truck that followed the pipe line. Under the law, as it was then, if I was killed, my widow, if I had one, was paid a pension. Also a big lump sum down, also a proper burial, etc. It was much better than our workmen's compensation laws today. But if I or anyone was willing to waiver his rights—that is, sign a waiver—saying that I had no wife or heirs and turning over all my effects to the company as my executor I made good wages and had other privileges. . . . I was one who did that."

Returning to San Francisco in May, Bridges shipped out again for what turned out to be the last time, as a quartermaster on a Coast and Geodetic Survey ship. While it was cruising up the coast he met his future wife, Agnes Brown, a Scottish girl who had been brought to the United States by her parents when she was twelve. Not long after, he quit the sea, settled down in San Francisco and got a job as a longshoreman. He liked the atmosphere of the waterfront, and he liked the work. Longshoring was, of course, the natural occupation for an ex-sailor, even though working conditions were wretched.

In order to get a job in those days a longshoreman had to go down to the Embarcadero at six in the morning, where he joined a growing throng of men who stood around in the street across from the Ferry Building, waiting for the hiring to begin a little before eight o'clock. From time to time, a hiring foreman would appear and the milling crowd would form into a shape–up around him. There were always two or three times the number of men he needed, so the foreman often picked his men in return for a kickback. "We were hired off the streets like a bunch of sheep," Bridges once recalled bitterly, "standing there from six o'clock in the morning, in all kinds of weather."

If the shape-up was still in progress at eight o'clock, the crowd of longshoremen in the street was an obstacle course for disembarking ferry passengers from the East Bay in a great hurry to get up Market Street to their offices. So another indignity was inflicted upon the men. "At the moment of eight o'clock," Bridges added, "we were herded along by the police to allow the commuters to go across the street from the Ferry Building, more or less like a slave market in the Old World countries of Europe."

To get steady work, longshoremen had to join a company union the shipowners had organized after breaking an AFL union in 1916. They called it the Blue Book and it was designed to prevent a *bona fide* union. The shipowners had signed a closed shop contract with it, to run until 1924.

Bridges was determined to stay out of the company union if he could. But how to do it and still get work on the docks was a problem. "I spent close to a couple of years," he has said, " 'pirating' on the waterfront, which means trying to find a job wherever and whenever it might be by standing around in front of the docks and waiting for a job. During this time I worked for many bosses, but I invariably lost my job because I wasn't paid up in the Blue Book."

Bridges was already in trouble because of his resistance to the Blue Book, but when the company union contract with the ship-owners ran out in 1924, he got in even deeper:

"There was an attempt in 1924 to revive the OLD UNION," he recalled in his first deportation hearing, "and I recall the case because I joined up just prior to Labor Day, 1924. And we entered in the Labor Day parade on Labor Day. Around 400 of us were members of the labor union, which was the ILA [International Longshoremen's Association, AFL] at the time. . . .

"And we paraded up Market Street in September 1924, and the company union agents stood on the sidewalk and took all our names down, all of those that they knew or could recognize, and we were all blacklisted for a couple of years, for the next couple of years, for about '25 and '26. We couldn't work at any of the regular jobs, and quite a group of us just got by, hit or miss, where we could. By and large, those who were citizens of the United States found employment out at the army transport docks.

"Those that were not citizens, and that is the category I was in, we generally picked up a little work at the old docks where the Japanese ships used to come in. Strange, but it happens to be true, that the only line that didn't do business with the company union, the Blue Book, was the Japanese lines. So there was always a few hours' work to be picked up down there.

"And then during the spring of the year, when the fishing vessels went to Alaska, they used to send up quite a fleet of big square-riggers at that time, as well as some steamboats later, and we could pick up a little work there. Then a few odd jobs, car–loading and one thing and another."

A few months after the Labor Day parade, Bridges married Agnes Brown. He now had three mouths to feed, for she brought with her a young son from an earlier marriage. About a year later they had a daughter of their own. 1925 was a bad year for Bridges in more than one way. The company union was firmly entrenched for another five years, having renewed its contract with the employers after the longshoremen's abortive attempt to replace it with a real union. Looking back on what it was like on the docks in those days, Bridges remembered it as a vicious speed-up:

> And when I say speed–up I mean it was pretty killing . . . . The men, the various longshoremen, both as individuals and as members of a gang, they were driven at a pretty hard pace. Because by that time the group of longshoremen on the waterfront were about evenly divided into two groups. You had one group of men that you might say worked steady, relatively speaking, and another group of men that worked casually. We used various names for them, but generally you had a situation like this: The men that were working steadily, they were in the docks working on the job, and twenty-four hours a day, certainly sixteen, eighteen hours a day, there was always a large group of men standing outside the docks, see, ready and willing to take the place of any person working inside that wasn't working fast enough. Now, in order to understand that, it should be borne in mind that the men standing outside willing to take a job of a so-called man working steady, merely had in mind making a living. They were pretty desperate, hard up, wanted to eat, hungry. . . .
>
> Speed–up simply means that every opportunity that presented itself, the number of men in the gang or the number of men per operations was reduced. And therefore, you had a situation where two men might be required to do the work of, say, eight men, where under normal circumstances without any pressure, or in the absence of any type of bona fide trade union organization, you would actually have eight men doing a job. But in order to save costs the men were knocked off and two men were pushed into doing the work.
>
> I worked down on that waterfront there in the hold of a ship where there was only two of us in the hold, stowing the ship.
>
> I would say, and I have found out since by research, that without a question of doubt, the output per man and per gang in San Francisco during those years or on the Pacific Coast during those years was higher than any other country in the world.

Longshoremen and employers who were on the waterfront in those days remember Bridges as a good worker, a skilled rigger and winch driver. In 1926 and 1927 he gave in and kept his dues paid up in the Blue Book Union. Late in 1927, he lost his job when an employer held back some of his pay and he asked the Blue Book delegate to handle the grievance for him.

One day he ran into Ras Karlson, a former shipmate who was now the boss of a steel–handling gang. Karlson invited him to join the gang, and he stayed in it until 1932. "My gang," Karlson told me after he retired, "handled the steel for the Fox Theatre [for many years a rococo landmark on upper Market Street until it was razed in the early sixties, to the accompaniment of anguished cries from old San Franciscans], the San Mateo Bridge, and cables for the Bay Bridge—they came in here on ships, did you know that?—rails for the Market Street Railway. When they had really big stuff to handle, that's when they called for Ras Karlson's gang.

"Harry was a good worker," Karlson said of him, "first rate. He was happy–go–lucky in those days. A good mixer." Bridges's own recollection of his days in the gang was much like Karlson's:

I worked in a steady gang for quite a number of years. You maintained your job in a steady gang because of your ability to keep going over a long period of time at a high rate of speed. In other words, we produced. I worked for many years for the steel company. We worked ships of the United States Steel, the Isthmian Line, and our gang was a great steel gang.

I was the rigger in the gang. So we used to be shunted around to the various jobs where we unloaded steel from the ships; that is, not only long steel, sixty or seventy–foot steel, forty–foot, but in addition prefabricated steel. I worked ships, for example, that unloaded quite a bit of steel that went into the Golden Gate Bridge and the San Francisco Bay Bridge. We worked almost all the steel that went into the Carquinex Straits Bridge.

And that was—that type of work we generally needed gangs there that were pretty highly skilled in their work so they could produce any tonnage at all. It was pretty dangerous work. Now, if you got a gang of workers that didn't know what they were doing, you could poke around all day on a ship and not haul out one piece of steel.

In the summer of 1928, Bridges remembered that he had been procrastinating about becoming a United States citizen since filing the first papers in 1921. Now, the seven-year limit for filing his final papers was almost up, so in June, he went to the immigration office in San Francisco. A clerk told him to appear in federal district court with his two witnesses on September 9th and he'd get his final papers. He appeared on schedule, flanked by his witnesses, only to be turned away. The clerk had misinformed him. All final steps, including the granting of the final papers, should have been taken in July, before the seven years had expired.

He re-filed for citizenship, and this time was told: "Come back in two years and apply for your second papers." When the two years were up, Bridges did not have the $20 he needed to take out the second papers. "At that time it took me two or three weeks to earn $20, and I had a wife and two children to support," he said later.

Another longshoreman who got into trouble with the Blue Book was Lee Holman, who was later to play a grotesque role in the campaign to get Bridges. Holman had been longshoring in San Francisco on and off since 1911. He had drifted down to the waterfront from the San Joaquin Valley, where his ancestors had pioneered. Holman's pioneer background made him feel superior to the more recent immigrants who, barely able to speak English, worked on the waterfront in large numbers.

In 1924, Holman was expelled from the Blue Book for supporting the AFL. Nevertheless, like Bridges, he stayed on the waterfront, picking up a job when he could. Then, in 1931, he was jolted by another effort to organize a real union on the docks. This time, it was spearheaded by the Marine Workers' Industrial Union but the campaign never got off the ground. Bridges explained why it didn't when he was on the stand in his 1950 trial (see chapter nine):

> . . . the Marine Workers' Industrial Union was an organization affiliated to what at that time was known as the "Red International of Trade Unions;" generally understood to be a Communist–affiliated or controlled organization. The Red International of Trade Unions or the TUUL (Trade Union Unity League) or TUEL (Trade Union Educational League), as it was known at that time, aimed at organizing longshoremen and seamen into one union, industrially . . . . But they didn't catch on at all because, although their program was pretty revolutionary, pretty idealistic, and . . . despite the fact that the people felt pretty desperate, they didn't cotton too much to . . . their political views.

To Holman, even the remote possibility of a communist–influenced union getting a foothold on the docks was alarming. He wrote Joe Ryan, president of the ILA in New York, to warn him that he had better get busy if he didn't want to lose San Francisco to the Communists.

Ryan's reply was only mildly encouraging—he sent neither organizer nor money—but in September, 1931, Holman met with eight other longshoremen to see what they could do about getting an AFL union started again. They decided to establish a permanent organization and to ask Ryan for a charter. They chose Holman as temporary president and business manager, and on his recommendation—Holman told them he had had a letter from Ryan advising him on organizing strategy—they decided not to begin recruiting members but to continue with a small membership until further orders from New York.

While Holman and his corporal's guard were awaiting orders from Ryan, the Marine Workers' Industrial Union tried a new approach. It started publishing a mimeographed bulletin, the *Waterfront Worker,* which concentrated on the problems and grievances of longshoremen rather than on the global issues which, in the past, had preoccupied its leaflets and throwaways.

The *Waterfront Worker* was launched from the rented room of a MWIU member. A used mimeograph machine was bought for five dollars, and there were plenty of unemployed seamen and longshoremen willing to get out the paper and peddle it on the waterfront. The paper had no official or permanent editor, only an editorial group whose membership fluctuated from issue to issue. No names appeared on the masthead, and news items and letters to the editor were signed by pseudonyms.

The first issue came out in December, 1932, and sold for one cent a copy. "We figured if we put a price on the paper," one of the editors has said, "people wouldn't throw it away." The 350 copies sold out in the first half-hour, and a second edition was run off and hustled down to the docks. Page one stories were about the ten-cent wage cut scheduled to go into effect on January 1, 1933, the employers' plan to get rid of older, experienced longshoremen and replace them with younger men, and the names of gang bosses and foremen who had scabbed in 1919 or who pushed the speed-up. Inside was a long historical piece which sought to show that the frame-up of Tom Mooney was directly linked to the 1916 longshoremen's strike. A good deal of space was devoted to news of what was happening in other ports on the Coast.

The impact of the *Waterfront Worker* was immediate. "There was an undercurrent of restlessness on the waterfront when we started putting out our paper," Mitch Slobodek, one of the editors, said, "but no direction. The paper gave one."

The second issue, which appeared in February, 1933, put forward the MWIU program: more men in a longshore gang, a fight against further wage cuts, a reduction in sling loads. Slobodek, who wrote the Tom Mooney story, had a piece entitled, "Lessons of the 1919 Longshore Strike." In 1919 the shipowners had had the cooperation of the mayor, "Sunny Jim" Rolph, a former shipowner, and the Chamber of Commerce, and the longshoremen had supinely allowed scabs to take their places. The article contended:

> Through their press, the shipowners made the claim that most of the men were against the strike, which they said was forced by a "radical minority" of the union calling for a rising vote instead of a secret ballot. . . . They followed this up with a refusal to meet in conference with the rank and file strike committee. On October 14th when the fatal mistake was made of letting the strike be taken out of the hands of the rank–and–file committee, the shipowners made even more arrogant demands that the negotiations be taken out of the hands of the officials and put into the hands of "appointed" men on the bigger docks, evidently having certain "safe" ones in mind. Compliance with these maneuvers added to the strength of the shipowners and gave them more opportunity to work within the union.
>
> Another factor in the final betrayal was the role played by the A.F. of L. officials. The Central Labor Council stabbed the longshoremen in the back by proposing that the shipowners' demand for a secret ballot be granted, and by urging a compromise without a fight. Casey of the teamsters by a subterfuge prevented his members from striking in sympathy. The same can be said of the officials of the International Seaman's Union.

From the first, the *Waterfront Worker* attacked the AFL and Andrew Furuseth, the eighty–year–old head of the West Coast sailors' union, for their opposition to one big union for all maritime workers. The paper was even more caustic in its appraisal of Joe Ryan, describing his ILA in the East as a racket, run by gunmen. Ryan's San Francisco branch, after Holman presented himself as its spokesman, came under continuous fire for general inaction and for Holman's refusal to call a meeting of the hundreds of longshoremen who had signed ILA pledge cards. The point that the *Waterfront Worker* was trying to make was an obvious one: the right union for the longshoremen was the MWIU. But while the paper helped whet the longshoremen's appetite for a union of their own in place of the Blue Book, it failed to persuade them that the MWIU was the answer.

Instead, the success of the AFL union was insured in mid–summer, when Ryan sent Holman the charter for a new San Francisco longshore local. It was designated Local 38-79 (38 was the number of the Pacific Coast District of the ILA). Within a few months, every longshoreman in San Francisco seemed to have an ILA button. But not everyone in San Francisco was as pleased as the longshoremen with the issuance of the charter.

A week or so after Ryan sent the charter out to San Francisco, Paul Scharrenberg, an official of the sailors' union who was also secretary of the California State Federation of Labor, wired Ryan, urging him to withdraw Local 38-79's franchise, and in its place to charter the Blue Book union as a local of the ILA. "Your strange maneuvering," he scolded, "will blast the prospects of organizing San Pedro and San Diego. Chartering the Holman group will cause bitter antagonism of shipowners. I therefore earnestly recommend that you revoke charter already issued."

Ryan ignored the telegram. The longshoremen, encouraged by getting the ILA charter, were even more encouraged when President Roosevelt signed into law the National Industrial Recovery Act, Section 7(a) of which put the New Deal on the side of unions by requiring industries to establish minimum working conditions and guarantee that workers could bargain collectively with their employers through unions of their own choosing.

To most San Francisco longshoremen, the question now became not whether they would have a union of their own instead of the Blue Book; the NRA made that a virtual certainty. Nor was it which union they would support, the ILA or the MWIU. The new charter settled that in favor of the ILA. Now they wanted to know what kind of a union their local in San Francisco was going to be and who was going to control it.

It was soon apparent that the ILA under Holman's leadership was not going to be aggressive enough to stand up to the shipowners. Once the NRA came into existence, Holman and his supporters took the position that if a man was fired for wearing an ILA button on the job, the solution was to report it to the local NRA board. The government, Holman contended over Bridges's opposition, would see that justice was done.

By July, 1933, three groups had emerged and were competing for control of the union. Holman's was the largest and attracted the conservative longshoremen, which included the Irish Catholics, a sizeable bloc on the San Francisco waterfront. A second group formed around two incongruous leaders, William Lewis and Fred

West. Lewis, known in waterfront circles as Burglar Bill because of a minor brush with the law in his youth, had been a member of the AFL longshoremen's union that had been broken in 1919. He was a unionist in the tradition of the AFL: militant on economic issues but politically a conservative. Fred West, by contrast, was a militant on both fronts. He was district organizer in San Francisco of the Proletarian Party, a small Marxist sect which fell ideologically somewhere between the Communist and Socialist Labor Parties. A coalition led by Lewis and West couldn't last, but they were temporarily thrust upon each other by their common aversion both to Holman's timid leadership of the ILA and the crimson hue of the MWIU.

A third group, the smallest, was a rallying point for the most radical longshoremen, including the handful of Communists who worked on the waterfront. It took its name from a building named Albion Hall where it held its meetings.

"There was never any question that Harry would head up 'Albion Hall,'" B. B. Jones, an Albion Hall member, told me in 1967. "He had a lot of good ideas, he was always there when meetings were called, and most important, he'd had more experience than any of the rest of us had had. Don't forget, he was in a sailors' union down in Australia for several years. Hell, he knew more about what to do than the rest of us combined.

"That goes for those of us who were in the Party, too. We used to study a lot, and we had a pretty good theoretical grasp of what it was all about, but when it came to practical knowledge and what to do from one day to the next, we just naturally turned to Harry. He always had an answer."

In his first deportation hearing, Bridges was asked why he had thought it necessary to organize Albion Hall instead of accepting Holman's leadership. He explained the shipowners' preference for the Blue Book and the support some AFL officials were giving it, as well as his belief that Holman was an employers' agent. If a militant group were not active within the local, he explained:

". . . we could see our union smashed, and there was great danger that the company union would be stronger than ever. It was necessary to organize a group of people to begin to lay down some policy in that union to overcome the disruption and the wrecking that was going on."

Albion Hall's first proposal was that the longshoremen's union should solve its problems by self–help: strikes, slowdowns and job actions, rather than relying upon the NRA as Holman proposed. It was the second part of Albion Hall's program that seemed revolutionary to the AFL old guard: The union should have regular meetings. Officers should render a financial accounting from time to time. And the local should adopt a democratic constitution.

From the beginning, Albion Hall was richer in leadership and organizing talent than the other ILA factions, foreshadowing Bridges's ability throughout the years to attract to his cause remarkably talented people such as lawyers, researchers, organizers and editors.

During the summer of 1933, the ineffective ILA leadership called no meetings in which the longshoremen could decide on policy, so Albion Hall began to call for job action.

"Before we got to be generally known along the waterfront," Bridges said in his 1939 deportation hearing, "we were letting our presence be felt on the docks where we regularly worked. We were the ones who received complaints from the men and then relayed them to the foremen. We took specific action against the speed–up by slowing up at the winches and in the hold. Soon the gains this rank and file group worked with became known as the beefers. Other men on the docks watched and saw that we were getting away with it and began to imitate us."

Meanwhile delegates from ports in Washington and Oregon were meeting in Portland to draft a proposal for an NRA hearing in Washington, D.C. to establish conditions for the maritime industry. By meeting more than two months before the hearing, the ILA delegates who drew up the labor provisions gave themselves ample time to circulate their proposal up and down the coast before it was to be presented in Washington. This served several purposes beyond the primary one. Perhaps most important, it provided a program around which the ILA recruited new members. Moreover, by submitting the proposal for discussion to its membership up and down the coast, the union gained rank–and–file support for its contention that longshoremen in all Pacific Coast ports should bargain as one coastwide unit.

After the hearing was held in November, 1933, the code was approved by General Hugh S. Johnson, national NRA administrator, but the President refused to give it his sanction. FDR never explained his reasons for not signing it, but a year later an Assistant Secretary of Commerce explained that a shipping code would run afoul of treaties with foreign nations whose ships used our ports. The code was lost, but the labor provisions which the ILA delegates had drawn up were easily transformed into a set of six bargaining demands of the union. These were: 1) that the ILA should be the exclusive bargaining agent for all Pacific Coast longshore-men; 2) that the contract should be coastwide instead of there being a separate contract in each port; 3) that employers and union representatives in each port should eliminate surplus labor by em-ploying only men who worked full–time as longshoremen; 4) that when employers needed longshoremen, they would hire them through ILA hiring halls, with ILA members getting preference in employment; 5) that the regular workday should be six hours, and the normal work week thirty; 6) that the straight–time hourly wage should be $1.00, with time–and–a–half for overtime.

While longshoremen in the Northwest were pinning their hopes on the NRA hearing in Washington, longshoremen in San Fran-cisco were having a disillusioning experience with the local branch of the NRA. Several times when Lee Holman went to the NRA office with complaints that men were being discriminated against because they were ILA members, the Blue Book counter–charged that the ILA was intimidating men to quit the Blue Book and join the ILA. Finally, the NRA turned the complaints over to a tripar-tite board appointed by George Creel, the NRA administrator in San Francisco.

A few days before the board handed down its decision, San Francisco longshoremen held their first election. Two slates of can-didates were put up. One was headed by Lee Holman, whose run-ning mate was Ivan Cox, who a few years later became the central figure in a bizarre attack on Bridges. Albion Hall's candidates for president and secretary turned out later to be equally erratic, though at the time they seemed sensible enough. Holman and Cox won, but two of the three business agents elected were Albion Hall candidates, as were a majority of the thirty–five–member executive board, including Bridges and Henry Schmidt, one of Albion Hall's most effective members, who continued to work closely with Bridges and the union until he retired in the late sixties.

A day or so later, the NRA board announced its decision that the Blue Book was a bona fide labor union, and its contract with the shipowners was valid. The board urged the Blue Book not to persecute longshoremen who had joined the AFL, but to let them work on the docks. Because most longshoremen had already left the Blue Book for the ILA, these findings were largely academic, but they confirmed Bridges's prediction that if longshoremen were going to have a union of their own, they had better forget about the government getting it for them and get it themselves through job action and economic pressure.

Within two weeks there was a test of the board's decision. It took place at the Matson Navigation Company pier, the largest employer in the port as well as the center of company union strength on the waterfront. One morning in mid–September longshoremen were starting to load a Matson freighter when the Blue Book delegate arrived to see if they were paid up. In the past, the longshoremen would have cooperated. But this morning, one after another refused to show his book to the delegate. He sought out the foreman, and together the two went from man to man, asking for their book. If they refused, the foreman barked, "Get off the ship!" The longshoremen ended up out on the Embarcadero, milling around, trying to figure out what to do next.

"Let's make a bonfire outa these goddam books!" someone shouted, heading for a vacant lot across from the Matson pier. The idea caught on and in minutes hundreds of books were blazing away. While the men stood around watching the last of the bonfire, the foreman came out of the Matson terminal and crossed the Embarcadero over to where they were. "OK, you men, I need three gangs to work that ship."

"What about the Blue Books?" someone called out from the crowd.

"Never mind the books. We've got to finish the ship."

For two weeks, all was quiet on the Matson pier, with longshoremen hired irrespective of ILA or Blue Book membership. Then, early in October, Matson struck back, firing four men for wearing ILA buttons on the job. One of the union's business agents went to the local NRA office to ask the agency to intercede for the men. The NRA turned him away with the excuse, "We can't do anything. We have no jurisdiction. You people don't have a code in your industry."

The four men who had been fired then went to Holman, but he was no more helpful than the NRA. "We don't want any trouble just now," he told them. "You fellows had better take whatever action you can as individuals."

At the next meeting of the local executive board, Bridges moved that the union strike Matson to force the company to put the four men back on the job. His motion was voted down. Then, on October 7th, a special issue of the *Waterfront Worker* (now being published by Albion Hall) called for rank–and–file support of the four men, even if the leadership of the local was unwilling to act.

Bridges described what happened next when he was testifying in his 1950 conspiracy trial:

> All we did was very simple; we went down there one morning, we lined up in the shapeup, and as the fellows started going to work, we stopped every one of them and said, "Look, fellows, four guys have been fired for joining the union. Let's have a program where they hire these four fellows back or none of us goes to work."
>
> So everybody stayed out. That affected the docks, and the strike lasted for five days. The Matson Company and the Waterfront Employers Association at that time went up to Skid Row and they hired a bunch of men from the employment halls, and of course we spoke to those men and got most of them to quit.

A federal conciliator who had viewed the burning of the Blue Books as a prank saw this as a sign that Communists were active on the waterfront. "My chief concern," he wrote Washington, "is that it is a forerunner of similar outbreaks. Please bear in mind that while the local ILA officers are not communistically inclined, there *are* communist elements inside the local union and outside of it, capitalizing on every situation that arises. I have before me samples of their handiwork in the form of mimeographed appeals to the workers on the waterfront, bearing all the earmarks of the Trade Union Unity League."

Holman's response to the Matson affair was to denounce the walkout as a wildcat strike. "If you men stay out on strike," he told Matson longshoremen sternly, "you do so without ILA sanction." At the same time, he wired Ryan in New York, asking him to file a complaint with the NRA's National Labor Board in Washington, charging Matson with firing the four men in violation of NRA policy. Ryan did so, and two days later, the secretary of the board, apparently forgetting that there was no code covering the shipping industry, told Matson that Section 7(a) of the NRA forbade discrimination of the kind the ILA complained of.

Simultaneously in San Francisco, federal officials, with the help of four members of the employers' association—*and* an ILA threat that locals in other ports would refuse to handle Matson cargoes if the company didn't rehire the four men—persuaded the company to get rid of the 150 strikebreakers it had hired, to take back all the strikers except the four whose discharge had precipitated the affair, and to agree to arbitrate the fate of the four. NRA Administrator

George Creel appointed a three–man board consisting of a municipal judge, a Catholic priest, and a professor of economics at the University of California. The board decided the case on October 17th, ordering Matson to put the four men back to work.

"That reestablished the union on the waterfront," Bridges said later.

That was the end of the fear and intimidation. After that—there was many, many of the men that was still maintaining their membership in the company union; they were afraid to join the new union, but after that, after we won the strike at the Matson dock and after we demonstrated No. 1, that you could join the union and wear your button, and if the company tried to fire you we had enough power to tie up that waterfront in order to enforce the demand. From that time on the union was established, it was recognized, it was in business.

Bridges was given a new problem to contend with when hearings on the NRA code for the shipping industry began in Washington early in November. The position of Pacific Coast longshoremen was put forward by an ILA official from San Pedro, whose presentation reflected the timidity of his constituents in Southern California but came as a shock to the class–conscious longshoremen in San Francisco and the Northwest. As if he had never heard of their campaign to organize all the maritime unions into a coalition, he urged the NRA to put the longshoremen under a separate code. "Longshoring," he explained, "is a special problem unrelated in its labor aspects to the problems of the entire shipping industry."

On the positive side, he proposed that the code provide for ILA–run hiring halls, joint union–management committees in each port to handle grievances, and a safety code to be supervised by another joint committee. Ryan, who attended the hearings as labor adviser to NRA Deputy Administrator William H. Davis, addressed the hearing briefly toward the end of the session. He said nothing about hiring halls, grievance machinery, or limiting the longshore labor force. Instead, he talked about the 85¢ an hour wages and forty–four–hour work week he had negotiated in the contract between the ILA and the shipowners in North Atlantic ports, which he thought highly satisfactory.

The president of the Blue Book was also heard from in a letter read at the hearing. He warned the NRA that sinister forces were at work in the West. "Since passage of the NIRA," he wrote, outside organizers, including Communists and well-known radicals, some with police records, have openly declared it to be their purpose to gain control of San Francisco longshore labor by breaking up the Longshoremen's Association of the Port of San Francisco and Bay District, ostensibly under an ILA charter for this purpose, and ultimately then gaining control of the ILA. . . .

Immediately following the passage of the NIRA these organizers, radicals and Communists, invaded the waterfront of San Francisco, where there had not been industrial troubles for a generation . . .

Bridges and the longshoremen might have expected the NRA to write that off as the death rattle of a dying company union. But a plan submitted by Boris Stern, a United States Labor Department economist sympathetic with the longshoremen, was cause for genuine alarm, for it would have put the government in control of the waterfront. A few years earlier, Stern had made an exhaustive study of longshore labor conditions in all important ports in the United States. In his report, he had presented a blistering evaluation of the shape–up as it operated on the East and Gulf Coasts. He had also criticized the hiring halls run by employers in Seattle, Portland, and Los Angeles for being designed to keep the ILA off the waterfront. He had concluded that because the conservative ILA leadership on the East and Gulf Coasts had no quarrel with the shape–up and employer domination, the only way to rid the waterfront of "the atrocious method of hiring longshoremen" was to put in a network of government–operated hiring halls. Under his plan, the Secretaries of Labor and Commerce would appoint directors of employment for each port who would supervise the halls with the assistance of union–employer advisory boards. The longshore labor force would be kept equal to normal manpower requirements by maintaining a register, and expenses of running the halls would be shared jointly by employers and the union in each port. The entire apparatus would be supervised by a national board, headed by the administrator of the NRA shipping code and a six–man union–employer advisory board.

Two weeks after the NRA hearing, ILA delegates from up and down the coast held a coastwide convention in Portland, Oregon. Two issues dominated the meeting. The first was the position they would take on the Stern plan. Ryan's spokesmen recommended going along with it. No one else spoke for it, but delegate after delegate arose to speak against it. Without coming to a vote, it died on the floor.

The other issue was what they were going to do to get a contract with the shipowners. The convention met this by electing a seven–member advisory committee to assist the coastwide officers, who were instructed to seek a meeting with the employers. If the employers did not reply by December 10, 1933, the district secretary and his advisory committee were to take a strike vote in all ports on the West Coast.

December 10th came and went without a meeting with the employers, but the secretary and his advisory committee failed to act. Some locals in the Northwest voted to strike on their own, but decided not to when shipowners agreed to discuss union recognition and other issues. The promise wasn't kept, but the union's district officers never did get around to calling the strike.

San Francisco longshoremen were less patient. They, too, waited one more month. Then, in January, 1934, they sent Bridges on a tour of the Northwest, along with a Holman man. Their assignment was to urge the locals there to support San Francisco in moving the date of the district convention ahead from May, as was scheduled, to February. Bridges took it upon himself to make certain the rank and file would be represented by delegates they would elect in their locals, as well as by their officers. He succeeded, despite opposition from old–line ILA leaders in the Northwest, who disliked a rank–and–file convention and who agreed with the shipowners that the convention ought to be postponed until a shipping code was signed by the President.

The convention met in San Francisco from February 26th to March 6th. Twenty–four ports, stretching up the coast from Los Angeles to Seattle, sent delegates. Officially, it was called the Twenty–seventh Annual Convention of the Pacific Coast Branch of the ILA, but actually it was the founding convention of a brand new union. The officers up front were tired old–timers, but the men on the floor were militant newcomers to unionism, eager for action.

The militants decided that the first thing they had to do was to tear up the old constitution and write a democratic one, so that the membership could control it. Next, they confirmed the old–timers' fears of what would happen if the rank and file were allowed a voice in policy-making. Bridges and other militants decided on a move that was sheer heresy to the old-timers, the creation of a federation of all the unions in the industry to give them more power when they met the employers. Furthermore, they argued that the union should not wait for the government to finish up the NRA shipping code but should tell the employers if they didn't negotiate, the union would strike on March 7th.

On March 3rd, the delegates heard a sobering report from a committee that had gone to talk with NRA Administrator George Creel about arranging a meeting with the employers. Creel said that the employers were not disposed to meet with the union. He added that if a strike did take place, "The government would stop it. Then the [NRA] regional labor board would hold an election to see if you people represent a majority." Then, just as the committee was leaving Creel's office, a telegram arrived from the NRA's National Labor Board in Washington saying that neither the national board nor its regional branches had the power to order an election for workers in the maritime industry because the industry was not covered by the NRA. Creel now told the committee that the shipowners and the union would have to arrange an election themselves, if one was to be held. And he was sure that the shipowners would not agree to an election.

The delegates heard an even more disturbing message when a telegram from Ryan was read to the convention. It was addressed to J. C. Bjorklund, secretary of the district:

> Am having considerable difficulty in getting Pacific Coast steamship representatives at this end to agree to meet with our Pacific Coast representatives to negotiate agreement stop They take position that due to fact that radical leaders are in control of our international on Pacific Coast and are expressing themselves as being dissatisfied with the Ryan and Bjorklund conservative type of leadership the employers may as well meet the situation now no matter what the cost stop Let me know what there is to this stop If this is sentiment of a certain port or ports and majority of ports are loyal to international the district should take the position they will negotiate conservative agreements and let the radical ports take whatever course they see fit.
>
> Joseph P. Ryan

Alarmed, the convention adopted a resolution reassuring Ryan that all Pacific Coast locals were 100 per cent loyal. Then, the delegates appointed a committee to meet with the employers who had assembled in San Francisco to plan counter–strategy. The committee was instructed to tell the employers that San Francisco longshoremen insisted on bargaining on a coastwide basis, that they were determined to get the closed shop and the six–hour day, that they were against arbitration, and that if their demands were not met by March 7th, they would take a strike vote.

That evening, the committee that met with the employers reported back with the employers' response. It was a declaration of war. They rejected the closed shop and all of the union's other demands. Moreover, the employers told the committee they had learned that sixteen of the fifty–five delegates to the convention were Communists.

The employers' contention that they couldn't agree to the union's demand for a closed shop because it was unlawful under the NRA was hypocritical, to say the least. In San Francisco, shipowners had long had a closed shop with the Blue Book and they were still trying to enforce it. Moreover, in Los Angeles, an NRA regional labor board had held an election in January in which longshoremen and ship clerks had had a choice between the ILA and Marine Service Bureau, the Los Angeles counterpart of the Blue Book. Of 1,294 votes, 1,262 had been cast for the ILA; only 32 for the Marine Service Bureau. After the election, Los Angeles employers, who were supported editorially by the influential *Los Angeles Times*, had taken the position that the election was not binding, and had signed a closed shop with the company union. In Portland, when the ILA had sought a meeting with the shipowners in November, 1933, the employers had hastily formed a company union and signed a closed shop contract with it, too.

The shipowners were right about the NRA position concerning sole bargaining rights and the closed shop. The question had come before the President in February, 1934, when he was asked to issue an executive order under which the union selected by a majority of workers voting in a National Labor Board election would represent all the employees eligible to participate in such an election. He did so, but two days later, General Johnson and Donald Richberg, the NRA General Counsel, countermanded the order.

In view of FDR's sympathy for organized labor, it may seem strange, that he did not correct the Johnson–Richberg interpretation. But FDR was ambivalent about giving one union exclusive representation. In mid–1934 he gave his views on the subject at a press conference, "7(a) says that workers can choose representatives. Now if they want to choose the Ahkoond of Swat they have a perfect right to do so. If they want to choose the Royal Geographical Society, they can do that. If they want to choose a union of any kind, they can do that. They have free choice of representation and that means not merely an individual or a worker, but it means a corporation or a union or the Crown Prince of Siam, or anybody."

"How do you feel on the point of minorities?" a reporter asked.

"The question of minorities is not a tremendously serious one," FDR answered, "because that has to be worked out in each individual case. If there is a substantial minority, it seems fair and equitable that the minority should have some form of representation, but that is a matter of detail depending on the individual case. In some industries it is possible neither side may want to have it."

"Suppose they do choose the National Geographic Society," the President was asked, "then do the employers have to trade with them?"

"Absolutely."

"About this Crown Prince of Siam, how is he going to get over?"

"If he is anything like the King of Siam," FDR replied, "he will be pretty good."

There was, of course, a fatal flaw in the shipowners' argument. There wasn't any NRA code covering the shipping industry.

While the convention committee that had met with the employers was answering delegates' questions in the evening session, Bridges waited until everyone else had spoken before he took the floor. It was his only extended speech of the convention, a quietly delivered but forceful plea that the delegates realize the employers would not recognize the union without a strike, code or no code. Then he turned to the employers' charge that the union had fallen under the thrall of radicals:

> . . . We have heard quite a bit about it in the last few days, what the shipowners thought of us and that the radicals didn't agree with the conservative policy. I notice today that we all are radicals, because the conservative policy was voted down. Nobody wanted to follow it any longer. Plan to wait for the code and for our future as the result of the settlement of that issue; that is the conservative policy, and I for one don't agree with that and have not for some time past. Also they all say this fighting and arguing and bickering will not get us anything, and so forth, and that is the question where the radical element comes up. That is why they class me under the radical element. I have never denied it. I am used to those things.
>
> . . . Now, brother delegates, I want to bring this out forcibly, we shouldn't take any notice of what the shipowners think or say

about us. They would shoot us if they had the chance or could get away with it without being discovered. We are putting them on the block and we should keep them there . . .

As the convention neared its end, delegates were told that Ryan had requested that they do nothing drastic until after March 22nd, when President Roosevelt was expected to sign the shipping code. The convention decided that if the employers did not meet the union's demands by March 7th, they would take a strike vote. If the majority voted to strike, and if employers were still holding out on March 22nd, they would strike the next day.

Their business accomplished, delegates turned to election of new officers. Bridges was not elected to any coastwide office, but he got in the last word of the convention. It was an instruction to the new executive board. Without argument, the delegates adopted it:

Since the shipowners have refused to meet with our Committee to discuss recognition of our union, and hours, wages, and working conditions, it becomes apparent that we will be forced into a strike, therefore, we must prepare to conduct a successful battle; therefore, the incoming Executive Board should be instructed to have ILA locals in each Pacific Coast Port call port conferences of all marine unions and marine workers, whether organized or unorganized. These conferences to be called for the purpose to organize united support behind our demands.

In mid–March, 6,616 longshoremen voted to strike, 699 not to, in a coastwide referendum. Nevertheless, it became increasingly obvious to San Francisco longshoremen as the deadline neared that they would have to take the strike out of the hands of their president, Lee Holman, or he would scuttle it. On March 20th, Holman wrote Ryan in New York, saying that he was against the strike and that he felt it had been forced upon the union by a radical minority. At a special strike meeting the next day, Bridges presented a plan that would circumvent Holman and put the rank–and–file in control of the strike. First, men who worked regularly at each dock in San Francisco would elect a member from their dock to a strike committee. Then, men who worked on the Oakland side of the Bay would elect members to the committee in the same fashion. Men who worked together in gangs but not regularly at a particular dock would elect three members. Finally, men who worked as casuals and were hired in the daily shape–up would elect six. The strike committee would thus have almost fifty members. Bridges's plan was adopted, and the next night he was elected chairman of the strike committee.

One of the longshoremen who voted to put Bridges in command of the strike has described how Bridges looked to him at the time:

> He came to the meeting in his working clothes with a cap on the back of his head and a cargo hook sticking out of his back pants pocket. He needed a shave and he looked rough. We had heard of this guy Bridges. The word was going around that he knew how to organize and we expected something special.
>
> Well, he damn near ran out onto the platform. We thought he was going off the other end, he came so fast. Then he stopped all of a sudden, looked us over and started talking and walking. For half an hour he walked back and forth, talking with his thumbs hooked in his belt. Aussie accent! Hell, we could hardly understand a word he said.
>
> That was Harry, in the old days.

On the evening of March 22nd, while San Francisco longshoremen were electing Bridges and making their preparations for the next morning when the strike would start, George Creel telegraphed FDR, asking him to intervene to stop the strike. The President responded immediately, asking the union to call off the strike and give him an opportunity to appoint a mediation board. Burglar Bill Lewis, President of the Pacific Coast District, called off the strike.

On March 23rd, Creel wrote a long letter to the Secretary of the National Labor Board, reviewing what had happened in the time from the Matson strike in October until March 22nd. He told him he had persuaded both sides to maintain peace until the adoption of a code:

> But the men broke away from their leaders and sent out a strike vote. It developed very quickly that the leaders on both sides were eager for a strike. The shippers were confident of victory and gave me to understand confidentially that even if they lost two or three million, it would be worth that to destroy the union. The International Longshoremen's Association, unfortunately, had put in new leaders, representing the radical element, rather than the conservative, who were committed to the strike by their own reckless utterances on the floor of the convention.

Creel deplored ILA president Ryan's inability to hold back the West Coast radicals, explaining that the Pacific Coast District was an autonomous unit, beyond control of the international union.

When the mediation board appointed by the President began its hearings, it first had to decide who represented whom, on both sides of the table. The employers contended that they could only speak for San Francisco, not for the whole coast. The union claimed to speak for the coast, but the shipowners argued there was no proof that longshoremen in all the ports actually supported the union. The board solved the argument this way: it called in employers from all the ports and told them they would have to accept coastwide bargaining if the union won a majority in the elections the board would hold up and down the coast. The board told the longshoremen it favored the Johnson–Richberg concept of proportional representation if some men voted for a union other than the ILA.

Neither side liked the board's recommendation. San Francisco employers were willing to recognize the ILA and to operate a hiring hall with the union, but they balked at a coastwide contract. Employers in the other ports refused even to recognize the union. Burglar Bill Lewis told the board he thought its proposal a workable one, but to Bridges and the majority of longshoremen on the coast, it was unacceptable. If the union went along with the board's recommendation, Bridges argued, it would be led into a labyrinth of negotiations with several minority unions. The longshoremen and their demands would be lost in the maze.

Bridges's view prevailed, and on May 9th, the great Strike began. In San Francisco, there was never any question that he was in charge. Then, as it became unavoidably apparent that Lewis and the other coastwide officials who had been elected at the convention weren't up to leading the strike, longshoremen in the other ports, too, turned to Bridges for leadership. It was a fortuitous choice. The time was right and he, having bided his time for more than ten years for this moment, was ready.

SOURCE NOTES

I SUPPOSE THE NOTE which prefaces this book makes it apparent that HARRY BRIDGES is built upon hundreds of interviews and on–the–spot observations, painstaking research in the union's archives, Presidential libraries, newspaper morgues and all the usual places where one searches for written material, published and unpublished, on his subject.

Nevertheless, in the interest of readability, I decided against including the usual paraphernalia of scholarship—those hundreds of little numbers, asterisks and daggers that would pepper the pages and, for most readers, only serve as a source of annoyance.

There are, however, readers who are annoyed when an author leaves them in the dark as to his sources. I hope they will find my solution satisfactory: inclusion in the text of the source where convenient, supplemented by an explanation relative to each chapter of the major sources not already mentioned in the body of the chapter itself.

Bridges told about his first experiences as a sailor in an interview with Byron Darnton, which appeared in the *New York Times* on February 5, 1940. He described the 1921 strike and his first encounter with the American Legion in his 1939 deportation hearing. The transcript is entitled: *Official Report of Proceedings Before the Immigration and Naturalization Service of the Department of Labor. Docket No. 55073/217. In the Matter of Harry Bridges. Deportation Hearing.*

Bridges gave his description of the 1924 Labor Day parade in his testimony in his 1950 trial. The transcript is entitled: *United States v. Harry Renton Bridges, Henry Schmidt and J. R. Robertson.* The Labor Day story is on pp. 5172–5173. His description of the speed-up comes from the same source.

Karlson's comments about Bridges in the early days were made in an interview with me in San Francisco in 1963. Bridges recalled his days in the gang in his testimony in his 1950 trial (pp. 5187–5188). His comments about the longshoremen's reaction to the MWIU were made in his 1950 trial (pp. 5202–5203).

The correspondence between Holman and Ryan is in the ILWU archives, as is the telegram from the AFL official (Paul Scharrenberg of the sailors' union, who was also secretary of the state federation of labor) to Ryan rebuking him for issuing a charter to the San Francisco longshoremen.

Stern's report is *Cargo Handling and Longshore Labor Conditions* (U.S. Bureau of Labor Statistics Bulletin No. 550, 1932). The reasons why Ryan and the AFL longshoremen's union liked the shape–up are described at length in my *Shape-up and Hiring Hall.*

President Roosevelt's remarks about the Ahkoond of Swat, etc., are in

"Presidential Press Conference No. 130 (June 15, 1934)," and are in the Roosevelt Memorial Library at Hyde Park, N.Y.

The description of Bridges in the strike meeting appears in a piece by Peter Trimble in *Frontier*, January, 1951. The speaker is not named.

Creel's letter to the secretary of the National Labor Board is in the Frances Perkins Papers, in the National Archives.

2

Neither Red Nor Dead

*We must all hang together, or most as-
suredly we shall all hang separately.*
                                BEN FRANKLIN

IN THE THIRTIES, strikes were sometimes more like civil wars than
labor disputes. It was a decade which, for wholesale violence and
the use of armed force, was without precedent in United States
labor history. This was the decade that produced the armed am-
bushes and guerrilla warfare in Harlan County, the Memorial Day
Massacre, the Flint sit–down strike, the Mohawk Valley Formula,
the massive use of labor spies, strikebreakers, industrial munitions
and, sometimes with fatal results, the National Guard.

The West Coast maritime strike was that kind of a strike. For it
was not merely an argument over a few cents more or less on the
wage rate. It was, on both sides, a matter of principle.

The shipowners saw themselves as defending property rights and
management prerogatives, against the intrusion of men they looked
upon as a rabble. "When we were all down at the heels and just
starting to organize," Bridges told a friend in 1950, "I used to tear
my guts out trying to tell them they were just as good as anyone
else around here; that they could become respectable members of
the community; that someday they'd be accepted. They weren't
afraid to fight for what they wanted then.

"Then they started to win better wages and conditions. They
started to buy homes, and then property, apartment houses especially. I kept telling them they could be respectable.

"And now," he added ruefully, "they've become too God-
damned respectable for me. Now they're starting to worry if I'm respectable enough for them!"

Moreover, to the shipowners and the business community, being confronted by a rank–and–file strike committee was a new experience, one they weren't prepared for. They had been used to dealing with the pliant Blue Book and the solid, reasonable men of the AFL—men they could do business with, who could sign contracts, tell their membership what was in them and that was that. But now they were faced with a new breed: men who had no respect for their traditional labor leaders, and who insisted that the rank–and–file had to ratify agreements before they would be bound by them. It was more than a little unsettling.

"What else we could have done to avert the strike, I do not know," T. G. Plant said after it was over, "except outright capitulation to union demands."

By the time the strike was in its fifth week, shipowners were convinced they were the shock troops of capitalism in a fight to the finish against communism. The view held by Roger Lapham, a leading shipowner, was typical of many: "I was convinced myself," he said later, "though I don't think the public was at that time, that this was a move that went beyond the aims of the usual accepted labor leadership. It was to get power. To get control, on the part of the Communist Party . . . control of the waterfront, control of transportation."

The longshoremen, on their side, were no less committed than the shipowners to principles they were prepared to fight for: the right to a union of their own choosing; above all, the right to control hiring so that they could make sure work was distributed equitably. "The hiring hall," the union has said repeatedly down through the years, "is the union."

Each side was convinced that its cause was blessed by the Constitution and the Supreme Court. The shipowners could invoke the thrust of the Fifth Amendment: "No person shall be deprived of the right to use his property as he sees fit without due process of law." The union could parry with the First: "Congress shall make no law abridging the freedom of speech . . . or the right of the people peaceably to assemble." Moreover, both sides seemed to have Sec. 7(a) on their side, depending upon who was interpreting it, General Hugh Johnson or the National Labor Board.

Both sides had their allies. The shipowners had the newspapers, the businessmen and organized farmers, the mayors of the port cities, the governors of the coastal states. "We used to have our conferences right here in my office," Lapham recalled. "When Rolph died and Frank Merriam became governor, Governor Merriam called on us, and we told him the conditions, or what we thought were the conditions, and he was simpatico." Local police, who thought the strike was the work of the Communists, were unequivocally on the side of the employers.

San Francisco's Chief Quinn thought the '34 strike presented a challenge to law enforcement that equalled the incendiary railway strikes of the 1870s. Two months after it was over, he said at a meeting of the state peace officers' association, an organization formed in 1933 to combat Communism:

> We found in our recent trouble in San Francisco that the riots we had there were programmed by Communists, programmed by these particular people, who, I believe, are the greatest propagandists that ever cursed this earth. They put out propaganda in that particular labor trouble that influenced the conservative men— and the majority of them in that strike were conservative labor men, desirous of bettering their positions, insofar as their hours of work and earning capacity were concerned. But unfortunately for them, when they got out on strike they found in some instances at least that their organizations were controlled by Communistic leaders and they were powerless to do anything but follow.
>
> We were quite fortunate in being able to anticipate their movements. We were quite fortunate in being able to offset their plans, with the result that in San Francisco . . . we feel a victory was won by the forces of law and order . . . .
>
> We faced a rather tough situation during that trouble in San Francisco. At times it looked quite bad for the forces of law and order. At one time, I think it was the last day that we had any trouble with them, we were faced by from five to seven thousand infuriated men, bent upon destroying not alone the police officers who were attempting to keep them out of their lines, but to advance through them onto the docks where they were going to wreak havoc upon the non-union men and then the property of the steamship companies, and then after that only the imagination can determine what they would have done in the way of sacking San Francisco . . .

The police chief of Piedmont, a well–to–do suburb of Oakland, followed Quinn to the rostrum with an account of an experience he had had during the strike:

". . . We received the tip–off that the boys were coming up to sack the homes of the shipowners. There are quite a number of ship–owners who live in our town. Within twenty–four hours after receiving that information we had 750 volunteer citizens, who took up the gauntlet against these fellows. We checked on everyone that came in and out of town."

When it was all over, either the source of the chief's tip–off had been misinformed, or the vigilantes frightened off the invaders. No one who seemed bent on sacking a shipowner's house had appeared at their barricades.

The longshoremen had, on their side, other unions, local and state AFL bodies, and, ultimately, the federal government. And the Communists.

The Marine Workers' Industrial Union, a TUUL affiliate, was the first to call its members off the job to support the longshoremen. Bridges, asked in his 1939 deportation hearing about the significance of the MWIU in the strike, put it this way:

> On May 10, 1934, the Marine Workers' Industrial Union struck. They, at that time, had the largest membership of any seafaring union . . . some two thousand. The International Seamen's Union [AFL], composed of sailors, firemen, marine cooks and stewards, had a total membership of some four hundred or five hundred.
>
> The sailors, or [AFL] seamen's unions . . . were forced to strike because of the pressure of the MWIU. The officials were mainly engaged in trying to keep the men on the ships . . . Finally, on May 15th, in a meeting I had a lot to do with, of twenty-four men, the International Seamen's Union officially voted to strike. But there were only twenty-four men in the meeting . . .

In some of the AFL shoreside unions, too, the Communists had small but active memberships which were able effectively to urge their locals to support the longshoremen. And when the longshoremen, convinced they wouldn't get fair treatment in the daily newspapers, shopped around for a printing press to get out a strike bulletin, the Party put the facilities of its newspaper, the *Western Worker*, at their disposal. The Party provided relief and food through its affiliate, the Workers' International Relief, and put up bond and provided counsel for arrested strikers through its legal agency, the International Labor Defense. Most important, perhaps, the Communists helped out by sending reinforcements to the picket lines, mobilized by the Party from unemployed councils, the Workers' Ex–Servicemen's League, and other front groups.

The appearance on the waterfront of thousands of unemployed workers marching shoulder to shoulder with striking maritime workers was of course a great help to the longshoremen. But it had its negative side, too. It reinforced the worst fears of their adversaries. "Actually, it isn't the Muscovite influence which the employers are most leery about," Arthur Caylor wrote in the *San Francisco News*. "It's the unemployed members of the unions. Privately, they point out that many of these men have had no work in many months, have little prospect of any, and have accumulated a vast feeling of protest." And the strike committee in San Francisco did not allay the community's mounting apprehension when it announced, "Although we are an anti–communistic organization, we will not refuse aid from any source."

Along with concrete help, the Communists proffered advice on strategy and tactics. The Communists were in a position, it would seem, to offer useful suggestions as to tactics. Sam Darcy, district organizer of the Party in San Francisco, had a labor background himself, had read extensively in labor history, and could put forward lessons drawn from earlier strikes. He had also been involved in a cotton strike in California's Imperial Valley a year earlier. Darcy said in 1965 that during the '34 waterfront strike he met frequently with key members of the strike committee. "Bridges asked me once, he said, 'Sam, how do you always know what to do next?' I told him, 'Harry, it's because I know where I want to see the working class go in the long run. I'm not just interested in winning a victory today and letting tomorrow take care of itself.' "

A question which came up over and over again was: How much influence did Darcy and the Communists have upon Bridges and the course of the strike? It is probable that their affect was minimal. Bridges, like Darcy, was an avid reader of labor history, and he had had more trade union experience. Darcy has said that one day during the '34 strike, after he had analyzed a strike development and suggested to Bridges what should be done, Bridges turned to him and said, "Hell, Sam, I learned all this in a school run by the Labor Party down in Australia." In his 1939 deportation hearing, Bridges was asked by the prosecutor: "Have you ever said at any time, so far as you can recall, that if your views and those of the Communist Party run parallel, that is something that shouldn't be held against you in any way, shape or form?"

"Lots of them I had before there was ever a Communist Party,"

Bridges replied. "I have been a member of a trade union since 1916. There was no Communist Party in 1916, and a lot of my views on trade unionism I had before there was ever a Communist Party. The labor movement in Australia is a pretty old one, and was a pretty militant and progressive one, and I learned a few things there that maybe came in handy later. So sometimes I get a little irritated when my views are ascribed to the Communist Party, because I had them before the Communist Party came into being."

Bridges had cause for irritation on this score on many occasions. One was in a meeting with the employers during the 1948 strike. Gregory Harrison, the employers' attorney, was presenting the case that Bridges was a Communist because his views sometimes ran parallel to those of the Communists. In the course of his exposition, Harrison read a passage written by William Z. Foster, onetime head of the Communist Party, on the necessity for socialism. Then he read an identical statement Bridges had made in a speech. "You see what I mean?" Harrison concluded. "Doesn't that prove Bridges is a Communist?"

"Somehow," one of the employers who was there said afterward, "Harry had copies of the statements Harrison was reading. So Harry said, 'I said that. I believe every word of it. But you're giving your people a false impression of what happened. You're suggesting that I followed the Party Line. Will you read the dates of those statements?'

"What do you mean?" Harrison stammered.

"Foster wrote that statement you read there in December. If you look at the date of my statement, you'll see it's June of the same year—six months earlier.

"What those statements show," Bridges concluded, "is that Foster knows a good trade union argument when he sees one."

One reason why Bridges's friends and foes alike may have overestimated the extent to which Communists, or others, for that matter, have influenced his actions was his unique method of thinking through a problem. Sam Kagel, West Coast longshore industry arbitrator, who knew Bridges since the days when they served together on the 1934 general strike committee, has described Bridges's technique: "Hell, Harry's as likely as not to discuss some questions he's thinking about with the bartender at Harrington's [an Irish bar on Jones Street, just around the corner from union headquarters in San Francisco, where Bridges habitually had lunch]. That's the way he works. He proposes his ideas and his policies, gets people's reactions. Then he decides what he'll do."

Scarcely a day of the strike went by unmarked by clashes between strikers and police. On May 9th, the first day, police broke up a crowd of strikers menacing two hundred strikebreakers who had been brought down to the Embarcadero in trucks to go aboard the "Diana Dollar," one of two passenger ships hired by the shipowners to house scabs during the strike. (The "Wilhelmina" wasn't yet available, having run aground on a sandbar as it was being towed down from Antioch. They got it off at high tide.) Then a call for help came from Pier 35, where strikers were threatening several gangs of strikebreakers loading a Grace Liner. The employers were able to announce, nevertheless, that seven hundred men were working in the port, with 275 more to be hired.

The strikebreakers housed on the "Diana Dollar" were a roll call of the victims of the Great Depression: carpenters, plumbers, farmers, bookkeepers, salesmen, accountants, graduates of law schools who had never been able to begin practice, lawyers without clients, even a small town G. P. With them on the ship were enough University of California football players to field more than three platoons of Golden Bears. They had been recruited by their coach, Navy Bill Ingram, who thought longshoring would be a good way for his boys to keep in shape while combatting Communism. Fortuitously for the athletes, their strikebreaking stint in San Francisco did not seriously interrupt their studies, for the term had ended and classes were out on the campus. And during their first week on the waterfront, understanding employers gave the boys time off so they could get over to Berkeley to take their final exams. A year later, when the Golden Bears arrived in San Francisco on the S.S. "Yale" from a post-season game in Hawaii, the longshoremen boycotted the ship and the athletes had to carry their own baggage down the gangplank.

On the second day of the strike, police were called to the strikebreakers' recruiting office on Main Street between Market and Mission when the strikers closed it down. The employers then moved the office to a new location on Mission, about four blocks up from the waterfront. But five hundred longshoremen marched on the new office, threatening the staff inside as well as the recruits lined up on the sidewalk. When the police arrived, a confrontation was fought with the classic weapons of street fighting: billy clubs on the police side, rocks and sticks on the strikers.' The police won, but at the cost of higher casualties. Five policemen were injured, three strikers. That afternoon, a somber communique came from police headquarters: "From now on, strikers will be shown no quarter."

Even so, San Francisco was relatively quiet compared with Seattle and Portland. In Seattle, in a similar engagement on the second day of the strike, longshoremen routed a squad of special policemen after taking their riot clubs away from them and sending five to the hospital with broken noses and bruised heads. In Portland, it was worse. By the third day of the strike, Mayor Joseph K. Carson and the Sheriff of Multnomah County were asking the governor to send in the Oregon National Guard.

Before a week was up, rioting in San Francisco and reports from cities up the Coast led San Francisco Police Chief Quinn to lay in a supply of tear gas. Actually, the decision to lay in the tear gas was an easy one for him to make. It would not cost the taxpayers anything, for the shipowners had quietly arranged to pay the bill and have the gas delivered to police headquarters. And it was as easy to get immediate delivery of tear gas equipment as it was to get it paid for. The two major munitions suppliers in San Francisco, Federal Laboratories and Lake Erie Chemical Company were both represented by resourceful, competitive salesmen who had been trying to get the police's business for some time.

On May 13th, Chief Quinn placed an order for tear gas with Ignatius H. McCarty, Lake Erie's man in San Francisco. It was delivered the next day. When Joseph Roush, the Federal salesman, learned of his rival's coup, he was as shocked at the ingratitude of the police as he was bitter about the loss of the sale. He had been calling on the San Francisco police department for almost a year and thought he had ingratiated himself with the chief by periodically inspecting and cleaning, without charge, all the tommy guns the department had in its arsenal. He had better luck with another client, though. This was T. G. Plant's assistant, Ashfield Stow, who bought a supply of munitions from Roush because, as he told the La Follette Committee, he thought Roush "a very peppy little salesman. . . . I met the kid and he made a hit with me."

Sometimes, competition between the two salesmen took a macabre turn. To show police how superior their products were, they formed the habit of accompanying the officers when they went out on riot duty. For McCarty and Roush, the arrangement was ideal; they could demonstrate their equipment on live targets, and besides, they liked their work. "Tomorrow we are going to have a hunger march here," McCarty wrote his home office, "and gas will be on hand, both by police and me. I am anxious for an opportunity to use our clubs and baby giants [a tear gas grenade]."

The enthusiasm with which San Francisco police approached

their work exposed a defect in one of McCarty's products. He called it to the attention of his president. "The police here," he wrote, "are strong for the long range guns and short shells as well as the candles. They are not sold on our clubs and think Federal clubs are superior as a club but admit it is not so hot as a gas weapon. These cops here when they hit a man over the head are not satisfied unless he goes down and a good split occurs. Our clubs are too light for this purpose. Should you contemplate making them heavier advise."

The McCarty–Roush rivalry reached a peak in July, when the employers tried to run a half–dozen trucks through the picket lines to open up the port. The longshoremen were out in force, and so were the two salesmen, each loaded down with his samples. Afterward, McCarty, distressed by the damage to his profession he thought would follow from the prodigal way his rival had fired off tear gas during clashes between police and pickets, wrote his superiors: "The first time Federal shot any gas was about July 3rd . . . The discharge of gas was wholly unnecessary and merely for advertising purposes as it occurred after we had driven the crowd back." Two days later, McCarty felt that Roush had embarrassed the profession again: "I saw them shoot $37.50 of long range shells in one burst at nothing. They shot at least fifty long range shells in the big battle when we used twenty–six of ours. . . ."

Unaccountably, McCarty failed to mention Roush's most newsworthy action of the day. Roush reported it to his home office, however, in a letter to the vice–president in charge of sales:

> I started in with long–range shells and believe me they solved the problem. From then on each riot was a victory for us. During the middle of the day we gathered in all available riot guns that I had and long–range shells and proceeded to stop every riot as it started . . . .
>
> I might mention that during one of the riots, I shot a long–range projectile into a group, a shell hitting one man and causing a fracture of the skull, from which he has since died. As he was a Communist, I have had no feeling in the matter and I am sorry that I did not get more.

His vice–president was impressed. "I have just read your five-page report regarding which I wired you yesterday," he wrote back. "The report is splendid and we think enough of it to excerpt a large portion of it to send out to the men, so you will be well known when you come in September first." Roush's report also struck a favorable note with the president of the company, who, at the beginning of the 1935 sales season, wrote Federal salesmen around the country, "We expect this summer will see a continuation of labor unrest, and you have a real service to offer the police departments in assisting them to handle their particular problem in a humane way. I want to especially compliment Baxter, Roush, Baum, Greig, Fisher and those boys who have given their personal services to direct the activities of the police in the use of this equipment during times of emergency."

San Francisco police evidently felt the same way Roush's employers did about his contributions to their work. After he bagged his supposed Communist, they made him a special officer of the department. They also made McCarty an honorary member of the special police officers' association.

Roush's exploit came to the attention of the staff of the La Follette Committee when they were going through Federal Laboratories correspondence subpoenaed for an investigation of the use of industrial munitions. Intrigued, they questioned Roush, located a man who had seen the shooting and finally tracked down the victim himself. As it turned out, he was neither dead nor a Communist.

The Committee's description of what happened differed sharply from Roush's version. Their investigation revealed that a large crowd of strikers had gathered near Pier 22, where the "Diana Dollar" was docked. Police had driven them off, using tear gas. Then, after the Embarcadero was cleared, three men armed with long-range tear gas guns appeared in the street and began lobbing shells into the Seaboard Hotel, where some of the strikers had taken refuge. At this point, James Engle, twenty–six–year–old longshoreman, appeared on the sidewalk in front of the hotel. Roush aimed his grenade launcher at Engle and squeezed the trigger. Engle went down. Then, as an eyewitness told it, "He half rose to his feet, felt the side of his head with his hand, looked at the blood and then collapsed. His arms and legs flapped like a chicken whose head has been cut off." He lay in the gutter until after several minutes, some of the men in the hotel dashed out and carried him back in.

Engle described how it had all looked to him in a deposition he gave the La Follette Committee in 1937 in Battle Creek, Michigan, where he was then living:

On July 5, 1934, at about 2:45 o'clock in the afternoon, I was walking along the Embarcadero Street between Folsom and

Howard Streets, with a friend whose name was Charles Rullard. Although there had been some disorders during the day, it was quiet at that time; in fact, we were really the only persons on the street. We were walking along the west side of the Embarcadero going north, and as we neared the vicinity of a hotel which is on the Embarcadero, we noticed an automobile parked at the curb in which a friend of ours was sitting. We stopped to talk to him . . . My back was toward the center of the street.

We talked for about five minutes, when I happened to notice out of the corner of my eye a group of men standing in the center of the street . . . two uniformed policemen and a man in civilian clothes. They were approximately twenty-five or thirty feet away from me. I noticed that the man in civilian clothes was carrying a large gun. I paid no particular attention to these men, inasmuch as I was minding my own business and there were no fights or disorders going on in that vicinity. The next thing that I remember is that I was lying in the gutter . . .

At the hospital, it was found that the shell had pierced Engle's skull behind his right ear, making a hole about an inch and a half in diameter.

When Engle himself gave a deposition about the incident to the La Follette Committee, he said: "Although I was a member of the International Longshoremen's Association, I was not at that time, and never have been, associated with any communist or radical organization. I was causing no disturbance at the time I was shot, nor was anybody around me causing any disturbance."

By the second day of the strike, hope that the ports could be kept open began to fade. Despite repeated urging by teamsters' union officials that drivers should honor their contracts and go through the picket lines, the men in the ranks came over almost immediately to the longshoremen's side and refused to haul cargo out of pier warehouses if it had been brought there by strikebreakers. Even so, San Francisco shippers were better off than their counterparts in Portland and Seattle. San Franciscans had a partial substitute for trucks in the state–owned Belt Line Railroad which runs parallel to the Embarcadero, with tributaries running across the street onto the piers. Before the strike, it took about 3,500 railroad cars a month to handle cargo coming off the docks. In May, the first month of the strike, twice the number of cars was needed, and in June, 10,380 Belt Line cars were pressed into service to handle freight to and from the piers.

West Coast sailors, too, who had helped break earlier strikes by doing longshoremen's work, this time came off their ships to support the dockers. Even more surprisingly, the ships' officers came off with their men. By the middle of May, all the maritime unions on the Coast were on strike, pledged not to go back to work until the demands of all the others were met.

When it became clear that the strike was going to close down the Coast, farmers and businessmen appealed to city and state governments to intervene. By the end of the first week the governors of the three Coast states made a joint request to Secretary of Labor Frances Perkins to end the strike. On the same day, two newspaper stories added force to their appeal. One came from San Pedro, where Dick Parker, a twenty–year–old striker, had died of a bullet through the heart as he and three hundred others stormed a stockade where strikebreakers were housed. Tom Knudson, a long–time member of the union, died later from wounds he received in the same attack. The other report, from San Francisco, was that for the first time in history, no freighters left Pacific Coast ports that day.

Frances Perkins responded to the request by sending Edward F. McGrady, an Assistant Secretary of Labor and the department's trouble shooter, to San Francisco. Her action seemed a sensible one because McGrady had wide experience in labor affairs and was highly thought of by Secretary Perkins, FDR, and the American Arbitration Association, which had given him a medal for distinguished service in labor arbitration.

General Hugh Johnson, for whom McGrady had worked briefly, thought well of him, too. "There was not a better man in the country to send," Johnson wrote later in his book about the NRA, *The Blue Eagle*, "except that he was a professional labor man and hardly to be regarded as wholly unbiased. . . . I knew at the time that his official connection with the Department of Labor was not conducive to agreement because employers were bound to think him prejudiced."

In San Francisco, however, McGrady got on better with the employers than he did with the strikers. Perhaps it could not have been otherwise, in view of his background and the inflammable ideological atmosphere in San Francisco when he arrived. For McGrady was the very model of the AFL craft union politician. Sixty–two–years old when he was sent to San Francisco, he had grown up in the Irish Catholic ambience of the Boston trade union movement and had worked as a foreman in the print shop of the *Boston Traveler*. Later, he became president of the pressmen's local.

He went on to head the central labor council, then to a seat on the Boston Common Council, and from there, to the Massachusetts House of Representatives.

During World War I, he headed the labor division of the Massachusetts Liberty Loan drive, establishing an enviable sales record. As if that did not adequately establish his credentials as a home–front patriot, he proposed that Boston unions expel all members who were not citizens unless they took out first papers. After the war, Sam Gompers appointed him to be the AFL lobbyist in Washington, where when the New Deal came in, he entered government service.

McGrady's experiences equipped him admirably to deal with old–style AFL craft unionists, but he was as unprepared as were West Coast shipowners to cope with the new unionism of the mid–thirties, in which a vocal, sometimes left–wing membership was active in making union policy. From the time he got to San Francisco on May 17th, he drove a wedge between himself and the strikers. Instead of meeting with the strike leaders when he arrived, he closeted himself with local businessmen and two mediators who, at FDR's request, had been trying to help resolve the dispute. The next day, still not having talked with the strikers, he asked both sides to give their negotiating committees full power to act on a settlement and forego the right of their memberships to approve any proposals the committees might agree on.

The employers replied that they were willing to give their committee such power, so long as the committee did not retreat from the conditions they stipulated for a settlement: the open shop, employer-operated hiring halls, elections in each port to determine whether or not the longshoremen wanted to be represented by the International Longshoremen's Association and port–by–port bargaining.

The longshoremen also limited the authority of their negotiators. Any proposals for settlement and any tentative agreements the union negotiating committee thought acceptable would have to be referred to the entire membership on the Coast for approval. Secondly, the longshoremen would not return to work until the other maritime unions settled their disputes. Bridges, as chairman of the strike committee, told McGrady of the union's decision and gave the story to the press on May 19th.

The employers' response apparently seemed reasonable to McGrady, but the union's answer nettled him and he told the press:

San Francisco ought to be informed of the hold of the Red element on the situation. A strong radical element within the ranks of the longshoremen seems to want no settlement of this strike. I have observed that Communists, through direct action and by pleas made in the widely circulated Communist newspaper here, are trying to induce the strikers to remain out despite our efforts to arbitrate.

We are very far away from a settlement. On Friday we believed the Executive Board of the ILA had power to act for the strikers along the entire coast. By that same night the rank and file of the strikers stripped them of that authority. The Executive Committee appears to me to be helpless to do anything with the men they represent, or to combat the radical element in the longshoremen's union.

McGrady's statement inevitably worsened the situation. He was, after all, an Assistant Secretary of Labor, a man of wide experience in labor matters who had access to police and FBI reports. People assumed that such a man would not make a grave charge if the evidence was not overwhelming.

Even the White House was alarmed by McGrady's statement. Upon hearing of it, Col. McIntyre, the President's confidential secretary, called the Labor Department to ask what they knew about the matter. A day or so later, he got a reply from Turner Battle, executive assistant to Secretary Perkins:

I am attaching herewith a confidential copy of a telegram received from the District Director of Immigration and Naturalization, relative to the longshoremen's strike at San Francisco. We are keeping in touch with the situation in accordance with my conversation with you:

Two cases investigated aliens connected with longshoremen's strike stop Frank Cameron a Canadian arrested by police in strike disturbance entered from Canada unlawfully year twenty three and showed by Army service and otherwise has been here continuously stop Harry Bridges entered lawfully from Australia year twenty stop applied for citizenship New Orleans year twenty one and again San Francisco year twenty eight stop has wife here and daughter Betty born December year twenty four stop has followed occupation stevedore with two known local firms from May year twenty three to June year twenty eight stop only indication as to Communistic connection is that two witnesses in naturalization proceeding were candidates on ticket of communistic party stop only direct report is quote he is captain and chief agitator in longshoremen strike unquote aliens arrested by police investigated but no direct approach made to aliens involved in strike.

HOFF

San Francisco

This reassurance by immigration authorities on the scene allayed whatever fears the President and his chief adviser, Secretary of Labor Perkins, might have had. For the rest of the strike they treated with suspicion the stream of telegrams and phone calls from the Coast warning that Communists had seized control of the waterfront.

Nevertheless, fears of Communist influence kept mounting on the West Coast. So far as the newspapers were concerned, McGrady's statement put the federal government's imprimatur on the charge of communism, and it became the standard explanation of the longshoremen's every move. Two days after McGrady's statement, a telegram from the San Francisco Chamber of Commerce to the President was published in newspapers up and down the Coast:

> The strike is not a conflict between employers and employees —between capital and labor—it is a conflict which is rapidly spreading between American principles and un–American radicalism . . .
>
> The longshoremen are now represented by spokesmen who are not representative of American labor but who desire a complete paralysis of shipping and industry and who are responsible for the bloodshed which is typical of their tribe . . .
>
> There can be no hope for industrial peace until communistic agitators are removed as the official spokesman of labor and American leaders are chosen to settle their differences along American lines.

With the influence of the Communists foremost in their minds, San Francisco businessmen decided the strike was too important to be left to the shipowners. They would have to take it out of their hands and settle it for them. The Industrial Association of San Francisco, which saw the waterfront strike as only one phase of a wider war, would be their agent. Paul Eliel, the association's research director, explained their reasoning in a letter to the secretary of the National Labor Board in Washington: "The fact remains that the ILA in San Francisco at the present time, is absolutely and unequivocally in the hands of a group of Communists. You know I am not a Red–baiter and I more or less laugh at these Communist scares. In the present instance, however, I am convinced that the ILA has definitely been taken over by a Communist group."

The association moved in quickly. At the next bargaining session, three of its representatives were at the bargaining table alongside the shipowners. Across from them were the eight officers of the longshoremen's West Coast executive committee, which, as McGrady had noted earlier, had been stripped of authority by the strikers. Chief spokesman for the union at the meeting, nevertheless, was William Lewis, titular head of the West Coast District. Behind him, his chair tilted back against the wall, sat Bridges, a mute observer. "The chairman of the strike committee is sitting in, checking up on Lewis," McGrady told Frances Perkins when he phoned that evening to report on the day's progress. "There is apparently some friction among the men. There is a vigilante movement on foot," he continued. "The papers are talking of turning the radicals out of town and are playing up the Red scare."

With trouble brewing and negotiations at a standstill, the West Coast eagerly awaited the arrival of Joseph Ryan, the union's international president, who was on his way out from New York. With his experience and prestige, it was hoped that he could find a way to reach the compromise that McGrady and the mediators had not been able to achieve.

Ryan was one of the more flamboyant personalities of the old AFL era. In his youth a handsome, 200–pound six–footer, by the 1930s years of rich living had made him look like an overweight ex–prize fighter. He was an imposing figure, expensively if flashily tailored, genial, ready at the slightest encouragement to render "Danny Boy" in a passable Irish tenor. On the walls of his office were photographs of mayors, governors, business leaders, labor leaders, inscribed by the donors to their good friend, Joe Ryan, as well as plaques testifying to his Americanism given him by the American Legion and the Veterans of Foreign Wars.

His career as a longshoreman had begun in 1912 when he started working on the docks in New York. After about a year, he was hurt on the job and elected to office in his local union. He went from job to job on up through the union hierarchy, becoming international president in 1927. In 1928, he was elected president of the AFL Central Labor Council in New York City. Two years later when a fifty–member committee appointed by the mayor looked into charges of corruption in the city, it reported that one of the most lucrative fields for racketeers was the waterfront. The shape–up, the committee thought, was primarily responsible for the evil conditions there. One member of the committee wrote a minority report, contending that the majority was unfair to the waterfront employers of New York. The dissenter was Joseph P. Ryan, president of the longshoremen's union.

Then, when repeal of Prohibition removed rum–running as a lucrative field for hijackers and gangsters, Ryan's waterfront became a haven for hoods. Just at the time they were casting about for new areas of activity, Ryan was propitiously chairman of the New York State Parole Board. Through his good offices, scores of displaced hoodlums were paroled to the waterfront. Some got jobs in management. "If I had a choice of hiring a tough ex–convict," one employer said, "or a man without a criminal record, I am more inclined to take the ex–con. Know why? Because if he is in a boss job he'll keep the men in line and get the maximum work out of them. They'll be afraid of him." Some were given jobs in the union, where they kept the members in line for Ryan.

Ryan should never have come to San Francisco. His East Coast experience left him unprepared for the kind of union members he encountered on the West Coast, and the way they talked and acted led him to agree with McGrady that they were under the influence of Communists. Not only did some of the strikers greet him with acid comments about his leadership of the union, but he also had great difficulty comprehending their goals.

He was a strong defender of the shape–up in East Coast ports and never grasped how deeply his West Coast members felt about putting a hiring hall of their own in its place. He also failed to understand their demand for a coast–wide settlement because on the Atlantic and Gulf Coasts bargaining was on a port–by–port basis, with wage rates and working conditions varying from one port to another. Moreover, Ryan moved in circles in which the old AFL philosophy of craft unionism was dogma. This led him to view as heretics the longshoremen he met in San Francisco who were hoping that alliances made in the strike could be preserved at its end and converted into a permanent federation of maritime unions, ultimately perhaps, one big union for all maritime workers.

Ryan and Bridges were publicly at odds within two days after his arrival. Their dispute began when Ryan told the employers that the union would drop the closed shop demand if they would recognize the union and give preference in employment to union members. This, he pointed out, was the arrangement the ILA had in its contracts in East Coast ports. "It has worked there for nineteen years," he said. "Why not here? And," he added, "it has kept Communists and radicals from infesting the piers of the employers."

Ryan's remarks only confused matters. Shipowners thought his proposal a subterfuge that would give the union a closed shop under another name. The longshoremen thought he was selling them out. Ryan gave others this impression, too. "Mike Casey tells me," Paul Eliel of the Industrial Association wrote the Secretary of the National Labor Board, "that Ryan isn't anxious to see the hiring hall adopted as a method of registering and routing labor because he feels that registration will be limited and therefore recruiting to the ILA will be limited."

Ryan's West Coast members knew, moreover, that in the East Coast ports Ryan referred to, the preference in employment he talked about was an illusion. Men who worked on the docks were hired in a shape–up, with local union officers cut in on the kick–back the hiring boss demanded as the price of the job. Only a favored few among the ILA membership had any real claim on a job.

Ryan further alienated many of his West Coast members by his belief in craft union separatism:

"We are not going to leave any men in the lurch if they struck in sympathy with us," Ryan told reporters. "But if they struck because of grievances of their own it is up to their own locals and internationals to settle for them. If the employers let this strike go on much longer, every trade in the industry may become welded together in a transportation organization, which would strike and present all their grievances at once. It would be a much more complicated situation to handle, and one for which the employers would have to blame themselves."

San Francisco longshoremen immediately repudiated Ryan's proposal to give up the closed shop. Bridges, now regularly being referred to in the newspapers as the leader of the left–wing element, went farther, repudiating Ryan as well. "Settlement for mere recognition may mean a lot to national heads of the International Longshoremen's Association who get fat salaries," Bridges asserted. "But the workers are going to hold out for nothing less than a closed shop."

McGrady listened to Ryan rather than to Bridges, and on May 28th, he asked the shipowners' committee to meet with him and a group that included Ryan and a few other West Coast ILA officials, but not Bridges. When the meeting ended, they told reporters they had agreed on a basis for settling the strike. Employers would recognize the union as the bargaining agent on a port–by–port basis; hiring halls would be established, at employers' expense, in which union and non–union men would be hired without preference; employers and the union in each port would negotiate the rules governing registration and dispatching of longshoremen; the union could have one of its members in the hiring hall to see that there was no discrimination against its members. Wages and hours would be settled later, by arbitration.

Everyone at the meeting was pleased with the arrangement. "Never in my many years of labor work," McGrady said delightedly, "have I seen a finer spirit than was displayed at the meetings which led up to this agreement. There was a spirit of cooperation and give–and–take which I have never seen equalled. . . ." Ryan was equally pleased: "This gives us exactly what the longshoremen have fought for and is all we want. It gives recognition to the ILA in all disputes and provides for collective bargaining. I hope and believe that it will be adopted unanimously by the locals." Angelo Rossi, San Francisco's mayor, assuming that the arrangement ended the strike, added happily: "To my knowledge, with the exception of the minor localized disturbance of Monday, this was the most peaceful waterfront strike in San Francisco."

Everybody was happy with the May 28th agreement, it seemed, but the longshoremen. To them, it was a sell–out. Bridges described it as an attempt by the employers to sound out the weak spots in the union. San Francisco longshoremen shouted it down at a meeting the next day and wired other locals to follow suit. When the news reached Seattle, Dave Beck advised longshoremen there to forget the rest of the Coast. "Make the best deal you can for yourselves," he told them. "There is no chance of getting an agreement as long as Los Angeles takes the attitude it does now. Merchants and shippers down there will never stand for union labor. They are able to move cargo there while other ports suffer."

To someone looking at the matter from the perspective of one port or even one region, Beck's advice must have seemed sound. Industry and agriculture in the Northwest were hard hit by the strike, and some of the damage looked as if it might be permanent. With Portland and Seattle completely closed down, freight customarily shipped in and out of these ports was being diverted to the south. Already, several shipping companies and fish–packing houses in Seattle were threatening to move to Los Angeles, where the union was weak and their competitors were either actually benefitting from the strike or getting by with only minor interruptions.

Heartened by Beck's support, Ryan set out for the Northwest. "San Francisco opposed the peace settlement," he told reporters at the Portland airport, "and it is up to the locals of the Northwest to vote down San Francisco and save that local from itself." At the meeting that night, Portland longshoremen listened respectfully to their international president. Then, refusing even to debate whether or not to take a vote on Ryan's settlement, as he and McGrady had asked them to do, they shouted it down.

Ryan continued up the coast to Tacoma to meet with the Northwest strike committee, only to discover once again that San Francisco was not, as he had thought, marching to a different drummer. When the committee gave him the floor, they listened quietly for forty–five minutes while he earnestly pleaded for their support, then voted him down.

San Francisco longshoremen, unlike those in the Northwest, went along with McGrady's request that they take a secret ballot on Ryan's proposal, scheduling the vote for May 31st. In the meantime, the police, oddly enough, became more violent. The longshoremen were not permitted to picket at the piers because of an anti–picketing ordinance that had been enacted after the 1919 strike, so they had been marching daily from their union hall on Steuart down to the Embarcadero, then along the length of the waterfront. They had to make arrangements with the police for each parade, with a two–hour notice to police headquarters. On May 30th, a parade moved out from the union hall, headed down Mission to the Embarcadero, turned left toward Fishermen's Wharf. They had only gone about a block and were just coming abreast of the Ferry Building when the police ordered them to cross over and march on the inland side of the street. They didn't move fast enough and the police charged, swinging their clubs. Several longshoremen went home with bruises, but there were no serious casualties.

The next day, while they were lining up to vote, the longshoremen witnessed another disturbing incident only half a block away from the union hall. May 31st had been designated as Youth Day by the Communist Party, and three hundred members of the Young Communist League had marched down to the union hall to hold a rally in solidarity with the strikers. For some reason, they had neglected to get a permit for the march. The police let them parade to within sight of the union hall, then, without warning, they broke it up, sending twenty-four young people to the hospital.

Community reaction to the incident was divided. To the Chamber of Commerce, it was a transparent ruse by Communists "to start a disturbance in order to provoke an attack by the police." Some longshoremen felt the same way:

"I was in the office," Henry Schmidt has recalled, "when the boys and girls of the YCL came parading down Mission to hold a demonstration in front of the office in support of the ILA. There must have been several hundred of them. Some seemed to be singing, some were sort of dancing along. When they were about half a block away, as they were passing a vacant lot with a five–foot fence running along the sidewalk, the mounted police came charging out of a side street and rode down on them, hitting at the kids with billy clubs.

"I turned to the guy in the window with me and said, 'Isn't that a helluva way to treat those kids?'

" 'Ah, hell,' the guy said. " 'They're just a bunch of Commies.'

"You might be interested in the sequel to that story," Schmidt continued. "About a week later, several hundred guys were milling around in front of the office, when the cops showed up with tear gas and shotguns loaded with buckshot. When they opened up, the longshoremen went running off in all directions. It happened that I was in the office that day, too, and I saw down on the street the guy I'd been watching with the other time.

"He took off up Mission, but there were cops at the next corner. So he started over the fence. Just as he was going over, a cop fired. That guy's ass was riddled with buckshot!

"I never got around to asking him how he felt about the cops after that."

The get–tough policy of the police did not influence the longshoremen's vote on Ryan's proposal. Two thousand, four hundred and four voted to reject it, eighty–eight to accept. They were almost as firm in their support of the other unions. Two hundred and fifty–eight were in favor of a separate peace, but 2,154 voted to stay on strike until the demands of the other unions were met.

Ryan stayed on in Seattle after his tour of the Northwest, trying to build up support among longshoremen there and to cement his relationship with Dave Beck. While he was there, two threatening developments occurred. One, of primary concern to the longshoremen, was a McGrady suggestion that the government should take the quarrel out of the hands of the shipowners and longshoremen by setting up hiring halls and running them itself. The other was a potential threat to all the maritime unions. This was an announcement by the mayor of Seattle that he and the mayors of Portland, Tacoma, and three smaller cities had made plans to open the ports, using whatever force was necessary.

Ryan and Beck, urged on by their eagerness to avert these dangers, produced a peace plan which Seattle employers accepted. It provided for hiring halls run jointly by the employers and the longshoremen, recognition of the union as the bargaining agent (but not a closed shop), wages and hours to be decided by arbitration later. Without waiting to see how Northwest longshoremen reacted to it, Beck and Ryan left for San Francisco to offer it there. In San Francisco, their settlement plan was greeted enthusiastically by everyone except the longshoremen.

The shipowners thought the Beck–Ryan plan excellent, as did the Industrial Association, whose original insistence that the shipowners hold out until the longshoremen surrendered unconditionally had seemed an insurmountable barrier to a negotiated peace. So on June 16th, an interesting group gathered in Mayor Rossi's office. T. G. Plant, the shipowners' lone representative, was there, flanked by three officers of the Industrial Association. On the union side of the table were Joseph Ryan and three West Coast officers of the union. They were flanked by three Teamsters: Dave Beck of Seattle, Mike Casey and John McLaughlin of San Francisco. In the middle were the President's mediators, except McGrady who had returned to Washington. Everybody who had a stake in the strike was represented except the strikers. Their spokesman, Harry Bridges, hadn't been invited.

At the beginning of the meeting, T. G. Plant turned to Ryan, "Do you suppose any proposal made to the longshoremen would be acceptable to the majority of them here in San Francisco?" "I don't think so," Ryan responded. "This local has been captured by radicals and Communists who don't want a settlement."

"Then what's the point of our reaching an agreement here," Plant asked, "if it's going to be rejected as soon as we announce it?"

"I give you my unqualified assurance," Ryan told Plant, "that I can make an agreement on behalf of my membership that will be effective." Casey, McLaughlin and Beck then assured Plant that they would guarantee any agreement Ryan made. Plant reported this to the employers in the other major ports, who then authorized him to negotiate a coastwide agreement on their behalf.

When the meeting adjourned, an agreement had been signed by T. G. Plant for the shipowners and by Ryan and a Los Angeles official of the ship clerks for the longshoremen. Then a singular rite was performed. The rest of the mayor's guests came forward and one after the other solemnly signed the document, guaranteeing performance by the parties they presumably represented. Giving assurance that the longshoremen would live up to the contract were Dave Beck, Mike Casey, John McLaughlin, Mayor Rossi, and the mediators. Observance of the contract by the shipowners was guaranteed by John F. Forbes, president of the Industrial Association. To those present, at least, the occasion was impressive. Nonetheless, what it would mean in practice was far from clear. No bonds were posted, to be forfeited if one side or the other failed to live up to the bargain.

In retrospect, it seems surprising that the signatories thought the longshoremen would ratify the agreement. Instead of the union hiring halls longshoremen were demanding, the hiring halls the agreement gave them were to be run jointly by the employers and the union, with no provision for distributing jobs so as to equalize earnings. And in the face of the longshoremen's resolve, repeated over and over again, to stay on strike until all of the unions supporting them won their demands, the agreement would have been a separate peace for the longshoremen. Even worse, it contained a no–strike clause that would have prohibited longshoremen from stopping work if necessary to support the unions that had struck in sympathy with them. Finally, Ryan, Plant and the guarantors all agreed that it would not have to be ratified by the union membership.

Moreover, if the signers' euphoria had not clouded their vision, they might have been disturbed by the failure of two of the men in the room to sign the document. One was Burglar Bill Lewis, the chief officer of the union's Pacific Coast District, which under the terms of the ILA constitution was an autonomous body. The members on the Coast could thus be bound to an agreement only when their own district officers, in accordance with district rules, signed it. Lewis refused to sign, reminding the others that he could not do so until the agreement was ratified by the membership. The other West Coast longshoremen who were present refused to sign on the same grounds.

Nevertheless, for a day or two, it looked as if the strike were over. San Francisco employers began paying off their 1,600 strike-breakers. Ryan wired McGrady in Washington: "I signed an agreement today which terminates the longshore strike that has been in effect on the West Coast since May 9th. Terms are: wages and hours to be arbitrated, joint control of hiring halls and a union recognition clause which is satisfactory, considering that the men are newly organized."

Early in the strike the Industrial Association had hired McCann–Erickson, the advertising agency, to handle its press relations. Now, the investment paid off. The June 16th agreement was greeted with favorable editorials in every Bay Area newspaper, portraying the agreement as eminently fair and urging longshoremen to accept it. Then, when the longshoremen rejected it, the press explained their refusal as the work of radicals and Communists.

It is of course probable that the newspapers would have treated the strike the way they did without any help from McCann–Erickson. A. J. Liebling, in his irreverent book about American newspapers, *The Press*, has given us an explanation for what sometimes seem to be publishers' conspiracies:

"When they appear to take positive action with common accord, it is by instinct, like a school of mackerel chasing sardines, rather than by predetermined plan, like warships chasing an enemy fleet. The common objects of their ire, unions, taxes, public welfare and the Democratic Party, require no pointing out by scout planes."

President Roosevelt's calm during the most trying days of the strike seems to have been due, at least in part, to his acceptance of the Liebling thesis. In September, after the strike was over, he was having a press conference in his study at Hyde Park with three or four White House correspondents and Lord Illiffe, owner of the *London Telegraph* and other English newspapers. Illiffe expressed surprise that American employers were still fighting unions when, he said, employers at home had accepted collective bargaining since 1926, after the British general strike. The President used the '34 longshoremen's strike as an illustration of the backward state of industrial relations in the United States:

"This is off the record completely, just conversation between us," he began.

I kept in pretty close touch . . . It appeared very clear to me, that just as soon as there was talk of a general strike, there were probably two elements bringing about that general strike.

One was the hot–headed young leaders who had had no experience in organized labor whatsoever and said that the only thing to do was to have a general strike.

On the other side was this combination out there on the Coast of people like the editor of the *Los Angeles Times*, for instance, who was praying for a general strike. In other words, there was the old, conservative crowd just hoping that there would be a general strike, being clever enough to know that a general strike always fails. Hence there was a great deal of encouragement for a general strike.

That is why I have to say this off the record because, if you put me in court, I could not prove it from the legal point, but it was there. For instance, this Hearst man who operated among some of the newspapers in San Francisco and along the Coast, and they all agreed to work together, all the publishers of all the papers, for a general objective, and the objective was to encourage the general strike.

That is the fact, as I say, although I could not produce legal proof of it in court. But the fact remains that they did discuss and encourage it among themselves. In other words, they baited the other fellow into it, not by offering him money but by baiting him into it.

The June 16th agreement and its repudiation by the longshoremen drove the employers and the men further apart. Both sides, confronted now with the inevitability of a long struggle, regrouped their forces. The strikers formed a joint strike committee, consisting of five delegates from each of ten unions: longshoremen, ship clerks, deck officers, engineers, firemen, sailors, cooks and stewards, boilermakers, machinists, caulkers. Bridges was elected chairman.

The Industrial Association, now fully in command of the employers' strategy, responded with a plan to open the port that it had had under consideration from the beginning of the strike. They arranged the complicated logistics: rented warehouses, leased a small fleet of trucks, obtained assurances from the police that the drivers would be protected. When these details were worked out, the association called together 150 San Francisco businessmen, who endorsed the plan.

Then one of the shipowners had an idea. Why not buy this fellow Bridges off? He has never had much money, he argued, and he's on relief right now. If the price is right, he'll scuttle the strike for us and we can forget about this messy business of opening the port by force. The scheme made sense to his colleagues. They hit upon a figure of fifty thousand dollars and located an ex-prizefighter who could act as a go-between to meet Bridges and hand over the money. The fighter got word to Bridges that he wanted to see him privately about an important matter. When they met, he told Bridges he had fifty thousand dollars in cash to give him if he agreed to call off the strike. For a moment, Bridges has said, he thought to himself: "Why don't I take the dough and put it in the strike fund?" But only for a moment. "Hell, if I had taken that money, I'd have been dead two minutes later. Then my body would have been found with the fifty thousand dollars in my pocket. I would have been dead and the union would have been dead, too."

The story of the bribery became the opening chapter in a Bridges legend. "You can say what you like about Bridges being a Communist or a fellow-traveler," people on the West Coast have said, "but you have to give the guy this much. He's absolutely incorruptible."

Inevitably, Bridges's critics questioned that the incident ever occurred. Their contention was that Bridges or his supporters made up the story and repeated it over and over again until it became a myth. But Randolph Sevier, a Matson executive, told me in 1963, "Oh, we tried to bribe him all right. The money was put up by an officer of this company."

Just as the combatants were readying themselves for what would unavoidably be a clash costly in lives and property, Congress gave the President more peacemaking authority. The instrument was Public Resolution 44, empowering the President, when labor disputes obstructed interstate commerce, to appoint special boards authorized to investigate, hold representation elections, mediate, and if the parties were willing, to arbitrate. On June 26th, FDR used his new power for the first time to appoint the National Longshoremen's Board.

Members of the board clearly had to be chosen carefully. Federal mediators on the scene advised the President to appoint non-Westerners who would be more impartial than residents of the Coast. Mayor Rossi advised the opposite; to gain confidence, board members should be local men, preferably old San Franciscans. The board FDR appointed—Archbishop Hanna of San Francisco as chairman, Oscar K. Cushing, a San Francisco lawyer, and Edward J. McGrady—was a compromise.

Archbishop Hanna was seventy-three, a scholarly, thoughtful man, known and respected for fairness. He had gone to college in the United States, then been called by the Vatican to the Propaganda College in Rome. From there he had been sent to study at Cambridge University and the University of Munich. From 1893 to 1912, he had taught theology at a seminary in Rochester, New York. While there, he had been appointed Coadjutor Archbishop of San Francisco. For five years Rome held up confirmation of his appointment because of charges he was guilty of Modernism. When he was cleared in 1912, he came to San Francisco as auxiliary bishop. The next year he was appointed Commissioner of Immigration for California. He became Archbishop of San Francisco in 1915. Active in civic affairs and in the liberal National Catholic Welfare Conference, he was frequently called upon as a mediator and arbitrator in labor disputes. In 1933, he had been chairman of a three–man board appointed by the governor to help settle a strike of farm workers in the San Joaquin Valley.

Cushing, the son of a California Forty-Niner, had been practicing law in San Francisco since 1894. He was president of the Legal Aid Society, had served on a committee appointed by the governor to study unemployment, and, at the time of his appointment to the longshoremen's board, was on the State Emergency Relief Committee. He was more liberal than much of the business community he presumably represented on the board.

The employers and the newspapers reacted favorably to FDR's appointments, but the strikers didn't think much of them. Their experiences with McGrady did not inspire confidence in him, and assuming that the board was tri–partite, he was the member who was presumably intended to represent them. "Who suggested the names of the board to the President?" Bridges wanted to know when McGrady met with the strike committee on June 27th. McGrady's answer was not entirely reassuring. He replied only that the President was undoubtedly in touch with the situation and knew whom he wanted to appoint.

"Don't you fellows trust me?" he asked.

"No," they answered, "we don't trust anybody."

The board's first job was to prevent the blood–letting that would undoubtedly take place if the Industrial Association went through with its plan, to open the port, now scheduled for June 28. The board succeeded, despite grumbling by the Association that this was the fourth time it had postponed action at the request of public officials.

As the board began day and night mediation sessions, Ryan left San Francisco for the East. His parting comments were equally harsh on the employers, whom he thought unreasonably obdurate, and Bridges, whom he thought obstructionist. "The executive committee of the Pacific Coast District agreed to a policy," Ryan said, referring to the June 16th settlement, "and it should be adopted. But Bridges opposed it and is influencing the men to oppose it. It looks like Bridges doesn't want the strike settled. My firm belief is that he is acting for the Communists."

Bridges denied he was a Communist, adding: "Anyone who says I am will have to prove it. Of course I want the strike settled. Everyone on the waterfront wants the same thing. But I want it settled on a basis favorable to the men. And don't forget that the men will have to vote on any proposal the executive committee signs, unless it meets the demand for a closed shop."

Bridges was, by this time, becoming accustomed to being called a Communist. But now came a wildly outlandish accusation. Someone suggested that perhaps Bridges wasn't a missionary from Moscow after all. He was a liegeman of London. A Bay Area newspaper speculated editorially on the possibility:

> It may be fantastic to suggest that the spectacle of a Britisher leading the group of striking longshoremen 'irreconcilables' is a British plot to tie up and effectively undermine American shipping and commerce.
>
> But to many, the port tie–up itself, despite the concessions offered the men, seems so fantastic that additional fantasies seem almost credible. Especially since British efforts to capture Pacific coast and South American trade are so well known.
>
> Here the strike leader is not even an American citizen but a native of a British dominion . . .
>
> Whether the shipping paralysis has been under the leadership of London, of Moscow, or under no leadership at all, the effect has been equally detrimental to Pacific coast business and to thousands of innocent American workers whose livelihood has been jeopardized by this foolhardy "beter–'oler" attitude.

NOTES

Lapham made the comment that he thought the strike was a Communist scheme in an oral history interview he gave in the 1950s. The transcript is in the library of the University of California at Berkeley.

Darcy recalled his conversations with Bridges during the strike in an interview with me in 1963. Landis's comment about support given the strikers by the Communist Party is in *In the Matter of Harry Bridges: Findings and Conclusions of the Trial Examiner* (Government Printing Office, 1939), p. 124.

The source of Bridges's denial of Gregory Harrison's contention that he followed the Communist line was Hubert Brown, a Pacific Far East Lines executive, who recalled it in an interview with me in San Francisco in 1963. Kagel described Bridges's way of making up his mind in an interview with me in San Francisco in 1964.

The shipowners' arrangement to pay for the tear gas used by the police is reported in *Violations of Free Speech and Rights of Labor, Report No. 6, Part 3* of the La Follette Civil Liberties Committee of the U.S. Senate, pp. 46 and 66. Stow's comment that he took a fancy to Roush is reported in the La Follette Committee *Hearings, Part 15-D*, p. 7105. McCarty's letter about the San Francisco police preference for Federal billy clubs is reproduced in the Committee's *Report No. 6, Part No. 3*, p. 34.

McCarty's letter criticizing his rival salesman for wasting tear gas is in the Committee's *Hearings, Part 15-D*, p. 7222. Roush's letter about shooting a Communist is Exhibit 921, the reply is Exhibit 922, and the president's letter to salesmen Exhibit 917, in the Committee's *Hearings, Part 7*.

The Committee's description of the incident in which Roush said he had bagged a Communist is in its *Report No. 6, Part 3*, p. 161 ff.

Engle's description of being shot by Roush is in the Committee's *Hearings, Part 15-D*, pp. 7100–7101.

Perkins's and FDR's opinion of McGrady's qualifications is in President's Personal File Number 1715, in the Roosevelt Memorial Library. Battle's letter to Col. McIntyre is in the file of NLRB Case File No. 76, also in the Roosevelt Memorial Library.

Records of McGrady's memos and phone calls to Secretary Perkins are in NLRB Case File No. 76.

For a description of hoodlumism in the ILA, see my *Shape-up and Hiring Hall*, pp. 19–24.

In 1943, Ryan was elected president of the union for life. For the next ten years, life was good to him: he had a good salary, which employers augmented by paying into a fund he maintained "to keep Communism off the waterfront," top businessmen and political figures came annually to testimonial dinners held to honor his labor statesmanship and to fatten his purse. Then, in 1953, his world fell in on him. The AFL expelled him and his union for corruption and for perpetuating the archaic shape–up, and after that the ILA pensioned him off. A year later, he was sentenced to six months in federal penitentiary for violation of a provision of the Taft–

Hartley law making it a crime for a union representative to take a bribe from an employer. He stayed out of jail, miraculously, when a federal court of appeals reversed his conviction, ruling that the word "representative" in the law meant the union itself, not an official. So Ryan wasn't guilty. That same year, Ryan went on trial again, charged with looting the union treasury of forty–eight thousand dollars. This time, the jury deadlocked. By the time the government got around to re-trying the case, Ryan was too old and sick to stand trial. In 1962, friendless and alone, he died in New York at the age of seventy–nine.

Eliel's letter to the National Labor Board is reproduced in his *The Waterfront and General Strike, San Francisco, 1934.*

President Roosevelt's explanation of the role of the press in the 1934 strike is in "Presidential Press Conference No. 141, September 5, 1934," in the Roosevelt Memorial Library.

The source of the story about the money being put up for the attempt to bribe Bridges was Randolph Sevier, former president of Matson, in an interview with me in San Francisco, in 1963.

The newspaper that speculated that Bridges was a British agent was the *Oakland* (Calif.) *Post-Enquirer*, which published the editorial on June 28, 1934.

3

Where Did You Study
Military Strategy and Tactics

*Stronger than any army is an idea whose
time has come.*

Victor Hugo

In strikes, as in wars, there sometimes comes a moment when the
outcome is irreversible. Paradoxically, it sometimes comes just at
the moment when the side that loses in the end has scored its greatest victory. Opening the port was such a time. Bridges remembered
it this way when he was on the stand in his first deportation hearing:

> When they talked about opening the port, it meant that they
> were going to hire strikebreakers for teamsters and remove the
> stuff from the docks. And on July 3rd we sent out an emergency
> call to all unions in the city to come down and string a mass
> picket line along the entire waterfront. When that was done the
> police charged the picket line and removed them and they ran a
> little bit of freight out of two or three of the docks and utilized it,
> of course, to proclaim in very glaring headlines that the port at
> least was open, mainly all directed, of course, to breaking the
> morale of the strikers.
>
> Well, I remember at that time I knew that they had made a
> foolish move. It was all very well to use strikebreakers and a lot
> of publicity on us, and the old Red scare, but when they started
> to put strikebreakers in the place of teamsters' union, which was
> an old established and conservative union, and started to call the
> teamsters a bunch of Reds, it just didn't work.
>
> So we got then the full and complete cooperation of the team-

62

sters, and that is when we really started to get organized, and that was the beginning of the spread of the strike, from July 3rd on.

The curtain went up on Scene I on the morning of July 2nd, when San Francisco newspapers carried the story under banner headlines that the port was going to be opened at three that afternoon. Plenty of police would be on hand to hold back the pickets, and trucks would be driven across the Embarcadero into Pier 38, where they would be loaded with goods that had been sitting there since the strike began. Then they would go back across the picket line to deliver their cargoes at a heavily guarded warehouse two blocks inland. The port would be open.

Early in the morning, longshoremen began gathering in front of Pier 38. By noon, there were fifteen hundred of them, waiting and wondering what they would do when the trucks started across the street, heading for the pier. While they waited, an engrossing scene was being enacted in the Mayor's office. Present were officers of the Industrial Association and the Chamber of Commerce, the Chief of Police and several of his lieutenants, and Mayor Rossi.

The Mayor was trying to persuade the businessmen to hold off opening the port. It's sure to cause bloodshed, he contended. People might even get killed. For three hours he pleaded, getting nowhere with the businessmen, who contended they had a right to get their goods out of the pier warehouses. They had trucks and drivers standing by, they reminded him, and men ready to unload them at an inland warehouse. All they needed was police protection, and it was the Mayor's duty to provide it. The argument surged back and forth, neither side giving ground. But when three o'clock came, the Mayor was still standing firm, so once again the Association had to put off opening the port until the next day.

By late afternoon, most of the crowd had drifted away from Pier 38. Suddenly, a squadron of mounted police cantered into place, forming a corridor across the Embarcadero. Five trucks came out of a side street, roared across, into the warehouse on the pier. As the last one disappeared inside, the heavy steel door clanged down. A police launch took the drivers off the end of the pier, landing them down the beach at a deserted dock.

By eleven the next morning, there were five thousand longshoremen and their sympathizers in front of Pier 38, waiting for the trucks to come out. The police drove the crowd back until they had cleared an area two blocks inland, and along the waterfront from

Pier 46 to Pier 34. (On the frontispiece map you can delineate the area cordoned off by running a line from Pier 46, where headquarters of the 185th infantry is shown, to the Southern Pacific Depot, then over almost to Rincon Hill, and from there back down to the Embarcadero at the foot of Beale Street.)

A little after noon on July 3rd, the trucks rumbled out of the warehouse, crossed the Embarcadero, headed up a long block on Townsend to Second Street. There, they turned left, then right at the next corner. Their destination, a warehouse on King Street, was now only half a block away. From behind the police line near the Southern Pacific Depot at Third and King, another half–block inland from the warehouse, twelve hundred longshoremen watched as the trucks unloaded their cargoes (the first one carried packaged birdseed, coffee, and automobile tires) and headed back for more, again and again, until the longshoremen could stand it no longer. "Like toy leaden soldiers, motionless, aloof, almost indifferent, they watched," the *San Francisco News* reported the next day,

But suddenly they moved into action, heading toward the police. The blue–coated line wavered as a barrage of bricks whizzed about them . . .

Gold braid glistened in the sunlight as chief and captains led the attack. Police reinforcements came sprinting up, wielding clubs. Rocks pattered about them, gashing their faces, ripping their uniforms, but they waded into the melee, swinging their clubs. The strikers scampered up Third and Townsend Streets, dribbling like quicksilver into surrounding streets and alleys . . .

An advance guard of four policemen, looking like grotesque Martian monsters—they wore khaki gas masks, hard black helmets, and brandished tear gas hand grenades and tear gas guns —cleared the way for the mounted officers and their club-wielding comrades . . . Sometimes the grenades didn't go off, and the strikers pounced on them, tossing them back at the police.

Shots were fired by a policeman as the bluecoats tried to disperse the crowd at Second and Townsend Streets. Eugene Dunbar, union seaman, was struck in the ankle, and Bertram Holmes, a bank teller in the Third and Townsend branch of the American Trust Company, was hit over the left eye by a bullet that pierced the bank window.

The casualty list for the battle included thirteen policemen and twelve others; one horse was cut on the forehead by a flying rock.

One man died that day, San Francisco's first fatality in the strike. After a minor fight between longshoremen and strikebreakers at the corner of Clay and Embarcadero, several long blocks from the main battle zone, he was found lying in the gutter, bruised and bloody. Doctors at the Harbor Emergency Hospital nearby learned that his name was Argonne Riley and that he was thirty-three. He told them he was a strikebreaker from Los Angeles. He had come ashore for a few drinks, he said, and had been beaten by several men. The doctors treated him for cuts on his chin and nose before he was transferred to the police station where he was booked as an alcoholic and put in the drunk tank. At midnight he complained of severe head pains. About an hour later, the police took him back to the emergency hospital, where he died nine minutes after his arrival. Only then was it discovered that his skull had been fractured.

Because the Fourth of July was a national holiday, the Industrial Association gave its truck drivers the day off, and Pier 38 was quiet. Trouble did break out, however, on the state–owned Belt Railroad which was loaded with fourteen cars of cargo, mostly fruits and vegetables, plus a shipment of polio serum, to be delivered to a Matson freighter scheduled to sail at 4:00 p.m. for the Philippines. As the train started toward the Matson dock, the longshoremen swarmed aboard, bringing it to a stop. The railroad superintendent alerted the harbor commissioners and the Governor in Sacramento, then went to strike committee headquarters, where he tried without success to get the train released.

To Governor Merriam, this was revolution. "The State of California has the power," he thundered, "and the Belt Line Railroad is going to operate. I will call upon the National Guard, the citizens of San Francisco and every citizen of the commonwealth to support the government. I will not send the guard in tonight," he went on, "but unless I receive word that the strikers have modified their attitude, I shall call out the National Guard tomorrow."

Events had already gone too far for the Governor's warning to be heeded, and July 5th was a day of battle on the San Francisco waterfront. Men who were there remember it as Bloody Thursday, the way old soldiers remember the Battle of the Bulge or Iwo Jima. Joe Rosenthal, the *San Francisco Chronicle* photographer who took the famous shot of the marines raising the flag on Iwo Jima, saw his first action on July 5th. "I was more scared taking pictures on the Embarcadero during the '34 strike," he said in 1957, "than when I

was on Iwo Jima." He had good reason to be. On Bloody Thursday
he was stoned by strikers, tear gassed by police, and beaten so
badly that he was hospitalized for a week.

At 8:00 a.m., a Belt Line locomotive slowly pushed two railroad
cars toward the Matson docks at Pier 30. Three thousand pickets
watched silently. "Move back!" the police called out. No one
moved. As the police advanced, the pickets threw themselves
fiercely into battle. Forcing the police back with a barrage of rocks,
they surrounded the boxcars and set them afire. When firemen arrived to put out the fires, police commandeered their fire hoses,
turning them on the strikers and forcing them inland. "At times,"
General David Prescott Barrows, who commanded the National
Guardsmen later sent to San Francisco, wrote in the July–August
(1934) *California Guardsman*, "the fighting extended as far north as
Pacific Street, the old 'Barbary Coast,' but police rounded up the
rioters and drove them south of the slot."

Many of the strikers climbed up on Rincon Hill (it was actually a
high knoll, bounded by Bryant, Beale, Folsom, and First Streets,
rising to a height of a four–story building) where they could get a
good view of what was happening down on the Embarcadero. This
was how it looked to Henry Schmidt, one of the strike leaders:

> Thousands of strikers were lined up near Piers 38 and 40. Scab
> trucks were to haul freight from them to a nearby warehouse.
> Hundreds and hundreds of police armed with clubs, revolvers,
> rifles, and tear gas guns were there to hold back the pickets.
>
> At 10:00 a.m. the 'Battle of Rincon Hill' was in full swing. I ar-
> rived at the foot of the hill at about 9:30 a.m. The strikers were
> retreating towards the hill, being driven by the police who were
> using their firearms freely and laying down a barrage of tear gas
> bombs. The bombs set fire to the dry grass on the slopes of the
> hill and the Fire Department arrived to extinguish the flames.
>
> Barricades were erected by the strikers across Bryant Street.
> Being attacked by the police from the rear, all the strikers re-
> treated towards the top of the hill. A steady rifle fire was directed
> towards the top of the hill and several strikers were shot. None
> were killed, however, at this point. Being without arms of any
> sort, the strikers were soon dispersed and proceeded to their
> union hall about a half mile from Rincon Hill and were promptly
> followed by the armed allies of the employers . . .

In 1962, at a party for Schmidt and another longshoreman who had just retired from the union executive board, Bridges fell to reminiscing about the Battle of Rincon Hill. He recalled that when the longshoremen retreated inland from Pier 38, Schmidt took charge of the men on Rincon Hill, Bridges himself taking charge of another group nearby. As the mounted police advanced toward the hill, Bridges heard Schmidt call out, "We'd better build some barricades, boys!" Several brick buildings had recently been torn down on the hill to make way for the massive concrete anchor for the cables of the Bay Bridge, the bricks stacked in neat piles by the wrecking crew. Under Schmidt's direction, the strikers quickly rearranged the bricks into a wall high enough to keep the mounted policemen from the crest of the hill.

As the police charged up the slope, the longshoremen waited behind their wall until the police were almost upon them. Then they lobbed their bricks over the parapet, driving the horsemen back. At the foot of the hill the police dismounted and attacked on foot, only to retreat again under a barrage of bricks. They called for reinforcements, who were rushed to the scene in squad cars. As the police cars approached, a group of strikers detached themselves from the main body and posted themselves on the overpass with a supply of stones and bricks. As the police cars passed underneath, the stones crashed down, smashing windshields and disabling some of the cars.

Before making a third assault, the police laid down a fog of tear gas. Putting on their gas masks, they struggled up through the smoke. This time, they made it. But when the sweating police, gasping for breath inside their gas masks, breached the barricade, the longshoremen were gone. They had abandoned their positions while the police were regrouping for the third assault.

Some longshoremen manned an especially formidable weapon. Ignatius H. McCarty of the Lake Erie Chemical Company described it in a letter to his home office:

> What has been done towards securing more long range guns in case of a sudden order? Green band grenades are of course wonderful but can't compare to the long range shells in the type of fighting indulged in by the longshoremen here.
>
> I don't know if I told you about the giant slingshot they have composed of inner tubes from automobiles and attached to 2' x 3' poles. This slingshot will throw a cobblestone weighing from 1 to 3 lbs. for a distance of 300 to 400 feet. Getting close enough to

use green band grenades in this case would be dangerous . . .
All in all it was a bad morning for the police.

After the retreat off Rincon Hill, the waterfront was compara-
tively quiet until after the noon hour. Several thousand longshoremen drifted down to the union hall where they stood around on
Steuart Street and in the open lot across the way where mass meetings were held during the strike. The police viewed any crowd as a
potential danger and appeared in force at both ends of Steuart to
execute a pincers movement against the trapped strikers. One de-
tachment moved south from Mission Street, the other advancing
toward it from Howard, at the other end of the block. In a professional military action, the objective would presumably have been to
take the men prisoners. But the police apparently had no well–
thought–out–plan. As General Barrows, the Commanding General
of the National Guard's 40th Division, described the action, "Police fired at the milling mob. There was a wild pounding of feet. Police followed. The crowd rallied. Another volley scattered it." The
police and their volunteer assistants Roush and McCarty opened
up with tear gas grenades and shells. As the men ran from the
smoke, the police fired at them from behind with rifles and buckshot.

In the midst of all this, three men fell to the sidewalk, blood
spurting from their wounds. The official police report described the
incident as follows:

> A general riot of about six thousand men broke out at Steuart
> and Mission Streets in the middle of the afternoon. At this time
> all radio patrol cars were ordered to this area. Two inspectors of
> police, while responding to this call found themselves sur-
> rounded by these rioters before the arrival of the other officers.
> The rioters blocked the car and shouted "Kill them," and at-
> tempted to overturn the police car. During this time the inspec-
> tors were being struck by showers of bricks and rocks. Feeling
> that their lives were in danger, the officers fired two shots from a
> shotgun and several shots from their revolvers at the men who
> were attempting to overturn the car. The two men who were
> struck with the bullets from the inspectors' guns later died.

One of the fatalities was Howard S. Sperry, a striking sailor who
had been working in the union relief kitchen on the corner of Mission and Embarcadero, just a block from the union hall. The lunch

period over, he was on his way to 113 Steuart Street to have his strike card punched when he was hit by a bullet only a few doors from his destination. The other was Nicholas Counderakis, an unemployed cook from uptown. A Communist who was known in the Party as Nick Bordoise, he, too, had been on duty in the strikers' kitchen. Counderakis was found, dying, near the corner of Mission and Spear, a block away from where he was hit.

The third man who fell, shot in the arm, face, and chest, was Charles Olsen, a longshoreman. He disappeared after the shooting and was given up for dead, but he appeared at the coroner's inquest a few weeks later, where he described the shooting as he had seen it: "The police had driven us up from the Embarcadero. I was standing next to Sperry when I saw a policeman start shooting at the crowd across the street. I started to run and he must have turned the gun our way. Sperry went down. Then something hit me. I fell and remember trying to crawl away."

Two Southern Pacific employees were watching the affair from their office a block away, on the corner of Market and Steuart. "The crowd had the policeman hemmed in," one of them said. "He got out of his car, wearing civilian clothes. A piece of brick hit him in the leg. He fired his shot gun without even raising it from his hip."

Irving Moore, a leasing agent, saw the shooting from still another vantage point:

"No bricks were thrown when the policeman opened fire. The only threats were shouts of 'let's tip his car over!' He jumped out of his car. He was nervous and excited. He shouted, 'If any of you sons–of–bitches want to start something, come on!' Then he dodged around his car like a man shooting birds. The shooting was unwarranted."

Bridges was finishing his lunch in the strikers' relief kitchen when the shots rang out. "I was standing," he testified in the coroner's inquest, "in a restaurant at the Embarcadero and Mission Street. I could see the police driving the men along both streets. There was no one throwing any bricks at the point where Sperry was killed. The men were just trying to get out of range of fire."

No one noticed Counderakis, as he staggered off down Mission, but a crowd collected around Sperry and Olsen. The police ran over, yelling, "Get back, you sonsabitches, or you'll get the same thing!" The crowd moved back, then stood frozen, as they looked down at the fallen men. The son of the manager of the service station across the street came over to see if he could help. "Get the hell out of here!" an officer shouted, "or you'll get what they got!" An ambulance arrived to take Sperry and Olsen to the hospital, where Sperry died moments after their arrival.

When the ambulance pulled away, strikers chalked off a 12–foot square where the fallen men had lain, banked flowers and wreaths around it, and placed the American flag and the union banner up against the wall. Minutes later, a paddy wagon pulled up. Three policemen and a lieutenant climbed out. Quickly they scooped up the flowers, threw them into the wagon, wiped away the chalk, and left. Almost as quickly, the graffiti and the flowers were back, with strikers standing guard. This time, the police let them stay.

After the inquest, the coroner's jury found that Sperry's death was justifiable homicide: "He died of buckshot wounds inflicted by an unknown police officer while said officer was engaged in suppression of a riot." The verdict in Counderakis's case was: "Shot by party or parties unknown to the jury."

Just around the corner, the union headquarters had taken on the appearance of a front–line medical aid station as the wounded and gassed were carried or stumbled up the narrow stairway to the second floor hall, where they were laid in rows on the floor. A doctor was found who was willing to treat them and as he moved among the wounded, a tear gas shell came crashing through a window, to spew its sickening smoke in the room. Someone had bolted the door to protect the wounded from the police, who insisted that they were going to take the casualties to the emergency hospital. Over the racket of the shots and the shouting outside and the moaning of the wounded inside, the men heard an insistent pounding on the door. The upper half was frosted glass, and they could see a head and shoulders silhouetted against it. "Don't let him in!" someone shouted, "It's a goddam cop!" Then, as the man outside turned toward the stairs, a cry went up, "Hey, you guys! Look at that nose! It's Harry! It's Harry! Let him in!"

At almost the precise moment that the intersection of Steuart and Mission was being turned into a battleground, the Adjutant General of the National Guard in Sacramento was calling Major General David Prescott Barrows, Commanding General of the 40th Division to order the guard to the waterfront. "By midnight," Barrows has written (in the *California Guardsman*), "steel helmeted soldiers were on guard in front of every dock from Fisherman's Wharf [the long dock at the extreme left on the frontispiece map] to China Basin, equipped with rifles, bayonets, automatic rifles, machine guns . . ."

General Barrows was pleased with the disciplined demeanor of the guardsmen under his command, and of the mastery of tactical and administrative detail demonstrated in the occupation of the waterfront. "Fourteen years of preparation," he admitted modestly, "have gone into our work of entering the San Francisco Bay waterfront with dispatch, and I am glad to say, efficiency."

For division headquarters, General Barrows used the "Fort Sutter," a river boat which his quartering officer found for him and tied up at Pier 3, near the Ferry Building. The 159th Infantry Regiment was strung along the docks from Fisherman's Wharf to the Ferry Building. The 250th Coast Artillery was guarding the area from the Ferry Building to the Matson dock at Pier 32. The 185th infantry held the most difficult sector, where the trucks ran the gauntlet from Pier 38 to the Industrial Association's warehouse. It ran inland from Pier 32 along Brannan to Third Street, then down Third to the China Basin. The 184th infantry took the area from there to a few blocks south of Islais Creek. The General had also called out two battalions of the 160th infantry and a tank company, but these never had to be used. On the Oakland side of the bay, General Barrows placed the other battalion of the 160th and headquarters company of the 184th at Parr Terminal (now occupied by an army base), with one battalion of the 143rd field artillery in reserve.

With the arrival of the national guard, the waterfront quieted down.

"Next day [July 6th] and for three days thereafter," General Barrows wrote, "there was peace. The Embarcadero became a No–Man's Land for strikers. All the steel doors of the docks were flung wide; the Belt Line moved 203 cars; trucks ran back and forth with impunity . . . Reason for the sudden peace was that Harry Bridges, Australian chairman of the strike committee, had told his followers, 'We can't stand up against police machine guns and National Guard bayonets.' "

Bridges's action was consistent with a position he had taken earlier when company guards and police, rather than the National Guard, were on the other side of the barricades. If strikers fired on police, he argued, it would be suicidal, for it would invite a retaliatory massacre. Moreover, nonviolence was a *sine qua non* of public sympathy with the strikers' cause. "In the 1934 strike, Bridges said later, "I stood there, with guards, and all of the men were rolled, every single man in our union, to see if they had guns. We found a few, maybe, and they were thrown in the safe."

As the national guard was moving into position, a message was on its way from Marvin McIntyre, FDR's confidential secretary at the White House, to the President who was vacationing on the USS "Houston" in the Pacific:

> Authorities in San Francisco today forced picket lines back by troops without real need, injuring two or three people. Perkins ought to, I told her, take the mail away and John Lang ought to threaten to put the shipowners under [the NRA] code and refuse clearance papers to firms which did not come under the code and live up to it. The attorney general is afraid of the legality but the federal government is given control over foreign shipping by the Constitution and in the past for very trivial reasons clearance has been refused. They need a hard jolt to frighten them, I think, or they will fan flames into life again.
>
> The patience and forbearance of the longshoremen, whom I was violently prejudiced against at the start, has been amazing to me. I hope you will back any efforts decided upon to put the fear of God into the shipowners and get the strike situation cleared up. Perkins agrees and I am convinced that on the theory that union labor has not prepared to carry the general strike through, the shipowners deliberately planned to force a general strike throughout the country and in this way they hoped they could crush the labor movement.
>
> I have no proof but I think the shipowners were selected to re-place the steel people who originally started out to do this job . . . .

McIntyre's message went unanswered.

When July 5th was over, the known casualties were two dead, thirty treated for bullet wounds, forty–three clubbed, gassed and stoned. There were even men missing in action. George P. Hedley, a summer preacher at the Stanford chapel who had gone up to San Francisco to see what was happening for himself, has described a conversation with a stranger that he had on July 6th:

"I sat down beside him in an 'I.L.A. Supporter' lunch room. He was not young, and was rather better dressed and groomed than most of us. Despite the place in which he had chosen to eat, I won-dered what his sympathies were. Tentatively I remarked on the mounted police across the Embarcadero.

" 'Yes,' he said, 'they shot my boy yesterday.' "

" 'They did, eh? How badly?' "

" 'I don't know. Paper said through the hand.' "
" 'Where did it happen?' "
" 'I don't know. Paper said he was in the lobby of the Seaboard Hotel.' "
" 'You haven't seen him?' "
" 'No.' "
" 'Where is he now?' "
" 'I don't know.' "
"Wearily he got up and went out."

The next day the dénouement McIntyre feared in his message to FDR moved a step nearer when Bridges asked all the unions in the city to meet on Saturday, July 7th, to discuss calling a general strike. Almost all responded, although the last thing San Francisco's union officers wanted was a general strike. Hoping to head it off and to have a moderating influence on the strikers, they authorized the president of the Labor Council, Edward Vandeleur, to appoint a committee of seven to work with the presumably less experienced members of the Joint Marine Strike Committee of fifty. Vandeleur appointed himself, John O'Connell, the council's secretary, and five other members of the San Francisco labor establishment. The committee of seven met with the shipowners, then with McGrady and Cushing of the President's board, only to find the shipowners as obdurate as Bridges had said they were in their opposition to union hiring halls and to meeting with the offshore unions.

While the AFL establishment was vainly seeking roads to peace with the employers and the Industrial Association, the rank and file of union after union was edging away from its leaders. On Sunday, July 8th, teamster locals in San Francisco and Oakland voted to strike on the coming Thursday if the maritime strike were not settled by then. Mike Casey urged the truckdrivers not to, reminding them that if they did, they would be violating the rules of their international union. Nevertheless, 1,220 San Francisco teamsters voted to strike, only 271 not to. In Oakland, 369 teamsters voted to strike, 54 against. "Nothing on earth could have prevented that vote," Casey said later. "In all my thirty years of leading these men, I have never seen them so worked up, so determined to walk out." In accordance with their rules, the teamsters scheduled a second vote for the coming Wednesday, to confirm the first. "The vote Wednesday will be a standing vote, and not a secret ballot as was today's," Casey decided. "Such a ballot would be unnecessary."

Monday, July 9th, was a day of intense drama. In the morning, members of the National Longshoremen's Board began public hearings to mediate the situation. In the afternoon, one hundred people crowded into the little union hall for a memorial service which the longshoremen held for Sperry and Counderakis. Their bodies had lain in state in the hall since their deaths, banked by wreaths and flowers. Because Sperry was a member of the veterans of Foreign Wars, his coffin was draped with the American flag and men in Army and Navy uniforms stood guard by it. Counderakis's coffin was bare. On the wall was a picture of FDR. The sermon was read by Alex Walthers, a former longshoreman. Someone asked Bridges if he would say something. "He shook his head," a reporter noticed, "too distraught to utter his feelings."

After the ceremony, the caskets were carried down the narrow steps to the street. There, they were placed on separate flat–bed trucks and flowers and wreaths were arranged around them. Following were three more open trucks loaded with flowers. Next came the car bearing Counderakis's widow and his young son. Then came the marchers, fifteen thousand of them, eight abreast, the longshoremen in their black Frisco jeans, hickory shirts and white caps. At their head were Bridges and William Lewis, president of the union's Pacific Coast District. Behind these four marched an honor guard, with the American flag and the union banner. Slowly they marched off Steuart Street onto Market, where they turned left and headed up Market to 17th Street, five miles away.

It was the most impressive procession the city could remember. The longshoremen had obtained a permit from the Police Department for the march and had asked that their own marshals be allowed to police it. Chief Quinn agreed, laying down two conditions: Communist contingents must be kept out of the procession, to avoid provocation of spectators, and there must be no picket signs that might inflame onlookers and lead to riots.

Paul Eliel wrote in his book about the strike:

. . . The funeral cortege formed in the most orderly fashion. The procession was orderly and quiet. Every marcher walked with bared head. Not a word was spoken. None smoked. The ranks were well formed and the cadence of the marchers' feet was set by the slow music of a Beethoven funeral march played by a single band. Tens of thousands of spectators lined the streets as the files of strikers, extending for more than a mile and a half down Market Street, swung slowly past. At each intersection volunteer traffic officers from the strikers' ranks controlled the crowds and the movement of the marchers through the intersection. Not a police officer nor a National Guardsman was in evidence from one end of the long line of march to the other.

It was one of the strangest and most dramatic spectacles that had ever moved along Market Street. Its passage marked the high tide of united labor action in San Francisco. Its dramatic qualities moved the entire community without regard to individual points of view as to the justice and righteousness of the strikers' cause. It created a temporary but tremendous wave of sympathy for the workers. Only after two or three days passed did San Francisco awaken to the fact that its sympathies had been aroused by a brilliant and theatric piece of propaganda. It provided the impetus that made the events which followed as inevitable as though the human beings involved in the subsequent drama had been moved by vast physical forces over which they had no control.

As the last marcher broke ranks, the certainty of a general strike, which up to this time had appeared to many to be the visionary dream of a small group of the most radical workers, became for the first time a practical and realizable objective.

The business community suffered another demoralizing experience the next day, when Bridges testified before the National Longshoremen's Board. He reiterated the two points on which the longshoremen would not retreat: the union hiring hall, and staying out until the demands of the other unions were satisfied. Then he explained why the men had repudiated the June 16 agreement and stated Ryan had no authority to sign agreements covering the Pacific Coast District.

Bridges also read a letter that had been written on June 21st by T. G. Plant to Eugene Mills, who was in charge of recruitment and housing of strikebreakers in Los Angeles harbor.

Dear Sir [Plant began]:

Our membership at today's meeting expressed themselves very forcibly on the subject of expense at San Pedro.

A statement which was studied indicated an average expense of approximately, $7,000 per day up to June 11th, after taking out the cost of preparing the housing ship . . .

The item of guards, cost of boarding, amounting to about $100,000, is one which we think should be borne by the city.

Here the police in ample numbers are supplied without cost, and the only guards employed are those needed on the housing ships. . . .

As Bridges talked, a mood of anxiety fell upon his listeners. Eliel wrote:

"Bridges made an extraordinary presentation before the Board, speaking without notes and extemporaneously. He showed not only unusual command of the subject matter but of the English language as well. Employers were able for the first time to understand something of the hold which he had been able to establish over the strikers both in his own union and in the other maritime crafts." Moreover, the employers could see clearly enough that Bridges's presentation was an effective appeal to the people of San Francisco.

The crucial teamsters' meeting came the next night at Dreamland, a large ballroom and auditorium. Bridges and a thousand longshoremen and seamen were there early, waiting outside the hall. "Stick with us, boys!" they called out as the truck drivers went in. As the meeting was beginning, someone noticed some wires and microphones near the stage. "Hey! They've got dictographs in here!" he yelled. "They're listening in on everything we say!" Several men rushed forward and were busily ripping out wires and mikes when a Dreamland employee managed to make himself heard. The place wasn't bugged, he assured them. The wires were part of a system that had been installed to broadcast political speeches.

For two hours, Bridges waited outside with the others. From time to time a sympathetic teamster would come out to tell them what was going on inside. It wasn't encouraging. Casey, Vandeleur, and George Kidwell, an officer of the bakery drivers' local, were pleading with the two thousand teamsters not to strike. Then suddenly, the door flew open and a teamster burst out. "Bridges! Bridges! Get Bridges right away!"

Bridges was located down the block and he rushed up to the entrance and pushed his way into the hall. As he hurried down the aisle to the stage, a cheer went up. He spoke in his usual quiet manner, carefully reviewing events of the strike, reminding the teamsters of past defeats at the hands of organized employers: the 1901 strike, when the newspapers called Casey "Bloody Mike"; 1916 and the Law and Order Committee; 1919 and the industrial relations committee of the Chamber of Commerce. And now, he said, it was the Industrial Association. "The entire labor movement faces collapse if we maritime workers are defeated," he concluded. "If you fellows join us, you will double our power."

Casey then asked for written questions for Bridges to answer. "Is it true," came one, "that you were run out of Australia and were identified with a Red organization there?"

"If it were true," Bridges replied, "I would have been exposed long ago. I took ship from Australia several years ago and came here. I have worked and been a law–abiding citizen. If anything could have been pinned on me to associate me with Communism, it would have been found out long ago and exposed."

Another questioner wanted to know where Bridges stood on arbitration. The employers had told the National Longshoremen's Board the day before that they were willing to let the board arbitrate their dispute with the longshoremen. "What about you?" Bridges said he was personally against arbitration but that the membership would vote on it.

When Casey called for the strike vote, two thousand hands went up in favor. Reporters covering the meeting saw only two or three hands go up when he called for the noes. Then came some questions for Casey to answer. "Can I report my C.O.D. meat deliveries before I quit?" one driver asked. "You'll go out like gentlemen," Casey assured his members, "with nothing to be ashamed of. Of course, you'll be allowed to do the decent thing. Don't worry, the children can eat and have their milk. Retail food deliveries won't be affected. And bless you, San Francisco may have its beer. The brewery drivers are a separate group." At this, the two thousand teamsters poured out of the hall, shouting euphorically: "We're out! We're out!"

All week long, from July 9th to 13th, San Francisco unions held special meetings where, one by one, they followed the teamsters' example. The typographical union decided not to go out, however, because it had just signed a new contract with a pay raise in it. This meant that newspapers kept publishing during the general strike. Then, on Saturday, July 14th, came the crucial meeting of the San Francisco Labor Council. There was only one item on the agenda: To strike, or not to strike? One hundred and fifteen unions were present, each represented by five delegates. As they spoke, it was clear that sentiment for a general strike was overwhelming. Only one delegate, a representative of the building trades unions, spoke against it. He talked of their strike in 1920, when the Industrial Association had defeated them so handsomely. "We haven't recovered from that beating yet," he warned. "Let's not do it again."

When the motion was put, "All unions out on Monday," 315 delegates, representing sixty–three unions, voted to strike. 245 delegates, representing forty–nine, abstained, explaining that they had not yet been authorized to vote on a general strike. Only fifteen voted no. The Central Labor Council's committee of seven was ignored, and a new one proposed which would have wider power and would direct the general strike.

Before deciding how large the committee itself would be, the delegates elected its chief officers. Vandeleur, president of the Labor Council, was elected chairman. Then Henry Schmidt nominated Bridges for vice–chairman. A conservative officer of the ferryboatmen, the only maritime union not on strike, was put up against him, giving delegates a clear choice between a militant and a conservative. They chose the conservative, giving him 262 votes to Bridges's 203. An official of the bakery drivers who, like the ferryboatmen, weren't on strike, was elected secretary. For the moment, at least, AFL grayheads could breathe easily. The establishment would be running the strike.

Having lost control of the committee officers, the militants tried to gain control of the committee itself. If the committee were large enough, they had a chance of dominating it. Then they would be running the strike. For two days the general strike waited while the delegates fought over the size of the committee. Although the militants won the argument the grayheads out–maneuvered them in the end. A committee of fifty was agreed upon, but the president of the Labor Council was authorized to appoint its members. As he read down the list of his selections it began to look as if he were not going to appoint Bridges. A cry went up, and Bridges's name was added. That gave the longshoremen two members out of fifty.

The stage was set, the cast chosen. When the curtain went up—it was set for July 16th—the general strike would be on.

"The general strike," Bridges explained when he was asked about it in his first deportation hearing,

> was brought about by us and deliberately planned by us as a mass protest against the killing and the murder of the men on the waterfront . . . .
>
> When we organized for the general strike and put the leaflets out all over the country, some two hundred thousand–odd, the leaflet contained the fact that there would be no attempt to inter-

fere with such things as lights, electricity or gas, there would be no attempt to interfere with the movement of foodstuffs, the operation of creameries or bakeries, but all of those other things were going to be struck, and that is the way it eventually worked out.

Of course, the city took the opportunity to cry a lot about taking over the country and taking over the city, and all that, and set up an emergency state of affairs, but it wasn't necessary. . . .

Most San Franciscans were much less calm about the turn events were taking. A more typical impression was passed on to Washington by James Moffett, a Department of Commerce man stationed in San Francisco. On the night of July 14th, with the strike only two days off, he called his friend Col. McIntyre at the White House to give him an on–the–spot report. His information, he told McIntyre, came mainly from a conversation with Kenneth Kingsbury, President of Standard Oil. Moffett was almost beside himself, but McIntyre managed to get most of it down:

There are 117 unions that went into session at ten o'clock this morning and they all voted to join the strike. There are forty-four out of the seventy-seven that will cast their vote individually. Kingsbury expects they will all vote to strike and there will be a general strike on Monday morning. He says he cannot impress upon me the seriousness of the situation; that they are all Communists and reds and they are out against the Government. He said they have two thousand national guardsmen on the waterfront; that they have a police force of nine hundred fifty; that they have two thousand guardsmen outside, ready for call. But he said that with the general strike and with the character of the men, who are red and Communists, that the guardsmen plus the police will not be able to cope with the situation. He says that at the Presidio there are something like five hundred–odd Federal troops. He said that this thing has been planned for months; it is not spontaneous; that Portland and Seattle will be faced with the same situation; that if they get away with it in San Francisco, unquestionably it will move to Los Angeles; that while Los Angeles is a little more open shop, it will sweep right through.

He says that at the Union Club, where he is staying, that there are about six pickets who are picketing the club; that there is no transportation; that all the taxicabs are out, although he can walk from there to his office; that they have shut off all food and there is no question but that there will have to be Federal troops to feed the people or they will be up against it . . .

As a matter of fact, Mac, my guess is that the leading citizens of San Francisco probably have their wives out of town, and some of them are penned up in that club which is up on the Hill, and they are even picketing that.

John Francis Neylan, Hearst's man in San Francisco, agreed with Moffett. At the moment Moffett was on the phone to McIntyre, Neylan was calling the publishers of all the major newspapers in San Francisco and Oakland, asking them to come to his suite at the Palace Hotel for an emergency meeting. They all came, except one.

"We publishers," Neylan told the group as he opened the meeting, "have a responsibility to protect our community from Communism. What we need is a committee that can clear editorials and stories about the strike." After a perfunctory discussion they all agreed without bothering to ask whether Neylan had any evidence that the strike was actually a Communist plot.

Paul C. Smith, who was then financial editor of the *San Francisco Chronicle*, was appalled at what the publishers were doing. "The newspapers, in my view," he says in his autobiography, *Personal File*, "had been putting on one of the least creditable performances in a series of incredible performances by the community leadership." He then describes the editorial cabal set up by Neylan, and his reaction to it: "I went to see Mr. Cameron [publisher of the Chronicle] to tell him I thought the arrangement was disgraceful, and while he said he saw my point, he said he felt that the press had to be unified in its fight against the Communists on the waterfront. It seemed that all this business had been whipped up by some agitator named Harry Bridges, and that all we had to do was get rid of him and the situation would be brought under control. . . ."

Smith was a most uncommon financial editor. A bachelor, some of the time he stayed as the house guest of ex–President Herbert Hoover in Palo Alto. Often on weekends he would drive in his red Cadillac convertible down to Carmel to visit his friend Lincoln Steffens, whose other guests were often radicals. Sam Darcy, who was, on occasion, a fellow visitor with Smith at the Steffens's, later remembered a conversation between Steffens, Garet Garrett, then editor of the *Saturday Evening Post*, and Smith, after Smith became editor of the *Chronicle*. Steffens was berating Garrett and Smith for the poor quality of their publications. Garrett defended his editorial policy by asserting that he'd like to publish a more liberal magazine, but he couldn't.

"I have the same problem at the *Chronicle*," Smith sympathized. "If we put out a liberal paper, we'd lose circulation."

Steffens lit into him. "Paul," he argued, "you're dead wrong. I don't ask you to do a liberal paper. Just print the facts about unions and issues the other papers don't cover. You'll be surprised. Your circulation will go up, not down."

Smith lived a cosmopolitan, bohemian life, with friends in every part of San Francisco and from every calling. Moreover, as a youth he had worked briefly on the waterfront, and, although as financial editor the strike was off his beat, he was fascinated by it. Night after night he went down to the docks and talked with the strikers.

"Word of mouth rumor and biased editorials seemed to have saturated people with a fear of the waterfront," Smith wrote later, "but I found these men invariably friendly and anxious to talk with an outsider about their troubles . . .

"The rank–and–file bitterness toward the press was deep and universal. Most of the men said that I was the only one from any of 'the big papers' with whom they had ever had a chance to talk, and they often told me that even if I couldn't 'get any of it printed' they were pleased that someone like me would come around and 'bat the breeze' with them."

Smith's first meeting with Bridges was just before the general strike. He went to see him with Ray McClung, a fellow newspaperman who had Bridges's confidence. Despite McClung's endorsement, Bridges was short with Smith, answering his questions curtly.

"He was a thin, wiry, almost frail man in his early thirties," Smith recalls.

He had a strong Australian accent, but his speech was replete with pure American idiom. He had a strong, lean, sharp face that looked just as completely honest as I found him to be over the next twenty–five years of what I regard as a cherished friendship . . . .

The first conversation did not flow easily, however. Bridges obviously was not prepared to put much trust in a metropolitan newspaperman, and he seemed openly perplexed that he should be sought out by someone calling himself a financial editor. Even his monosyllabic responses began to wane, so as a gag, I said, "Tell me, Mr. Bridges, just how serious do you think the class war is in America, and what stage is it in?"

He turned slowly in his chair and looked past me at McClung. Arching a thin eyebrow, he said, "Kee–rist, you don't mean to tell me there's anybody on the *San Francisco Chronicle* who knows there's a class war in America." From that moment on, Bridges and I always found it easy to talk.

As it turned out, Smith couldn't get his reports of the strike printed, even the interview with Bridges. The managing editor favored publishing it, but the publisher ruled against it after checking with Neylan's committee.

In view of the frightening picture of the strike created by West Coast newspapers, the Moffett–type reports Washington was receiving, and, later, the fervid calls from the Governors of Oregon and Washington for help from the White House, one might wonder why the federal government did not send federal troops into San Francisco or take some other kind of drastic action. Some high officials in Washington were, in fact, strongly disposed to do so. The President had gone on vacation on the first of July, cruising down the Atlantic Coast on the U.S.S. "Houston," and through the Panama Canal, heading for Hawaii. When the general strike broke, he was out in the Pacific, enjoying the fishing. The cabinet had discussed the strike just before he left Washington, and he had said that Frances Perkins, Secretary of Labor, was in charge of the problem. He had full confidence, he had added, in her ability to handle it.

"One morning," Frances Perkins has written in *The Roosevelt I Knew,*

Secretary Hull [Secretary of State Cordell Hull, who was Acting President in FDR's absence] called and asked me to come to his office at once. I arrived and found the Attorney General and the Secretary of State surrounded by law books and looking very solemn indeed. It was their opinion, based on a definition in the *Encyclopaedia Britannica*—in the article written some thirty years earlier by P. Tecumseh Sherman, an elderly gentleman who had once been Commissioner of Labor Statistics in the State of New York—that the situation in San Francisco was legally a "general strike." Under the laws of the United States and the State of California, drastic action could be taken in case of a general strike.

A "general strike," I protested, was a strike of a large body of workers planned and co–ordinated in advance to force the Government to take a position on some matter of interest to them.

Secretary Hull and Mr. Cummings appeared to think that the National Guard and Army should be called and the "general strike" put down. I pleaded that this was in no way an alarming situation and that the likelihood of anything more than a brief strike of delivery and transportation services was remote, and I thought it unwise to begin the Roosevelt administration by shooting it out with working people who were only exercising their rights under our Constitution and laws, to organize and demand collective bargaining. At any rate, I insisted that before any action was taken we must communicate with Roosevelt, and I sent him a message through Howe [Louis Howe, a Presidential secretary].

Secretary Perkins's message advised the President not to interrupt his vacation because of the strike: "Think only danger San Francisco strike," Howe cabled on July 15th, "is that Mayor is badly frightened and his fear has infected entire city and vicinity . . . . Mayor has made country a little nervous by foolishly going on national hookup last night giving situation undue importance . . . ."

The next day, when the general strike was underway, Howe again cabled FDR:

> See no reason to change my judgment of yesterday. Strike so far proceeding in very business–like and orderly way with no violence up to tonight and a singular absence of hot temper on either side . . . .
>
> Suggest the "Houston" might move toward West Coast, then if situation becomes serious you can move fast to San Diego, summon both sides to a conference aboard ship . . .
>
> Still feel so long as public think you are not worried there is no danger, no general panic, but that general panic might easily be brought about if public once think you are frightened yourself.

The President had arranged before he left that the way to communicate with him on the "Houston" would be to send the message to the White House, where Presidential aides would decide if it was important enough to send on. The system didn't work very well. "In the San Francisco strike a lot of people completely lost their heads and telegraphed me, 'For God's sake, turn the ship around,'" Roosevelt said later. "Stephenson and Roddan and Fred [three White House correspondents with whom FDR was on intimate terms. Fred was Fred Storm] would not let me turn the ship around. They insisted on Hawaii.

"Everybody demanded that I sail into San Francisco Bay, all flags flying and guns double-shotted, and end the strike. They went completely off the handle."

One official who went off the handle was Julius Meier, Governor of Oregon, who sent a wire on July 16th directly to the "Houston," endorsed by Joseph Carson, Mayor of Portland, the Portland Chamber of Commerce, and the publishers of the city's three newspapers. "We are now in a state of armed hostilities," Meier informed the President. "The situation is complicated by communistic interference. It is now beyond the reach of state authorities." He ended by recommending that Roosevelt should either return to the Coast and handle the situation himself or give General Hugh S. Johnson authority to act "to prevent insurrection which if not checked will develop into civil war."

Roosevelt was annoyed. "Call Governor Meier," he cabled Howe with an acerbity unusual for him, "and tell him I got his long telegram. If he made public his copy tell him I do not consider such action advisable and to communicate with me hereafter through the White House . . . ."

Governor Meier's suggestion was palpably presumptuous. He was asking the President to risk alienating organized labor by sending federal troops to the Portland waterfront, when he himself had not sent in the Oregon National Guard. And while Meier was no doubt unaware of the fact, his choice of a Presidential surrogate was unfortunate. General Johnson was one of the more bizarre personalities in the New Deal galaxy, with an unsurpassed talent for making trouble rather than mediating it. As NRA administrator, he had attempted to settle several important strikes, and had succeeded only in worsening them. Indeed, Johnson himself knew that he wasn't good at labor mediation. He says in his book about the NRA that after several disastrous experiences as a mediator manque—all before the maritime strike: "I determined that I was never going to get into another strike settlement."

He forgot that resolve in mid-1934 when, on a national speaking tour, he found himself in San Francisco during the general strike. The University of California, his old alma mater, invited him to give a speech in the Greek Theater on the campus, after which he would be given an honorary Phi Beta Kappa key. When Johnson got there, the overflow crowd of five thousand awaiting him was rewarded by an electrifying Jekyll-and-Hyde performance. At the outset, the speaker was Hugh S. Johnson, an old grad who had become a high government official, lecturing them on the dramatic changes being wrought by the New Deal. All over the country, he told them, workers were taking advantage of Sec. 7(a) of the NRA, which gave them the right to join unions and bargain with their employers through representatives of their own choosing.

As he saw it, one of the causes of the strike on the West Coast waterfront was the shipowners' refusal to move with the times. "If the shipping industry does not fully and freely accord these rights," he said sternly, "then on its head will lie every ounce of responsibility for whatever may happen here. I think their present position is extreme and unreasonable and must be tempered if we are to have peace."

Then, as he began to talk about the strikers, he was suddenly transformed into General "Iron Pants" Johnson, the rough–riding cavalryman who, if he had his way, would make short shrift of troublemakers. His remarks about the employers had been an appeal to reason. This was an appeal to the mob.

"There is another and worse side to this story," he rasped, his gravelly voice rising. "You people are living out here under the stress of a general strike. And," his face turning crimson as he pounded the rostrum, "a general strike is a threat to the community. It is a menace to government. It is civil war.

> When the means of food supply—milk to children, necessities of life to the whole people—are threatened, that is bloody insurrection. . . . this ugly thing is a blow at the flag of our common country and it has got to stop.
>
> I lived in this community for many years and I know it. If the Federal Government did not act, this people would act, and it would act to wipe out this subversive element as you clean off a chalk mark on a blackboard with a wet sponge.
>
> But this is not primarily a duty of the community, much less a duty of the National Government. It is a duty of responsible labor organizations . . . They must run these subversive influences out from their ranks like rats . . .

To many who heard him, Johnson's address was a call to organize a vigilante committee, as San Franciscans had already done twice before. Their inclination to take the law into their own hands was reinforced by what they read in their newspapers, which day after day pounded away at the theme that official Washington had deserted them.

Indeed, even as Johnson was speaking, vigilante activity was starting. It was prefaced with a raid on headquarters of the Marine Workers' Industrial Union, just off the Embarcadero. National guardsmen with machine guns mounted on trucks took up positions at each end of the block, while a squad of police moved in to make the arrests. They bagged eighty-five prisoners. Then, for almost a week, police and vigilantes went on a spree, roaming from one union or left-wing social hall to another, where they piled everyone who happened to be on the premises into paddy wagons, then went back and systematically smashed everything in sight.

At the station house, the prisoners were booked on vagrancy charges. Cooperative judges set bail at $1,000 cash or $2,000 bond. For most, it might as well have been $10,000. While the strikers certainly weren't vagrants—some, like Harry Jackson, MWIU secretary, were seized in their own living rooms—they were out of work, many on relief. The International Labor Defense bailed out as many as it could, but its bail fund was quickly depleted. And the jail kept filling up. When the police finally decided their job was done, they had three hundred men behind bars, most of whom stayed there for several weeks. It was all patently unconstitutional, of course, and painfully reminiscent of the Palmer Raids.

No general strike has ever lasted for more than a few days, and so it was with this one. The end was in sight by the evening of the second day, when the general strike committee, over Bridges's vehement objections, urged the longshoremen and shipowners to let an arbitrator settle their differences. Next morning, the shipowners agreed to arbitration of their dispute with the longshoremen, but not the seamen. "How can we arbitrate differences with those workers," they asked, "until we hold elections to determine who represent them?"

A majority of the general strike committee was also in favor of arbitration. But there were almost as many in favor of holding out. The argument surged back and forth for another day. Then, at noon on the third day of the general strike, the committee brought it to an end by a vote of 191 to 174.

The general strike was over, but the strike on the waterfront went on:

"The longshoremen's strike committee," Bridges declared, "still assumes its original stand for recognition for seafaring unions, abolition of company–controlled hiring halls for seamen, and control of longshoremen's hiring halls by longshoremen.

"The sentiment of the men is very solid. And in going out on general strike the unions of San Francisco proved that they would not stand by and see the maritime unions crushed."

The next day Neylan invited some of the waterfront employers to meet with his newspaper publishers' committee at his home in Woodside, a suburb south of San Francisco. After an all–day session they issued a press release, reiterating the willingness of the waterfront employers to arbitrate all differences with the longshoremen. More significantly, the press release then went on to commit the shipowners (without having gotten their approval) "to bargain collectively with the maritime unions if and when they select representatives under the direction of the President's Board." Neylan's gambit was brilliantly designed to bring the strike to an end. Shipowners could not continue to refuse to talk with the seamen's unions after the public statement attributed to them, for they would appear to be needlessly prolonging the strike. The seamen's unions were equally out–maneuvered. After the shipowners' putative promise to bargain, the seamen would lose what public sympathy they had if they stayed out on strike.

Then, a few days later, the National Longshoremen's Board made a move that forced the longshoremen's union, also, to retreat from its position that longshoremen would stay out until they got their own hiring halls and until the seamen got hiring halls of their own. The board's strategy was to take a coastwide vote—after trying unsuccessfully to get the longshoremen to do it themselves—on the question: "Will the International Longshoremen's Association submit to arbitration by the National Longshoremen's Board the issues in dispute in the longshore strike and be bound by the decision of the Board?" Six thousand, five hundred and four longshoremen voted "yes." Fifteen hundred and twenty–five voted "no." Everett, a lumber port north of Seattle, was the only port that rejected arbitration. There, the vote was 109 'yes', to 110 'no'. In San Francisco 2,316 longshoremen voted for arbitration, 759 against it.

Even as the men were voting to accept arbitration, vigilante activity was stepped up in Northern California, with raids against suspected Communist meeting places reported in San Francisco, Sacramento, Stockton, Berkeley, San Jose, Oakland, Alameda, Piedmont, Hayward, Richmond, Salinas, and Carmel. In the middle of it all, General Johnson laid a mantle of respectability on the shoulders of the vigilantes.

I think it is about time for an America First campaign on this subject. I do not know the accuracy of the statement and I have no means to check it, but it has been said to me with at least the circumstances of verity that if the jobs of aliens and non–declarants were given to citizens and the former were deported, the unemployment and destitution problems of the United States would be reduced by at least one–third.

That sounds like a pretty harsh remedy. But so is the distress of our own people harsh. I do not suggest such a move, but I do suggest that any alien who pretends to lead an economic group of our people in the direction of strike and bloodshed has no place here and should be no more tolerated than an armed enemy under a foreign flag.

What our people have got to understand is that there is a far more effective weapon against their rights than guns or gas—and that is economic strangulation. If a foreigner walked down our streets with a machine gun to enforce some antisocial demand we should know exactly what to do with him. But if he comes enforcing influence such as you have just repudiated on the Coast, we are loath to act. Let's rid ourselves of them. Let us not recognize or have anything to do with a man in a responsible American economic position that would not be eligible to a responsible American political position—that would do the trick . . . .

After the vote was in it took a week to get the longshoremen back on the docks. On July 27th, waterfront employers assured the National Longshoremen's Board that they were laying off all strikebreakers, that they would not discriminate against any longshoreman because of his union or strike activities, and that working conditions that had existed before the strike would be maintained pending the arbitration award. They added that they were prepared to bargain with the seamen's unions if the unions won elections conducted by the board, and that they would accept arbitration. They would not, however, agree to take back all the seafarers who had gone on strike.

On the evening of July 29th, the longshoremen told the board they would be on the docks at 8:00 a.m., Tuesday, July 31st, ready to work. Those who, like Bridges, would have stayed out until all their offshore allies were assured they would get their jobs back were somewhat mollified when the board promised the seamen's unions it would use its influence to have the shipowners take back everyone who had struck. In view of this promise and of the longshore vote, the seamen had little choice but to go back to their jobs along with the dockworkers on July 31st. The board reported later that, "While most of the unlicensed seamen who struck were returned to work after the strike, a smaller proportion of the licensed officers were reinstated or reemployed."

John Francis Neylan, proud of the publishers' role in ending the strike, wired his chief at the castle in Glamorganshire where Hearst was on holiday: "San Francisco crushed the general strike more thoroughly and promptly than London did. There has been no compromise of any character or description. As a San Franciscan you have a right to carry your head even higher than you did last week."

On August 8th, the National Longshoremen's Board began its arbitration sessions in San Francisco. Bridges was only one of a score of ILA members and officials who testified, but he was on the stand almost as long as all the rest combined. He was called on the 13th and answered questions all day long, describing the shape–up and explaining myriad technical longshoring operations and working conditions.

While he was testifying, press releases sent out by two groups meeting in the city reminded San Franciscans that the hysteria generated by the strike had not abated. One was from the San Francisco Merchants' Committee which announced a campaign against radicalism. "Our goal," the merchants said, "is to strengthen immigration laws to prohibit persons of Communistic tendencies from entering the United States; to register, fingerprint and photograph all persons over eighteen; to amend the Constitution to include seditious propaganda within the definition of treason; and to prohibit teaching Communism in the schools." The other was from the California State Convention of the American Legion, which had adopted three resolutions introduced by the San Francisco Americanism Committee of the Legion. One censured Frances Perkins for not deporting suspected Communists during the strike. Another expressed confidence in the 100 per cent Americanism of the American Federation of Labor. The third was a bit extreme, even by Legion standards. It asked the state legislature "to enact a law punishing radical agitation by death or one hundred years in jail."

If proponents of these proposals hoped to prejudice the members of the National Longshoremen's Board against Bridges and the militants in the maritime unions, they were disappointed. The board went on, unmoved, with its longshore hearings and the representation elections it was holding for the seafarers. As it was doing so, a new controversy confronted it. This one was between the ship clerks who had joined the longshoremen's union and the waterfront employers, who refused to bargain with them, contending that ship clerks were part of management. They did not belong in a union, especially a longshoremen's union. The board disagreed and finally persuaded the employers to bargain with the clerks if a majority of them voted for the union in elections the board would supervise. The clerks wanted a coastwide bargaining unit like the longshoremen's, but the employers held out successfully for company–wide bargaining units. An employer would have to bargain with the union only if it won a majority of the clerks on his payroll.

The election results confirmed the shipowners' shrewdness. In San Francisco, 249 of the 331 votes went to the union. In Los Angeles, it was ninety–three for to thirty against. One hundred and sixteen clerks in Seattle voted for the union, forty–three against. In Portland, it won by a vote of seventy–one to twenty–seven. Thus, almost three–fourths of the clerks in the four major ports voted for the union. But of the ninety–seven companies whose clerks participated in the election, only forty–one, as it worked out, ended up having to recognize the clerks' union.

On October 12th, the board handed down its award in the longshore case. It was a masterful job of compromising the seemingly irreconcilable principles that brought on and prolonged the strike and arriving at a solution all concerned could live with. Indeed, the basic structure of the hiring system established by the award is still intact, after thirty–eight years of vigorous collective bargaining.

The most intractable issue—the longshoremen's insistence on a union hiring hall—was resolved by providing for jointly–operated hiring halls in each port, with expenses to be shared equally by the employers and the union. All longshoremen were to be dispatched from the halls without discrimination or favoritism because of union or non–union membership. Surpluses and shortages of longshoremen were to be avoided by maintaining a register kept by a joint labor relations committee composed of three employer representatives and three from the union. Moreover, the award went on, "No longshoreman not on such list shall be dispatched from the hiring hall or employed by any employer while there is any man on the registered list qualified, ready and willing to do the work." A longshoreman whose name was on the register but who was not a member of the union was to pay to the labor relations committee "a sum equal to the pro rata share of the expense for the support of the hall paid by each member of the International Longshoremen's Association."

In two ways, the award satisfied the employers' contention that a hiring hall of the kind the union was seeking would take away their freedom to choose their employees. First, it stipulated that employers would have the right to have dispatched to them the longshore gangs in their opinion best qualified to do the work. It also provided that they would be free to choose their men when they hired them individually rather than as members of a gang. At the same time, the award met the longshoremen's argument that a hiring system of the kind the employers wanted would expose them to the favoritism and disparities in earnings they had struck against. First, it instructed the labor relations committees supervising the hiring halls to dispatch men and gangs so as to equalize earnings as nearly as practicable. Even more significantly, the board ordered: "the dispatchers in the hiring halls shall be elected by the union."

The award, moreover, laid the foundation for a remarkable system of industrial government. The joint labor relations committee in each port was instructed to serve as the second step in the grievance procedure, under orders to meet within twenty–four hours of a request from either side. Then, in each major port the parties were to appoint an arbitrator, who would hear appeals from decisions of the committee. If the longshoremen and employers couldn't agree on an arbitrator, they were to ask the U.S. Secretary of Labor to designate one for them. Before the contract had been in force very long, they asked the Secretary to appoint a coastwide arbitrator to preside over the whole system.

The award gave longshoremen the coastwide contract they coveted and a six–hour day, with time–and–a–half for work beyond six hours a day or thirty hours a week. Instead of the dollar an hour they were after, they got ninety–five cents.

Some longshoremen were disappointed in the board's decision because they had not won their main goal, a union hiring hall. They still had cause for rejoicing, however. Their union had survived an eighty–three day strike after lying dormant for fourteen years, and they had won their coastwide contract. Wages and hours were improved, and joint hiring halls, especially with dispatchers elected by the men themselves, were a great advance over employer control of hiring.

The terms on which the prolonged, violent strike was settled were similar, to be sure, to some of the proposals for settlement made before the strike began. Looked at from this point of view, it might seem that the strike served no purpose. But in the broader context of collective bargaining, the strike was both unavoidable and necessary. In collective bargaining, the administration and policing of an agreement is as important as the substance of the agreement itself, sometimes more so. And considering the many years of skillful employer domination and hostility to unionism that preceded the settlement, it is doubtful if the longshoremen could have stood up to employer opposition and have maintained the benefits they got from the contract without the demonstration of solidarity and the new leadership that came out of the strike.

An effective union leader has to have a variety of talents. He must have more, in fact, than the employer he faces across the bargaining table. To run his union, he has to be, in the best sense of the term, an effective politician. To negotiate contracts, he has to have the skills of a diplomat. To establish and preserve strategic alliances with other unions and to hold the support of the community, he has to be something of a statesman. Not least, to lead a strike, he must have the tactical and strategic competence, the iron nerve, of a military commander.

Because the longshoremen and their supporters in the Battle of Rincon Hill carried out their defense with such effectiveness and then retreated in such good order some people ("Including," Sam Darcy said in the sixties, "several FBI men who have spoken to me in recent years.") have thought that there was some type of military direction of the men on the hill, that the longshoremen's union or perhaps the Communists had been running schools for street fighting and guerrilla tactics.

A few weeks after the strike ended, the Marine Corps Commandant of the San Francisco area phoned Bridges. "I'd like very much to have a talk with you," he said. "Could you come to my house for dinner?" Bridges accepted, and they agreed on a time. When the day came, a Marine Corps limousine pulled up in front of the dingy union office on Steuart Street, and Bridges was driven down the Peninsula to the Colonel's house in Palo Alto. Only the Colonel and his family were there.

After dinner, the Colonel and his guest retired to the study, and his reason for inviting Bridges was revealed. "You know, Mr. Bridges," he said, "my office is on the top floor of our building on Harrison, overlooking the waterfront. And of course, it's right across the street from Rincon Hill. During the strike I spent a good deal of my time watching what was going on down on the Embarcadero through field glasses.

"I was particularly impressed with the way you deployed your men behind those barricades on Rincon Hill, maneuvered the police into attacking, drove them off several times, and then retreated when their reinforcements arrived and defeat was inevitable."

The Colonel leaned forward, lowering his voice to ask in a conspiratorial whisper, "Would you mind telling me, Mr. Bridges, where did you study military strategy and tactics?"

NOTES

Governor Merriam's statement about the Belt Line Railroad is Exhibit VV, in Eliel's book (cited above) about the general strike. Joe Rosenthal's experiences in the strike are described in William Camp's *San Francisco: Port of Gold.*

Hedley described his conversation in the strike lunchroom in a talk entitled "The Strike as I Have Seen It," which he gave on July 19, 1934 in Berkeley.

Schmidt's description of the battle on Rincon Hill is in Herbert Resner, *The Law in Action During the San Francisco Longshore and Maritime Strike of 1934.*

McCarty's letter about the slingshot is in the La Follette Committee *Hearings, Part 15-D,* p. 7223.

The police report of the shooting at Steuart and Mission was included in a telegram from McGrady to Secretary Perkins on July 7, 1934.

Olsen's, Bridges's, and the other witnesses' descriptions of how they saw the shooting are from the coroner's inquest as reported in the *San Francisco News* on August 2, 1934.

McIntyre's cable to the President on the "Houston" is in FDR Official File 407-B, in the Roosevelt Memorial Library.

Plant's letter about the cost of boarding the strikebreakers is in the transcript of the mediation hearings (July 9, 1934) held by the national Longshoremen's Board.

Moffett's phone call to McIntyre is in FDR Official File 407-B.

Darcy told me of the conversation between Lincoln Steffens, Garrett and Smith when I visited him in 1964.

FDR's account of appeals made to him that he intervene in the strike is in Presidential Press Conference 141 (September 5, 1934) in the Roosevelt Memorial Library.

Gov. Meier's cable to FDR is in FDR Official File 407-B. Gen. Johnson makes his rueful comment about staying out of strikes in his *The Blue Eagle* (p. 320).

The story of Johnson's Greek Theater speech is from the *San Francisco News*, July 17, 1934. For the part played by Bay Area newspapers during the strike, see Earl Burke, "Dailies Helped Break General Strike," *Editor and Publisher*, August 28, 1934.

A useful source for events that occurred after the longshoremen voted to end the strike is the *Report to the President* of the National Longshoremen's Board. Neylan's cable to Hearst after the strike is in the Bancroft Collection in the library of the University of California at Berkeley.

For a description of how the longshore hiring halls operate on the West Coast, see my *Shape-up and Hiring Hall.*

Lincoln Fairley, former ILWU research director and, upon his retirement, arbitrator in the port of San Francisco, has described the longshore arbitration system in *Labor Law Journal,* Sept., 1971.

Bridges has told the story of his visit to the Marine Colonel's house after the strike on several occasions to his cronies, who related it to me.

4

Armed Truce

*Celui que entre en guerre s'engage dans une
aventure incalculable, contre des forces inde-
terminees, pour un temps indefini.*

PAUL VALERY

LEARNING TO LIVE with the new union Bridges headed was a trying
experience for the employers. Before the arbitration award that
ended the strike had been in effect a month the *Waterfront Worker*
carried this story:

"Struggle along the docks has succeeded very largely in keeping
off scabs and cutting down on the speedup. . . . No more do the
docks of San Francisco hear the booming echo of some boss's
voice, the winches do not groan with their heavy loads as before,
although it would do no harm to make the loads still smaller. . . ."

A few months later, Bridges said in a progress report to the longshoremen:

> The union, not the employer, is going to decide on the Pacific
> Coast whether a man can work or not. There has not been one
> man fired off the docks since the general strike for union activity.
> The union has a delegate in every gang on the waterfront. It's his
> job to see that every man has an I.L.A. book and that there is no
> discrimination. Before the strike the longshoremen were slinging
> two to three tons. Now the union has cut this down to 1800
> pounds . . .
>
> We won those conditions through our strike. We won them by
> fighting on the job. . . . If the union conditions are violated,
> everybody, including other marine workers, walks off the job.

Actually, the longshoremen's goals and grievances were only one of several reasons for the work stoppages that seemed to occur somewhere along the waterfront at least once a day. Another was the seamen's award at the end of the '34 strike which gave ship-owners the option either to hire sailors at the pierhead or to call the union hall when they needed men. In retaliation, the seamen made a mutual assistance pact with the longshoremen. When longshore-men refused to cross the seamen's picket lines, it didn't take a ship-owner long to get on the phone to the sailors' hall and ask for a union crew.

There was also the problem of hot cargo which began to plague the longshoremen as soon as they had their own union and were automatically caught in the crossfire of the labor wars flaring up all around them. In one industry after another, a pattern kept repeat-ing itself: the newly–organized employer would refuse to bargain, the workers would strike, the employer would hire scabs and strike-breakers and go right on operating. Unable to stop production at its source, the strikers would follow the company's shipments to the waterfront, where they would appeal to the longshoremen not to handle the cargo.

What was Bridges to do? He could, of course, assume the states-manlike posture of Mike Casey and Dave Beck and tell the long-shoremen to live up to their contract by crossing the strikers' picket lines and loading the cargoes. But that would have meant repudiat-ing everything he had learned about the need for working–class sol-idarity since he first went to sea. Inevitably, his unfailing willing-ness to help other unions was one more reason for employers to conclude it was hopeless to try to do business with Bridges, that he was a Communist, hell–bent on disrupting the industry. Some of Bridges's own statements reinforced that belief. "If to place the support of union men above any agreement, and to stick by other unions even if an agreement has to come second is communistic," he said when asked if disregarding the contract with the shipowners wasn't a Communist tactic, "then yes, that's our policy. Unionism must come first and agreements second."

Already unhappy with the work stoppages and Bridges's radi-calism, the shipowners also found out that they had lost their most prized prerogative, control of hiring. The President's board had provided that while the employers and the union would jointly op-erate the hiring hall, the men who would dispatch the workers to their jobs would be elected by the longshoremen. "It was supposed to be joint control," Lapham said later, chuckling as he thought back on the position the employers were in. "But the dispatcher was the man who really had the power. We shared the expenses, but when it came to getting new men on the payroll, we felt that no new man came on unless he had been thoroughly screened by Bridges. We used to think that only a Communist could get on as a new longshoreman."

When it came to getting men off the payroll, employers were equally abject. In 1965, when Bridges was discussing in a union meeting the case of a Los Angeles longshoreman dropped from the industry for repeatedly disrupting work, he reminded his listeners that this was the first time since 1934 the employers had fired a longshoreman over the union's objection. The man was taken back in 1969.

With union–elected dispatchers deciding who to send out on jobs, the employers also found they couldn't even choose the men or the gangs they wanted when they called the hall. Nor would the union allow the employers to hire men on a steady basis. "A major purpose of this hiring hall," the union told them, "is to spread the work evenly so as to equalize earnings. The way to do that is to dispatch men in rotation. The man or the gang with the lowest earnings goes out first. You take the men the dispatcher sends you."

The employers protested, pointing out that permanence on the job promoted efficiency, and that if an employer could have the same men work for him every day it would lighten the burden of dispatching. It would also, they added, save the longshoremen the trouble of having to report to the hiring hall to get their jobs. "You've got a case," Bridges admitted. But he went on to argue that the very virtues of permanence the employers were arguing for pointed up the countervailing vices of favoritism and inequality:

"Equalization is the fundamental objective of the union, and equalization includes equal requirements of reporting, equal division of the desirable jobs, equal acceptance of unpleasant tasks, equal regularity as well as quantity of employment, and equal sharing of the work when times are bad."

For the employers, all of this was frustrating enough. But there was more to come. "There is every indication," Lapham wrote Secretary Perkins, "that the same leadership now dominating the longshoremen's union is seeking control of the officers' unions, the seamen's unions, and recently the teamsters' unions, and already has a stronghold in these unions. The objective is plain—a vertical union embracing all workers in any way connected with maritime operations, thus forging a stronger weapon to advance their political aim."

Lapham was referring to Bridges's latest attempt to launch a permanent alliance of maritime unions. Bridges began by asking interested unions to come to a meeting in Seattle in April, 1935. The response was exhilarating. Looking out over the crowd as he called the opening session to order, Bridges saw men from every maritime union: longshoremen, sailors, deck officers, cooks and stewards, marine engineers, coal passers, radio operators, shipyard machinists and boilermakers, even teamsters. When the convention was over, there was a new coalition on the West Coast, with a name— the Maritime Federation of the Pacific—and a motto—"An Injury to One is an Injury to All." That could lead both its friends and enemies to believe that the one big union Bridges and the longshoremen were working toward was at hand. And it did indeed look as if it finally was.

Old–line maritime union officials, suspicious of entangling alliances with other unions, reacted to the federation as apprehensively as the employers did. One who felt this way was Burglar Bill Lewis, who in 1935, with sixty–nine convention votes to Bridges's fifty–one, was re–elected president of the Pacific Coast District of the union. Another was Paddy Morris, who, up in Tacoma in the bleak Twenties, had held onto the only ILA enclave on the West Coast. When Bridges proposed that the longshoremen take the lead in getting the federation started, Morris asked him acidly, "Is this another Commie scheme to establish soviets on the waterfront?"

Unruffled, Bridges responded with a mild rebuke, telling Morris, "Let's look at the record." It was a tactic which was to become a Bridges trademark in parrying red–baiting questions and challenges as to the accuracy of reports he was making to the membership. Invariably, when he came to a meeting, he carried with him a briefcase bulging with the transcripts and records of earlier meetings where some controversial action had been taken. "Paddy," he replied softly, like a disappointed teacher correcting an errant pupil, "you should know better than that. This idea was tried, and it worked, on the San Francisco waterfront in 1901, when they established the City Waterfront Federation. Look it up, Paddy. It's in the minutes."

As Bridges spoke, the future for the federation seemed auspicious, but a question hung over the gathering nevertheless: Could this federation survive the long–standing rivalries between the maritime unions that had torn its predecessors apart?

Another of Bridges's causes that seemed Communist-inspired even to some of his labor colleagues and the business community was his espousal of social security and unemployment insurance. In the early 1930's, the American labor movement, still in thrall to Sam Gompers's attachment to laissez faire capitalism, was opposing unemployment insurance on two grounds: it was socialistic; and it would wreck unions by doing a job unions themselves should do by softening the effect of unemployment and making workers beholden to the government. Ignoring official AFL policy, Bridges in 1934 became a member and, in time, chairman of the AFL Rank-and-File Committee for Unemployment Insurance and Relief. The Committee had two goals: to raise support for an unemployment insurance bill then before Congress; and to pressure AFL leadership to change the AFL stand on social security.

The leadership of the AFL thought the committee was Communist-inspired. It may have been. "A very important feature of the TUUL unemployed work was its support of the left-wing AFL Committee for Unemployment Insurance Relief . . ." William Z. Foster says in *From Bryan to Stalin*. "This rank-and-file body carried on a wide agitation in the trade unions for unemployment insurance and relief and against the reactionary Green [William Green, President of the AFL] policies of stagger plan, local charity, relief, expulsion of unemployed from the unions for nonpayment of dues, etc. . . ."

In 1935, the year social security was adopted by Congress, Bridges was invited to speak to a mass meeting arranged by the committee in the Manhattan Opera House. Ryan ordered him to turn down the invitation, threatening to rescind his recent appointment as an organizer on the international union payroll, a position supplementing Bridges's modest salary as president of the San Francisco local. Bridges spoke anyway. The next day Ryan told him curtly, "You're no longer an international organizer."

Bridges's leadership of the strike and, perhaps even more, the masterful way he consolidated the union's power once the strike was over made the business community determined to get rid of him. Paul Smith has told of a secret meeting of ten or twelve prominent San Franciscans he attended at a local hotel:

"When I arrived at the designated room," Smith relates in his autobiography, *Personal File*,

it was pointed out to me that I had been asked to come as a friend whose views were respected if not agreed with and that of course I was not to publish anything I heard there nor discuss it with any other newspaperman. Intrigued, I fully agreed. The unstated question before the assemblage was how to go about cleaning up the waterfront, how to rid it of Bridges and the Reds. It did not take much conversation to reveal the depth of the conviction that this man Bridges was responsible for the troubles that had come to San Francisco and that the solution lay in his disappearance from the scene.

It suddenly dawned on me what they were talking about. It seemed incredible to me. These were not evil men. They were good men, all sincerely interested in the community. Yet they believed that the murder of a labor leader would be a dedicated service to their city and their country.

Smith exploded. "You're going to have to count me out!" he burst out. "I'm leaving for the waterfront, where I'm going to volunteer as one of Bridges's bodyguards." He started angrily from the room and was heading down the hall when the man who had invited him to the meeting caught up with him. "You took what they were saying too literally, Paul. Come on back."

Smith went back and the talk continued. Some of the men insisted he had misconstrued their meaning. Others, their eyes avoiding Smith's, said nothing. Thirty years later, when he was writing his memoirs, Smith was still convinced his outburst narrowly averted an assassination.

Frustrated in this attempt, the employers turned to the government to get rid of Bridges for them. He was, after all, an alien and, they believed, a Communist. That would make him deportable. Early in 1935, a group of businessmen led by Roger Lapham went to Washington to urge Secretary Perkins (in those days, the Immigration Service was in the Labor Department) to remove Bridges.

San Francisco businessmen chose wisely when they picked Roger Lapham to mobilize their defense against the new longshoremen's union. A congenial cosmopolite whose picture appeared more often in the society and sports pages of San Francisco newspapers than in the shipping news, at various times he was president of the California and the national amateur golf associations. He was also a determined opponent of Bridges.

Born in New York City in 1884, Lapham came from a line of Quakers who ran clipper ships in the Atlantic trade. His career in the maritime industry began when he graduated from Harvard in

1905 and went to work as a freight checker at one of the family's docks on the New York waterfront. A quarter–century later, when he was President of the American–Hawaiian Steamship Company, a reporter asked him, "What would you do if you went broke?" Lapham answered without hesitating, "I'd go down to the waterfront and get a job checking cargoes . . . I'd be down there with the cargoes, the ships, the dockhands."

When Lapham died in 1966, Bridges said of him:

> A very important piece of San Francisco history dies with Roger Lapham. I never had anything but admiration for him. We fought on opposite sides of the labor–management fence. We had our bitter fights and our private and public debates, but there was never any doubt in my mind that he honestly represented his class and whenever we reached agreement, his word was good.
>
> I am terribly saddened by his passing. I hope I last as long and do as well for my people as he did for his.

One of the public debates Bridges might have been thinking of took place in 1936 during a prolonged maritime strike, when Lapham chagrined his fellow employers by accepting Bridges's challenge to debate before an audience of ten thousand strikers. "Were you afraid of personal violence when you went up there?" he was asked. "Absolutely not," Lapham replied. "Having asked us, they couldn't afford not to give us a decent reception. They had the building policed themselves with their own men. It was very orderly."

At one point in the debate Lapham took the offensive, bluntly announcing he was against the union hiring hall. There was a roar of boos and catcalls. Lapham peered over his glasses at his hecklers and said with a grin, "Well, that was at least an honest statement, wasn't it?" Amused, the crowd gave him a burst of applause. The debate was a stand–off, but from then on Lapham was increasingly drawn into public affairs. In 1943, he was elected Mayor of San Francisco.

He was an unusual mayor. During his term, anti–Japanese feeling was high in West Coast cities as well as on the U.S. Supreme Court, which in 1944 held in the *Korematsu* case that rounding up all persons of Japanese ancestry on the Coast and putting them in concentration camps did not, as jurists say, offend the Constitution. With the war against Japan still raging, the city's Civil Service

Commission, faced with a shortage of streetcar mechanics, hired a
Nisei named Miyama who had just been released from the camp at
Tule Lake. When Miyama showed up at the carbarn, the other mechanics, their home–front patriotism reinforcing their racism,
downed their tools and marched off to City Hall. Crowding into the
Mayor's office, they declaimed to Lapham: "We're not going to
work with a Jap!" "Why don't you fellows go back to work," he
countered, "while I look into this?" When they left, he called Jack
Shelley, then President of the San Francisco Labor Council, to ask
his help.

Shelley felt the way Lapham did, and he went to the carbarn,
where he argued with the mutinous mechanics for several hours. In
the end they gave in, agreeing to let Miyama stay on the job. "I got
150 letters about that," Lapham said afterward, "mostly from over-
seas. Ninety per cent agreed with what Shelley and I did."

After the Miyama incident, Lapham decided that San Francisco
should have a citizen's committee to help solve the general problem
of race relations in the city. His approach to the make–up of the
committee was extraordinary, even for San Francisco. In the accepted manner, he first appointed members of ethnic, religious
business and labor groups. Then he asked Maurice Harrison, a
businessman he had appointed as chairman, "How about a Communist?" Harrison was taken aback. "Well, maybe," he replied.
"Whom would you appoint?"

"During my campaign," Lapham said later, "there was a woman
named Oleta Yates. She was a graduate of the University of California, a Phi Beta Kappa. I'd listened to her campaign. She'd made
no bones about it. She came out and said she was a Communist
and running as a Communist.

"A well–educated, good–looking woman. So I said to Maurice,
'How about Oleta Yates? If we're going to have a cross–section of
every kind.' And he agreed.

"She was the last person I appointed, and I called her in. And I
put it to her. I could see she was so surprised she didn't know what
to make of it. She asked if she could have time to talk to some of
her people. She came back and said she would."

In 1945, when the United Nations was organized in San Francisco, Lapham made another controversial appointment when he
named Bridges to the advisory committee for the session. Bridges
remembered the incident when he was reminiscing with a *Chronicle*
reporter at the time of Lapham's death: "He was a formidable ad-
versary, but he never held a grudge. Why, when he was Mayor, he

appointed me to the advisory committee for the first UN session here. And if you know how his buddies felt about me, you know that took guts."

In 1946, Lapham's administration bought the privately–owned Market Street Railway, merged it with the city–owned streetcar system and then raised fares to pay for the acquisition. Some of the indignant streetcar riders started a recall movement. When a crowd of reporters came to his office to get his reaction, Lapham asked if anyone had one of the recall petitions with him. Somebody produced one, and as the reporters looked on in surprise, Lapham signed it. "I'm signing this so this matter can be brought to a vote," he told them, adding, "I urge all good citizens to do likewise." He was kept in office by a comfortable majority. Ten years later, in the mid–fifties, Lapham startled San Franciscans once again, when he became a director of the Fund for the Republic at a time when it was engaged almost exclusively in combatting McCarthyism.

One might wonder why a man like Lapham would have led a campaign against Bridges. The answer is simple, if paradoxical. He was convinced that Bridges was, if not a card–carrying Communist, at the least a fellow–traveler bent on disrupting the maritime industry. Even so, Lapham's ardor for the get–Bridges crusade did not last long. When he was asked in 1956 in the oral history interview, "Do you think San Francisco employers ever participated in efforts to deport Harry Bridges?" he answered, "Well, of course, many of them were working day and night to bring that about." "How did you feel about it?" "Well," Lapham replied, "the more I got into it, the more I felt—it might have taken some time to develop this feeling—that it was a move that would only stir up more trouble, would tend to make him a martyr. And that was the case . . ."

Waterfront employers next tried to get the longshoremen's union to purge itself of Bridges. They wrote a letter to Burglar Bill Lewis, complaining that San Francisco longshoremen were violating the provisions of the arbitration award "willfully, deliberately and repeatedly." They told Lewis that between October 12, 1934, when the arbitration award was handed down, and June 1, 1935, on 150 separate occasions San Francisco longshoremen had pulled quickie strikes or refused to work because they were respecting some other union's picket line. "We are convinced," the employers continued, "that radical and destructive elements dominate the San Francisco local, and that no peace is possible while such an element is in control." The letter ended with a threat that unless the San Francisco local purged itself of its radical leadership, the employers would have to throw their collective bargaining agreement into the wastebasket. Then, scarcely giving Lewis time to act, they began running the letter in full page ads in San Francisco papers.

With the deadline for renewing the contract getting close, Frances Perkins asked P. A. Donoghue, a National Labor Relations Board official in San Francisco, to find out what he could about the employers' intentions. "The employers told me," Donoghue reported, "that they won't renew the agreement unless the radical and Communist leadership in San Francisco is removed . . . They also said they had assurances from officers of the union that, if necessary, the charter of the San Francisco local would be revoked to eliminate present leadership. A new local would then be formed with a more responsible leadership." At his press conference that same day, President Roosevelt was asked if he had suggested to the Labor Department that it should try to eliminate the radical wing of the longshoremen's union on the Pacific Coast. "I've never even heard of a suggestion that that be done," he replied.

It was a good question nevertheless. The same day's newspapers carried a story that Ed McGrady was calling West Coast shipowners and maritime union officials to Washington for a joint meeting. "I am especially anxious," he told reporters, "to interrogate Bridges before employer–employee groups as to the underlying reason for Pacific Coast maritime unrest, what and who promoted it, what is the object of its continuance, and how closely does it dovetail, if at all, with Communist plans for a labor uprising on the Coast in September, as divulged by Sam Darcy in Moscow."

This last was a reference to a widely reported speech Darcy had made in a Comintern meeting in Moscow. In it, he credited the Communist Party with a crucial role in the '34 strike and, while denouncing conservative AFL officials as labor fakers, praised Bridges for his leadership. Darcy ended the speech with a prediction that when maritime union contracts expired on September 30th, West Coast shipping would be shut down again. This time, Darcy promised, the shutdown would be better organized, for the unions and the Party had had months to prepare.

"How does Sam Darcy get in and out of this country?" FDR asked his Secretary of Labor. "I think he is not a citizen but a native of Russia. Also, how about Harry Bridges? Is he not another alien?"

McGrady's meeting didn't come to much. Employers and national union officers who were present agreed, for the most part, with his notion that Reds were responsible for the turmoil out in the West. But some of the younger union leaders from the Coast dissented, arguing that the trouble on the docks was a carryover from the fury of the '34 strike and that the employers were at least as responsible as the workers for the hostility and suspicion that envenomed their relations. Furthermore, they contended that what McGrady talked about as purposeless sympathy strikes was the unions' way of defending each other against hard–boiled employers determined to break the unions and bring back the open shop.

The labor uprising that Darcy predicted never materialized. There had never actually been much likelihood that it would. In 1935, Bridges and the other leaders of the maritime unions had only the modest goal of reaching September 30th without doing anything that would provoke the shipowners into retaliation. If they could extend existing agreements for another year, they felt, they would be doing as well as anyone could reasonably hope for.

In mid–August, however, a group of sailors led by Harry Lundeberg drafted demands they wanted in the new contract and asked the longshoremen to support them by refusing to renew their contract until the sailors were ready to sign theirs. But the longshoremen's union disappointed them, just as it had in '34. It also disappointed Bridges:

"We renewed the longshore agreement [in 1935]," he said in his 1939 deportation hearing, "over my protests, that is, the officials renewed them over my protest . . . in 1935. It disregarded entirely the interests of the seamen. In other words, as long as the information was out in advance that the longshoremen had renewed their contracts, that put the seamen at a great disadvantage so far as their strength behind collective bargaining was concerned. It ultimately ended up that they were forced to renew their contracts, although they deserved improvements on the ships . . ."

One might have thought the weak front the unions were putting up would have reassured West Coast businessmen. But they wre filled with foreboding, remembering 1934 when they had worked out agreements with union officials only to have the rank–and–file reject them. As September 30th neared, a rising stream of telegrams and letters reflecting their pessimism and their fears reached the White House. One was from James Moffett, the Commerce Department's man in San Francisco who had sent back such alarming reports during the '34 general strike. On September 12th, returning to San Francisco after an absence, he wrote his friend Marvin McIntyre at the White House:

The minute I arrived here, Stanley Dollar and other ship-owners as well as businessmen generally started to talk about the threatened strike on the waterfront and the activity of the radical element.

I met with a group and listened to their troubles and believe me it makes your blood boil when you think that a damned lot of alien communist agitators, few in number by gorilla [sic] tactics, have been able to set up a so–called union, the Maritime Federation . . .

Radical control is centered in San Francisco where longshore-men and sailors under Bridges dominate longshore and seamen's union meetings and by force and intimidations have driven off conservative union men and leaders. Bridges has been de-nounced by Joseph Ryan, International President of I.L.A., by W. J. Lewis, President of the Coast I.L.A., by Andrew Furuseth, International President and by Victor Olander, Secretary–Treas-urer, of the International Seamen's Union, and by Green, Presi-dent of the A.F. of L., also by leading labor leaders in San Fran-cisco and California State.

. . . This whole picture is communistic dictation and backing, in my opinion. If not stopped now, it will continue to grow as a running sore and as the President of the California State Federa-tion of Labor told me yesterday, will mean machine guns and death out–rivalling Chicago and other spots, as the shipowners have given all and more than he would have, in their place.

Other writers reminded the President that waterfront employers were pledged not to extend the longshore contract so long as Bridges and the radicals headed the union. Alarmed, FDR sent Frances Perkins another memo on Bridges and Darcy: "Will you talk with the Assistant Attorney General in regard to these two cases and also in regard to the case of others against whom we can prove propaganda directed at the destruction of the government?"

A letter from Ben Grey, a prominent Democrat and fund raiser for the Democratic Party, may have prompted this request, so un-characteristic of FDR.

"I am reliably informed," Grey wrote, "that the immediate cause of the present existing difficulties is the fact that large numbers of well–known malcontents and definitely known Communists, who are fomenting the disorders are, in one form or another, being maintained on relief rolls of the Federal Government. If the Ad-ministration would assure the recognized labor organizations that such sabotage will not be countenanced and supported by Government funds, it undoubtedly will prove most effective.

"Madame Perkins and Ed McGrady, I am informed, are in possession of full documentary evidence, supported by affidavits, of the facts and personnel above mentioned . . ."

A week later, Miss Perkins reported to the President that the letter from Grey, who lived in Washington, D.C., was not actually based on his own personal knowledge but upon information sent to him by Robert Malone, a West Coast shipping executive. Nor did she have the documentary evidence or the affidavits Grey had heard about. Furthermore, at her request, Labor Department representatives on the Coast had looked into his charges. There wasn't anything to them. Few longshoremen or sailors were on relief rolls and there was no record of any sabotage.

September 30th finally arrived, and the contracts were renewed, unchanged and without incident. But friction on the waterfront persisted, and the shipowners stepped up their plans to match the union's coastwide organization with a permanent coastwide association of their own. Now it was Bridges's turn to look to the White House for help. In January 1936, he wrote a long letter to the President, telling him that West Coast employers were laying plans for a last–ditch fight with the maritime unions. As evidence, he quoted Louis Stark, the respected *New York Times* labor reporter, who had written in December, 1935: " 'Employers on the Pacific Coast virtually have completed a coastwise vigilante organization to protect their interests in the event that they find themselves unable to obtain redress from the government . . . The Pacific Coast owners are said to be in constant contact with the Atlantic operators, and it is probable that a meeting of both groups will be held in San Francisco.'

"That meeting," Bridges added, "was held on January 7th."

FDR sent Bridges's letter over to the Labor Department, asking Secretary Perkins to draft a reply for his signature. She sent back a short, noncommittal note which thanked Bridges for calling attention to the developments on the Coast and expressed the hope that they would not lead to a costly confrontation of the kind he anticipated. At the bottom of the President's file copy of the letter he was to sign, someone had added in pencil: "See our file on Bridges, who has been described as a Communist and an agitator." Unmoved by this intelligence, FDR signed the letter, adding "Very" to the "Sincerely yours" above his signature.

By the opening months of 1936, the employers had their forces in readiness for the all–out fight Bridges had written the President about. All that was needed now was an incident, an excuse to open hostilities. They got it in April, when the S. S. "Santa Rosa" arrived in San Francisco with a non–union crew recruited on the Great Lakes to replace Atlantic Coast sailors who were striking for the wages and working conditions their union had negotiated on the West Coast. Passengers leaning over the rail found themselves looking down on three hundred sailors massed on the dock, picketing in protest against the ship's scab crew. Out on the Embarcadero, they could see another mass of white–capped longshoremen. The whole affair could hardly have been better staged if a Hollywood director had planned it.

The shipowners, declaring that the time had come to make their stand, dramatically announced that they were closing the port. "And it's going to stay closed," they added, "until Harry Bridges is no longer the head of the union."

The maritime unions closed ranks behind Bridges, but in the end it was the patriarch of the San Francisco labor movement, "Bloody Mike" Casey of the teamsters, who frustrated the employers' hopes. After the port had been shut down for a week, Bridges, desperate and uncertain, went to see him. "What do you think I ought to do, Mike? I can't leave the men out of work just because I'm unacceptable to the employers. Maybe I ought to give up the presidency of the local." "No!" Casey shot back. "You can't do that. We can't let the employers tell a union who shall lead it."

The next day Sam Kagel, a young staff member of the Pacific Coast Labor Bureau, a private research and consulting firm with unions for clients, was in Casey's office on other business. "Sam," Casey said, "write me a motion I can put before the Labor Council tonight on the waterfront lockout." Kagel, one of whose other clients was the longshoremen's union, was delighted. "I wrote what I thought was a strong motion," he said later. "But it wasn't strong enough for Mike."

That night at the Central Labor Council Casey presented a motion from the floor unequivocally supporting the longshoremen and censuring the employers. "We can't let employers tell us who will represent us," he argued in the debate that followed, "no matter what we may think of the particular leader who happens to be in question."

The next morning, the port was open.

Another test of Bridges's leadership came almost immediately.

The Presidency of the Pacific Coast District of the union was coming up for election, and he decided to run. He and his supporters were pretty sure a majority of longshoremen on the Coast shared his beliefs about the kind of union they should have. But they couldn't forget the disquieting experience of a year earlier when convention delegates had decisively chosen Burglar Bill Lewis over Bridges, whose record was too radical. To the insurgents, what they would have to do to win was clear: They'd have to change the election procedure. Convention delegates should be allowed to nominate candidates for district offices, but the final election should be put in the hands of the membership, who would elect the officers in a referendum vote. They were wildly successful. Their procedure was adopted, Bridges was nominated and elected in the coastwide referendum by a handsome majority.

When the longshoremen chose Bridges to lead them, he became, *de facto,* the spokesman for all the maritime workers on the Coast, for of the dozen or so unions in the industry, only one had produced a leader to rival him. It was Harry Lundeberg, who had been an unknown minor official of the sailors' union in Seattle when, early in 1935, Bridges tapped him for the presidency of the Maritime Federation of the Pacific. He held that office only briefly, leaving it to head the sailors' union. Almost at once, relations between the two men began to deteriorate, and in time conflict between them and the unions they headed wrecked the maritime federation. Ultimately, Lundeberg became a sworn enemy of Bridges, a collaborator in efforts to deport him.

What went wrong? The poison in the relationship apparently was Lundeberg's resentment over having to play second fiddle to Bridges. Lundeberg, a six–foot two–inch, muscular two hundred pounder, was an ambitious, effective labor leader of the old two–fisted–we'll–settle–this–out–in–the–alley type, but he was no match for Bridges either as a strategist or on a public platform, and it rankled him. Lundeberg was deeply embittered when, after he persuaded his sailors to vote for CIO affiliation in 1937, John L. Lewis nevertheless chose Bridges to be the CIO's first West Coast regional director. When Lundeberg learned he had been passed over by Lewis, he destroyed the sailors' ballots on CIO affiliation, and the sailors stayed in the AFL. From then on, as far as he was concerned, the CIO was a Communist front.

Lewis chose Bridges on the recommendation of John Brophy, a high CIO official he had sent from Washington to the Coast to talk with Bridges and Lundeberg and to report back as to which one had more promise. "I had no trouble deciding," Brophy said in the early sixties. "Bridges was head and shoulders over Lundeberg in ability." When asked how Bridges got on with Lewis, he responded with a laugh. "Not always too well. Bridges sometimes got on Lewis's nerves. Here was Lewis, with all his years of experience, and this brash young upstart from the West Coast would come into his office, perch on the edge of his desk and lecture him on strategy, politics, and so on. The old man wasn't used to being talked to that way."

Thirty years later, after Lewis had gone into retirement, Bridges dropped in for a chat with the old man. "I said to him," he said later, " 'John, I understand you're writing a book about your life.' He said, 'No, I've had publishers offer me big money to do that, but I'm not going to.' It took some urging on my part to get him to say why he wouldn't, but finally he said, 'Harry, you and I have both made promises we couldn't keep and wouldn't want anybody to know about. And we've done a lot of things that would take a lot of explaining before people would see why we did what we did. You know that.'

"I said, 'Yes. And the difference between you and me is, you made about a hundred times as many as I did.' "

When Lundeberg died in 1957 of a heart attack, the *San Francisco Chronicle* said of him in an editorial:

Harry Lundeberg was a throwback to a vanished race of labor leaders: a hard–talking, rough–acting, tempestuous but highly effective man in whom diplomacy or the tempered approach had no foothold. He neatly split all mankind into two groups; those with whom he agreed, who were "all right," and those with whom he disagreed, who were rats, finks, richly described Commie so–and–sos, or any combination thereof.

This newspaper frequently found itself flung into the latter bin as its editorial policy happened to run counter to Lundeberg's views . . . Of late years, however, his vocal and printed denunciations were fewer and more placid; either he, or we, had mellowed . . .

Paul St. Sure, who as head of the shipowners' association had known Lundeberg well, was less favorable. "Lundeberg?" he said. "He was a phony. Shore gangs, super–patriotism, calling everybody who crossed him commies or commie–lovers. . . . [Shore gangs] were hoodlums Lundeberg had on the payroll to beat up people on the waterfront. He used to hire them out to employers or whoever wanted to hire them to get somebody in line."

To refresh his memories of life as a sailor, Lundeberg shipped out in 1947 as an able seaman on the "Marine Jumper," a converted troopship carrying American students to Europe. A *Washington Post* reporter was aboard and reported a conversation between Lundeberg and some of the students.

"Mr. Lundeberg," a high school teacher asked, "how do you think we should act toward the Russians?"

The granite face hardened. "Things have gone too far. We've been too gentlemanly. We got to get tough."

"You don't mean we should fight? What about the United Nations? Liberals have to believe in it." "You call yourself a liberal. Man, you're way behind the times. You sound more like a Commie . . ."

A college student spoke up. "Harry, why is it that the CIO maritime unions let in Negroes and your union doesn't?"

"Why, those Commies will let anyone in. But my men don't want them. You theorists talk a lot about mixing with Negroes. But do you eat and sleep with them?"

In his latter years, Lundeberg became a conservative Republican living in Hillsborough, a fashionable suburb of San Francisco, but he could, had he thought of it, have needled Bridges by telling him, "The trouble with you, Harry, you don't come from the working class." For Lundeberg did. Two of his brothers, deckhands like himself, were lost at sea, his father was a syndicalist, his mother a crusader for women's rights. Lundeberg himself shipped out at fourteen, sailed under a half–dozen flags, joined a syndicalist union in Latin America, for a time held a card in the Australian Seamen's Union. He came to the United States just after World War I, made Seattle his home port, and joined the Sailor's Union of the Pacific. In the early thirties he sounded and acted as if he had brought his father's radicalism along when he landed in Seattle.

"We'll fight the capitalists to a finish unless they give us our rights," he promised the Maritime Federation when he was elected President in 1935. And he was without question an ardent practitioner of the wobbly tactic of job action.

"[In 1934] when the longshoremen decided to arbitrate, and the teamsters voted to call off their strike," Lundeberg told the 1936 Maritime Federation convention, "the sailors agreed to do likewise in order to all go back together and maintain unity, although they went back with nothing in the way of gains for themselves. Instead, they were forced to fight inch by inch through job action up and down the Coast in order to establish conditions." And when, at the same convention, a resolution was passed committing unions in the federation to consult with the others before they struck, thereby putting all the others out on the bricks with them, Lundeberg declared, "F— you guys. When the S.U.P. wants to strike, it'll strike."

As the date approached for renewing the maritime contracts in 1936, the time seemed at hand for the showdown that had been building up since '34. The workers had what appeared to be an effective fighting organization in the maritime federation, and the employers had regrouped their forces into a coastwide counterpart with a battle–hardened veteran of '34, T. G. ("Tear Gas," the workers called him) Plant, at its head.

The longshoremen wanted to formalize their *de facto* operation of the hiring halls into full union control. The shipowners were equally anxious to regain the power to choose their workers. They were also hoping to get rid of an expensive feature of the longshore agreement—the six–hour day, which they viewed as a Depression spread–the–work measure that was no longer needed. The longshoremen were equally set on not giving it up. They had, since 1934, been working a nine–hour shift, three hours of it at time and a half, and they had gotten used to the earnings it produced.

Sea–going unions—even the licensed officers—were also, like the longshoremen, demanding full union control of hiring. And the sailors had an economic demand that worried the shipowners: payment in cash at time and a half when they worked overtime at sea, rather than compensatory time off. All in all, it looked as if another '34 was shaping up.

Early in September Frances Perkins sent Ed McGrady out to the Coast again, this time on a reconnaissance mission. He made his report directly to the President, on September 20th. It was a sobering analysis, but this time Bridges was not the only culprit:

> After two years of bickering and violations of the contracts on the part of both sides, hatred has developed, and there is a determination on the part of each side to smash the other.
>
> Two years ago the strike was between the longshoremen, joined by other maritime trades, and the shipowners. It was bad, but if this strike takes place it will be worse because the ship-

owners have joined with organizations consisting of farmers, wholesale businessmen, manufacturers, and industrialists, from the Canadian border down to San Pedro. All of them are determined "to smash radicalism and communism," but in reality to destroy the maritime unions. They believe the fight might as well take place now and have it over with.

The leaders of the maritime unions are not without blame. They have repeatedly allowed violations of the contracts . . .

McGrady's letter ended with an observation about the shipowners' objectives that was interesting, although probably not surprising to FDR, who was campaigning for reelection with most businessmen and 90 per cent of the nation's press against him. "It is my impression," McGrady suggested, "that in addition to their desire to defeat the unions, they would like also to defeat the present Administration."

The shipowners, confident that this time, unlike 1934, they had public opinion with them, offered to arbitrate. The unions, convinced that the employers' assessment was correct and that an arbitrator's decision would go against them, turned the offer down. They put the strike off for a month, however, when FDR's newly–established maritime commission asked for a chance to try its hand at mediation. "Harry held the strike off for a month," one of Bridges's critics later said disapprovingly, "to help Roosevelt win the election." That may indeed have been Bridges's motive, for in 1936 he, like John L. Lewis, was an admirer of the President, whose New Deal was still in its pro–labor phase. But an assist from Bridges was scarcely necessary. When the nation's voters went to the polls, seven days after the strike began on the Coast, they gave FDR majorities in every state but Maine and Vermont.

Just before the strike was to start, twenty–seven eastern and foreign steamship companies offered the longshoremen a separate peace, on the union's terms. It was a tantalizing offer, because acceptance would have thrust a wedge in the employers' front and given some longshoremen work during the strike. But it would have destroyed the spirit of unity in the maritime federation. "It's useless [for the employers] to make such an offer," Bridges replied as he turned it down, "unless the sea–going unions are granted what they ask: hiring halls and cash overtime pay."

The longshoremen's response shored up the federation, but it worsened the creaky relationship they had with their parent union on the East Coast. Back in July, Bridges had asked Joseph Ryan and officers of the ILA Atlantic and Gulf districts to meet with him in New York to discuss strategy and terms of the contracts they wanted in September. It was a tense meeting, with mistrust barely below the surface, primed to explode if Bridges or Matt Meehan, the secretary of the Pacific district, made a wrong move. Ryan had plenty of reason to hate Bridges, whom he blamed for humiliating him in '34, and everyone there except Bridges and Meehan was wedded to the AFL philosophy of craft unionism and separatism. Viewed from that perspective, the Maritime Federation of the Pacific looked like a Communist conspiracy.

Maud Russell has described what happened at the meeting in *Men Along the Shore*, basing her account on talks with some of the East Coast officials who were there and on the manuscript of an autobiography Ryan began but never finished, *My Forty Years on the New York Waterfront*. According to Russell, after the group had discussed their demands and pledged mutual support if any of the districts had to strike, Ryan summed up: "Then if the three districts negotiate satisfactorily, we'll all sign up on October first." He wheeled on Bridges and Meehan, "Is that correct?"

"Bridges told Ryan flatly," Russell wrote, "that no matter how good an agreement was secured for Pacific Coast longshoremen, they would not sign a contract until all other maritime unions on the Pacific had won satisfactory agreements from the shippers. After a second of stunned silence, the room suddenly filled with shouting voices; everyone was talking at once, tempers that had been held in check for months now burst to the surface. The five other union leaders accused Bridges and Meehan of following the Communist Party line in forcing a nationwide strike and of sacrificing the welfare of longshoremen for the sake of a phantom 'working class unity.' Bridges was warned that neither the Atlantic nor the Gulf would support a strike whose settlement depended on agreement of half a dozen unions, at least two of which were Red-controlled . . ."

The strike began on October 29, 1936. It was fifteen days longer than the eighty-three day '34 strike and more effective; not a single port stayed open. Yet, there was neither the violence nor the stridence of the earlier strike. Shipowners didn't try to operate behind the picket lines, and in their public statements they stuck to explanations of their stand on the issues of the strike, carefully avoiding personal attacks on union leaders. And because the weapons appropriate to this kind of strike were non-violent—pamphlets and leaflets, radio talks, public debates—rather than strikebreakers and mass picketing, there were neither the broken heads nor the police violence of '34.

The first breach in the strikers' ranks came on the fifty–second day, when the sailors signed a separate agreement. "We want to show the other unions the way home," Lundeberg explained. The sailors' defection was, of course, in the every–man–for–himself tradition of maritime unions. (The marine firemen followed soon after.) It was consistent, too, with the behavior of Atlantic and Gulf longshoremen, who were unconcernedly working cargo diverted from West Coast ports. But it left Bridges and the longshoremen in an exposed position. Nevertheless, they reaffirmed their decision to hold out until the other five unions also got their hiring halls.

The shipowners, who had had a whiff of victory when they signed with the sailors and firemen, were now faced with a choice between giving in on the issue of hiring halls or letting the strike continue indefinitely. And in view of FDR's landslide victory, they couldn't expect help from the government. They gave in on the seamen's hiring halls.

Soon after, on January 6, 1937, Bridges and his negotiating committee met for the first time with the employers. Three days later, FBI director J. Edgar Hoover sent the Attorney General a report on how the strike was progressing. He reported that Lundeberg and a conservative group were making steady progress within the sailors' union. "But," he observed, "Harry Bridges, aided by Communist organizers and sympathizers, is doing his best to discredit Lundeberg." After a month of negotiating, longshoremen voted in a coastwide referendum to accept a new contract, and on February 4th, the ships began moving.

Who won the '36 strike? The shipowners thought they did. "In my mind there was absolutely no cause for it," Roger Lapham said later. "Except the wish of Bridges to extend his power. As I recall, the longshoremen got nothing out of the strike." Lapham was right in one way, wrong in another. The strike was a test of power, and Bridges did wish to extend the power of the union. He was also hoping to strengthen the Maritime Federation. And it was true that the longshoremen did not achieve their main objective of gaining complete control of the hiring halls. Nor did they get a wage increase.

But Lapham underestimated the gains the longshoremen did make. The new contract gave them both job security and more control over the hiring halls. They retained the right to elect the dispatchers from their own ranks, and they kept their six–hour day, assuring three hours of overtime when they were dispatched to a job. They also spread the work by limiting sling loads to 2,100 pounds. Moreover, in the new contract employers agreed to give union members preference in employment.

Soon after the ports were working again, Roger Lapham, fatigued by the ordeal of the long strike, went off on a five–month cruise around the Pacific, touring among others the country he'd been longing to send his opposite number to, Australia. It was a grand trip, he told the *Examiner's* society editor when he got back, marred only by his having pulled a leg muscle on the dance floor the first week out. He was still limping slightly as he came down the gangplank.

For Bridges, the end of this particular skirmish with the shipowners provided a chance to pay attention to some personal and union problems. For one thing, he had been having trouble with his health. 1934 had given him an ulcer, and while Lapham was off on his cruise, Bridges was having part of his stomach removed. As he was being wheeled into the operating room, two longshoremen who had appointed themselves his bodyguard drew the surgeon aside. "We just want you to know, Doc," one of them whispered hoarsely, "if Harry doesn't come off the operating table, you'll get yours, too."

One of the major problems the union faced was the fight that was working up between the longshoremen and the West Coast teamsters under Dave Beck. Beck, like Lundeberg a conservative Republican, was also a product of the working class. Born in 1894, he left school at seventeen to work in the Seattle laundry where his widowed mother was employed. "Mom and I used to work ten or twelve hours every day," he once recalled. "I would tell her as we walked home at night that I was going to do something so that people wouldn't have to work away their lives as we were doing. And by God, I have!" He joined the teamsters' union six years later, in 1917, when he moved up to a job driving a delivery wagon. After several years with the AEF in Europe in World War I, he came back to Seattle, where he again became active in the union. In 1925, Dan Tobin, the teamsters' national president, made him a general organizer.

Beck quickly demonstrated his skill as an organizer, as well as his grasp of economics. Within two years he had a contract with the laundry association in Seattle, a model for contracts he was to negotiate in other fields. It gave increased wages to the laundry workers, higher commissions to the drivers, and a price list ensuring satisfactory profits to the laundry operators. Under Beck, Seattle businesses organized by the teamsters operated as vest–pocket cartels with the union as the policing agency.

San Francisco narrowly escaped a similar fate. In 1933, Mike Casey described the Seattle system to Paul St. Sure, at that time secretary and legal counsel of the San Francisco laundry owners' association. When Beck was next in the city, he had dinner with St. Sure and some of the laundry owners. He had brought his agreement along with him and told the group that under its terms laundries employed only union drivers, and union drivers worked only for members of the association. "That means," Beck confided, "our members work only for laundries that maintain the price list." The lawyer in St. Sure was stirred. "How do you do this?" he inquired. "We have an agreement," Beck replied. "I noticed that copy you showed us wasn't signed," St. Sure said. "Do you have an original, that's signed?" "You don't sign it," Beck explained, producing a decision by a Seattle judge who'd ruled that a plaintiff who had filed a charge of collusion between the teamsters and launderers hadn't been able to prove his case because he couldn't produce any incriminating documents. "You don't sign it," he repeated. "You enforce it."

"I advised my people," St. Sure said afterward, "that Mr. Beck's arrangement was not legal, but they could have one if they wanted to on an 'enforcement basis'—if they wanted to get in bed with the teamsters' union. They didn't want to go that far."

Most businessmen on the Coast liked Beck. "When he addresses the Chamber of Commerce," *Time* said in a cover story it ran on Beck in the 1940s, "the members applaud like trained seals." The faculty at the University of Washington, where Beck was chairman of the university's governing board in the 1940s, liked him, too, for Beck was an enthusiastic supporter of higher faculty salaries. A few had misgivings about him, however, especially when Beck favored firing several professors who had invoked the privilege against self–incrimination before a state legislative committee hunting for Communists on campus. "Nobody who takes the Fifth Amendment," Beck said sternly, "has any right to be in a position of public trust."

Beck was as unimpressed with democracy as a way to govern a union as he was with Constitutional safeguards. "I'm paid $25,000 a year to run this outfit," he said in the mid–forties. The "outfit" he referred to was the union's eleven–state western division. "Unions are big business. Why should truck drivers and bottle washers be allowed to make big decisions affecting union policy? Would any corporation allow it?"

In 1947 Beck assumed the newly–created job of executive vice president of the teamsters, a post created to enable him to run the union while Tobin, the aging titular head, rested at the estate the union bought for him in Florida or took trips around the world, also at union expense. Five years later, Tobin formally retired and Beck assumed·the title as well as the function of presiding over the union. He was an effective president. During his term, when membership in most unions was levelling off or declining, teamster membership, and the union treasury continued upward, partly because of Beck's shrewd investment of union reserves. When Beck began laying a foundation for national bargaining in the mid–fifties, *Fortune* said of him: "In view of his potential membership and the strategic position of the teamsters in controlling transportation, Beck may live to be the most powerful labor leader in the United States."

Beck was just rounding out the final year of his first five–year term as president and riding high, when a Senate committee headed by Senator McClellan of Arkansas began investigating him and other teamster officials on suspicion of mishandling union funds and other malpractices. Beck appeared voluntarily before the committee, but to the undisguised glee of the committee's general counsel, Robert Kennedy, he invoked the Fifth Amendment repeatedly in response to questions. "Do you plan to resign your office in your union because of invoking the Fifth Amendment?" asked Senator John Kennedy, a member of the committee. "I certainly do not!" bristled Beck. As the head of the largest and richest union in the country, Beck was without doubt the most influential member of the AFL–CIO Executive Council, but a few days after his appearance before the McClellan committee, a majority of his colleagues on the council decided he had been right about the Fifth Amendment when he favored firing the professors who had invoked it. "Any official of an AFL–CIO union who takes the Fifth Amendment when asked about his conduct as a union officer," they declaimed as they dismissed him from their midst, "is unfit to hold union office."

Teamster officials persuaded Beck not to run for reelection, which came up a few weeks later. They assured him he would get his $50,000 a year pension, despite his early retirement. Jimmy Hoffa was elected in his place. Then, on December 6, 1957, the AFL–CIO, acting on charges of misconduct lodged against teamster leadership by the McClellan committee, expelled the union from the federation. Eight days after that, Beck was convicted of pocketing $1,900 from the sale of a union–owned Cadillac and sentenced to fifteen years in state prison. Two years after this conviction, he was sentenced in federal court to five years in the federal penitentiary for filing false income tax returns on behalf of the union. He was acquitted on a third charge that he had failed to pay income tax on several hundred thousand dollars of personal income. His lawyer successfully argued that the government had not proved that he had not embezzled the money from the union. If Beck had stolen it, the lawyer contended, he shouldn't be required to pay taxes on it. In 1962, his appeals from both convictions exhausted, he entered McNeil Island prison. After thirty months, the federal parole board let him out for good behavior. Members of the state parole board, of which Beck had once been chairman, were even more generous, deciding that because he was now seventy years old, the time he had served on McNeil Island would satisfy his fifteen–year sentence.

Released from prison, Beck went back to Seattle, where he busied himself with his investments. It was rumored that he was a millionaire, a speculation he neither affirmed nor denied, although he did tell a reporter after he retired: "I'm going to show everybody I can make money, and I don't have to work for the Teamsters. . . . I made 10 times as much on real estate as the Teamsters ever paid me." He illustrated his instinct for business by pointing to the teamster parking area across the street from where they were standing:

"You see those two lots. Four years ago the Seattle First National Bank was offering me $125,000 for them. I wouldn't take it. Then the Teamsters wanted them. I would not sell, but they said, 'It's your duty to the union.' So I said, 'O.K., if it's my duty, you give me anything over $125,000, and I'll sell.' The Teamsters gave me $135,000. Just twelve years ago I'd paid $28,000 for that property."

Beck was instinctively hostile to the West Coast longshoremen because their militancy rankled his conservative nature, but Bridges crystallized Beck's latent opposition by moving into an area of potential teamster jurisdiction. Warehousemen in San Francisco had been in the longshoremen's union since 1934, and in the middle of the '36 strike, Bridges proclaimed, "The longshoremen's union is not going to stay on the waterfront. It is going inland." Until this time, the teamsters had not shown any interest in warehousemen. Indeed, in the thirties, Tobin looked with disdain even at over–the–road truck drivers, whose admission to membership, he felt, diluted the craft purity of the teamsters' union. But Beck immediately started an organizing drive of his own among warehousemen. In those days he had some good friends on the AFL executive committee who decided that warehousemen belonged to the teamsters. Under the AFL rule that each union in the federation had exclusive jurisdiction over a craft or a class of workers, the longshoremen should have stopped organizing warehousemen and turned their warehouse members over to the teamsters. Joseph Ryan was willing to do so, but not his Pacific Coast District, which was now moving away from the AFL and towards the CIO.

Most West Coast businessmen, and especially those in the Northwest, viewed the prospect of longshoremen marching inland, of the CIO organizing lumberjacks, aircraft workers, even cannery workers and field hands—and all of them with Bridges at their head—as a frightening prospect. Beck's good friend, John Dore, the mercurial Mayor of Seattle who had had trouble in the past making up his mind where he stood on Bridges and the longshoremen, typified the widespread apprehension of the new development. In 1934, he called the strike a soviet of longshoremen and threatened to open the port by force. Two years later, he praised Bridges in public speeches, and announced on the eve of the '36 strike, "If the shipowners use guerrilla guard tactics, I'll give 'em a touch of hell." Then, in 1937, after the longshoremen went into the CIO, he had still another change of heart.

"When the CIO–AFL fight got hot in the city of Seattle," he told the 1937 AFL convention, "I announced as Mayor of that city and as a private individual that I was going to do everything humanly possible to make that an AFL city . . . The Mayor of Seattle has great executive powers . . . and I have laid down a rule and have enforced it relentlessly that there will be no picketing in that city by anybody unless that picketing is approved in writing by the Seattle Labor Council."

For many businessmen, therefore, Beck and his teamsters were a reassuring refuge. "Beck is a top labor statesman and an outstanding civic leader," the president of the Northwest's largest private utility told a *Time* writer in the forties. "He's absolutely tops. With him we've had labor peace when it might have been hell."

In San Francisco, where Beck's influence was relatively weak, the longshoremen's march inland was an immediate success. There, the teamsters weren't standing in their way, at least at the outset. Also, wages and working conditions in the Bay Area's two hundred warehouses were a union organizer's dream. In some, wages were more than twice what they were in others. Almost all the organizer had to do was show up at the door, tell the workers about wages and conditions in the warehouse down the block, and hand out applications. Within a year, the longshoremen's union had most of the warehouses under contract.

Then, in the summer of 1938, when it came time to start talking about new contracts, the warehouse operators made a proposal that put the union in a paradoxical position. By now, employers were well-organized in the Association of San Francisco Distributors, and they wanted a master contract to replace all the separate contracts they had signed when the union first organized their employees. One might have expected the union to welcome the employers' proposal, in view of its hard fight only a few years before to get a master contract on the docks.

But the union faced different conditions in the two industries. In longshore, a master contract protected it by preventing shipowners from playing one port off against another. But in warehousing, the crazy-quilt of wage rates and working conditions gave an advantage to the union, which, by bargaining warehouse-by-warehouse, could play one employer off against another. So the union held out for separate bargaining, publicly denouncing the employers' proposal as a scheme to wreck the warehousemen's union and bring back the open shop.

Insistence on consistency for its own sake has never been one of Bridges's weaknesses.

"In 1947, when Harry was trying to persuade the pineapple people and the Hawaii Employers' Council to accept arbitration," Phil Maxwell, president of the council, said in 1964, "we were meeting in a room in the Moana Hotel. Harry was arguing why we should arbitrate when a call came for him from his office in San Francisco. He took it right there in the room. 'You tell them the hell with that,' he told whoever was on the line. 'We won't go for arbitration. Look, our union is in a good, strong position with those employers. We'll do all right if we strike. If we let them take us to arbitration, we can only lose.'

"When he hung up," Maxwell said, laughing, "he turned back to us and picked up right where he'd left off, telling us why we should let him take us to arbitration."

After a brief propaganda battle the union forced a showdown by going to Woolworth's and demanding renewal of the contract covering its Bay Area warehouses. Woolworth's refused to be split off from the other warehouses, and the union shut down its warehouses. At this point, somebody in the distributors' association had a clever idea. A Woolworth executive crossed the picket line into the warehouse, got a box of pencils off the shelf and put it in a boxcar. Then the boxcar was shunted over to another warehouse to be unloaded. The point of this was to see how the union responded. If they unloaded the pencils, the workers would see that the union was weak because no union with any self–respect would allow its members to unload goods from a struck warehouse. And if they refused, they would be shutting down an employer they had no quarrel with. It would look like a secondary boycott.

The union fell headlong into the employers' trap. As soon as the pencils were tossed into the boxcar and the big sliding door slammed shut, one of the pickets took a piece of chalk and wrote in big letters on the side: HOT CAR. For a couple of months, the boxcar was shunted from warehouse to warehouse, even taken over to the Oakland side on the rail ferry, with the warehousemen walking off the job wherever it appeared. By October, retailers' shelves were bare, and San Francisco was feeling the pinch.

Paul Smith, who was now editor of the *San Francisco Chronicle*, reacted as the employers hoped, too. "Although I understood the position of the unions in the growing struggle," he says in his autobiography, "I strongly supported the employers because they were fighting the devastating technique of the secondary boycott. . . . I began to editorialize somewhat brashly on the front pages, usually from the point of view of the 'public'. . . ."

One day in October, Eugene Paton, the president of the warehousemen's local, was in a bar with Sam Kagel, going over Smith's editorial in that morning's *Chronicle*, muttering angrily as they read. "We were sitting there, having a drink," Kagel recalled later, "wondering what we could do, when one of us said, 'Look! That bastard Smith thinks he knows how to settle this damn thing. Let's make him put up or shut up. Let's ask him to mediate it.' So we ordered a couple more drinks and wrote him a special delivery letter right there on the bar. And then, to make sure he couldn't back out, we sent a copy to the employers."

To their surprise, Smith accepted. "While I was trying to figure out a logical answer to such a challenge," Smith has written, "the leading spokesman for the employers telephoned me to say that . . . of course they would be delighted to accept me as a mediator.

Since both sides apparently had agreed on something for the first time in four months of strife, I couldn't very well duck the challenge." He chose an unused courtroom in the old Post Office as a neutral ground for the meetings, and he and the two dozen union and employer negotiators met there for several days, not getting very far because the employers held out for the master contract and the union just as firmly said no. Then, without warning, Bridges, whose troubles on the waterfront had kept him from the warehouse meetings until the last moment, broke the impasse.

"Gene and I were laying it on as hard as we could," Kagel said later, "that the employers' insistence on the master contract was unfair, that they were trying to bust the union, bring back the open shop, and all that, when without having said a word to either of us, Harry spoke up. 'You know, fellows, the employers are right about this. A master contract does make sense for this industry. We'll go for it.'

"He'd been sitting there listening to the talk and it suddenly dawned on him that our position was OK in the short run, where we could whipsaw the employers," Kagel replied. "But in the long run, they were bound to gain strength, and then one contract covering all of them would make more sense for us, just as it did in longshoring. And it would be a buffer against the teamsters raiding our membership in warehouse, too.

"Actually," he went on, "I think Harry's action shows the greatness of his leadership. He's always been pragmatic, always willing to change his position if conditions change or if somebody comes up with new facts.

"I think, too, he'd been thinking about the kind of union the ILWU was going to be. His heart has always been with the longshoremen, and he'd pretty much left the warehouse division up to the other officers. But it hit him that if the union didn't branch out and have a strong warehouse division, in time it would be nothing but a labor trust with a dwindling membership on the waterfront. Like some of the craft unions in the AFL.

"And you know, if the union hadn't branched out into warehouse, I doubt if it could have organized Hawaii."

"Older and wiser heads among the shipowners said even in 1934 that Bridges was far and away the ablest labor leader that had emerged in years," George West, a *San Francisco Chronicle* reporter, wrote in a profile of Bridges in 1936. "But they predicted that in a few years he would be wearing diamonds, attending the weekly fights and running for the Board of Supervisors like other San Francisco labor figures."

That notion should have been dispelled by Bridges's first report to the membership when he took office in 1937, as President of the Pacific Coast District of the longshoremen's union. He began by answering longshoremen's complaints that they hadn't gotten as much as they should have out of the 1936 strike, reminding them that their bargaining position had been undercut by the defection of the sailors and firemen. He reminded them further that they had done the same thing to the sailors and firemen in 1935, with even worse results for the seafarers.

Then came several portentous recommendations. "I propose," Bridges wrote, "that the district reiterate its pledge of full support to the campaign and aims of the CIO . . . and demand that Joseph Ryan conduct a national referendum on CIO affiliation." The proposal must have bemused Ryan when he heard about it. Some of the longshoremen's locals on the Atlantic Coast hadn't held local union meetings or elected officers for decades. And Ryan's union had never held a referendum on anything. Bridges also urged the longshoremen to participate in Labor's Non–Partisan League, the political arm of the CIO, and to do everything they could to bring the warehousemen into their union.

His final recommendation did the most to invalidate the ship-owners' prediction that he would end up a typical union pie card. "My salary of $75 per week is, of course," he observed, "far more than any rank and file ILA man earns on the job, and the membership should make known, through their various delegates, their wishes in regard to continuing this salary or reducing it."

Bridges's insistence that he and other ILWU officials should be paid frugal salaries, in contrast to the bountiful amounts received by most American union officers, gave him a deserved reputation for incorruptibility. Sometimes, it was inconvenient. In the late 1950s, a San Francisco Cadillac dealer who was an admirer of the longshoremen's union found himself overstocked at the end of the model year. He called Howard Bodine, an official he knew at ILWU headquarters. "Look, Howard," he told him, "I've got to get these cars off the floor in a hurry to make room for the new models coming in. I'm going to take a loss on 'em no matter who I sell 'em to, so if you and any of your friends down there want one, let me know. I'll give you a real good price." When two of Bridges's fellow officers showed him the Cadillacs they had bought, explaining that they had paid less for them than the list price of a new Chevy or

Ford, for a few days he considered taking advantage of the dealer's offer. He was driving an old Dodge, and he needed a new car. His interest died as quickly as it had awakened when he discussed the deal with one of his associates at lunch. "For Chrissakes, Harry," the friend exclaimed in horror, "you can't be seen driving a Cadillac!"

He ended up with a Falcon two–door, Ford's cheapest model.

After the sailors' and marine firemen's defection in the '36 strike, the Maritime Federation didn't seem to have much of a future. Hope revived when delegates to the federation's 1937 convention endorsed the CIO, instructing member unions to hold referendum votes on whether or not they would affiliate. Ultimately, about as many stayed with the AFL as went into the CIO.

Besides the CIO endorsement, the 1937 convention was memorable for Bridges for another reason. During a recess, he was in the lobby of Portland's Multnomah Hotel where he was staying, talking with friends about how U.S. Immigration officials at the border had harassed some Canadian delegates who had been held at the border until the federation put up a bond guaranteeing their return to Canada. They were still being harassed by U.S. agents at the convention itself. Suddenly someone exclaimed, "You know, Harry, I'll bet those bastards've got your room bugged!" They went up, and Charles Krolek, a ship's radio officer, volunteered to see if he could find it.

"First he looked all around, and then he passed his hands over the walls while we stood there, impressed with the expert way he was going at it," Henry Schmidt said afterward. "Finally, down near the floor, he pulled back a strip of wallpaper, and there was the bug. For years, we wondered how he'd been able to find it, it was so cleverly hidden, even though we always suspected there was something phony about the guy.

"Then, when the trial [the Bridges–Robertson–Schmidt conspiracy trial of 1949–1950] was beginning, Krolek showed up in the witness section. I nudged Harry, 'Look who's here. Is he going to testify for us or against us?' 'Wait and see,' was all Harry would say. Well, Krolek testified for the government. And we finally found out how he'd been able to find that bug. It came out in his testimony. That sonofabitch had installed it himself!"

While the longshoremen were strengthening their union and the bonds between all the maritime unions, the shipowners were busily reorganizing themselves. As soon as the waterfront settled down after the '36 strike, they strengthened their association, renaming it the Waterfront Employers' Association of the Pacific Coast. T.G. Plant went back to his old job at American–Hawaiian, and Almon E. Roth, a member of a West Coast shipping family, came up from Stanford, where he was Comptroller, to head the new association.

Roth's term of office started off well with the negotiation of the 1937 contract, arrived at amicably even though the employers made a significant concession to the union, agreeing not to introduce labor–saving machines without the union's permission. In the 1960s, when the union finally gave up the restrictive working rules it got in that 1937 contract, Bridges commented on how effectively the union had practiced feather bedding: "We did as good a job— maybe a better job—as any union in the country in holding back the effects of mechanization. We had eight–man gangs on the job when maybe two or four men were needed."

Roth was still settling in on his new job when he found himself dealing with a brand-new longshoremen's union. In August, 1937 the longshoremen, in a coastwide referendum, voted overwhelmingly to go into the CIO. The Pacific Coast District thereupon broke away from Ryan and the ILA to become the International Longshoremen's and Warehousemen's Union–CIO. Now, instead of being a semi–autonomous branch of a corrupt national union, the ILWU was independent, free to develop in its own way.

One of the first departures from the old union's custom was a provision in the new constitution that if 15 per cent of the membership signed a petition calling for the recall of an official, he would be suspended pending a trial by the union's executive board. "I propose," Bridges had urged in his first report as ILWU president, "that the present recall provisions be liberalized and strengthened, making it easier to immediately suspend or remove any official using or attempting to use his authority to exercise dictatorial or top control."

The system of government Bridges proposed for the ILWU was popular with the rank and file, but it exasperated the leadership of many other unions, reinforcing their view that Bridges and the longshoremen were somehow subversive. The ILWU was just two years old when Arthur Eggleston, a *Chronicle* labor reporter, writing about the 1939 California AFL convention, observed: "There is very good reason why the old–line leaders in California and elsewhere hate the Pacific Coast waterfront unions, the longshoremen's union and some of the rest. Referendum election of officers, referendum votes on agreements, referendum votes on practically everything of importance and extremely easy methods of recalling officers constitute a grave threat to the less risky method of machine and convention control."

Although the new union and its CIO affiliation had undeniable benefits for the longshoremen, it also presented certain problems. It got the union into arguments with the shipowners and with other unions, and it almost sent Bridges to jail.

It wasn't long after the union joined the CIO before the shipowners raised doubts about the contract. They contended they had signed a contract with the ILA–AFL, not the ILWU–CIO. They also claimed they weren't sure the new union actually represented a majority of the men on the Coast, pointing to Tacoma, Anacortes, and Port Angeles, where the longshoremen were violently opposed to John L. Lewis and CIO affiliation.

Bridges's response was to propose an NLRB election in which all West Coast longshoremen could decide whether the new ILWU would be their bargaining agent. The shipowners, remembering their success in holding back unionization of ship clerks in 1934, insisted that each company should constitute its own bargaining unit and determine individually whether it would be represented by the ILWU, the AFL, or by no union at all. The labor board resolved the argument in the ILWU's favor, noting that for years shipowners had coordinated their labor policies on a coastwide basis, and that from the turn of the century longshoremen had wanted coastwide bargaining.

After the argument was resolved, the anti–CIO feeling in the three Washington State ports created new problems when Tacoma longshoremen went on strike to force employers to sign a port–wide contract with their old ILA–AFL local. The employers responded by saying that much as they might like to, they were bound by the NLRB order certifying the ILWU. That didn't satisfy Tacoma longshoremen, who refused to go back to work. Wayne Morse, Dean of the University of Oregon Law School, who had been appointed in 1938 by Frances Perkins as permanent arbitrator for the industry, was called in to settle the argument. He decided that the employers were right and that the longshoremen had to go back to work.

But the truculent Tacomans defied Morse, too, and the port stayed down. The NLRB finally came to the rescue, reopening the case and ultimately certifying the AFL union in the three ports. For years until the AFL locals joined the ILWU in the 1950s, it was a handy arrangement for the shipowners. When they had trouble with the ILWU, they could divert ships from an ILWU port to Tacoma, where the AFL longshoremen would handle their cargoes. It was useful for Beck, Lundeberg and Ryan, too, for it gave them an AFL enclave in ILWU territory.

They needed one, for in the late thirties the issue of AFL or CIO affiliation, which often became a fighting matter, made a crazy quilt out of collective bargaining in the maritime industry. On the West Coast, longshoremen were CIO but sailors were AFL. On the East Coast, sailors were CIO, longshoremen AFL. On both coasts, deck officers were AFL, engineers CIO. West Coast cooks and stewards were CIO, firemen and oilers unaffiliated. If one union put up a picket line, it might be able to count on perhaps half the others to support it. Some of the other half would send flying squads down to the docks to breach it, either to get the strikers' jobs for themselves or for members of another union in their federation.

Having CIO longshoremen on the West Coast was an asset to a new East Coast CIO sailors' union that broke away from the old AFL seamen's union in the mid–thirties. Called the National Maritime Union, it was led by a brawny, energetic young sailor named Joe Curran and became an immediate success. When sailors started to desert the AFL for the CIO in a growing stream, William Green, AFL president, organized a rescue operation, putting Joseph Ryan in charge. Ryan declared the leaders of the AFL seamen's union morally unfit to hold union office, and called upon the union to clean itself up under AFL supervision. The seamen's union proved unable to purge itself, and in 1938, the AFL revoked its charter, creating in its place the Seafarers' International Union and appointing Lundeberg President. Ironically, in the 1950s, Ryan himself was denounced as morally unfit to hold union office, and his union was expelled from the AFL. His chief critic was Dave Beck, who headed an AFL committee to clean up the East Coast longshoremen's union.

The ILWU also lost the support of a loyal old-time longshore leader. Burglar Bill Lewis, understandably bitter about the direction the union took after Bridges defeated him for District President, refused to go along with the new order and stayed on Ryan's payroll as West Coast organizer, maintaining an office in San Francisco, where he gathered around him a forlorn cadre of diehard AFL loyalists. From time to time they issued pronouncements that the old AFL union was on the brink of launching a massive drive, under Lewis's leadership, to liberate West Coast longshoremen from the ILWU and get them back into the AFL. Nobody paid much attention.

A group of AFL longshoremen in San Pedro, the harbor for Los Angeles, though never numerically strong, proved more troublesome than the San Francisco loyalists. When three thousand Los Angeles longshoremen moved over into the CIO, fifteen stayed behind. Pointing to the AFL longshoremen's constitution and the articles of incorporation of the original local, which allowed a group as small as theirs to hold onto the local union charter, they insisted that they, not the ILWU, were the owners of the union treasury and the hiring hall. Then, using the same reasoning the employers had used earlier, they argued that because the shipowners had a contract with the ILA–AFL, they were obligated to give AFL longshoremen preference in employment. The employers ignored them, so they asked the county court in Los Angeles for a court order enforcing their claims.

Their appeal was heard by Judge Reuben Schmidt, who ruled that the AFL group did own all the property of the local union and controlled the contract with the shipowners. It followed, he held, that they were entitled to run the hiring hall, and in dispatching men to the waterfront to give jobs first to AFL longshoremen. To make his ruling effective, the judge appointed a receiver to see that it was all properly carried out. Then, to give the ILWU a chance to reply, he agreed to hold off enforcement of his order for a few days.

Bridges replied with a long brief reviewing the history of the ILWU, asking the judge for a new hearing and a reversal of his ruling. Simultaneously, he sent a telegram to Secretary of Labor Perkins, a copy of which the union's publicity man gave to Los Angeles and San Francisco newspapers. They published it the next day:

"This decision is outrageous," Bridges was quoted as telling the Secretary,

considering ILA has 15 members [in San Pedro] and the International Longshoremen–Warehousemen's Union has three thousand. International Longshoremen–Warehousemen Union has petitioned the Labor Board for certification to represent San Pedro longshoremen with International Longshoremen Association denied representation because it represents only fifteen men. Board hearing held: decision now pending. Attempted enforcement of Schmidt decision will tie up port of Los Angeles and involve entire Pacific Coast. International Longshoremen–Warehousemen Union, representing eleven thousand of the twelve thousand longshoremen on the Pacific Coast, does not intend to allow state courts to override the majority vote of members in choosing its officers and representatives and to override the National Labor Relations Board.

The Los Angeles County Bar Association was as outraged by what Bridges had done as he was by the judge's ruling. The lawyers felt that Bridges's telegram and its publication in the papers was a wanton challenge to judicial authority, and they asked the judge to hold him in contempt. The judge agreed, fining him $125. Bridges appealed his conviction to the California Supreme Court, contending that it violated his Constitutional right to freedom of speech and of the press. He lost again. "Freedom of speech doesn't permit comment on a case pending before a court," a majority of the court replied, upholding his conviction, "if such comment will affect the orderly administration of justice." One justice dissented, noting that Bridges's criticism of Judge Schmidt hadn't been voiced in the courtroom, nor did his telegram actually interfere with the court's proceedings.

Supported by the American Civil Liberties Union, Bridges took the case to the U.S. Supreme Court. On the day after Pearl Harbor, the Court, by a vote of five to four, reversed the conviction. Even before that, longshoremen and shipowners in San Pedro had quietly agreed that the hiring hall and the contract were the property of the ILWU, not the corporal's guard of AFL loyalists.

The ILWU was not only caught in the crossfire between the AFL and the CIO but also, in the thirties and forties, it had to contend with the ramifications on the waterfront of the rise of fascism in Europe and militarism in Asia. In 1936, within a week of the longshoremen's promise to the shipowners that they would stop using job action, they had to decide whether or not they would load scrap iron on a ship bound for Italy.

Mussolini, fresh from his victory over Ethiopia, needed the scrap iron to make the guns and bombs he was sending to General Franco, who needed them for his campaign to overthrow the democratically elected government of Spain. The longshoremen, torn between their contractual responsibility to load the ships and their sympathies for the Spaniards who were fighting to defend their government, decided in favor of the Loyalists and left the cargo on the dock until an arbitrator ruled that they had to load it.

In 1937, with the war in Spain going badly for the loyalists, longshoremen in San Francisco shut down the port for a day to take part in a protest against America's policy of non–support for the Republican government of Spain. The longshoremen's protest made no sense at all to the shipowners. They viewed it as a Communist-inspired tactic:

"If the majority of the membership of the maritime unions have become so social-minded," Almon Roth observed, "that they are prepared to sacrifice their own earnings and the stability of their own employment for the common cause of 'the Communist party' it is apparent that the sanctity of contracts and such items will mean but little.

"Personally, I do not believe, however, that the majority of longshoremen are looking for trouble for trouble's sake or are prepared to make such a sacrifice."

Roth underestimated the depth of the longshoremen's political and humanitarian commitment which was demonstrated soon again when Japan invaded China. Early in 1938, the longshoremen, meeting in their first convention as the ILWU, passed half a dozen resolutions condemning Japanese aggression. After the convention, a Greek ship, the "Spyros," and a British freighter, the "Beckenham," called at San Francisco to pick up scrap iron for Japan. Longshoremen were starting to put it aboard when two thousand boys and girls from Chinatown marched onto the dock to protest the shipment. The longshoremen swarmed off the ships, and for almost a week the scrap iron lay untouched on the dock.

The employers called in the arbitrator, insisting that the union was violating its no–strike pledge. "Our union wants to live up to its contract," Henry Schmidt answered for the local, "but we cannot expect self–respecting men to push Chinese children out of the way and load scrap iron that will be used to slaughter their countrymen." The Chinese community solved the problem by pulling the picket line off the dock just as the arbitrator was getting ready to open a hearing on it.

Leaving the waterfront on the fifth day, the children marched back up to Chinatown behind a banner reading: "Thank you, longshoremen." On their way, they stopped off at the longshoremen's headquarters. Henry Schmidt made a brief speech:

"The fact that you are withdrawing your picket line, and that we longshoremen will proceed to load scrap iron for the 'Spyros' and 'Beckenham,'" he told them, "does not mean that this movement to halt shipments of war materials for Japan has ended.

"On the other hand, the movement is just beginning. Ahead is a nation–wide campaign by labor for Congressional action to declare an embargo against such Japan–bound shipments. That's the only way you can do it."

"Rah, rah, rah, longshoremen!" the children chanted when Schmidt finished. Hoisting their banner and their signs, they set off for the Waterfront Employers' Association, where they sang a Chinese war song. Then, with a parting boo for the shipowners, they trudged on up the hill.

After the war, John Gunther, in San Francisco to gather material for *Inside USA,* was waiting outside Bridges's office for an interview. Glancing about, he noticed a scroll on the wall:

In Appreciation to the
International Longshoremen's and Warehouseman's
Union For Upholding the Principles of Righteous-
ness in Refusing to Load Scrap Metal For Japan in
December 1938, As a Protest Against Japan's Unde-
clared Aggressive War Against China.
The Chinese People of San Francisco
June 8, 1945

The scrap iron issue posed a major problem for Bridges. Pulling him in one direction were the picket lines manned by the Chinese, reinforced by ministers and pacifists, which were at one time after another thrown around scrap iron ships in a dozen West Coast ports. Against that was his responsibility as the union's chief officer to urge his membership to live up to their contract with the employers. It was an excruciating decision, and he vacillated at length before he finally made up his mind.

A few months after the "Spyros"–"Beckenham" incident, Bridges was in Astoria, Oregon when a ship put in to pick up a cargo of scrap iron for Japan. If longshoremen refused to load the ship, the employers warned they were prepared to lock out the port until they got a firm commitment from the longshoremen that they would live up to the contract in the future. Under the circumstances, there didn't seem to be anything the union could do but capitulate, for the employers had the arbitrator on their side and, presumably, the law as well, for the longshoremen would be breaching their contract. "I don't think it would do any good to tie up all the scrap iron on the Pacific Coast," Bridges said reluctantly. "It would then go through Vancouver, B.C., the East Coast or the Gulf, and our ports would get it in the neck."

But when the union met in April for its 1939 convention, Bridges reverted back to his original position. In his opening remarks to the delegates, he urged them to take a stand on foreign policy and to boycott German vessels and ships carrying scrap iron to Japan. "I can't see any reason why German ships should run to our ports," he said. "None of us will want to profit from them. That's blood money, and we don't want any of it."

In 1939, Roger Baldwin, chairman of the American Civil Liberties Union, toured the country assessing the state of civil liberties. Toward the end of his tour he was in San Francisco, where he remarked that he had found peace on the labor front everywhere but in California. "Here," he continued, "you have an exceptional state of affairs, because the state is the center of a vast change. Its industrial situation is not fixed, as in the East. Its population is rapidly growing. Your agricultural feudalism, open shop temper of big employers, and struggle on the waterfront have created excessive strife." Baldwin's visit to San Francisco followed closely a series of incidents that had the appearance of yet another last–ditch stand by the shipowners. As before, the business community was supporting them, this time through a new organization, the San Francisco Employers' Council.

To Bridges and the longshoremen, the employers' council was their old enemy, the Industrial Association, in new clothing. All the employers and corporate farmers who had been in the Industrial Association were in the new council, along with bankers and insurance executives. Its president was Almon Roth, who had been sounding an increasingly belligerent note as head of the shipowners. Almost immediately, the longshoremen's impression of the council was confirmed. In 1938, they and the shipowners had negotiated a new contract with almost no difficulty. In 1939, with the new employers' council on the scene, a strike was unavoidable. Just before negotiations got under way Roth and Frank Foisie, who was now president of the waterfront employers' coastwide organization, set the tone by stridently berating Bridges, accusing him of being irresponsible, a chronic troublemaker with ulterior motives.

Foisie was a lamentable choice to head the shipowners, especially to confront the militant, left–wing union he had to deal with in the ILWU and the union leader he encountered in Bridges. Foisie had been in the longshore industry since the early twenties, when, fresh from Harvard, where he had studied social work, he arrived in Seattle. The shipowners had just driven a longshoremen's union off the waterfront, and they were looking for somebody from outside the industry with new ideas about how to avoid labor problems to head their association. Foisie got the job. He proposed a scheme designed to improve working conditions and keep the union out, as well. It combined an employer–controlled hiring system then in use in British ports with a company union much like the employee representation plan William MacKenzie King designed for Rockefeller after the Ludlow Massacre in Colorado.

Foisie's system worked pretty well in the open shop atmosphere of the twenties. Jobs and earnings were divided fairly equally among the men, and from 1929 to 1933, when jobs became progressively more scarce, Foisie added only three men, all sons of Seattle longshoremen, to the roster of longshoremen in the port. His scheme kept the union out until 1933. But when NRA and Section 7a came along, it turned out Seattle longshoremen didn't think much of company unionism. Nor did they think much of the employer–run hiring hall and its creator, whom they referred to, venomously, as Fink–Hall Foisie.

To Foisie, who was unable to understand the grievances of the longshoremen, the only palatable explanation for all this was that Communists were behind it. In 1934, he had told reporters the day before the big coastwide strike began he'd been talking with the men on the waterfront and he was sure of their loyalty. "I don't think the walkout will affect Seattle," he concluded. He carried his conspiracy theory of the longshoremen's behavior with him to San Francisco when he moved there to head the coastwide employer's organization. He held the job for almost ten years, until the shipowners decided that if they were ever to have peace on the waterfront, Foisie would have to go.

He was invited down to Stanford in the summer of 1939, just after he succeeded Roth, to talk to a business conference about the kind of leadership he was going to give the shipowners. Bridges's deportation hearing was opening that day on Angel Island, and the newspapers were full of it. "Won't things go better if union leadership changes on the waterfront?" one of the students asked Foisie. "The only thing that would do any good," he replied, "is for Bridges and his crowd to be discredited. Thank God that day seems to be approaching. However," he added darkly, "you must remember that Bridges is only the symbol, not the head."

The Foisie–Roth denunciations of Bridges were echoed, soon after, by an even stronger one from the San Francisco Chamber of

Commerce. "This city," it asserted in a full-page newspaper ad, "and that means everyone in it—employer, laborer, white-collar workers, everyone—has stood all it can stand of hell on the waterfront." The ad went on to remind readers that the employers had said they would accept arbitration in case of a strike, but the ILWU had balked. It ended on a sinister note:

"There is basis for suspicion that industrial peace in San Francisco is contrary to the aims of those leaders who talk of 'economic pressure.' There is substantial evidence in their open avowal of class hatred, that destruction of industry is of more importance to them than is the welfare of the workers they represent and their families."

Bridges answered the Chamber with an open letter he sent to the two newspapers he thought reasonably fair, the *Chronicle* and the *News.* "What the employers want in the contract," Bridges contended, "will take away so much of the union's gains in the last five years that the longshoremen will be set back to where they were before '34. We are against arbitration as to whether we should keep these gains," he conceded, "but we're willing to work beyond the present contract termination date while we negotiate a new one. What worries us," he wrote, "is that Roth has been saying the employers intend to give the ILWU a fight to the finish." He had reason to worry, for as he was writing, the port of San Francisco had been shut down for a month because of the shipowners' refusal to bargain with the ship clerks' union, a branch of the ILWU.

San Francisco's four newspapers gave the employers and the Chamber of Commerce the better of the argument. This was to be expected, except for the *Chronicle*, where Paul Smith had moved up from the financial page to the editor's chair. Smith still admired and liked Bridges, but on this issue he was convinced he was wrong. He said so in an open letter addressed to Bridges which was published as a front-page editorial:

> Your letter is full of unadulterated bunk. . . . What Roth said the employers would fight to a finish is the union's constant breaking of contracts.
>
> On the basis of the record up to the moment, such moral weight as we may have stands squarely behind the employers in their present position. . . .
>
> And let me lay this on the line: I strongly suspect that the motives behind your present position are not primarily in the interest of better wages and working conditions for your men. [The

union was demanding that wages be increased from 95¢ an hour to $1.10; that the six–hour day be continued, with overtime starting at 3:00 p.m. instead of 5:00; that employers share with the men any savings accruing from the use of labor–saving machines: and that longshoremen be free to respect picket lines on the docks without being penalized.] I would hazard a guess that there has been involved a "strategy" which you think will expand your sphere of influence. To put it more bluntly, I would go so far as to suggest that it would be a "good idea" to have the ships tied up in port when the sailors' union elections come off in October, in the hope that you could "depose" that particular leadership which has been such a thorn in your side.

There was, of course, another explanation for the impasse that Smith may or may not have considered: that it was the shipowners who were stalling, hoping that Bridges's deportation hearing described in the next chapter, would go against him.

NOTES

Bridges's comments about how the union was going to control hiring and limit sling loads were quoted in the *Waterfront Worker* in July, 1935.

Lapham's letter to Perkins asserting that Bridges sought to establish one big union for maritime workers is in the Perkins Papers. His meeting with Secretary Perkins exploring the possibility of deporting Bridges is described in his oral history memoir. Bridges's comment about Lapham after his death in 1966 was reported in the *San Francisco Chronicle* on April 18, 1966.

The Korematsu decision is *Korematsu* v. *U.S.*, 323 U.S. 214 (1944).

Donoghue's memo is in the Perkins Papers.

FDR's question to Perkins as to Bridges's citizenship is in File No. 1750 ("Harry Bridges") in the Roosevelt Memorial Library. His second query, about Bridges and Darcy, is in FDR Official File 407-B. Grey's letter is in the Perkins Papers. Bridges's letter to the President and FDR's reply are in FDR Official File 407-B.

The source of the story of Bridges and Casey is Sam Kagel, who told the story in an interview with me in San Francisco in 1964.

McGrady's report to the President on the West Coast maritime situation in 1936 is in FDR Official File 407-B. J. Edgar Hoover's report on the 1936 strike is in the Justice Department file in the National Archives.

The *Time* cover story on Beck was in the issue of November 29, 1948.

Beck's remark about how to run a union is quoted in Romer, *The International Brotherhood of Teamsters.* The description of Beck's appearance before the McClellan Committee is in Robert Kennedy, *The Enemy Within.*

Eggleston's comment about the AFL officials' resentment of ILWU democracy is in the *San Francisco Chronicle,* August 23, 1939.

The NLRB decision establishing the West Coast as the appropriate bargaining unit is in 7 NLRB 1041 (1938). The board decision certifying the AFL in the three Northwest ports is in 32 NLRB 668 (1941).

Bridges's telegram to Secretary Perkins about Judge Schmidt's decision is reproduced in the Supreme Court decision, *Bridges* v. *California* (3.4 U.S. 252 (1941)), reversing his contempt conviction for sending it. The California Supreme Court decision is *Bridges* v. *Superior Court,* 14 Cal. 2d 464 (1940).

Roth's comment about the longshoremen's protest against American neutrality was quoted in the San Francisco *Daily Commercial News,* May 24, 1937. Henry Schmidt's remarks about the longshoremen's refusal to load scrap iron for Japan were quoted in the *San Francisco Examiner,* December 20 and 21, 1938.

Bridges's comments about the scrap iron issue were quoted in the *San Francisco Chronicle* on March 3 and April 8, 1939.

Roger Baldwin's evaluation of the labor scene in California were quoted in the *San Francisco News,* November 6, 1939.

Foisie has described his employee representation plan in *Decasualizing Longshore Labor and the Seattle Experience.* It is summarized in the *Monthly Labor Review,* December, 1922. His remarks at Stanford about the need to remove Bridges were quoted in the *San Francisco News,* July 18, 1939.

5

That's Against the Constitution!

*His first reaction was that of the ordinary
American liberal.*
*"What's the idea?" he asked. "Has he done
anything to overthrow the Government?"*
"No," I admitted.
*"Then why in the world," asked the Presi-
dent, "should a man be punished for what he
thinks, for what he believes? That's against the
Constitution."*

FRANCES PERKINS, in
The Roosevelt I Knew

IN *The Roosevelt I Knew*, Frances Perkins says that when demands
were first made that Bridges be sent back to Australia, it was "difficult to say whether the problem of the deportation of Harry
Bridges was a problem in industrial relations or a plain problem of
justice." She had met him once, briefly, in 1934 when she was in
San Francisco for the AFL convention, and Bridges sent word he
would like to see her.

"I suggested that he come to the back of the platform of the convention hall immediately after I made my address," she recalled
thirty years later.

I have a clear memory of him. He was a small, thin, somewhat
haggard man in a much–worn overcoat, the collar turned up and
pinned around his throat, with a cap in his hand. He was polite,
deferential, hardly finding the voice to make demands for the
striking longshoremen. His suggestions seemed practical and reasonable. I recall putting down in my mind that he was a typical
British worker.

In the course of the next six months Bridges became an important and dominating factor in the West Coast industrial picture. As he established himself as a leader of the longshoremen, there began to be violent protest against him locally and nationally.

To answer the protestors, who deluged her with demands that she deport Bridges, she asked San Francisco immigration officers to investigate the repeated charges that he was a Communist. They reported that there was no evidence to show that Bridges was connected with either the Communist Party or any other radical organization. One of the investigators' discoveries much amused FDR when she discussed the case privately with him. The investigators had been told by the landlady of a boardinghouse Bridges had lived in in the early twenties that he was quiet, orderly, worked regularly, and paid his rent promptly. "What did he do in the evenings?" they asked. "I don't know much about that," the landlady replied. "Mostly he went to his room after supper and played his mandolin until bedtime." Over the years, when the Bridges case came up in the newspapers, the President would ask Miss Perkins with a chuckle, "How's your mandolin player getting on?"

And the Bridges case kept coming up. Early in 1936 it was injected into a hearing before the House Appropriations Committee by Congresswoman Florence Kahn, a conservative Republican from California, when Daniel McCormack, the Commissioner of immigration, was defending his budget.

"The San Francisco Police Department has followed him unremittingly for years, and our men have also," McCormack said. "He either is not a Communist or he has so carefully guarded his utterances that there is no legal ground for his deportation."

When anyone wrote to Secretary Perkins that Bridges was a Communist, it was her practice to ask him for documentary evidence or an affidavit. For three years, none was forthcoming. Then, one day in the fall of 1934, two immigration officials on the West Coast wrote her asking for a warrant for Bridges's arrest and deportation, supporting it with affidavits made by four men who said they had seen Bridges participating in Communist Party activity. They also sent along a photostatic copy of a CP membership card issued to one Harry Dorgan, the implication being that because Bridges's mother's maiden name was Dorgan, that was his name in the Party, and this was a copy of his card.

The request put Frances Perkins in a quandary. For one thing, none of the affidavits corroborated the others, and she recognized one of the signers as a man with a notorious reputation for anti–labor activity. Moreover, the copy of the Harry Dorgan card was only tenuously connected to Bridges. And strangely, the request didn't come from San Francisco, but from Raphael Bonham and Roy Norene, who headed the Seattle and Portland immigration offices.

San Francisco officials reported that they still had no evidence on which to deport Bridges unless they charged him with moral turpitude, using as evidence some recordings made by Portland police when they bugged Bridges's room during a maritime federation convention in 1937. Larry Doyle, one of the affiants, worked closely with a Portland police captain named John Keegan, and had taken advantage of the relationship to take the recordings from the files. He had approached Edward Hoff, director of the San Francisco immigration office, offering to sell him the recordings. "They've got a lot of interesting stuff on him," he told Hoff. Including, he went on, a conversation between Bridges and a delegate's wife he'd entertained in his room. "Should I use this?" Hoff asked Washington. "It might be useful." "No," James Houghteling, head of the Immigration Service, wrote back. "We get plenty of valuable information, but not by such methods."

Suspecting that Bonham and Norene might have been taken in by their informants, Miss Perkins sent Gerard Reilly, her general counsel, out to the Coast to see for himself if the men who had signed the affidavits were trustworthy and to ask Bridges, under oath, if he were a Communist. Bridges replied without hesitation, "No, I am not."

Herbert Mills, one of the four witnesses, was a member of a sailors' union goon squad. Lawrence Milner, the second, was a major in the Oregon National Guard who had found the skills he had learned in military intelligence useful in labor espionage. Not much was known about the third man, John Leech, until he testified in the hearing. The fourth was Larry Doyle, who had rounded up the other three. Nevertheless, no doubt infected by Bonham's and Norene's enthusiasm for the case, Reilly reported back to Washington that they would be effective witnesses. The copy of the membership card seemed authentic, too, he told the Secretary.

Miss Perkins still hesitated, because, she has said, "I recognized that this was no ordinary deportation case, since the man was an important labor leader with whom settlements and bargains were being carried on constantly." She called Homer Cummings, the Attorney General, asking him to find out from J. Edgar Hoover, director of the Federal Bureau of Investigation, what information the FBI had on Bridges. On January 15, 1938, a surprising answer came back: "The FBI has nothing in its files on Bridges."

Early in February, Bridges wrote Secretary Perkins that he was aware immigration authorities were considering holding a hearing to decide if he should be deported. "If such a hearing is going to be held," he wrote, "I believe I'm entitled to a bill of particulars." She answered that a hearing in his case was under study, and that if the department decided to go ahead with it, he would of course get a statement of the specific charges against him so that he could prepare a defense.

A few days later, Reilly appeared in a closed session of the Senate Commerce Committee to bring its members up to date on the Bridges case. The chairman, Royal S. Copeland, an old–line Democrat from New York, was delighted with Reilly's testimony, for it confirmed what he had said in a Senate speech almost a year earlier, in April, 1937. At that time, he had been discussing the 1936 maritime strikes which, he told his colleagues, were the work of Communists.

"There is in this country," he had added, "one Harry Bridges, an alien and an avowed Communist. He is the leader of a movement on the Pacific Coast that I believe is dangerous and subversive. . . ." On February 9, 1938, the day after Reilly's appearance before his committee, Copeland triumphantly held a press conference. "Reilly told our committee," he informed reporters, "that the Labor Department has enough evidence on Harry Bridges to make a *prima facie* case for his deportation."

Bridges decided not to wait until Perkins set a date for the hearing, for it would give Copeland and other Congressmen time to inflame the public against him. He wired Miss Perkins on February 11th—two days after Copeland's press conference—asking her to schedule the hearing immediately, before his Congressional critics convicted him in the newspapers. She agreed, and on March 5th, he and Lee Pressman, the CIO general counsel, went by prearrangement to the immigration office in Baltimore, where a warrant for Bridges's arrest and deportation was served on him. The four charges in the warrant were scarcely the bill of particulars he had asked for.

The four seemingly repetitive charges were: 1) that after he entered the country, he became a member of an organization that believes in, advises, advocates, and teaches the overthrow by force and violence of the government of the United States; 2) that after he entered the country he became affiliated with such an organization; 3) that after he entered the country he became a member of an organization that causes to be written and circulated printed matter advising the overthrow by force and violence of the government; and 4) that after he entered the country he became affiliated with such an organization. The hearing was set for April 25, 1938 in San Francisco.

Out on the West Coast, Raphael Bonham was aghast when he learned that the hearing was going to be held in San Francisco. "I have received a great many protets over this," he wrote his superiors in Washington, "and several of our witnesses have asked me if we can protect them from rough stuff during the hearing." Two weeks later, he wrote again, suggesting a change of venue from the Federal Building in San Francisco to Angel Island in San Francisco Bay, where the Immigration Service had its West Coast headquarters. Witnesses against Bridges could thus be housed in government buildings on the island, while everyone else connected with the hearing would go back and forth each day by government boat.

Bonham's objections also persuaded Secretary Perkins to renege on her promise to Bridges that she would furnish him with a bill of particulars. When more than a month had gone by after the warrant for his arrest was served on him at Baltimore and the bill of particulars still hadn't come from Washington, Bridges sent Miss Perkins a formal request for it. To prepare his defense, he reminded her, he needed to know for sure what was the organization named in the warrant, the date he was alleged to have become a member, the place where he was believed to have joined it, the written documents, if any, tending to prove his membership, the manner in which the government claimed he became affiliated with the organization—indeed, what acts or conduct constituted "affiliation"—and the printed matter advising the overthrow of the government which the organization published and distributed.

It did him no good. The Labor Department, worried by the second thoughts some of its witnesses were having about testifying, decided that its case would be endangered if it gave Bridges their names or if it answered questions about the dates and the other points of evidence he asked for. All the government would tell him was: "The organization is the Communist Party of the United States of America."

Both sides were frantically preparing for the trial, but the lack of a bill of particulars posed especial difficulties for the defense. Aubrey Grossman, one of the attorneys who represented Bridges, has explained how they prepared for cross-examination of the government witnesses when they didn't know whom they would be.

We decided we'd make up a list of all the people who *might* be used, and we'd prepare dossiers on them. We began by listing everyone who'd turned against Harry. So we went to him, and he gave us some names. Then we made up a list of people the government had something on. And here was where Harry's lousy judgment of people showed up. In one case after another, when we brought up a name he'd say, "Aw, c'mon, he'd never fink on me!" And then that guy would turn up as a witness against him!

Then we went to the Communist Party. "Give us a list of the people in the area you've kicked out in the last year," we asked them.

By the time we finished, we had a steamer trunk and two suit cases full of dossiers on possible witnesses. On top of that we had an extensive card file, with the names of all the possible witnesses cross-indexed. When the government put somebody on the stand, we'd look him up in our card file and prepare our cross-examination on the spot. Of course, we missed some. We couldn't anticipate them all.

And we kept some of their witnesses honest, too. We'd managed to get some stuff out of Harper Knowles's files, and they knew we had it.

With less than three weeks to go before the hearing, a federal court of appeals reversed a deportation order against an admitted former Communist, Joseph Strecker. Strecker, a self-employed merchant, had come to the United States from Poland in 1912. For some reason, he never took out naturalization papers. Then, in 1932, with the country wallowing, rudderless, in the trough of the Depression, and with both major parties seemingly incapable of getting the economy on course again, he joined the Communist Party as a gesture of support for William Z. Foster, who was running for President on the Communist ticket. As an alien he could not, of course, vote for him. Strecker paid dues for three and a half months. Then he forgot about the Party. In 1933, he decided to file for citizenship.

That was when his troubles began. He innocently told the immigration officer at the first interview about his brief encounter with the Party. The officer reported it to his superiors, and the deportation machinery started turning. In no time, the government had Strecker processed for deportation, but Poland, then in the hands of a rightist dictatorship, threw a monkey wrench into the immigration machinery by telling our government that it wouldn't allow him back in. Reprieved by Poland's rejection, Strecker made arrangements for an appeal to the courts.

In the appeal, immigration authorities used arguments that had won judicial confirmation in a long line of earlier cases where Communists had been deported and won this one in the federal district court in New Orleans. But when Strecker appealed the decision, the Fifth Circuit Court ruled in his favor: "It seems to me," Judge Hutcheson said for the court, "to be a kind of Pecksniffian righteousness, savoring strongly of hypocrisy and party bigotry, to assume and find that merely because Strecker joined the Communist Party of America, he is an advocate of, or belongs to, a party which advocates the overthrow by force and violence of the government of the United States."

The *Strecker* decision put the case against Bridges in a new light. If Communist Party membership wasn't a ground for deportation, there wouldn't be much point in going ahead with the April 25th hearing. For unless the *Strecker* decision was reversed, the charges against Bridges, even if proved as Miss Perkins has said, had no legal significance whatsoever. Gerard Reilly, therefore, wrote Attorney General Homer Cummings a long legal memo, calling his attention to more than a half–dozen decisions where other federal circuit courts had held that CP membership was sufficient ground for deportation. Reilly concluded by expressing the hope that the Justice Department would appeal the *Strecker* decision to the Supreme Court. Then, for two more weeks, Frances Perkins pondered what to do now about the Bridges case. Finally, on April 19th, she called the hearing off until the Supreme Court acted on the *Strecker* question.

To most people, the action Miss Perkins took was reasonable, in view of the uncertain state of the law on which the Bridges case was based. But the National Executive Committee of the American Legion demanded on May 6, 1938, that the Labor Department proceed with the deportation of Harry Bridges. Coincidentally, Bridges had another brush with the Legion at about the same time. He had been invited to speak in a high school auditorium near Los Angeles, setting off a controversy over whether an alien radical should be permitted to speak in a public building. In the end, he was allowed to speak.

Just as he was about to begin his talk, a color guard of American Legionnaires appeared. They marched up onto the stage and came smartly to a halt. Their officer, bemedalled and resplendent in his blue and gold uniform, stepped resolutely to the center of the platform, grabbed the mike away from Bridges and shouted, "We're going to open this meeting with the Pledge of Allegiance to the Flag! Repeat after me," he commanded.

"I pledge allegiance to the flag," he intoned. "I pledge allegiance to the flag," the crowd repeated. Then, overcome with emotion, he couldn't remember the rest. Bridges moved over, took the mike from his hand and continued with the crowd repeating after him: "and to the country for which it stands . . . one nation, indivisible . . . with liberty and justice for all." He turned to the Legionnaire and, placing his hand over his heart, said, "You know, when I say that pledge, it comes from here."

As the months went by and Secretary Perkins waited for the Supreme Court to rule on Strecker's deportation, the House Un–American Activities Committee, complaining that she was coddling Communists, introduced a motion to impeach her in the House of Representatives.

"I didn't like the idea of being impeached and was considerably disturbed by the episode," Frances Perkins says in her book about Roosevelt. FDR made light of it, no doubt because he knew the resolution would die, as it did, in the House Judiciary Committee, which was safely in the hands of New Dealers. "It's all nonsense," he told Miss Perkins at a Cabinet meeting early in 1939, where the President asked Miss Perkins to review the facts of the Bridges case.

"There was not a single one in the lot," Harold Ickes, the maverick Republican who was FDR's Secretary of the Interior, noted in his diary, "that would justify the arbitrary expulsion of Bridges from the country." Nevertheless, when Miss Perkins finished her summary, James A. Farley, Postmaster General and National Chairman of the Democratic Party, burst in, according to Ickes, with a defense of the deportation:

. . . whether Bridges was a Communist or not, the people of the country believed that he was and believed that he ought to be deported. He declared that failure to deport him was doing great harm to the Democratic Party. In effect, [Farley] said that whether he was deportable or not, Bridges ought to be sent out of the country for the sake of the Democratic Party. I was on the point of bursting out with "the primary function of a government is to protect the weak" when the President took the ball and made it clear that Bridges ought not to be deported unless there was legal justification for it.

Three weeks after the judiciary committee cleared Frances Perkins, the Supreme Court decided the *Strecker* case on April 17, 1939. The Court held that Strecker could stay in the country, reasoning that an alien who, after entering the country, becomes a member of the Communist Party ". . . is not deportable on that ground if at the time of his arrest his membership has ceased."

The Court did not rule directly on the question posed by the decision of the Fifth Circuit Court: Was or was not the Communist Party dedicated to the overthrow of the government? The implication of *Strecker* was clear enough, however. The Fifth Circuit Court was overruled. If Strecker had been a Party member on November 25, 1933, when the warrant was issued for his arrest, he would have been deportable. It followed that if the government could prove that Bridges was a Communist in March, 1938, when the warrant was issued for his arrest, he would be deportable.

This time, the Labor Department moved fast. Just four days after the *Strecker* decision came down, while Bridges was addressing a meeting of the Maritime Federation of the Pacific in Everett, Washington, Raphael Bonham presented him with a new warrant for his arrest. The hearing was set for July 10, 1939, at the immigration station on Angel Island.

Now came two awkward questions. The first was: Who should preside at the hearing?

"It was suggested," Frances Perkins has said,

that inasmuch as the ranking officers of the Department had already been smeared as being pro–Bridges, and the West Coast officials of the Service had been smeared as anti–Bridges, and that since the evidence in the case was highly conflicting and depended primarily upon the relative credibility of the witnesses already interviewed, it was highly desirable that a lawyer of distinction and ability, having no ties with any of the West Coast factions, and whose standing was such that his judgment would be beyond suspicion of possible influence by the Secretary, the

Administration, or *employee* groups, be appointed to sit as trial examiner.

Secretary Perkins found her man in James M. Landis, Dean of the Harvard Law School. A specialist in administrative law, he was fascinated by an opportunity to preside over a pioneering administrative hearing. As the co–author with Felix Frankfurter of a casebook in labor law, he was intrigued by the labor side of it. Conveniently, the hearing was to begin in mid–July and ought to be over in a month, six weeks at the most, before the fall term would begin at the law school.

"I had a summer free," he recalled in an oral history interview at Columbia. "I didn't know much about Harry Bridges. I hardly knew who he was. But I made two conditions for taking that job. One was that whatever happened, my report would be public. The second was that I would have complete control over the courtroom in which the hearings were held. Nobody else would have the right, except myself, to admit people or not admit them . . ."

Not quite forty, Landis already had behind him a distinguished record as a legal scholar and public servant. The son of a Presbyterian minister, he was born in Tokyo, where he had lived until he was thirteen. In 1925, after Princeton, Harvard Law School and a year as a law clerk for Supreme Court Justice Brandeis, he joined the law faculty at Harvard. In 1933, he went to Washington as a New Deal brain truster, after which he was appointed to the Federal Trade Commission. He went from there to the Securities and Exchange Commission, becoming its chairman in 1935. In 1937, he left the SEC to go back to Harvard as Dean of the Law School. Everyone, even the Hearst newspapers, whose owner had a passionate aversion to New Dealers, agreed that in Landis, Secretary Perkins had found just the man to preside at Angel Island.

Bridges thought so, too, though he may have had second thoughts one afternoon when he was coming back to San Francisco in the government boat. He was in the stern, showing a friend how to tie sailors' knots, feeling pretty good about the way the case was going. Landis and several other passengers were in the wheelhouse, chatting with the captain. When the captain left the wheel for a moment and stepped outside, Landis grabbed the helm, and, heading the boat toward the Golden Gate, called out, "Hang on to your hats, boys! We're off to Australia!"

The other question was: Should the hearing be open, as Bridges wanted, or closed, as the government insisted? Bridges's view was supported by California's liberal governor, Culbert Olson, and the *San Francisco Chronicle*, which suggested that it was important for the public to be able to see for itself the kind of case the government had against Bridges, especially who its witnesses were, and how they held up under cross-examination.

Landis struck a compromise. "As a matter of strict law," he said as he ruled that the general public would not be allowed into the hearing, "no right even to any kind of open hearing attaches to proceedings of this nature. Deportation has always been held by the courts again and again to be a civil proceeding to which the requirements of the Sixth Amendment . . . calling for an open trial, do not apply." He also pointed out that opening the hearing would break with precedent because every deportation hearing ever held had been closed. But he partially opened this one by issuing passes to eighteen reporters, including several magazine writers. Among them were Estolv Ward, who covered the hearing for the Bridges Defense Committee and wrote a book about it, *Harry Bridges on Trial*; Ella Winter, who sent her dispatches to the *Manchester Guardian*. Dean Landis also admitted representatives of the American Civil Liberties Union, the American Legion, the Associated Farmers, the International Labor Defense, the King–Ramsay–Conner Defense Committee, and a few others with a serious interest in the proceedings. His academic leanings were revealed on the first day, when he allowed three law school students from Yale to sit in "to further their education by observing an administrative hearing in action."

Although the people of San Francisco were barred from the hearing, they were kept abreast of the proceedings through the extensive coverage in the city's four major newspapers. What they learned about the hearing depended, of course, upon which paper they read. The Hearst *Examiner* treated events on Angel Island as if it were covering a war in which our fresh, victorious forces steadily advanced against a demoralized, poorly led enemy. To the *Examiner*, Bridges's lawyers were always weak, imcompetent, their arguments irrelevant. Carol King, his chief defense counsel, was depicted as screaming, smoking in defiance of No Smoking signs, wearing sensible shoes, dressing mannishly, and trying, the *Examiner* said, to be tough. According to the *Examiner*, the defense attorneys browbeat witnesses and were continually being caught off balance by the brilliant government counsel. Witnesses testifying for the government, by contrast with witnesses for the defense, were believable, experts on communism, patriots.

The locally-owned *Chronicle* was more straightforward, with no discernible editorializing in its news stories. Indeed, it reprinted verbatim testimony so extensively that it had to publish a special index to its coverage. The Scripps-Howard *News*, like the *Chronicle*, offered straight reporting. It summarized the testimony each day, with pictures of witnesses and highlights of their appearances on the stand. In contrast to Hearst's *Examiner*, the Call-Bulletin, his afternoon paper in San Francisco, also covered the hearing fairly. It offered much feature material on the hearing, with well-done summaries and a generous use of pictures.

The one aspect of the hearing all the papers agreed on was Dean Landis. They uniformly presented him as an Olympian figure, "one of the nation's most brilliant legal minds, a keen lawyer," whose conduct of the hearing was always above reproach.

"In an atmosphere of uncertainty and excitement," Ward says in his book about the hearing, "friends, strangers and bitter enemies gathered about the gangplank to the little ferry 'Angel Island' at Pier 5 early in the morning of July 10th." Ward himself was there, as was Dean Landis, and the two dozen or so observers and reporters. So was Bridges, accompanied by his fourteen-year-old daughter, Betty, who stayed at his side for the duration of the trial. Bridges's youthful San Francisco attorneys, Richard Gladstein and Aubrey Grossman, were on the dock, sweating and out of breath from lugging their steamer trunk, the suitcases filled with dossiers, and their card index down to the gangplank. With them was Carol King, the country's leading expert on deportation law. She had also participated in many of the nation's most celebrated civil liberties trials, including the defense of Sacco and Vanzetti, the Scottsboro Boys, Angelo Herndon, and Joseph Strecker. She had told a *Chronicle* reporter when she arrived in the city that she thought the Bridges case more important than that of Tom Mooney. She also saw the case as different from the other *causes célèbres* she had defended. "Here we have a direct attack on the labor movement," she said. "In the other cases interest was aroused afterward and the men involved became important because of their cases. They became symbols. But here is an attack on one of the most prominent labor leaders in the country." Asked to give her theory of the case, she replied: "I believe this is a fight to the finish between the forces of reaction and the liberal, forward-looking groups."

On the dock, too, were the four government lawyers: Bonham and Norene from the Northwest, A. J. Phelan of the San Francisco immigration office, and Thomas Shoemaker, sent from Washington to act as chief prosecutor. "Shoemaker was a nice guy," Aubrey Grossman said in 1967. "Remember, he was an attorney in the Immigration Service when it was in the Labor Department. He wasn't mean or out to get Harry, the way they were later."

As the ferry moved out into the Bay, Bridges leaned against the rail, Betty at his shoulder, Raphael Bonham just beyond her. "Bonham is a rat," Bridges observed to Betty. "He'd sell his mother down the river." "Bonham merely smiled," a newspaperman standing nearby noticed. "Then he said, 'Let the evidence tell the story.'"

The immigration station had partitioned off a small area of the dining hall, just off the kitchen, for the hearing. Almost all of the two hundred immigrants held on the island were Chinese, and for many in the hearing room the scents drifting in from the kitchen were tantalizing. But not for Landis. One afternoon, just after a recess, he firmly closed the door to the kitchen and, to make sure it wouldn't slip open, bolted it. "I don't like those chop suey odors very much," he explained. A moment later, there was a pounding on the door. It was Bridges, who had been in the kitchen drinking milk his doctor had prescribed for his ulcers.

Landis opened the hearing at 10:30, using a yellow pencil to tap for order. Shoemaker picked up his papers and was on the point of reading the warrant for Bridges's arrest, when Landis leaned forward. "May I interrupt you to inquire whether the alien is here?" "Yes," Bridges answered, from about eight feet away. Shoemaker read the warrant, in effect making an opening statement for the government. He then called Bridges to the witness stand:

"At this time, I wish to ask you but two questions. Are you an alien?"

"I am."

"Are you now a member of the Communist Party?"

"No."

"Or have you at any time in the past been a member of the Communist Party?"

"No."

Shoemaker turned to Dean Landis, "I have no further questions for the time being," he said, moving back to his place at the government's table.

Carol King made the opening statement for the defense. "Since 1934," she began, "Harry Bridges has been a stormy petrel around whom has raged such a storm as only the most violent labor struggles engender. He has become such a symbol of labor strength to certain employer groups that they have spent, and continue to spend, large sums of money to get rid of him. . . ."

She described the efforts of a private eye named Harper Knowles to persuade Frances Perkins to deport Bridges, and how, when Miss Perkins called upon Knowles to supply proof, he had none. Knowles's first effort having failed, she went on, the get–Bridges effort took a new tack. Knowles and his co–conspirators spread the word that they would pay generously for affidavits against Bridges, and in addition offered to fix the sentences of several men facing prison terms, if they would sign an affidavit placing Bridges in a Communist meeting.

"We shall show," she continued, "that this blackmail was carried out with the active assistance of high public officials. The most prominent participants of this type are Captain Keegan, of the Portland police, Lieutenant 'Red' Hynes, of the Los Angeles police, Clarence Morrill, director of the California State Bureau of Criminal Identification, and Captain Odale, of the Portland police force."

"This conspiracy needed and depended upon the cooperation of someone in the Immigration and Naturalization Service. We charge that R. P. Bonham . . . and his assistant, R. J. Norene, were also cogs in this complicated wheel. . . ."

Miss King was moving on to the aspect of the affair that had puzzled Frances Perkins, namely, why the case against Bridges came from Seattle instead of San Francisco. She was beginning to discuss the crucial role of Larry Doyle, who, she asserted, "has supported himself by this case for several years," when Landis broke in. "I do not like to interrupt you, Miss King, but the issues in this case. . . ." "I am coming to the issues," she answered before he could finish. She quickly concluded her opening statement, ending it with: ". . . the witnesses against Bridges are felons or labor spies, or both, and their evidence is not credible. . . ."

The government's first witness was Major Laurence Milner, one of the four whose affidavits were the basis for Bridges's arrest. At the outset, Milner was impressive. Ward describes him as "middle–aged, erect as a ramrod, hawk–nosed . . . he took the stand confidently. . . ." He had been a special agent of the military intelligence unit of the Oregon National Guard, he testified, from 1933 to

June, 1937, his assignment being to investigate subversive groups. He decided to pose as a Communist and get his information from the inside.

He said that in order to gain the Communists' confidence, he appeared as a character witness for Dirk De Jonge, a Party member who went on trial just as Milner was starting on his undercover career. De Jonge was on trial for organizing a protest meeting in Portland during the '34 waterfront strike after police fired on the strikers, killing and wounding some of them. He was sentenced to eight years in state prison for violating the Oregon criminal syndicalism act, but in 1937 the U.S. Supreme Court overturned his conviction, on a ground that had eluded the Oregon judiciary. In organizing and then speaking at the meeting, the Court ruled, De Jonge had simply been protesting the actions of the police.

After the De Jonge trial, Milner carried off his Communist masquerade so well that the American Legion took away his Legion button, and his former friend, "Big Bill" Browne of the Portland police Red squad, threatened to beat him up. Milner presided at radical meetings, and on occasion acted as an *agent provocateur* of mob violence. Having established his credentials as a super–militant radical, he was accepted as trustworthy by the Communists, who were only too glad to accept his offers to drive them to and from meetings in his seven–passenger car.

It was in this way, he testified, that he found out Bridges was a Communist. In April, 1935, he drove Bridges from Portland to Seattle, where Bridges was scheduled to speak. After the meeting, Milner and Bridges went to a restaurant with several others, who Milner was certain were all Communists. Harry Jackson, a Communist functionary in the Northwest, was in the group and, Milner said, asked Bridges for his Party dues. He testified that Bridges gave Jackson $2.50, saying he did not want a receipt. Milner offered two other items of evidence of Bridges's Communist affiliation. Once, he said, he and Bridges were looking at some U.S. battleships in Portland harbor and Bridges remarked, "We will see a day when we can sink those damn things because they are the enemy of the workers." At another time, he testified, Bridges described to him how waterfront goon squads beat up opponents of the Communist Party.

Aubrey Grossman began the cross–examination, spelled off by Richard Gladstein. Their curiosity was especially piqued by Milner's testimony in the *De Jonge* case. "Did you tell the complete truth in that case?" they asked. "Yes," Milner answered, "Yes, I did." Bridges's attorneys, unconvinced, felt sure that Milner, appearing as a character witness for De Jonge, would have told the court that De Jonge wasn't a Party member. Yet in this hearing, in answer to Shoemaker's questions on direct examination, Milner had said he had known De Jonge was a Communist four months before he testified for him in Portland. Grossman and Gladstein made a hurried call to Portland, asking that a transcript of the *De Jonge* trial be rushed down to San Francisco. Meanwhile, they hammered away at Milner, hoping to break him down. He refused to budge. "I told the truth in that case, and I'm telling the truth here," he insisted, over and over. At last, they gave up for the time being and moved on to cross–examine him on other aspects of his testimony.

When the attorneys got back to their office late that afternoon, there on a desk was the transcript of the *De Jonge* trial. Breathlessly, they leafed through it. They were right! Milner had testified he knew De Jonge well, and that he knew he was not a Communist. The next morning when they confronted Milner with the transcript, he admitted that he had lied, both in the *De Jonge* trial, and yesterday. "I considered it my duty as a military intelligence officer," he explained, "to do anything to gain my purpose without being disclosed."

It was in the *De Jonge* trial that Milner first met Larry Doyle, who had been hired by the state of Oregon as a special prosecutor for the case. Doyle sought him out, he testified, and tried to bribe him to change his testimony about De Jonge, but he didn't take to Doyle, so he refused. The next time he met Doyle was in 1937, when Doyle was helping Portland police plant the dictaphone in Bridges's room. Doyle invited him to collaborate in the project, but he declined. "I didn't like the set-up," he told the hearing. "He drank too much, and you can't trust anybody that drinks . . ."

"Too much," Landis interjected drily, before Milner could finish.

Landis was disgusted with Milner. Thursday morning, as the hearing opened, he told the attorneys for both sides that he was turning Milner's testimony over to the Solicitor of the Labor Department for possible perjury prosecution. Landis was especially put off by Milner's deliberate lying under oath, first in the *De Jonge* trial, again in this hearing. Moreover, much of what Milner testified to when Shoemaker was questioning him turned out under cross–examination to be inaccurate. And his most incriminating testimony—Bridges's conversations with him and his payment of $2.50 dues to Jackson in Seattle—was unsupported. Most exasperating was Milner's boast that in his four–year tour of duty as an under-cover agent, he had written seventy–seven detailed reports on Bridges's actions. He had them with him and referred to them repeatedly while he testified. But somehow, none of his reports mentioned either the dues payment to Jackson or the conversations with Bridges he talked about when he was in the witness chair.

"Milner's testimony in this proceeding is deserving of little if any, credence," Landis concluded in his report. "[He] can best be dismissed as a self-confessed liar, a man who has admittedly tried twice—once successfully—to make falsehood parade as truth."

On the second day of the hearing, the "Smolny," a Russian freighter, arrived at San Francisco and berthed at Pier 5, alongside the dock where the "Angel Island" picked up and discharged its passengers. The next morning, a *San Francisco News* reporter was standing next to Bridges as they waited for the ferry to take them aboard. "Bridges gazed at the Soviet flag and the ship," he reported, "and then he said to a companion: 'I'd like to go below deck and see the working conditions the Soviet maritime workers endure. I bet they're not so good as they're pictured.' "

John Leech, another of the four who had signed affidavits for Bonham, was the government's next witness. In appearance, he was very unlike Milner, whose military bearing and appearance had been so impressive when the major first marched to the stand. Leech's garments, by contrast, so fascinated reporters at the hearing that they described them in detail: "He wore a light tan checkered suit brightened by an orange handkerchief in the breast pocket, and a mottled orange tie. A small pink rosebud was in his lapel and his socks were gray with a pink design. His shoes were tan."

In more important ways, Leech was very much like Milner. He had something to hide, which came out in cross–examination; he contradicted himself as he testified; and he had perjured himself in the period just preceding the hearing by signing, under oath, two affidavits about Bridges that were diametrically at variance with each other. And his meanderings, like Milner's, put Dean Landis off:

"Leech was afflicted with verbal haemophilia," Landis said of him. "It seemed impossible for him ever to answer straightforward questions simply. Much of this was equivocation following upon Leech's being caught in earlier misstatements; much of it flowed from a curious pretence to knowledge about totally irrelevant matters; much of it, however, sprang merely from a habit of using ten words where one would have sufficed."

Leech's story was as bizarre as his appearance was unusual. He testified that he had joined the Communist Party in 1931, was on the Party payroll as an organizer in Southern California from 1934 to 1936, and had been expelled in the middle of April, 1937, for offensively bureaucratic behavior. "I have never seen documentary proof such as membership cards or other written data stating that Harry Bridges is a member of the Party," he said in the affidavit he gave the government which was read to the hearing before he testified, "but it was my common knowledge that he was, and that his Party name was Rossi."

Leech told a byzantine story about how the Portland police had tried to bribe him to testify against Bridges and how he had refused. Then, a man from the Oregon Chamber of Commerce, he said, came down to Los Angeles, where he lived, and offered a larger bribe. When he turned that down, Larry Doyle made arrangements to move him and his family to Portland, promising that the government would protect him and his family if he would be a witness against Bridges. That was what persuaded him to come forward, he said.

Cross-examination brought out another reason. He was in trouble with the law in California because he had been getting relief checks based on statements that he had no other income, at the same time that he was working for a roofing company.

The first two witnesses whose affidavits had led to Bridges's arrest were obviously of no help to the prosecution. The next two were even worse. Mills, despite his impatience in 1937 to get the Bridges hearing under way, could not be located in 1939. Doyle was in Minnesota at the time of the hearing and refused to come out to San Francisco. When he finally did appear, at the end of the hearing, he came only because he could no longer evade a court order issued at the request of Bridges's attorneys, who wanted to get him on the stand to cross-examine him after he testified for the government. He tied up the hearing for a day and a half wrangling about how much he should be compensated, and demanding that the hearing be thrown open to the public. When he finally subsided, the presiding officer turned to Shoemaker and asked if the government wished to call him as a witness. "No," replied Shoemaker.

"Doyle," Landis said with restraint, "proved to be a problem in contumacy."

Bridges's alleged Party membership card came up as the hearing started into its second week. "I also offer at this time a certified copy of membership book No. 54793, alleged to have been issued to Harry Dorgan by the Communist Party of the U.S.A. on January 1, 1937," Shoemaker said, handing it up to Dean Landis.

"We expect to make no use of that alleged membership book at this time because, frankly enough, we have not been able to establish its authenticity, and in fairness to the person charged we do not believe that it should be used in any way."

"You offer it merely for identification?" Gladstein asked.

"For identification only," Shoemaker responded.

Landis accepted it on that basis as government exhibit 25, and then, looking closely at it, said to Shoemaker, "If I may just ask a question or so in connection with this. There is a name, Harry Dorgan, on this . . . and also the name, W. Schneiderman. [Schneiderman had succeeded Darcy in 1936 as secretary of the Party in northern California.] Beyond that the exhibit is print. I assume that you have not been able to establish the authenticity of any of those signatures?"

"I haven't tried, your Honor," Shoemaker said, "so far as the signature of Mr. Schneiderman is concerned. You will notice that the name of Harry Dorgan is printed on there."

"Yes," Landis said. "I just wanted that explanation to be in the record. I think the press and the public ought to recognize that an exhibit marked for identification only is, from the standpoint of the record, not upon the record; in other words, that anything that is contained in it is not in evidence in the case. Now, what one may choose to do with material of that nature, from the standpoint of fiction, is not my concern."

"I presume your Honor wishes to add to that statement also," Shoemaker suggested helpfully, "that it will not be used in any wise in connection with any decision that is finally reached in this case."

"Well," Landis said quietly, "that would be obvious."

John Leppold, the government's next witness, was an ex–marine cook who had been expelled from his union in 1938 on charges of anti–union activity he was certain were trumped up by Communists. His testimony before Dean Landis suggested another reason for his expulsion. At the end of his union trial, Leppold testified, the trial committee had divided evenly, and the matter of his expulsion had gone to the membership for their decision. Before the membership meeting was held, Alfred Van Leakan, a fellow seaman, asked him if he would go along as a witness when he applied for naturalization. Leppold said he would. When the two got to the immigration office, one of the investigators took Leppold into a side room by himself and asked him if he would recommend Van Leakan for citizenship. "I told him no, I wouldn't. Not in this country, I wouldn't. The man has stated openly that he belongs to the Communist Party." Leppold then rejoined Van Leakan, and the two went before the chief immigration examiner, who told Van Leakan he was ineligible for citizenship, giving as the reason Leppold's statement to the investigator. Leppold saw nothing inconsistent in his behavior, but the union membership, after hearing Van Leakan's story on top of the trial committee report, voted to expel him.

Leppold said he knew that Henry Schmidt, one of Bridges's union associates, was a Communist because he happened to be in the San Francisco office of the Maritime Federation one day while Schmidt was counting the per capita payments sent in by the union in the district. "I heard Schmidt say," Leppold told the hearing, " 'The Moscow gold is pouring in.' " His basis for believing Bridges was a Communist was on the same probative plane. In the late thirties, the local branch of the Maritime Federation was discussing a motion to picket the German and Italian consulates and local Communist Party headquarters. Leppold seconded the proposal. "Bridges strongly opposed it," he testified, "calling it red–baiting."

By the time Leppold finished testifying, the government's case was floundering badly. To revive it, they called Aaron Sapiro, a Los Angeles lawyer. As he took the stand, Sapiro was, as Major Milner had been on his first day, an impressive witness. He was tall, dark-haired, with bright eyes, and, the newspapers said, a noted lawyer. It was clear that the government had high hopes for his testimony.

Early in his career, Sapiro had won a spectacular legal victory over Henry Ford, who had been waging a virulent campaign of anti–Semitism, using as his weapon his newspaper, the *Dearborn Independent.* For seven years, letters of protest from outstanding Jews were either rudely acknowledged or unanswered. Ford even ignored a public protest signed by such distinguished Americans as President Wilson, ex–President Taft, Jane Addams, Archbishop Carleton J. H. Hayes, and William Jennings Bryan. Then the *Dear-*

born Independent made a tactical error. It accused Aaron Sapiro, describing him as a Jewish lawyer and promoter, of fleecing his clients, members of farm marketing associations he was organizing across the country. Sapiro countered with a libel suit against Ford, asking a million dollars in damages.

Ford, represented by a battery of seven lawyers headed by a prestigious U.S. Senator, James Reed of Missouri, narrowly escaped what promised to be an adverse verdict when the judge declared a mistrial. The case was set for retrial, but before it came up Ford settled out of court and gave Sapiro a public apology. Ford, never a man to do anything by half, went on to apologize to the Jewish people as a whole, assuring them that never again would he allow anti–Semitic material to come from his printing presses.

In the early 1930s, a promising field for a man with Sapiro's combination of legal and organizing talents was small business. He moved on to New York and then to Chicago, where he organized both sides of the bargaining table: trade associations of merchants, laundry owners, cleaners and dyers, tailors, milk distributors, movie theater operators; labor unions of the workers his association members employed. Sapiro's clients happened to be in precisely the fields where gangsterism and labor racketeering were most often found in the post–Prohibition era, and in 1933 he was indicted in Chicago, along with officials of his trade associations and unions, for bombings, acid throwings and the like, to force holdouts into his organizations. He and his co–defendants were acquitted, but a year later he and one of his clients were charged with attempting to influence a jury. His client went to jail, but Sapiro was lucky. His only punishment was disbarment from practicing in the federal courts.

He thereupon went out to the West Coast, where he quickly lined up as clients half a dozen newly emerging maritime unions, among them the longshoremen's local in San Pedro. In 1936, he represented Harry Lundeberg, the West Coast sailors' union leader, when Lundeberg was having trouble with the national seamen's union. In time Sapiro became general counsel for Lundeberg's West Coast sailors. He got on well with Lundeberg, but not with Bridges, who distrusted Sapiro from the first because of his indiscriminate name dropping. And it quickly became obvious that Sapiro, claiming to be sturdily anti–Communist and at the same time a confidante of Party leaders, was working hard to poison Lundeberg's relations with Bridges.

Ironically, Sapiro acted as Bridges's attorney in December, 1936, when Bridges was involved in a traffic accident in Los Angeles. He was driving along with another longshoreman when a bicycle ridden by an eight–year–old boy named Joseph Miranda came hurtling out of nowhere and ran head–on into Bridges's car. The boy died almost instantly. The police held Bridges while they investigated and officials of the San Pedro longshore local called their attorney, Sapiro, to help out. The coroner's jury exonerated Bridges, finding the boy's death accidental and unavoidable. Sapiro claimed the credit for the jury's ruling, but Bridges felt that Sapiro's legal aid had been useless. Because he hadn't authorized Sapiro to act for him, he refused to pay the $1,000 fee Sapiro sent him for his services. "I was in jail and had nothing to say about who was going to get me out," he told Landis.

As Sapiro became more and more closely identified with Lundeberg, his relations with his other union clients deteriorated. By mid –1937, the only ones left were the West Coast sailors and a few rump groups of longshoremen that stayed with the AFL when the rest went into the CIO. On their behalf, he filed suits in Tacoma, San Francisco and San Pedro, vainly asking the courts to rule that the tiny AFL minorities owned the contracts and the hiring halls. In 1938, Sapiro lost his last maritime union client when Lundeberg dropped him as general counsel and in the process revoked his honorary membership in the sailors' union.

Sapiro came to Bonham's attention as a possible witness in September, 1937, when he wrote a long, bitter open letter to CIO president John L. Lewis in which he attacked Lewis for splitting the ranks of labor but particularly for letting Communists get into positions of influence in the CIO. Bridges was one of the officers Sapiro named in his letter and he threatened to prove his charges by legal action if Lewis didn't get rid of the Communists. A few weeks later, Bonham went down to Los Angeles to see Sapiro, to find out if he could be of use in the Bridges case.

Shortly thereafter, Sapiro had two more visitors from the Northwest, Captain John Keegan and Paul Mumpower, a Portland red squad detective, who told him they knew his talk with Bonham had been productive. Keegan called Sapiro from Portland a week later to tell him that Gerard Reilly was coming out from Washington and would be in Portland in a few days. The immigration people in Seattle and Portland, he told Sapiro, would like him to be there when they talked over the Bridges case with Reilly. Sapiro went up to Portland, where he met with Bonham, Norene, Reilly and several members of the Portland Police Department.

Once on the stand, Sapiro's behavior was, like Milner's, disappointing. He pictured himself as a dedicated anti–Communist, yet he claimed to be an intimate of Earl Browder, then head of the Communist Party, Roy Hudson, the Party's maritime specialist, and William Schneiderman, who had succeeded Darcy as the chief Communist official on the coast. Sapiro said he ran into Browder in a restaurant in 1936 and complained to him of Bridges's tactics in the maritime industry, which he said were undermining his efforts to build unity between the sailors and longshoremen. Browder replied, according to Sapiro, that Bridges was one of the hardest men to handle in the Party, but that he would order him to work with Sapiro. Hudson and Schneiderman, Sapiro added, confirmed what Browder had said.

Sapiro testified at length about clandestine meetings he said he had had with Bridges, and how Bridges followed the Party line in the differences that developed between the longshoremen and the sailors in the 1936 strike. Finally, he testified, Bridges once told him he must line up with him and not Lundeberg, or else Bridges would use his power in the Party to take all of Sapiro's union clients away from him.

On its face, Sapiro's testimony was damaging. One of the weaknesses in it was, however, that Sapiro's alleged conversations with Browder, Hudson, and Schneiderman were uncorroborated. Whether one believed that these men had made such statements to him about Bridges depended upon whether or not Sapiro was a believable witness. Browder and the others could, of course, have been subpoenaed, asked if they had made the remarks, and subjected to cross–examination. But the government declined to call them, contending that if Bridges contested the truth of Sapiro's testimony, it was his responsibility to call them.

Landis disagreed, pointing out that hearsay testimony about such conversations would not even have been admitted if the hearing were conducted strictly according to the rules of courtroom procedure instead of the looser rules of administrative hearings. It would be unfair to the defense, therefore, to require it to call witnesses to rebut normally inadmissible testimony. Landis consequently ignored Sapiro's stories about what Browder and the other Communists had supposedly told him about Bridges.

In the end, Landis decided that none of Sapiro's testimony was credible. "I'll never forget the third [sic] witness," he said in his oral history. "His name was Sapiro. He took the stand. I looked at him. I said to myself, 'You don't know me, but I know you.

" 'I met you about twenty years ago in Felix Frankfurter's office, in Cambridge. I was introduced to you as being one of the leading lawyers who would handle the cooperative movement in Michigan.' Of course, I didn't say this but I was thinking this. 'Finally, I thought, I'll get something I can rely on.'

"His direct stuff wasn't good. Then they opened up on him in cross. The cross examination went substantially like this:

'Mr. Sapiro, were you a member of the New York bar?'

'Yes.'

'Are you now a member of the New York bar?'

'No.'

'Were you disbarred?'

'Yes.'

'Disbarred for trying to influence a jury?'

'Yes.'

"Then they went on:

'Did you become a member of the Bar of the Supreme Court of Illinois?'

'Yes.'

'And were you at one time indicted?'

'Yes.'

'And was the indictment for racketeering under the antitrust act?'

'Yes.'

"It went on. 'Were these some of your co–defendants?' and they went down the line, Al Capone, etc.

"Then he went on to practice in Los Angeles and got involved in the same thing. The guy had just gone to pieces in twenty years."

Sapiro was followed by Joseph Marcus, who, in the middle thirties, had been the manager of Pierre's Chateau, a restaurant and bar near Golden Gate Park, not far from the Presidio. Marcus testified that when Bridges came to Pierre's, he usually sat with Arthur Margolis, the son of the owner, and Arthur's wife, Norma Perry, who was Bridges's secretary. Marcus said he often saw persons he believed to be Communists go upstairs to meetings, but he never saw Bridges anywhere except downstairs in the cocktail lounge. Gladstein and Grossman did not cross–examine Marcus when he finished, but Landis's curiosity was aroused.

"How did you know the meetings that went on upstairs were Communist meetings?" he asked. "Well," Marcus replied, "Mr. Margolis was worried, for one thing, because 40 per cent of the

Army officers at the Presidio patronized the Chateau, and he was afraid we'd lose their trade if they found out about the meetings. 'We're sitting on a keg of dynamite,' he said to me. 'My son Arthur hopes to be a great statesman some day; he hopes to be head of the Communist Party. That is why he holds those meetings upstairs.' "

Margolis had good cause to be worred about his son, but for another reason. In December, 1937, young Margolis was arrested by the Beverly Hills police and charged with thirteen counts of burglary. When the police discovered what an unusual second story man they'd bagged in Margolis, perhaps because he called Sapiro to come down to the station house and spring him, they called Captain Hynes of the San Pedro red squad. Hynes hurried over, went into the cell with Margolis, who was now calling himself Arthur Scott, and came out with a signed statement that the prisoner knew Bridges to be a Communist. Hynes gave several copies to Sapiro, who sent one to Captain Keegan in Portland, another to Harry Lundeberg in San Francisco.

Margolis, who was listed on the police blotter as Scott, was released pending trial and disappeared. The Beverly Hills police sent out a bulletin on him, and Captain Hynes wrote Keegan to be on the lookout for him in Portland. Keegan didn't trust Hynes, so he wrote the Chief of Police of Los Angeles, a personal friend:

> I am in receipt of a letter from the Beverly Hills Department of Police . . . that they hold a felony warrant for one ARTHUR J. SCOTT. . . .
>
> . . . this letter looks phony to me for this reason: Scott has been before our Immigration authorities here and made an affidavit regarding the deportation of Harry Bridges, and this letter looks to me as if somebody is trying to locate Scott through this department for the reason that he has been playing ball with us.
>
> I would like to know if you will make a confidential investigation to see whether or not these are the true facts regarding Scott as to his burglary activities, as you are well aware of what we are trying to do in regard to Harry Bridges. . . .

When Margolis (Scott) was found and put on trial, the judge dismissed eleven of the charges, allowing him to plead guilty to two. He was found guilty, and the judge ruled that the two sentences would run concurrently. "No deal was made," Keegan said when he testified later, "but the judge appreciated his valuable services to the government." Soon after Margolis began serving out his term, he applied for a commutation of his sentence. "I didn't know Scott," Keegan told Dean Landis, "I hadn't met him or even seen him." Nevertheless, when Sapiro asked Keegan to support Scott's application he was glad to help out. He sent six affidavits to the court in Los Angeles: four from detectives on the Portland red squad, one from Oregon's Governor, Charles H. Martin, and his own.

"I know the petitioner, Arthur James Kent [Margolis had given up the name Scott for "Kent"]," Keegan said in his affidavit,

> and that he has been of valuable assistance to the Immigration authorities of the United States Government, with which the Police Department of the City of Portland has cooperated. . . . I am convinced, from my personal observation of Kent and my knowledge of the work he has done, that without him the Immigration authorities would have been at a great loss to interpret the activities of the Communist Party and the members thereof, and particularly the acts of persons sought to be deported by reason of their connection with the Communist Party.
>
> Kent is a scholarly man and is thoroughly acquainted with all of the entire workings of the Communist Party.

California law enforcement authorities commuted Margolis's sentence to time served and let him out of jail.

By the time the hearing was in the middle of its second week, newspapermen covering it began wondering when Larry Doyle was going to take the stand. They discovered that the government had lost interest in having him testify, but that he had been subpoenaed, at the request of Bridges's attorneys, to appear later on. Doyle was finally found by a reporter in Lamberton, Minnesota, where he now had a law office. He told the reporter that despite the peculiarity of being called by the defense, "I am willing to appear, and I will show that Bridges was a Communist and guilty of moral turpitude."

After Marcus, the government called William Howard, who had briefly been an officer of the West Coast marine firemen's union and vice-president of a local branch of the Maritime Federation. He stopped shipping out in 1937 and went on WPA. Six months later, Congress cut back the WPA budget, and he was lopped off the roles. When the immigration people contacted him, he was on local relief. Howard testified that in 1936 he was talking with Bridges out on the sidewalk after one of the meetings of the maritime convention when Bridges warned him that certain delegates would be waving the red flag at him, telling him what a Commie Bridges was.

"I says," Howard testified. " 'That is neither here nor there with me, Harry. I don't care what they say.' "

"He says, 'Maybe I am a Commie. If I am, I might be damn proud of it.'

"I says, 'I don't care, Harry. It doesn't make any difference to me what you are.' "

Shoemaker asked Howard whether anything had occurred at the following convention of the Maritime Federation that would have led him to believe Bridges was a Communist. "Yes," Howard replied, "there was one thing in particular. Bridges's introduction of a resolution that all the unions in the Federation should join the CIO. We [the marine firemen] had made a study of the CIO," Howard continued, "and we come to the conclusion that the CIO was a Communist–controlled organization . . . We considered it [Bridges's resolution] as a deliberate attempt of the Communist Party to dissolve the unity that we held in the maritime federation."

That afternoon, as they were going back on the "Angel Island," a reporter from the *Chronicle* asked Bridges what he thought of Howard and his testimony. "He's the first honest witness they've put on," Bridges answered. "He's not a stool pigeon."

Eugene Detrich, the government's eighth witness, was one of the most interesting and one of the most colorful. As he entered the hearing room, he checked his revolver with the marshal at the door. He was living dangerously, he believed, for when San Francisco's 4,500 longshoremen went over to the CIO, he had stayed behind with thirty–seven others, holding the fort for the more conservative AFL. Indeed, at the time Detrich was testifying, he was on the AFL payroll as an organizer, with San Francisco as his territory. He was also a plaintiff in a suit pending before a San Francisco court, in which he was asking the judge to take the hiring hall away from the CIO longshoremen and turn it over to thirty–eight AFL loyalists. Detrich said that he had not known he was to testify at Bridges's deportation hearing until the government subpoenaed him on July 10th, when the hearing was already underway. A couple of days later, he gave an affidavit about Bridges to the attorneys for the government. "Was there a police officer present?" he was asked. Detrich was outraged. "No!" he shot back. "What do you think I am, a stool pigeon?"

Detrich's association with Bridges went back all the way to the Twenties, when they worked in the same gang at the steel dock. In the 1934 strike, when the union was born, he had been a member of the defense committee of the San Francisco local. That was when his differences with Bridges began. Their first disagreement was over the choice of a lawyer to defend longshoremen picked up by the police. Detrich had hired Leo Collins, who insisted on avoiding publicity and on conducting the defense according to the strictest canons of legal decorum. Bridges disagreed. He was convinced that in order for the strikers to arouse public sympathy, they would have to publicize in every way they could the wholesale arrests on vagrancy charges, the police brutality, the biased behavior of the municipal judges.

In his testimony, Detrich asserted that Bridges maneuvered the discharge of Collins, replacing him with George Anderson and the International Labor Defense. "I am familiar with what goes on in that Hall of Justice," Detrich said, "and I seen the defendants George Anderson usually defends. They are all the Communist element." Later, during the 1936 strike, Bridges worsened their relationship by publicly criticizing Detrich, at the time a longshoremen's business agent, for not contributing part of his $75 a week salary to the strike fund, as Bridges and the other officers were doing.

As Detrich testified, it became apparent that he thought Bridges was a Communist primarily because he supported what Detrich saw as Communist causes: the Scottsboro Boys, anti–war resolutions, Labor's Non–Partisan League, Tom Mooney, attacks on the AFL, refusals to load scrap iron for Japan, the *Western Worker*. In 1935, he recalled, the *Western Worker* asked the longshoremen to make a donation to the paper in the form of a full–page ad. "Bridges got up before the membership," Detrich said, "and stated that we have got the Communists to thank for a lot of our conditions, and virtually running the strike in 1934, and it wouldn't hurt us to go ahead and contribute a bit to them." The members, he recalled, voted not to take the ad.

Detrich's most dramatic moment on the stand came when he recounted a conversation he said he'd had with Bridges's wife, Agnes, in 1935 or 1936. Bridges was out of town, and Detrich, who was trying to locate him, called Agnes.

"She had a peeve on," Detrich said. "She says, 'I am going to show him up for what he is.'

"I said, 'What is that?'

"She says, 'Well,' she says, 'I have got his book.'

"And I said, 'What do you mean, his book?'

"She said, 'I have got his book in the Communist Party. Everybody on the waterfront don't believe he is a Communist.'

"I said, 'Aw, get off your foot, Aggie.' I was calling her about meeting with Mr. Bridges, so I could talk to her that way.

"She says, 'Well,' she had it, and she was going to flash it, give it to the world; she was going to call up one of the newspapers, I think at that time and give it to them, she says.

"I says, 'You haven't got his book.'

"She says, 'Yes, I have.' "

"Did you have any interest in it at all?" Shoemaker asked.

"None whatsoever," Detrich replied. "I naturally thought it was just a little war between he and his wife. They get these peeves on, you know. . . ."

"Was she telling you the truth or was she just talking?"

"At that time I never gave it a thought," Detrich answered. "I thought she was just talking."

"Have you given it any thought since?" Shoemaker persisted.

"Yes; quite a bit. . . . I believe now that she did have it."

"I am just anxious to know the date," Landis broke in. "You say that was sometime in '35; and as I remember your testimony, you said you did not believe her statement?"

"I didn't. I never even give it a thought. . . . She was just a little mad at Harry, because other times I have called her up, too, and Harry had been out of town a day or two, and I get a snappy answer; she bawls him out."

"Do you plan to call Mrs. Bridges to testify?" reporters excitedly asked attorneys for both sides during the recess. "No," Bridges's lawyers replied.

Shoemaker seemed unprepared for the tack Detrich's testimony had taken. "I had no intention of bringing family affairs into this case," he said. "She can testify if she wants to, but neither the government nor the defense can force her to testify if she declines."

After Detrich, almost anyone the government put on the stand would have been an anti–climax. The next two witnesses didn't have much to add anyway. Theodore Stark, an unemployed worker from Bellingham, Washington, was a weak witness, but he enlivened the hearing with a couple of interesting stories. One was that while he was in the Communist Party, to which he belonged from 1934 to 1937, he attended a meeting in Seattle at which a soldier from nearby Fort Lawton, dressed in his Army uniform but wearing a mask, appeared before the group to tell them about CP activities among the soldiers at the post. Shoemaker, thinking that he was on the scent of some significant Marxist intrigue, then questioned Stark at length about Communist infiltration into the armed forces. But all Stark could add was that two Party members were working as machinists in the big navy repair yard at Bremerton, across Puget Sound from Seattle.

Stark then told the hearing that in about 1936, he was in a meeting of a small group of Communists which was told by Morris Rapport, district organizer for the Northwest, "The way Comrade Bridges gets our literature on foreign boats is by dropping it down funnels, and putting it under the temporary floors longshoremen build in the holds when they're stowing cargo. When longshoremen in foreign ports unload the ships, they run onto our literature."

What was the nature of the literature, Bridges's attorneys asked Stark. "I was told by Rap, or Rapport, rather," he answered, "that it called upon the Chinese and Japanese to work against their miserable working conditions that they were being forced to work under in the Orient and to strive for better working conditions in general."

Did the literature urge them to organize unions, Stark was asked. "Yes, it did." "Did it ask them to join the Communist Party?" came the next question. "I couldn't say to that," he answered. "That wasn't discussed."

Merriel Bacon, the eleventh witness, had been a detective on the Portland red squad for almost ten years. He joined the force in 1930, he said, and four days later the chief of police ordered him to join the Communist Party and other radical organizations in order to look for violations of the Oregon criminal syndicalism law. At first, he did very well. The Party made him responsible for keeping its Portland membership abreast of new Marxist publications, appointed him secretary of the local branch of the International Labor Defense, and sent him as a delegate to a Party convention in San Francisco. He was in the Party about a year when he was exposed as a spy and expelled. He stayed on as a member of the red squad, was in on the arrest of Dirk De Jonge in 1934 and, as an expert on Communism, was the state's chief witness in De Jonge's trial.

"Where does the Communist Party get its money?" Shoemaker asked.

"They obtained their finances from dues collected from the membership, from the collection taken up at various meetings of the Party and subsidiary organizations, and they have advocated while I was in the Party," Bacon replied, "the seizure of property and funds by—for instance, one time we were instructed as to how the Communist Party in Russia had taken the money from the Czar's banks and used it to carry on the revolution. We were instructed that that is what we must learn how to do here, to carry on the revolution. They cited one instance in which they stated a holdup had taken place and they obtained $40,000 to carry on the Party work."

Shoemaker wasn't interested in following up this story, but Landis couldn't resist asking Bacon when Shoemaker was finished, "Where did the holdup take place?" "They said they held up a bank messenger and obtained $40,000," Bacon answered. "Where?" Landis repeated. "In San Francisco."

For a man with Bacon's tenure as a member of Portland's political police, he knew remarkably little about Bridges. And what information he was able to give the hearing was secondhand, based on a conversation he had had with a secret agent named Mickey, who worked for the state of Oregon. Mickey had so successfully infiltrated the Communist Party in Portland that he was its secretary from 1933 to 1935. Bacon testified that Mickey confided to him that not long after the '34 strike that he and a small group of local Communists had called on Harry Bridges at the hotel where he was staying in Portland. "At that meeting," Bacon testified, "he [Mickey] was told that Mr. Bridges, who is in this action, was doing a lot of good work for the Party. . . ."

On cross–examination, Bacon remembered that what Mickey had told him, more precisely, was that Bridges was described, not as having done good work for the Party, but as having done good work for "the cause." The people in the meeting, it turned out, had all been connected with the waterfront in one way or another (Mickey, himself, had run a strikers' soup kitchen in '34), and their short conversation with Bridges was about the maritime unions in Portland. Bacon said that when Mickey had told him about the meeting, he had not thought it important enough to include in his written reports.

Bacon was as casual in identifying organizations as Communist fronts as he was in identifying Bridges as a Red. During cross-examination, Grossman noted that in 1934, Bacon and Captain Odale had co–authored a pamphlet called, "Does America Want Communism?" One passage in it especially interested Grossman. "The American Civil Liberties Union claimed to stand for free speech, free press and free assemblage," Grossman paraphrased, "but in reality its main function was to protect Communists in the advocacy of force and violence to overthrow the government of the United States. Is that substantially what you said?" he asked Bacon.

"That is substantially my conclusion."

Several times during the hearing the newspapers commented on the calm, cool, aloof impersonality of both Bridges and Dean Landis in the face of the bitterness and emotionalism which was prevalent on Angel Island. The strain was taking its toll internally, however, on Bridges, who, on the day Bacon testified, had to be excused to be treated for an ulcer. And the government's next witness, a former marine fireman named James W. Engstrom, proved too much for the nerves even of the imperturbable Landis.

Engstrom had made a voyage in 1930 from Portland to New York on a ship with Roy Hudson, who was, at the time, an organizer for the Marine Workers' Industrial Union. He became friendly with Hudson, who tried to persuade him to join the union. Engstrom, who had been going to sea since 1926 and had not yet joined any union, held back because he thought seamen ought to be in the AFL. When they reached the East Coast, he and Hudson stayed in the same rooming house in Philadelphia for several weeks and Hudson took him along to several Communist meetings, vainly urging him to join the Party. Their friendship ended, Engstrom recalled, when they went together to a dance in Baltimore, where a high Communist Party official ordered a white girl to dance with a black. "I didn't approve of the races being instructed to mingle," Engstrom explained.

"Just what is the relevance of this testimony?" Landis demanded sharply of Shoemaker, who was questioning Engstrom.

"Just to show the practices of the Communist Party, your Honor," Shoemaker responded. "To show that to accomplish their aims and purposes they resort to any means."

Engstrom said he was approached in 1936 by a sailor named Walter Stack, who told him that if he would join the Party, he would get left–wing support for the presidency of the Seattle AFL Labor Council and Bridges's support for the presidency of the Maritime Federation. Stack assured him, Engstrom testified, that the Party wasn't going to make a major issue of racial equality and that he wouldn't have to support the Party line. Engstrom joined, but only on condition that his membership be kept secret.

He first met Bridges shortly after the '34 strike. The Seattle branch of the marine firemen's union, at Engstrom's instigation, and the sailors, led by Lundeberg, were removing Filipinos from the crews of ships owned by the Calmar and Shepard Lines as they tied up in Seattle. Bridges, who in Engstrom's opinion was acting on CP orders, came up to Seattle to urge the two unions to stop discriminating. He got nowhere, Engstrom told the hearing, because he and Lundeberg weren't pulling the Filipinos off the ships because of their race, but because under U.S. immigration laws, Filipinos couldn't become citizens. And only U.S. citizens could join the unions.

He saw Bridges again at the 1936 convention of the Maritime Federation, when Bridges and Earl King, secretary of the marine firemen's union, asked him to run for president of the Federation. He was certain, he testified, they supported him because they knew he was a Party member, and that he would be subject to Party discipline. King explained, when he testified later, that he supported Engstrom because, as a member of the progressive caucus in the Federation, his main concern was to prevent the AFL–oriented group from putting their man in the presidency.

"I was keeping my eyes open for some delegate that would show some promise," King said. "I wasn't particularly anxious about what group he came from. I kind of had a leaning towards a young fellow by the name of Jimmy Engstrom, who had been under me in Seattle, and whom I had practically taught unionism, as I knew it, from the ground up.

"He didn't know anything about it when he came out on strike. He was intelligent, and he seemed to have courage . . . And he was learning fast. . . ."

"Did you ever speak to Bridges about him?"

"Well, I think I have spoken to Bridges about him, probably half a dozen times or more. He was noncommittal; he says, 'Well, I think the guy is all right. I'm not sure.' Finally he said he was all right."

Bridges's reasons for supporting Engstrom were similar to King's:

One of the big grievances raised by the leadership of [the maritime federation], and it is still raised today, was that the shore unions, that is, unions like longshoremen, were opposed to unions that go to sea, and that they had too much control over the maritime federation. Therefore, our strategy was to answer that by saying, "All right, we will elect a seagoing man as president and as secretary of the Federation in order to keep it together. . . ."

Engstrom was a compromise candidate. We never trusted him, and we knew his weaknesses. That happens in inter-union politics just like it happens in any other politics. We knew at the time he was a pie card—a person in trade union circles who has got his eye on the job and the money in the job, more than the interests of the membership.

We knew that because he wanted the job he might not go along with one side entirely to hold the job and have the other side trying to throw him out. . . .

"Did you know he was a Communist?" Bridges was asked.

"I was pretty sure he wasn't. I know now; he has admitted it. . . . It would have been the farthest thing that I would imagine at that time, that Engstrom would be a Communist; maybe not because of his actions, but because of the weak type of individual that he was."

Landis, like Bridges, took a dim view of Engstrom. "Engstrom left a convincing impression," Landis wrote in his report, "that he was not telling the truth. Indeed, it is [my] conclusion that Engstrom never was a Communist."

Up to now, the government's case suffered from the failure of its witnesses to corroborate each other on any important point. But in Engstrom, despite his otherwise weak contribution, they finally had a witness who supplied an item for which the government had two other witnesses. In his testimony, Engstrom had said he attended a Communist meeting with Bridges in Seattle, during the 1936 strike. Bridges had come up to address a mass meeting of maritime workers, after which, Engstrom recalled, a small group of Communists met out on Magnolia Bluff at the home of Howard Costigan, Secretary of the leftist Washington Commonwealth Federation. Among those present were Costigan, Engstrom said, Rapport, Harry Jackson and Bridges. He couldn't remember who else was there or what subjects were discussed, but he was certain it was an important meeting.

Engstrom was followed by John Davis, an ex–sailor who said he, too, had once been a Communist and that he had been at the Magnolia Bluff gathering, which he also thought was a Party meeting. While his testimony supported Engstrom's, all in all, Davis was a poor witness for the government. Landis described his own reaction this way:

> Davis' . . . testimony is intrinsically weak. Its vagueness gave the impression of a subdued sense of stress that is difficult to appreciate apart from the visual impression created by his demeanor on the stand. Even the record as it stands discloses a man testifying to the minimum details necessary for the purpose, never going beyond to volunteer one item that would fill in with a background of realism the bare bones of his recital. His subsequent addition of Jackson and Rapport to the persons present at this meeting, two of the most prominent Communists in that region, at the time sounded suspicious. It appears in the same light as one reviews the whole of his testimony.

Gordon Castor, a lumberjack who, at the time of the Magnolia Bluff meeting, had been a minor official of the CIO union and, he said, a Communist, was put on by the government to corroborate Engstrom's and Davis's story. He recalled that fifteen or sixteen people were at the meeting, but he could remember by name only Bridges, Rapport, Jackson, Davis and a longshoreman named Pilcher. He was practically certain that Engstrom was not there. Engstrom must have been thinking of some other meeting, he said. And, in contrast to Engstrom's belief that the meeting was held in Howard Costigan's home, Castor didn't remember Costigan as even having been at the meeting at all. He was, however, certain it was a top fraction meeting of the Party.

The mystery of Magnolia Bluff hung over the hearing until weeks later, when the defense called Bruce Hannon, an officer of the Seattle longshoremen's local, to the stand. The meeting, he told the hearing, had taken place at *his* house on Magnolia Bluff, not Costigan's, who was his neighbor. When Bridges came to Seattle for the strike meeting, Hannon and Henry Geary, another longshoreman, had met him at the train, taken him to his hotel, then to a radio station for a broadcast, then to dinner and from there to the mass meeting. Afterward, he took Bridges to his home to relax. Several

THAT'S AGAINST THE CONSTITUTION

union officials and one or two of Hannon's neighbors dropped in and they sat around chatting, he said, being served coffee and doughnuts by his mother, while the wives of some of his guests played cards in the dining room.

Even after Hannon cleared up the mystery of where the Magnolia Bluff gathering took place, a cloud of uncertainty remained. He couldn't remember, either, exactly who had been at his house that night. His mother was there, of course, and his two brothers, and Henry Geary. Matt Meehan, secretary of the longshoremen's union, was there. But he couldn't recall whether Davis had been there or not, and he said he had never met Castor. He was positive neither Jackson nor Rapport was present.

Bridges's own memory of who was present was better than Hannon's. He also remembered the meeting as a social affair after the mass meeting, and that Hannon, Meehan, Costigan, Davis and Engstrom had been in the group. He couldn't remember ever having seen Castor, and he was positive Rapport wasn't present, because he distinctly remembered the first meeting he'd had with him. That was in April, 1937, after Bridges became West Coast Director of the CIO and he and Rapport met to discuss Labor's Non-Partisan Political League, the CIO's political arm.

What was the affair on Magnolia Bluff? A top fraction meeting? Or was it the sort of gathering that naturally follows a public meeting, where a speaker's host takes him home for an hour or two, inviting in friends for casual conversation? Landis accepted Hannon's and Bridges's view that it was the latter. He ended his analysis with the observation:

"That among this group Communists might be present is entirely plausible, but considering the established falseness of so much of the testimony presented in this connection, no conviction attends the attempt to transform this social gathering into a top fraction meeting."

After Castor, the government digressed briefly to lay a foundation for its argument that the Communist Party did in fact teach and advocate the overthrow of the government. Their next witnesses were two immigration officials. The first, from Seattle, brought with him a stack of books and pamphlets he had bought in a Communist bookstore there. The second had a boxful of publications he had picked up on a shopping tour of Communist Party bookstores in the Bay Area. Bonham then asked permission to put in evidence more Marxist publications, producing a library a Marxist theoretician might have coveted.

The newspapers, reasoning that their readers would find this bibliography dull reading, ran another story on Doyle on the day the two immigration officers were on the stand. Although the hearing was now going into its fourth week, Doyle was still in Minnesota. He told reporters that until the defense sent him $800 to cover his travel expenses and properly compensate him for the time he would lose from his law practice, he would refuse to go out to the Coast. The defense, after consulting with Dean Landis, proposed to pay Doyle the standard government rate for witnesses, which seemed reasonable enough. But from Doyle's point of view, the amount was preposterous. "They're only posting $4.50 a day," he protested, "and my time is worth $50."

When Castor left the witness chair, the government's case against Bridges was in. Their argument that Bridges was a Communist rested on what their witnesses, from Milner through Castor, had told the hearing. That was the evidence on which they proposed to deport him.

It turned out that the government lawyers did have one more witness on their list, and his identity gave the newspapers their biggest story so far. The government had decided to call Harry Bridges to the stand. The defense had objected strongly to his being called by the government, the press reported, for his attorneys wanted to have him testify in his own defense first, and then to let the government cross-examine him. But Landis had upheld the government's contention that in deportation proceedings it was customary for immigration authorities to question an alien first. After that, he could try to disprove the charges against him.

"Being an alien," a government lawyer was quoted as saying, "Bridges must answer all our questions as far as deportation is concerned, and these will include his affiliation with the Communist Party." Then, perhaps anticipating objections that the Fifth Amendment protects a person from having to testify against himself and that in a criminal trial, a defendant doesn't have to take the stand at all if he doesn't want to, the attorney added brightly: "He can, however, remain mute on any question that might result in his prosecution for a crime."

A layman, reading about events on Angel Island over his morning coffee and pondering the somber penalty hanging over Bridges's head if he gave wrong responses to questions he did have to answer, might have been reminded of a comment made by one of Dickens's characters in *Oliver Twist* when he was told of another lawyer's distinction–without–a–difference:

"If the law supposes that," Mr. Bumble said, "the law is a ass, sir, a idiot."

NOTES

The exchange of letters between Hoff and Houghteling is in the Perkins Papers. The FBI report that it had nothing in its files on Bridges is in the Perkins Papers.

Grossman described the problem of making up a list of probable prosecution witnesses in an interview with me in 1967.

Sen. Copeland's statement that Bridges was an avowed Communist is in *Cong. Rec.*, April 29, 1937, p. 3936. The deportation charges against Bridges are reproduced in Landis, *In the Matter of Harry R. Bridges*, p. *1*.

The Strecker decision is reported in *Strecker* v. *Kessler*, 95 F 2d 976 (1938); *Strecker* v. *Kessler*, 96 F 2d 1020 (1938); and *Kessler* v. *Strecker*, 307 U.S. 22 (1929).

6

Do You Believe in a
Capitalistic Form of Government?

*There are some supporters of Bridges who
are a little fearful that he is being allowed by
his own counsel to talk too much, to set forth
with too great fullness and too little restraint
his ideas on society, the State, industry, the
labor movement, the relation of politics to
labor, the relationship of the Communist Party
to the labor movement. . . .*

ARTHUR EGGLESTON

WHEN BRIDGES was put on the stand, the hearing took a new tack.
Government lawyers now set out to show, by Bridges's answers to
their questions, that he was affiliated with the Communist Party. It
was fairly apparent that the prosecution had struck out in its efforts
to prove he was a member.

Bridges, for one, felt that way. "We think the case is in the bag,"
he assured the national convention of the Newspaper Guild, which
was meeting in San Francisco. "We're not afraid of any group of
labor spies, perjurers and ex–convicts when their testimony goes
before a fair–minded person like Dean Landis of Harvard University. . . . Despite attempts being made to remove me from San
Francisco," he added, "I intend to be here a long time, because this
is the best city in the United States."

When Bridges finished his speech, Heywood Broun, the noted
columnist and founder of the guild, gave his theory of the case: It
was a frame–up. Bridges, like Eugene Debs, Big Bill Haywood and
others down through the history of the labor movement, Broun
said, was getting the treatment American business kept in store for

troublesome union leaders. "We all know the trial of Harry Bridges
has nothing to do with the issues being heard," Broun asserted.
"We know he's in a spot because he's an honest, efficient and able
labor leader."

That was how it looked to Woody Guthrie, too, so he wrote a
song about it. He called it "The Ballad of Harry Bridges," and it
was published in the San Francisco *People's World* on August 4,
1939, Bridges's third day on the stand.

> I'll sing you the Tale of Harry Bridges
> Left his parents and his home
> He sailed acrost that rollin' ocean,
> And into Frisco he did roam.
> > Now Harry Bridges saw starvation
> > Was a creepin' along that ocean shore,
> > 'Gonna get good wages for th' Longshoremen!'
> > That's what Harry Bridges swore.
>
> He went to the seamen 'long the ocean,
> He organized them day and night
> Most of the seamen follered Harry,
> Because they figured that he was right.
> > Hard times was bad along the ocean,
> > And there was a many an idle hand,
> > And there was a many of wives and children,
> > Going hungry in a Rich Man's land.
>
> Now the big ship owners they shook their timbers,
> They moaned and groaned and hung their head,
> They flapped their fins, and swore they'd get him,
> Because they figured that he was Red.
> > They carried him away to the Angels Island
> > It was there they had his trial
> > They sighed, and spied, and lied, and cried,
> > But Harry Bridges laughed and smiled.
>
> Old Harper Knowles and Captain Keegan
> Will some day sleep in a restless grave
> And old Red Hynes, and R. P. Bonham,
> Of men like these—no songs are made.
> > What a bloody old day was Bloody Thursday
> > What a bloody case of low disgrace
> > For every man that the police killed there,
> > Ten thousand rise to take their place.

> I've sung you the tale of Harry Bridges,
> Of Howard Sperry, and Nick Bordoise
> Of Helland, Daffron, Parker, Knudson,
> And all of the other Union Boys.
>> They fought and died to save the Union,
>> They fought and died for what is Right
>> The Union Way is the American Way,
>> By God, I figure I'm just 'bout Right!

The government's new approach raised a formidable problem of definition. On its face, the law Bridges was charged under was clear enough. It said that an alien who was affiliated with the Party was equally as deportable as if he were a card–carrying, dues–paying member. But what was not clear was the definition of affiliation. Landis considered several definitions and finally settled on one used in 1935 by a federal court of appeals in another deportation case, *Kettunen* v. *Reimer*.

"Affiliation," the court had said, "is not proved unless the alien is shown to have so conducted himself that he has brought about a status of mutual recognition that he may be relied on to cooperate with the Communist Party on a fairly permanent basis. He must be more than merely in sympathy with its aims or even willing to aid it in a casual, intermittent way. Affiliation includes an element of dependability upon which the organization can rely which, though not equivalent to membership duty, does rest upon a course of conduct that could not be abruptly ended without giving at least reasonable cause for the charge of a breach of good faith."

Bridges took the stand—it was actually a kitchen chair from the mess hall—as the session began on the morning of August 2nd. He stayed in it for three full days, rocking back against the wall, coming down with a bang as he leaned forward to gesture, looking to reporters on the scene, "like a dapper young capitalist." Shoemaker began by asking if he'd ever told anyone he was a Communist. "I have kidded people at times because it got to be such a joke on occasions," Bridges said, "But soberly and officially I never have."

"Have you ever denied that you are a Communist?"

"Plenty of times. The general strategy of stool pigeons, for example, labor spies, disrupters—in disrupting a meeting, is through a process of Red-baiting. When maybe a certain militant member or rank and file leader in the union gets up and proposes a program, one of these people might get up and say, 'Just a moment! I want to know if he is a Communist.' Of course, that is the lead–off. If the question is at all recognized, then the successive question is, 'Well, I don't think he should have the floor because of this, that and the other thing.'

"You can disrupt and ruin an entire meeting just from that beginning. . . . Now on those occasions, naturally, if I am asked, 'Are you a Communist?' the question is ignored. At certain open forums where I believe the question is asked from a sincere desire to get the information, the question is answered."

Shoemaker next asked about Communists in the labor movement, and if Bridges would name some he knew. He named four or five who openly admitted their membership. The prosecutor then asked Bridges if he believed in the teachings of Communism.

"I am not very familiar with the teachings of the Communist Party," Bridges answered, "only from a trade union point of view. . . . But the general question of, 'Do I believe in the teachings of the Communist Party?' as far as I have delved into them, they are pretty much a matter of theory, and our hands are so full of practical matters that I generally stay with the practical matters."

Later on, when Shoemaker put the same question again, Bridges said, "It seems to me that it might be all very well to talk about taking over the means of production, but . . . I am not concerned with that. I believe it will be thirty or forty years hence, and I do not think I will be around. There are plenty of things to be done today, for instance, the matter of getting simple recognition of trade unions and so on. There are areas in this country and in this state where we do not dare go in as trade unions."

In Bridges's three days in the witness chair, Shoemaker came back to this theme again and again, turning Bridges's social philosophy over and over, painstakingly studying its facets for a flaw.

"Do you know about Marxism?" Shoemaker asked.

"I have a knowledge of it; it is necessary in our work," Bridges responded.

"Will you tell us about it briefly?"

"Well . . . ," Bridges began.

"Very briefly," Shoemaker interrupted, for already he had learned that Bridges was not reticent.

"I think it would be impossible to say what I know about Marxism briefly," Bridges objected.

"Withdraw the question," the prosecutor said hastily.

But Bridges wasn't to be stopped. "I have read Marx's works," he went on, "and although I attempted to wade through Marx's

Capital, I didn't get very far. It seemed dry to me. Certain portions of it is tied up closely with our trade union work and I am familiar with that."

"Do you believe in social ownership of the means and implements of production?" Shoemaker next wanted to know.

"I certainly believe that, as far as the means of production are concerned, that we could have a lot more municipal or government ownership than we have now," Bridges replied. "And we couldn't do a much worse job with the means of production than private industry has been able to do." His answer was straightforward enough, and it made him sound anti–capitalist, but it was not really a direct answer to the basic question Shoemaker was asking: Do you believe in the Communist economic program? For at the time of the hearing, American capitalism was rounding out its tenth year of the Great Depression. Although the New Deal had administered Keynesian remedies, it had done so cautiously, in insufficient doses. Millions of unemployed were still dragging themselves wearily from one factory gate to another in a vain search for work, and Bridges's own industry was so depressed that even the forceful longshoremen's union he headed had not been able to get a wage increase in five years. In August, 1939, you had to be a Pollyanna or ignorant of what was going on in the world not to have doubts about capitalism.

Shoemaker digressed, momentarily, to ask, "Do you believe that the Communist Party is a subversive organization, an organization working against the interests of the government and, perhaps, the people of the United States?"

Bridges's answer was candid, if injudicious. "I can only answer that from the contacts or the knowledge that I have of it in my activities. My opinion would be that it isn't."

The questions then veered back again to Bridges's economic views. Shoemaker led off by asking, "Do you believe in our form of government, the democratic form of government?"

"I most certainly do," Bridges replied.

"Do you believe," came the next question, "in a capitalistic form of government?"

"The two things are entirely different."

"I will ask it again," Shoemaker insisted. "Do you believe in a capitalistic form of government?"

"If you mean do I believe—when you refer to a capitalistic form of government I don't exactly know what the term means, but here is my opinion of it. If you mean the capitalistic form of society which, to me, means the exploitation of a lot of people for a profit, and a complete disregard of their interests for that profit, I haven't much use for it. But that is a question entirely separate and apart from the government, as I understand it."

At this point, Shoemaker decided to ask Bridges a few questions about his experiences in the IWW. But Bridges's membership in the IWW was too brief, his view of the IWW's anarcho–syndicalism too negative for this line of inquiry to be useful to the prosecution. Moreover, Shoemaker's questions led Landis to strike up a discussion with Bridges about the Wobblies in which he treated Bridges more like a peer than a defendant. So Shoemaker got back to his main theme as quickly as he could. "If the workers should take over the government, do you believe that there should be compensation given to those persons who lose out?"

"Isn't that in the Constitution?" Bridges parried. "If I recall right it is. It is already provided for in the Constitution that nobody can be robbed of their property or have it taken away from them without compensation."

Shoemaker also asked a great many questions about Bridges's views about Communists in unions and his relationship with the Party itself. After Bridges had said he had no objection to Communists being in unions, Shoemaker asked, "Would you people take a man into the union who, for instance, believed in the overthrow of the government. . . . ?"

"There is nothing in our [union] constitution to discriminate against any person regardless of what their political beliefs are," Bridges replied. "If the constitution could be construed that the advocacy of the overthrow of the government by force and violence or in any other way was a political belief, it would be improper and illegal to hold that against a person."

"Wouldn't the union be concerned with it?" Shoemaker asked, as if he couldn't believe what he was hearing.

"They possibly would. I don't know. The issue has never come up. A man comes up before our union. They want to know, 'Have you ever been a strikebreaker? Have you ever been a stool pigeon? Have you ever been on the police force?' and a few other things like that."

"Then the whole paramount consideration from your viewpoint," Shoemaker summed up, "is just this: that a man has a right to any belief he desires in regard to anything, whether it be the overthrow of the government . . . or not, provided it does not conflict with his union obligations?"

"Yes," Bridges said. He thought for a moment. "I don't think anybody would dare get up in our unions to advocate the overthrow of the government by force and violence. They would throw them out on their ear."

"Suppose you have Party members in your union," Shoemaker asked. "How do you cope with them if the Party line runs counter to the interest of the union?"

"When we believe that individual members of the Communist Party, or possibly groups of them, have gotten out of line," Bridges explained, "the only way to correct that is to notify Party officials that we don't like it." He recalled an incident concerning the longshoremen's rule that local officials in their union could not hold office for more than two years. The Party thought that turning experienced men out of office was inefficient, and one of the Communists in the union was campaigning for abandonment of the rule. "I notified the Communist Party," said Bridges, "that I didn't like it. Of course, I would say that as far as the arguments that these fellows put up, they were somewhat logical and convincing."

"Did you do that orally or in writing?" Shoemaker inquired.

"Oh, orally. I don't write to the Communist Party. Not that I believe it shouldn't be done, but it would probably be up here in evidence to prove I am a member."

"Not at all," Shoemaker protested. "I don't think that necessarily would follow."

Bridges also said that he had asked the Party for help several times: to defeat Mayor Rossi when he ran for re-election in 1935, to kill an anti-picketing proposal in 1938, and to help union leaders who had been framed.

"Did you personally go up to the Party's headquarters?" Shoemaker asked.

"No," Bridges answered. "If I want to contact a Communist Party official, or any of them, I don't go up to Communist Party headquarters officially and for two reasons: First, I haven't a lot of time. Telephones are available. They can come down and see me. They might have a lot more time than me. Secondly, it might not be the most intelligent thing to do, although I'm not afraid, or anything like that, but your actions are misconstrued. There are many, many people around, apparently, who think that because you even talk to a Communist, they put you in the Communist Party."

"When you say you notified the Communist Party," Landis

broke in, "I would just like to get some concrete idea of what the mechanics are. If you asked me today, 'Notify the Democratic Party to do so and so', or 'Notify the Republican Party to do so and so,' I have to scratch my head and think how in thunder I could do that."

"It all depends," Bridges explained. "If I want to communicate with the Democratic Party with respect to a labor question, I get in touch with Dan Tobin [president of the teamsters], who is the labor representative on the Democratic National Committee. It is the same with the Republican Party. If you are a labor man and you want to go to the official heads of that party, you go to William Hutcheson, the president of the carpenters' union.

"Then, of course, so far as the political issues are concerned, you have your local committees. As far as the Communist Party is concerned, you look into the telephone book and you get the headquarters of the Communist Party, and I call up the headquarters and ask for them."

Shoemaker's next question was one most people, had they been in Bridges's shoes, would have liked to dodge. But again, Bridges's fluency was matched by his candor. "In your opinion," Shoemaker inquired, "is the influence of the Communist Party beneficial or detrimental to the labor movement as a whole?"

"I don't know," Bridges responded. "That's a pretty general question. I have known of instances where I believe if that was carried out to the logical conclusion I think it would be detrimental. I know of others advocated by the Communist Party where it has been distinctly beneficial.

"In my experience with the people I know who are members of the Communist Party, and from what I have seen of their actions in the unions, I found them good union men. They have generally fought for progressive and democratic trade unionism. I have very few complaints against the Communist Party as a whole, insofar as the trade unions are concerned, but they are not many. And if we look at it that way, I think the good the Communist Party does, if they have an influence over trade unions, which they don't over ours, would outweigh any bad things the other way."

Encouraged, no doubt, by Bridges's last remarks, Shoemaker turned to the heap of Marxist literature Bonham and his subordinates had piled up on the exhibit table. Picking up *Communism* by Earl Browder, he read:

"As the crisis becomes worse the more desperately will the Capitalists cling to their property and their power, the more murderous will become their attacks on the masses of the people. It must be emphasized that Capitalism will not simply come to an end. It can only be ended by the organized actions of the working class in collaboration with its allies from other sections of the population. The revolution does not simply happen; it must be made."

Shoemaker looked up from the book at Bridges. "Are you in accord with that view?"

"I wouldn't know. 'Revolution' brings to my mind a lot of force and violence, bloodshed, shootings and what not, and I am against any of that kind of stuff and I have never advocated it and I have always opposed it.

"That is Browder's opinion and that is his theory, and if it means that—although I can't conceive it—that this country is going to get to the point where the workers or the people get so desperate that they will take up arms, I think that that is a question for the future. I know that it will never reach that point as long as we have our trade unions and fight for wages, hours and working conditions, but I can understand how a situation like that happened in Russia, where the people were so miserable and desperate and under such terror that they had a choice of two evils: They could starve or be killed, or they could take a chance and go down fighting. And I think I would do the same in that situation.

"But I can't compare what happened in Russia or anywhere else with the United States. I think. . . ."

Shoemaker cut in before he could finish. "You don't think we have that same condition here, do you?"

"No," Bridges went on. "I think things are very bad in certain sections, but at least they are not that bad. You haven't had any millions of people starving to death yet. There has been attempts to starve them to death by the special interests, but you do have the WPA and the PWA and relief, despite all the efforts to put an end to them.

". . . I have no opinions on revolutions, except that they have happened in the past and they can conceivably happen in the future. . . . Leave them up to Earl Browder; that is apparently his job. But my job is hours, wages and working conditions, and any political or other activity that will strengthen the union and bring those things about."

Landis interrupted before Shoemaker could ask his next question. He had been fascinated by Bridges's declaration that unions and collective bargaining are bulwarks against revolution, and he now engaged Bridges in a discussion about the necessity of using and preserving democratic procedures—due process, free discussion, legislation—to bring about economic change. Shoemaker, impatient to get on with the interrogation and growing increasingly uncomfortable as he listened to the friendly tone of Landis's exchange with Bridges, fidgeted anxiously until, finally, Landis leaned back, signalling with his yellow pencil for Shoemaker to continue.

"Do you think the Communist Party would perpetuate the democratic move?" Shoemaker asked Bridges sharply.

"I don't know," Bridges answered, "and I am not particularly concerned with it. My observation of the individual members of the Communist Party, from my observation of them, I haven't seen them doing anything, or advocating anything that leads me to believe otherwise. But again, I am not fully conversant with their program, only through the few instances that I have seen myself."

Landis broke in again, almost as if he had forgotten for the moment where he was and as if he imagined that he, the witness and the prosecutor were three colleagues sitting comfortably in the faculty club at Harvard discussing political theory over highballs: "That is what I wonder about there, is whether or not that emphasis upon procedures is to be found in the literature of the type that has been read here."

Bridges fell in with Landis's mood. "It's all theory. It seems they are talking about what might happen, or could happen, but it just doesn't work. You can't give arguments like that to workers. When a person has finished working at the end of the day, when you try to give him arguments like that, you will probably get a laugh out of them.

"There are other serious-minded people, if you approach them and say, This might be good for the heart and soul or good for the mind, as a matter of study, along with the reading of detective stories,' and one thing and another, they might listen to you. But to come out with that as an immediate solution of their problems, the raising of their children and the keeping of their households, you can't get to first base with that kind of stuff, and no intelligent trade unionist would try it."

If Bridges believed that unions should be active in politics but the Communist Party was not the answer, what then, Landis asked, was his solution?

"I favor the endorsement and support of a labor party," Bridges answered. "It is all very well to have a small political party for the sake of principal . . . but you don't improve the lot of the workers.

. . . The trade union movement, or the people generally, should work to build such a party, or, if it's not possible to establish a new one, should work through the present established parties to liberalize them."

"It would be your idea to establish a labor party in this country somewhat according to the British Labor Party?" Landis asked.

"Or even better than the British Labor Party," Bridges corrected. "They have a good labor party in Australia. When you join a union in Australia, part of your dues go to the support of the Labor Party."

Bridges's rejoinder brought out the legal scholar in Landis. "But that is possible in England," he observed, "despite the Trade Disputes Act of 1927?" (He was referring to the "contracting-in" requirement in the British law under which, before a union could assess a member for its political fund, it had to get his written consent. The law was repealed by the Labor Government in 1946.)

"That more or less ruined trade unions when that Trade Disputes Act was passed," Bridges tartly retorted.

"No," Landis said firmly. "The President's Commission, for example, came to the conclusion that the effect of the Trade Disputes Act of 1927 was negligible, if I remember that report correctly."

Bridges was equally firm. "I remember the report. I discussed it with some members of the committee after it was written. But the fact remains that since that Trade Disputes Act was put into effect, the workers in Great Britain have not won one major fight."

Now it was Landis's turn to be tart. "That is a poor basis, I think, to infer that it is that which has made it responsible for that condition."

"I have another good reason," Bridges countered. "Our employers are heartily in favor of the Trade Union Act of Great Britain. If there were no other reason, that would help to convince me that it was no good."

"I was not suggesting that you should support the principle of the Trade Disputes Act of 1927," Landis said, retreating, "but that I think the inference you have drawn is an improper inference and is certainly in conflict with the President's Commission's conclusion, not that that necessarily establishes the conclusion. But your idea with reference to labor tactics is that trade unionism, as such, ought to become political . . . ?"

"It has got to be," Bridges said. "Otherwise, trade unions can only go so far and then they will be robbed of it by other means.

"We have many examples of it in this country. . . . When we

fought and won certain things that were sorely needed in the maritime industry and we became so firmly organized that our employer groups could not take those things away from us through economic struggle they immediately started pouring a lot of bills into Congress and every one of those bills was aimed at crippling our activities, crippling our unions. . . ."

When Shoemaker began the questioning again, his inquisition was an unconscious parody of an ideological catechism, with himself in the role of a frustrated instructor in Marxism and Bridges a balky novice who, holding the theoretical questions up to the mirror of his experience as a trade union leader, kept giving wrong answers. For a text, the prosecutor used the preamble to the constitution of the Marine Workers' Industrial Union. Handing Bridges a copy, he asked him to read aloud and comment on a marked section: "This fight between the marine workers and the shipowners, bosses, etc., is only one front of the class struggle which rages ceaselessly between the whole working class and the whole class of employers—the capitalists."

"I think, generally speaking, that is correct," Bridges said. He read on: " 'Victory in this struggle can only be won by the most relentless, militant and revolutionary struggle of the whole working class.' I don't agree," he commented. "We have won a couple of things in our trade unions and we didn't have to go through a relentless and militant struggle of the whole working class. We had to fight some of the working class, as a matter of fact. So, from the light of what I know by practical experience, I don't agree with that."

Shoemaker then reminded Bridges that in 1933 and 1934, he urged sailors to join the MWIU. How could he have done so, Shoemaker asked, in view of its political coloration? Bridges responded by saying that at the time there hadn't really been an alternative. The AFL sailors' union wasn't actively organizing, and he felt it wasn't militant enough to stand up to the shipowners on the West Coast. Besides, the AFL sailors' union wasn't supporting the strike at the outset and the MWIU was. "I advised many people to join this union," he went on, "and lots of times they used to say, 'Look at that preamble.' I said to them, 'Listen! The way you change it is by joining the union. You can't change it by not joining the union. . . . You are joining a trade union organization, you can change it.' "

Shoemaker then asked Bridges how he felt about the following phrase from the preamble: "[The MWIU] rejects and condemns the treacherous class–collaboration policy of the AFL, which seeks to delude the workers into believing that it is possible for them to live 'in peace' with the capitalists." Bridges's answer was most un–Marxist.

"Class collaboration can't be condemned in a flat, general statement such as that. Collective bargaining is class collaboration."

Shoemaker quoted another passage: "While striving constantly for the immediate betterment of all living and working conditions of the marine workers, the MWIU does not limit itself to immediate economic demands alone."

"That's quite proper, I think, and practical," Bridges remarked. "There are other things besides just wages, hours, and working conditions. There is the question of democracy, civil liberties; there is the question of the persecution of racial groups in other lands. They are all our business, and we definitely and are actively conscious of it. I believe they are correct, in my opinion, if that is what they mean in that respect."

Up to this point, the MWIU preamble was an unusually militant statement for an American labor union, but hardly a call to revolution. The tone sharpened in the next few sentences: "But [the MWIU] declares that the liberation of the marine workers or any other type of workers from exploitation is only one part of any struggle of the whole working class against the capitalist system."

"I would assume that that is correct," Bridges observed. "However, when it becomes a question of, say, the whole working class against the capitalist system, I think I would say that is correct, too. Regardless of whether we like it or not, there is a struggle against the present system. If that's regarded," he continued, coming back to Shoemaker's apparent belief that capitalism and democracy were one and the same, "as a struggle against the present government, I think it is incorrect. . . . However, when you get down to '. . . the struggle is directed toward the goal of the establishment of a revolutionary workers' government . . .' I will say that it takes further analysis and explanation. It is the method you are going to use, then, that we have to go into. If this means the establishment of a revolutionary workers' government by force of arms, especially against a democracy, I would not believe in it or support it, and would be absolutely opposed to it.

"If they mean, however, the establishment of a revolutionary workers' government by democratic means, I don't see who could object to it. If that is what the majority of the people want, they will eventually get it. As long as it is done in a democratic fashion, it seems to me that it is provided for in the Constitution or the regulations of any democratic set-up."

When the interpretation of the MWIU preamble was over, the questions turned to whether Bridges thought the Immigration Service, the American Legion, the National Guard, and the regular army were anti–labor. He answered that he didn't think the immigration people in San Francisco were anti–labor, but that those in the Northwest definitely were, and told how they had prevented Canadian CIO delegates from crossing the border to attend union meetings in the U.S. He said he thought the Legion and the National Guard were strike–breaking outfits, but the regular army was not. He was saying that the Governor of California during the '34 strike had been controlled by business interests when Shoemaker, thinking he saw an opening, darted in with a question.

"Would you change the plan, or the system, of selecting officers?" he demanded.

"Not at all."

"Or selecting candidates?"

"Not at all. You don't change or condemn the form of government because of the people who administer it. And that is what is the matter. If there is any criticism to be directed against the present democratic form of government in this or any other country, it is not to be directed against the form but it is certainly to be directed against many of the people that are supposed to administer it."

"Do you believe it would be in the interests of the majority of the people in the United States," the prosecutor now asked, "to scrap our present form of government?"

"I think it would definitely be to their detriment."

"Do you think the form of government in the Soviet Union would be any improvement over it?"

"I don't know much about the—what is the form of government in the Soviet Union?"

"Well," Shoemaker answered, "what they call communism, I believe."

"Well, the second question is, what is communism? Very frankly, my knowledge of the Soviet Union is general. I have worked on ships where the men have just come back from the Soviet Union; I have spoken to them . . . raised a lot of questions with regard to the dictatorship, the proletariat, and what not. I don't think the American form of government, as I read the Constitution and the

Bill of Rights, can be bettered any place in the world. It is a democratic form. I don't see how any time that you set up a form of government where the function is by democratic methods, a majority rule where problems can be taken to the people and voted on by majority rule—I don't think that can be bettered. It might be possible. It might work under some other circumstances. I have still got to learn."

"Is there any way you would amend the Constitution?"

"Yes. It should be amended so that it guarantees the right of members of the army and navy to vote, and overrules the rights of the states prohibiting people to vote, such as Indians. . . ."

Shoemaker, speaking in the condescending tone lawyers often strike with laymen, informed Bridges that soldiers, sailors and Indians already had the right to vote. Landis wasn't so sure, and he and Shoemaker had a long, inconclusive colloquy about the roles of the federal and state governments in determining voter eligibility. Finally, Landis turned to Bridges. "In other words, your suggestion is that something like the Thirteenth Amendment, or the Fifteenth Amendment, rather, which guarantees the right to vote without reference to race, color, or previous condition of servitude, should apply to people like Indians, and so forth?"

"Certainly," Bridges replied. "And should repeal the payment of poll taxes in the South, and should overrule the various legislation and restrictions passed by certain southern states that prohibit a great number of people in the southern states from voting today. . . ."

Landis was satisfied with the views Bridges put forward, until Bridges said that while he knew Russia was a dictatorship, "I wouldn't put it in with Nazi Germany and Imperial Japan."

"Then the difference is that in one type of society," Landis asked, "the dictatorship, its power to control without regard to democratic methods, lies in a few men, whereas in the other type, although it may lie in a few men, it has the ideal that it holds out to itself as operating for the benefit of the proletariat and, therefore, has different objectives?"

"I think," Bridges replied, "that under a dictatorship . . . if the dictatorship functions in the interests of the majority, I don't see how it can function without allowing a certain amount of freedom of expression, and so forth. If that continues long enough something is going to happen and I believe that the dictatorship would be overthrown and that democracy would take its place, or a democratic form of government."

To observers at the hearing, it was evident that Bridges had made a favorable impression on Dean Landis. His candor and forthrightness, even when his unorthodoxy about capitalism and about Communists in unions could be used against him, was like a salty breeze coming in off the Bay and clearing away the murk left by the prosecution witnesses the government had put on the stand before him. Arthur Eggleston, covering the hearing for the *San Francisco Chronicle*, summed up Bridges's testimony on August 7, 1939:

> For those who would like to keep Bridges a mythical monster and the labor movement something unknown and feared, the deportation hearing may turn out to be the worst thing that ever happened.
> There are some supporters of Bridges who are a little fearful that he is being allowed by his own counsel to talk too much, to set forth with too great fullness and too little restraint his ideas on society, the State, industry, the labor movement, the relation of politics to labor, the relationship of the Communist Party to the Labor movement. . . .
> Against that is the view that the hearing, the probing of Dean Landis, the government and the defense, and the full, unrestrained manner in which Bridges sets out his views is the best thing that ever happened to the labor movement.

If it had seemed odd for the government to call Bridges as a witness for the prosecution, the strategy of the defense, as they called its first major witness, seemed equally singular. It was Harper Knowles, who, according to a layman's logic, should have been called by the government to lay the foundation for its case. For Knowles was, as he told the hearing, "one of the foremost people on the Pacific Coast who have been demanding a hearing against Bridges."

At the time of his appearance, he was Executive Secretary of the Associated Farmers of California, an aggressively anti–union body that ostensibly represented only growers and processors but was actually a front organization financed by a cross section of California business up and down the state: the Industrial Association, public utilities, railroads, sugar refiners, oil companies, manufacturers of paper products, cans, and so on. Knowles's interest in radicalism began, he related, during the '34 strike, when he was commander of the American Legion branch in San Francisco. He and his Legion comrades, having persuaded themselves that Communists were behind the strike, organized a committee to keep the subversives under surveillance. After the strike, the committee expanded rapidly under Knowles's enthusiastic leadership. In no time, he had hundreds of informants all over the state sending in reports on individuals and organizations they believed were radical. Before long, his committee, centrally located in San Francisco's Civic Center, became a clearing house for records and reports sent in from up and down the coast by a score of public and private agencies which were keeping an eye on union organizers and supposed leftists.

Knowles testified that he shared information reciprocally with employers and outfits like the Associated Farmers, but that while he gave information to Army and Navy Intelligence and the immigration people, they didn't give him any. The Director of the State Bureau of Criminal Identification was more cooperative, and Captain Hynes of the Los Angeles red squad carried out *ad hoc* investigations for Knowles. The phone company was helpful, too, releasing to Knowles phone numbers and addresses of people he wanted to get a line on.

In 1935 and 1936, Knowles kept up a brisk correspondence with Frances Perkins, sending her second–hand allegations and rumors that Bridges was a Communist. In 1936, he dropped this campaign in favor of a new tactic, primarily because of Miss Perkins's insistence on documented proof. Another reason came out in Knowles's testimony. At the 1936 Legion convention, a report, allegedly written by Charles Wyzanski, Reilly's predecessor as legal adviser to the Labor Department, was circulated among the Legionnaires. It reviewed Knowles's letters to the Secretary, advised her that what Knowles had submitted was worthless, and criticized his attitude as prejudiced, his language intemperate and overbearing. After that, Knowles, with Doyle and the Portland police, started looking for ex–Communists and anybody else they could get to swear he knew Bridges was a Red.

The net they threw out brought up some queer fish. One was Ivan Cox. In the early days, when he was secretary–treasurer of the San Francisco longshoremen's local, he favored direct action and was highly thought of by the militants in the union. As the years went by, however, he drifted further and further to the right of Bridges, whom he thought too radical, finally breaking openly with him over affiliation with the CIO, which Cox thought was a Communist front. Cox was defeated for re–election as secretary–treasurer in 1937. When his successor took over, he found a shortage of $800.

Cox claimed he hadn't taken the money and was being framed by Bridges and the Communists. He went to the U.S. Secret Service for help, but they didn't know what to do with him, so they sent him to Navy Intelligence. Navy Intelligence was equally at a loss, so they passed him along to the Presidio, to talk with Army Intelligence. At the Presidio, an officer told him the place to go was the American Legion office in San Francisco's Civic Center. "They conduct investigations into matters of this kind," he told Cox, "and we rely on them authentically."

When Cox phoned for an appointment, Knowles's office told him, "Don't call us. We'll call you." Sure enough, a few days later, Knowles's partner, Larry Doyle, was at Cox's house, offering to help. He led Cox to believe that he represented the Governor of Oregon and the FBI, and that he worked closely with Knowles. "We have forty agents in the Party right now," he told Cox. "Before twenty-four hours are over we'll have forty reports on this very thing, and I'll know if [the frame-up] ever existed or not." That same night, Doyle came back to see Cox, bringing with him Harper Knowles and a man Cox thought was from Navy Intelligence.

Not long after that, Doyle told Cox he had checked out his story, and he should do three things. One was to tell the San Francisco longshoremen about Bridges's scheme to frame him. Cox agreed, and Doyle wrote a long speech for him, blaming the financial shortage on Moscow agents and ending with a comparison of himself with Christ, Cox's cross being Marx and Lenin. Cox gave it to an unsympathetic audience at a meeting of the San Francisco longshoremen's union in November. Afterward, he quit the local and left the waterfront altogether.

His second assignment was to make an affidavit stating that he'd been in a CP meeting with Bridges. Compliantly, he did so, witnessed by Knowles, Doyle, Raphael Bonham, and Captain Keegan of the Portland police, who came down from the Northwest for the occasion. Cox's third task was, in a way, the most dramatic. Using papers prepared by Doyle, he filed a conspiracy suit charging a Communist Party plot to dominate the West, working through unions, the schools, and the movies. Defendants were Harry Bridges, the 13th district of the Communist Party, the San Francisco director of the National Labor Relations Board, movie stars Frederick March and Mary Astor, and five thousand Jane and John Does. Doyle told Cox to ask for $5,100,000 damages. If he won, he was to turn $5 million over to the people of California, keeping $100,000 for himself as payment for defamation of character. When Cox finished signing the papers, Doyle took him over to the office of the secretary of the California Federation of Labor, who gave him one hundred dollars on the spot and put him on the payroll as an AFL organizer.

The suit never came to anything. Before it came up in court, Cox made out another affidavit on August 31, 1938, this time in the presence of Ernest Besig of the ACLU and Richard Gladstein. In this one, he repudiated both the affidavit about Bridges he'd given Bonham and the $5,100,000 conspiracy suit. "I told Doyle I didn't even know the movie stars and some of the people named in the suit," he said as he signed the new affidavit. "But he told me, 'Don't worry about that. You're helping the government, enabling it to construct its case around what you actually know.'"

Bridges's attorneys also drew from Knowles a story of how in 1937, during a fight between the longshoremen and teamsters in the early days of the march inland, he helped destroy a union official. The teamsters had announced that they wouldn't carry any merchandise to or from docks worked by CIO longshoremen until the longshoremen's union backed off from its drive to organize inland warehousemen. AFL sailors were supporting the teamsters, and they asked the marine firemen's union, a neutral in the AFL–CIO civil war, to cut off steam from the ships' winches and make it impossible for the longshoremen to unload the ships. The secretary of the firemen, John Ferguson, supported the sailors and teamsters against Bridges and the CIO, but was afraid he couldn't get a majority of the firemen to go along with him, so he asked Doyle if he had any suggestions. Doyle talked it over with Knowles, and then suggested to Ferguson that he round up a hundred men along the waterfront who were out of work, give them books in the firemen's union and pay them a few dollars to vote in the union meeting to support the AFL.

Bridges found out about the scheme and on the night of the meeting, he went to the firemen's hall accompanied by three hundred longshoremen and demanded the right to speak. When the hall quieted down, Bridges accused Ferguson of issuing membership books to "more than one hundred gas–hounds, vigilantes and waterfront bums picked up along the 'front to vote against us in this meeting. . . ."

Ferguson could only mumble that the presence of Bridges and the three hundred longshoremen was part of a Communist plot.

"All right," said Bridges. "There are approximately 104 men here with forged books. I'll give them a chance to leave the meeting before I present my proof. Those who leave will do so in complete safety." Sixty to seventy men scrambled to their feet at once and left the hall. The membership thereupon voted down Ferguson's proposal, and then, not long after, expelled him from the union for 99 years for his part in the plot.

Knowles proved to be an effective witness for the defense, not so much because of what he had to say, but because, as had been true of Milner, Sapiro, Leech, and the other witnesses called by the government, he had nothing incriminating to tell. Landis said in his report on the hearing:

"Knowles' relationship to the issues presented by this proceeding is not always clear. He was neither a candid nor a forthright witness. His memory tended too frequently to become beclouded when answers might have proven to be too revealing. Recollection, even when it existed, tended at times to be suspiciously faulty. Because of these tendencies it becomes necessary on occasion to disbelieve him and also to treat a hesitant qualified admission tortuously wrung from him as far more significant than would be the case with an open witness."

The next witness, Captain Keegan of Portland, also turned out to be an effective witness for the defense.

"He is a trained police officer with years of service," Landis said, summing up Keegan's testimony. "Yet he swears falsely in behalf of Scott. His contradictions are both frequent and with regard to major matters, not in respect to minor uneventful details. He is required again and again to devise explanations, crude in character, when documentary evidence and other testimony directly contradict his original recitals. He misled the examiner again and again only to be forced by documentary evidence and the testimony of others ultimately to reveal a wholly different story of his activities and the activities of his men than he first sought to portray. . . ."

Keegan began by saying that his investigation of Bridges had been routine, the same kind he would run on a suspected housebreaker: "Bridges isn't any more to me than anyone else." He first got interested in Bridges, he said, when Larry Doyle told him in 1937, just before a Maritime Federation of the Pacific convention in Portland, he was investigating Bridges for the state of Oregon, and asked if Keegan could lend him a good man.

Big Bill Browne was a natural for the assignment, Keegan decided. Browne was a member of the Red squad and, like Knowles, with whom he was in frequent touch, he was chairman of the Legion's Americanism Committee for his state. "I didn't have to give Browne any specific instructions when I assigned him to work with Doyle," Keegan said. "I had absolute confidence in Doyle's integrity and judgment. I still do."

On the second day of Browne's new assignment, Keegan told the hearing, Browne came to him to report that Doyle wanted him to help hide a microphone in Bridges's room at the Multnomah Hotel. "I see," Gladstein said when Keegan recalled the incident. "What did you say, 'O.K.?' " "I says," Keegan answered, "All right. Get all the information you can."

Keegan said he decided that while Browne and Doyle were otherwise occupied, he should cover the convention himself, with the help of several of his plainclothesmen. He had never attended any other union meeting, but until the maritime workers organized, he hadn't had to worry much about unions. "We had a bitter experience during the 1934 waterfront strike," he explained, "because we weren't properly prepared. . . . I wanted to know what was going on, and I couldn't find out much from the newspapers, especially what was going on in the caucuses." That seemed plausible, but later, under Gladstein's persistent questioning, Keegan admitted that he and his men hadn't paid any attention to strike talk. What they were after, he conceded, was proof that Bridges was a Communist.

If the Bridges investigation was routine, as Keegan insisted over and over that it was, Portland police deserved high marks for perseverance. They were also unusually generous in the lengths they were willing to go to help the federal government, for Bridges's activities were not under the jurisdiction of municipal law enforcement authorities. If what Bridges was doing and saying were properly the concern of government at all, only the immigration authorities could have acted. But Keegan could not concede that he and his colleagues were an unofficial investigative arm for Bonham and Norene, anymore than he could own up to his collaboration with Harper Knowles and the Los Angeles red squad. Such a confession would have confirmed the existence of the get–Bridges conspiracy that Carol King had pointed to in her opening statement.

No wonder, then, that Keegan was evasive when he was asked to describe how, for a couple of years, several of his men and he, himself, ranged up and down the coast, interviewing possible witnesses and following up leads for use against Bridges. And how it hap-

pened that he put up the money to bring witnesses from Los Angeles and San Francisco to Portland so Bonham and Norene could
talk to them, maybe get an affidavit. And why the city should have
paid the bill for his junket to Washington to testify in a Dies Committee hearing that the Portland red squad had found Bridges to be
a Communist.

All of this raised another sticky question for the squirming captain. Those trips had cost somebody a lot of money. Where had it
come from? From his chief of police, Keegan answered, who always met his requests for cash, and never asked how he used it. Not
a dime, he testified sturdily, came from outside the police department. But once again, he was forced to recant. After much spar-
ring, he finally admitted that the teamsters' union, for one, had
generously underwritten some of his expenses. Keegan's denial of
outside assistance, moreover, hurt the feelings of one of the donors,
an official of the teamsters' warehouse local in Portland.

"I personally would contribute money right today," Jack Ester-
brook said when he testified later in the hearing, overlooking the
fact that it had been the union's money he'd given Keegan, not his
own, "towards any fund to investigate anybody that was a Communist, providing they are a Communist. . . . And why Captain
Keegan should take the witness stand and swear under oath that he
didn't receive any money from me is beyond my comprehension. If
I was Captain Keegan, I would be very proud of the fact that there
was money paid in by citizens that were willing to do these things."

After Keegan had testified, defense lawyers had to resolve a matter of strategy. In view of all the exhibits and testimony the government had put in to prove that the Communist Party advocated violent overthrow of the government, the defense had to decide
whether to ignore that contention or try to counter it? "Harry
wasn't sure it was a good idea to get into the question of Communism," Aubrey Grossman said later. "He wasn't sure how the rank–
and–file in the union would react if we put witnesses on the stand
for that purpose. 'They may get the idea we're defending Communism rather then me.' We debated for quite a while, but finally we
convinced him that you might look like a red if you defend communism, but we'd better take that chance. What if some fink's testimony convinces Perkins, we argued, that you've been in the Party?
If we haven't challenged the government's contention about the
Party, you're as good as gone."

Miss King called to the stand Harold Chapman Brown, a professor of philosophy at Stanford, to discuss Marxist theory and to give an opinion on the prosecution's contention that the Communist Party advocated violent overthrow of the government. An old–fashioned scholar, Brown claimed a reading knowledge of Latin, Greek, French and German. He could also read Italian and Russian with the help of a dictionary, he said. An admirer of John Dewey, Brown's interest in Marx had grown out of his discovery of similarities between Dewey's concept of levels and Marx's dialectical materialism. Once interested, he had plunged on to read the fifteen volumes of Lenin's work.

Miss King was still qualifying Brown as an expert on Marxism–Leninism, as a preface to asking his views of the books and pamphlets the prosecution had piled up on the exhibit table, when Shoemaker interrupted to argue that the theory of Communism wasn't relevant. It was the practices of Communism that counted. Landis ruled that expert testimony as to Marxist theory was relevant, if it dealt with the intentions of the writers of official Marxist documents, and the effect of their writings on the minds of ordinary human intelligence. Brown thereupon read a fifty–page essay on Marxist theory.

When he was done, Shoemaker began his cross–examination with the question: "Are you a Communist?"

"No."

"From your study of these books, do you believe that force and violence is contemplated by the Communist Party in their activities in the United States?"

"I do not believe that the Communist Party intends or has any plans," Brown replied crisply, "to initiate force and violence."

"Then how do you explain this?" the prosecutor demanded, reading from Olgin's *Why Communism?* a blood–and–thunder description of how, when the revolution came, the workers would have to build barricades and defend themselves to the death.

"Oh, when I read that," Brown replied easily, "I felt it was mostly froth and not much beer."

Walter Thompson, the next expert witness, was also from Stanford, where he taught political science. He had read much of Marx, some of it in German, though by no means as much as Brown. He had with him a thirty–six page manuscript he was planning to read, but on Shoemaker's fervid plea that it would take too much time, Landis had it inserted in the record and Thompson summarized it. He supported Brown's view of the Communists' peaceful intentions, and in his testimony he contributed an interesting footnote to intellectual history.

Marx's economics, he said, owed its central concept, the labor theory of value, to an American. "The first sensible analysis of exchange value as labour–time," Thompson read from Marx's *Critique of Political Economy*, "made so clear as to be almost commonplace, is to be found in the work of a man of the New World . . . That man was Benjamin Franklin, who formulated the fundamental law of modern political economy in his first work when a mere youth and published in 1721: 'Trade,' Marx quoted Franklin as having written, 'in general being nothing else but the exchange of labour for labour, the value of all things is . . . mostly measured by labour.' "

After Knowles, Keegan, and the professors, the next witness provided a change of pace although his testimony was of no value to the defense. It was Charles C. Bakcsy, who told an entertaining story of his experiences as a private detective and of how he was hired by the waterfront employers to get the goods on Bridges. When the bailiff called him to the stand, he gave his name as Captain Bakcsy. Dean Landis, intrigued by the witness's appearance— he was a short, stocky man with a broken nose, cauliflower ears, a Van Dyke moustache and beard—asked, "Where did you get the term, 'Captain'?"

"I was captain of the four–masted bark 'Lisbeth,' a big sailing ship," Bakcsy answered. He explained that he had been a sailor on the vessel when, as they were rounding the Horn in a furious storm, the ship began to leak. The real captain, convinced the ship was lost, went below and brought up rum, so that all hands could go down happily. He and his first mate drank themselves into a stupor, but Bakcsy and a few others stayed sober. "We took charge of the ship, us sailors, and tied the captain and the mate down, and I was captain of the boat and sailed her to the Falkland Islands, and from there we took her to London, England."

Bakcsy also told the dean that he'd been a professional boxer, fighting as Young Sharkey, and a professional wrestler, under the name of Strangler Schmidt. He had shanghaied sailors, he said, and had been a bodyguard for Queen Liliuokalani of Hawaii. His greatest triumph as a private eye, he testified, was when he wormed his way into a job in the office of Big Bill Haywood, chief officer of the IWW, while at the same time he was on the payroll of General

Leonard Wood's intelligence bureau, reporting on Haywood's activities.

T. G. Plant of the waterfront employers hired him in April 1935, Bakcsy related, to see if he could get something on Bridges. The assignment took him to Carmel, the art and beach colony down the coast from San Francisco, where Lincoln Steffens, the noted muckraker and admirer of the Soviet experiment, lived with his wife, Ella Winter. In her autobiography, *And Not to Yield*, Miss Winter has explained why Bakcsy was dispatched to Carmel: "Someone had sold San Francisco industrialists on the idea that 'all the money'—for the waterfront troubles, the maritime strike of thirty–five thousand, the general strike, the 'agitation' in the agricultural fields for higher wages—came from Moscow, that the Soviet Consul brought it to Carmel, and Stef gave it to Harry Bridges."

Steffens, a boxing buff, was an easy mark for Bakcsy, who introduced himself as Young Sharkey when he called on the writer carrying copies of Steffens's *Autobiography* and Ella Winter's *Red Virtue*, to be autographed. With Steffens as his sponsor, Bakcsy was soon moving in the galaxy of liberals, radicals, Hollywood movie stars and writers, which revolved around Steffens. Bakcsy rented a large beach house, fitted it out with hidden microphones and cameras, and launched into a series of large parties where the liquor never seemed to run out. He talked like a radical, and he soon had a bulging file of quotes from his guests whom he entrapped into discussing "the coming revolution," which he invariably worked into his conversations with them.

Bakcsy testified that while he was on the Carmel assignment he reported regularly to the waterfront employers in San Francisco, who had hired him. He never was able to get anything they could use against Bridges, and after about six months, they cut him off.

He was also, he said, working closely with Knowles and Doyle and their coastwide espionage network. His relationship with them was never comfortable, he said, for they nagged him even more persistently than the waterfront employers to turn up something incriminating about Bridges. He broke with them, he told Dean Landis, when they threatened to tell the waterfront employers to fire him unless he would perjure himself by signing a statement that Bridges was at a meeting at Steffens's house when Bakcsy knew he had not been there.

Actually, Bakcsy had gone first to Bonham when the hearing was already underway, offering to testify for the government, but he had been turned down. Bonham, who was handling the cross–examination, loftily told the hearing, "We haven't used and don't intend to use any witness who had any connection with the shipowners."

Landis decided not to give any weight to Bakcsy's testimony. "It is impossible to separate truth from fiction in [it]," the dean said in his report. "It was bizarre and at times fantastic."

Doyle, still missing, was in the news for another reason the day Bakcsy was testifying. Because Doyle was ignoring the order of a federal court to appear at the hearing, it was up to the federal marshal in St. Paul, Minnesota, to arrest him and ship him out to Angel Island. But for some reason the marshal didn't seem able to find him. Reporters assigned to the case thought that a bit odd, for they had no trouble finding him at all.

One, taking a photographer along, went to the American Legion convention in Minneapolis, just across the river from the marshal's office in St. Paul, and sure enough, there was Doyle, chatting with his comrades. He lightheartedly posed for a picture, freely admitting that he was dodging the subpoena. He was going to keep on doing so, he added, as long as it was the defense that wanted him. "It's obvious what Bridges's lawyers are up to," he explained. "They want to get me on the stand and get all of my evidence, and then they'll bring in a troupe of witnesses who'll deny every statement I make." But he added, "I'm willing to come out voluntarily if the government wants me to testify."

Looking back on the hearing, one gets the impression that Bridges's lawyers arranged the order of appearance of their witnesses the way a playwright might bring his characters onstage in a play that taxes the capacity of his audience to absorb the intensity of the drama, giving their emotions respite from time to time with a comical or a tranquil scene. After Knowles and Keegan, the defense had called the two professors, "an interlude," as Ward puts it, "that caused the boys at Terry's bar to turn their backs on the radio and concentrate on social life. No more did the radio speak of spies and lies and plots, pardons and perjury. It spoke instead in . . . academic language. . . ." Then Bakcsy came on with his burlesque turn, followed by handwriting experts and others testifying about technical details. Then, with the next several witnesses, the hearing zoomed back up to fever pitch.

The defense now wanted to call Earl King and Ernest Ramsay, to show the lengths to which Knowles, Doyle, and Bonham had been willing to go in their effort to get Bridges. But to put King and

Ramsay on the stand, Bridges's lawyers had to get the cooperation of the state, for King and Ramsay were in San Quentin Prison. In 1936, during a campaign to organize marine firemen, George Alberts, a chief engineer who had been fighting the union, was found knifed and beaten to death in his cabin on the "Point Lobos," while the ship lay at anchor at Oakland. Three officials of the marine firemen's union, King, Ramsay and Frank Connor, were charged with conspiring to hire a pair of goons to beat him up—to dump him, as they say on the waterfront. According to the theory of the case put forward by Earl Warren, then District Attorney, the goons did their job too well, and Alberts died. Warren, who as District Attorney had a less libertarian view of trial–by–newspaper than he had later as Chief Justice of the Supreme Court, also saw the Communist Party casting its sinister shadow over the case and referred to King when he discussed the case with reporters as "the communistic leader of the marine firemen's local union."

The arrest and trial of the three men had the classic earmarks of a frame–up. King and Ramsay insisted they were innocent. And while Connor confessed immediately after he was arrested that he had gone aboard the ship and pointed out Alberts to the goons, he later repudiated his confession. With the case of Mooney and Billings fresh in people's minds, the King–Ramsay–Connor affair became a *cause célèbre* in labor and liberal circles on the Coast. Nevertheless, the three men were convicted and sentenced to from five years to life, with the Board of Prison Terms to decide if their sentences should be extended after they had served the five years.

In 1942, after the men had been in prison five years, Governor Olson commuted their sentences to time served. Connor went back to sea, Ramsay took up his job again as port agent for the firemen in San Francisco, and King became a licensed marine engineer and an official of the marine engineers' union.

The warden, uncertain about the propriety of letting his prisoners make the trip to Angel Island, asked the state Attorney General if he had authority to do so. By coincidence, in 1939, the Attorney General was Earl Warren, who as District Attorney had put King and Ramsay in jail in the first place. Warren's answer was "no." Landis solved the problem by taking the hearing to the prison. But before that, the defense called three other witnesses.

The first was Garfield King, Earl's brother, sixtyish, respectable, a successful solicitor and barrister in Vancouver, British Columbia. He had a fascinating story to tell. He testified that one day in February, 1938, he was called on by a U.S. Immigration Service officer named Shearer who was stationed in Vancouver. Shearer had just had a letter from his boss, Raphael Bonham, saying that there was some doubt about Earl King's guilt. If Garfield King could help persuade his brother to make out an affidavit establishing that Bridges was a Communist, Mr. Bonham might be able to use his influence to get Earl pardoned. Senator McNary of Oregon was a friend of Mr. Bonham, Shearer added, and he could use his influence with certain judges. Shearer also told King: "Bonham comes from a distinguished family, [and] has a high reputation for honesty and integrity."

King refused to cooperate. "I had the impression that Shearer regarded his task as dishonorable and was relieved at my refusal," he told the hearing. When Shearer left, King immediately made notes on the conversation. For two weeks, he pondered what he should do about his caller and his disturbing proposal. Then he decided to act. He made out a declaration in the form prescribed in the Canada Evidence Act, had it notarized, and told his brother about it. The prosecution, thrown off stride by King's testimony, did not challenge it.

The next witness was Gwendolyn Ramsay, Ernest Ramsay's wife. Bonham's blackmail attempt having failed with King's brother, Doyle then had asked John Ferguson, who stepped into Ernest Ramsay's union job when Ramsay went to prison, if there might be a way to get to Ramsay. Ferguson told Doyle that the best approach would be through his wife. "She's just a kid," Ferguson said, "and they'd only been married about a year when he went up. She must be pretty lonely." They decided Ferguson should talk to her first. Then he could bring Doyle in.

Gwendolyn Ramsay was only eighteen—"a pretty little girl," Ward describes her—and was living with her mother, when Ferguson, who as far as she knew was a friend of her husband, invited her one day in August, 1937, to come with him to meet a man named Doyle who might be able to help Ramsay. Doyle made her a tantalizing offer. If she would sign a statement saying she knew Harry Bridges was a Party member, Doyle would get her husband out of prison. At the time of the conversation, Ramsay had been in jail a year, and could be facing twenty-five more unless he was lucky. Nevertheless, she refused. "I couldn't sign a statement like that. I don't know that about Bridges," she told Doyle.

When Ferguson finally took her home, Mrs. Ramsay testified, he put the proposal up to her mother, urging her to make Gwendolyn see how sensible it was, and how she could help the government while helping her husband and herself. But Gwendolyn's mother backed up her daughter. "I wouldn't think of letting her do such a thing," she told Ferguson firmly.

A few days after that, Ferguson was back again. Gwendolyn told the hearing that this time he asked her whether she would be willing to go to San Quentin with him and Doyle and Doyle's wife to talk with her husband, even if she wasn't willing to sign a statement herself. She agreed, and they went across the Bay to the prison. When they got there, she noticed that Doyle seemed to know the guard at the gate and the captain where visitors were checked in. She especially noticed that Doyle wasn't required to sign a visitor's card. Later in the hearing, a prison official testified that the general rule was that unless authorized by the warden, visitors were required to sign in at the gate. He knew of no instance, he said, where a man was allowed in to visit a prisoner without signing in. When Ramsay came down to the visitors' room, the Doyles and Ferguson went off by themselves, leaving Ernest and Gwendolyn alone to talk over Doyle's proposal. After a bit Doyle came back and Ramsay told him he wouldn't sign the statement.

Shoemaker was visibly shaken by Mrs. Ramsay's story. "I have no questions," he said when it came his turn to cross–examine. "I couldn't question you," he said to her during the next recess. "You've had enough trouble in your young life, without my adding any more."

Before the hearing moved over to San Quentin, the defense sandwiched in a character witness. One can imagine Landis's curiosity quickening as Grossman qualified him as competent to testify. It was a fellow law school dean, Wayne Morse of the University of Oregon. He was about the same age as Landis, and there were interesting parallels in the careers of the two men. Born and raised on a Wisconsin farm, Morse had gone to the university at Madison, where he was a successful student politician. He stayed on for a master's in speech, then went to Minnesota for his law degree. From there he went on for a doctorate in law at Columbia, taking work in addition with John Dewey and Raymond Moley. In 1931, two years after he went out to Oregon as a lowly assistant professor, he was dean of the law school—the youngest in the country.

Morse, describing himself as a progressive Republican (at the time, Oregon was a one–party Republican state), testified that in 1938, after he had been doing *ad hoc* labor arbitrations for several years, Secretary Perkins appointed him arbitrator for the longshore industry in the Columbia River area. Then, in January, 1939, she promoted him to the top arbitration position for the coast, which made him a kind of one-man longshore industry supreme court, reviewing appeals from decisions of port arbitrators below. At the same time, she made him responsible for arbitrating disputes in the coast's prime trouble spot, San Francisco.

Morse testified that he knew Harry Bridges well, but only in a professional way. Bridges had appeared before him in some twenty to thirty arbitration proceedings and had been a party to ten or fifteen more. He hadn't had any other contact with Bridges. "As I have told the parties to these arbitrations on many occasions," he said gravely, "I look upon an arbitration proceeding as a judicial process entirely." Grossman, who was questioning him, tried persistently to get into the record a statement from Morse that Bridges had a reputation for veracity and trustworthiness. But time after time, Landis ruled that Morse could not answer the question because he would only be giving an opinion, not testifying to a fact. Grossman did succeed, finally, in getting into the record a statement from Morse that he knew from his own observations and from talks with waterfront workers that among the longshoremen, Bridges had a reputation for being truthful.

Grossman now brought up the issue that hung over the hearing and in doing so, provoked the kind of litigious colloquy that mystifies laymen but seemingly conveys meaningful distinctions to lawyers. The issue was: What questions could he ask in order to find out if Morse, on the basis of his own dealings with Bridges, assumed that he was or was not a Communist. "Have you observed any conduct on the part of Harry Bridges," he asked, "as either a witness or as an advocate in any of these arbitration proceedings which would cause you to conclude that he is a member of the Communist Party?"

"That is a matter of opinion again," Landis interrupted before Morse could answer. "If you want to ask whether the witness knows any facts which are relevant to the issue, I have no objection to that."

For once, Landis's ruling seemed unduly legalistic. "I would like to make this plain," Grossman said, his voice showing his puzzlement. "Obviously, I am not asking this question of the witness as a character witness, but with reference now to the record. There is plenty of testimony in the record, based on no facts whatsoever. For instance, there has been evidence offered that Harry Bridges is a Communist based on his conduct, and nothing else. If that evidence is relevant on one side, it should be on the other."

"There is testimony in the record that he is reputed to be a Communist, a great deal of that type of testimony," Landis conceded. "There is testimony of the type that a witness says, 'I know him to be a Communist,' and when the basis of that knowledge is examined in a particular instance, it may turn out that the basis for the witness' inference in that particular case has been the fact that Mr. Bridges supported a particular motion, we will say, to picket the German Embassy, or something of that nature. What is purported to be knowledge in some of these situations has been knowledge based upon an inference drawn from items of that type.

"Now, if you want to ask the witness what knowledge he has upon which he would indulge an inference that he is a member of the Communist Party, or that he is not a member of the Communist Party, what facts he can testify to along that line, I think that is relevant."

Grossman made one more try. "Is there anything about the position taken by Harry Bridges, either as a witness or as an advocate before you, which could cause you to draw the conclusion that he is a member of the Communist Party?"

The law dean in the witness chair turned to the law dean on the bench. "May I answer that?"

"Yes, you may answer."

Morse swung back to Grossman. "No."

The day the hearing party sailed over to San Quentin was warm and cloudless, the bay sparkling in the sun. For a hearing room, the warden let them use the auditorium of the prison guards' recreation building. After lunch, he invited everyone on a tour of the prison, the main attraction being San Quentin's smoke house, as San Quentin inmates call the gas chamber. They all went, except Bridges and Carol King, who waited for the others on the steps of the recreation hall, in the warm sun. "It's too morbid," Bridges said, as the warden led the others away.

Ernest Ramsay was brought down first. He testified that Doyle had told him, "I am connected with the Governor's office in California here, Governor Merriam's office, and with the Governor of Oregon, and with the Immigration Department. We have an affidavit here we want you to sign." Ramsay refused, saying he had no evidence that Bridges was a Communist.

"Maybe we both know that," Doyle countered, "and maybe we

know you're in here on perjured testimony. And maybe there's a couple of other unsolved murders I know about that might just be pinned on you if you don't cooperate."

Ramsay stood fast, and Doyle finally gave up and left.

Earl King was older and a more important figure in the labor movement than Ramsay. Born in Canada in the 1890s, he had been a seaman all his life, a union member since 1920, a naturalized citizen from 1935. At the time of his arrest, he was secretary of the marine firemen's union and Vice-President of the Bay Area Branch of the Maritime Federation. He was honorary President of the Federation at the time he was testifying.

He said that for some reason Doyle had not approached him until two months after Doyle and Ferguson had been to see Ramsay. In the meantime, Ramsay told King about Doyle and Ferguson coming to see him. King was shocked.

"I had heard things about Ferguson," he told the hearing. "I didn't believe them. Ferguson was a man who was somewhat similar to Jimmy Engstrom, whom I had more or less taught the handicraft, you might say, of the officialdom in the trade union movement and who had been, when I was there, a good friend of mine, a good supporter of mine, and who seemed to get along with and agree with me and my trade union viewpoint. I trusted him, and you might say he was my choice to take my office when I was arrested."

When Doyle did get around to calling on him, King was expecting him. "I was the prosecutor in the De Jonge case," Doyle told him (King hadn't heard of it), flashing his gold State of Oregon special agent's badge. "Now, I want to get Mr. Bridges out of the country. I have connections with the right people, and if you'll give testimony that you sat in top fraction meetings with Bridges, in places and dates I'll give you, I'll see that you get out." Without hesitation, King told Doyle he wouldn't do it. Unable to understand King's refusal, Doyle kept after him, threatening him, as he had Ramsay, with being framed for another murder, until King said, "If you want me to, I can explain why I won't do it." "I will be glad to hear why you won't," Doyle replied.

"Well, I am forty-five years of age," King told him. "I have been to a lot of places, and done pretty near everything I wanted to do, had a good time, had good friends. Nobody can make me perjure myself."

At this point, the memory of his encounter with Doyle became too painful for King and he broke off, sobbing audibly. Landis hastily ordered a recess. After a few moments, King nodded to Landis, indicating that he could go on. He and Doyle had talked further, he said, and finally Doyle got up to go.

"He shook hands with me and started off, and he turned back, and he says, 'Say, what has Bridges got on you?'

"I says, 'Bridges hasn't got anything on me.'

" 'Well,' he says, 'what is the matter with you?'

" 'Well,' I says, 'I told you. I am not going to lie,' I says, 'against Harry Bridges just to get out of here.' I says, 'I don't care what happens to me now,' I says, 'I have only got my self–respect left. I am going to keep that. Nobody is going to take it away.'

"So he left."

When the hearing resumed on Angel Island, Carol King called Bridges back for cross–examination. Several government witnesses who had said they were with him in Communist meetings had been meticulously precise about the dates and time of day of the meetings, so she began by having him produce documents establishing that at the very time they said he was with them, he was in a union meeting or some other place where a record of his presence was kept.

He also told about a meeting he'd wanted to attend but hadn't been able to get into. It took place in 1938, when Senator Copeland used his Senate Commerce Committee as a platform from which to label Bridges a Communist. He had gone to Washington, Bridges recalled, loaded with documents: Leech's twenty–six page statement, Garfield King's declaration, statements from WPA workers whom Doyle and Ferguson had hired to pack the meeting of the firemen's union, the letter written by Captain Keegan about Arthur Kent. He even had evidence, although he didn't say how it had come into his hands, showing that the shipowners had made a generous contribution to Senator Copeland after the Senator introduced a bill designed to weaken maritime unions which later failed to pass. Bridges said that he had asked to appear before the committee to defend himself, but Copeland had refused even to let him into the hearing room.

Harper Knowles was brought back for further questioning when Bridges finished. This time, he brought his own lawyer with him. Knowles's lawyer was on his feet almost continuously with objections to Gladstein's questions, but once again Bridges's lawyer extracted from Knowles an uncanny tale. In 1936, he said, he had set up a meeting between Arthur Kent and a Colonel Henry Sanborn to discuss getting evidence against Bridges. Which was the more bizarre, the participants or the setting for their meeting, would be hard to say. Colonel Sanborn was the publisher of *The American Citizen*, an uninhibited rightist tabloid dedicated to exposing the Red menace in labor unions. On the side, he commanded a vigilante army, which he trained in the hills north of San Francisco. The arrangements Knowles made for the Colonel's conversation with Kent were thorough, if unusual. He reserved a room for them in a San Francisco hotel so they could have a private talk, but then, without telling them, he rigged up a bug and connected it to the next room. While Sanborn and Kent compared notes and made their plans, Knowles, accompanied by Larry Doyle, a San Francisco Police captain, and two officers of the Industrial Association, listened in in the next room with a stenographer, who took it all down.

The hearing was starting into its ninth week when Landis declared a holiday to allow Bridges to march in the Labor Day parade. It was a magnificent affair. Thirty thousand CIO marchers, with Bridges at their head, paraded up Market Street from the Ferry Building to the civic center. Just behind Bridges were eight thousand longshoremen, eight abreast, stretching back farther than the eye could see, all wearing the dockworkers' uniform: white caps, hickory shirts, black Frisco jeans. At the civic center where Bridges spoke, his theme was AFL–CIO unity: "Despite certain differences, we know that basically, the objectives of labor unions are the same, and that eventually we will all agree together." Sharing the platform with him was California's liberal governor, Culbert Olson, who talked of the need to liberalize social security, to achieve the widest public ownership of water and power resources, to give the poor a better break under the tax system, and to establish a one–house legislature in California "because the [State] Senate is an undemocratic institution."

AFL unions held a separate meeting on Treasure Island, out in the Bay, where Mayor Rossi told them that their organization had the respect of the American people, implying that the CIO did not. Then he launched into an attack on "subversive influences in labor, radical and un–American leaders, and outright Communists."

In the last week of the hearing, Landis listened to half a dozen more defense witnesses and twice that many put on by the government in rebuttal. The most interesting was Major General David

Prescott Barrows, called by the government as an expert on communism to rebut the testimony of the two Stanford professors.

Barrows was a formidable witness. "Gray, a perfect picture of a military gentleman of the old school," Harry Lang described him in the *San Francisco Examiner*. "He knows Communism, he knows Marxism, he knows Leninism—not only as a pure theorist, as the Stanford professors who testified for the defense, but also from the practical side, as a man who encountered it on its own chosen field —the bloody field of violence!"

Barrows had, indeed, had an extraordinary military career. It began in Mexico in 1911, where he was, he said vaguely, "more or less with the Madero forces." In World War I, military intelligence sent him to Siberia during the Russian Revolution to make an estimate of the military situation there. When he got to Siberia, he attached himself to the White Army. After the Russians signed the treaty of Brest–Litovsk and pulled out of the war, he regarded the Bolsheviks as an enemy, he said, because their leaving the war aided Germany. Then, when the American–British–French–Japanese Expeditionary Forces invaded Siberia to help the White forces put down the Bolsheviks, Barrows stayed on as assistant chief of staff in the intelligence section.

Barrows liked military life and kept up his connections with the army after the war. He said that, when he commanded the guardsmen sent to the waterfront during the 1934 longshoremen's strike, he was a Brigadier General of the Line, a Major General of the Army, commissioned by the President, and a Major General in the National Guard, commissioned by the Governor. "Although this was the largest assembly of any troops that I think ever occurred in the history of this country in a civil disorder," he recalled with pride, "it was successful from the important standpoint that those troops didn't kill a man."

But Barrows was more than just a military man. He was also a professor of political science at the University of California, where he had been teaching, he said, "since 1910 or 1911." He was president of the university from 1919, when he got back from his Siberian adventure, until 1923. He also testified that in the academic year 1933–1934, he taught political science at the university of Berlin.

Barrows's students must have found his lectures stimulating, if a speech he gave to the American Legion three weeks before he took the stand at Angel Island was typical of his style.

"Fifteen hundred delegates to the American Legion convention rose to their feet and tumultuously cheered," the *San Francisco Chronicle* reported, "when Major General David P. Barrows, USA, retired, told them:

" 'To all communists I deliver this message from the American Legion: "If you start any rough stuff, such as you did in Europe, we shall kill you first!" '

"While the California Legionnaires were still shouting their approval," the newspaper went on, "the former President of the University of California continued:

" 'Testimony in the Harry Bridges deportation hearing has brought out the fact that the one secular civilian group standing in the way of the communists is the American Legion. . . .' "

The general's preoccupation with communism was longstanding, and it had led him into some uncouth associations. In 1934, he wrote a manual on communism and how to deal with it for the California Peace Officers' Association. The association, not having enough money in its treasury to publish the manual, turned to friends outside. One was Joseph Roush, the Federal munitions salesman. Roush sold his sales manager on the manual, and Federal put up part of the money. "How much . . . and what effect publication of *Barrows Manual* had on his business," the La Follette Civil Liberties Committee reported, "does not appear in the record."

Barrows's testimony on Angel Island consisted of a long lecture, which he gave without a prepared manuscript, on Marx, Lenin, and the theory and practice of communism. When he finished, Landis summarized Barrows's view of Communist tactics as consisting of three stages: "First, the softening of the mechanism of the state—causing disaffection in the armed forces, for example; second, taking advantage of some crisis such as defeat in war, or a severe economic depression; and third, taking over the state as the opportunity arises."

"Would you say," Grossman asked, "that such a thing as a general strike, in the setting that it occurred in in 1934, was part of the softening–up process that you have been discussing?"

"Well, no," Barrows answered. "I would say that a general strike . . . was a poor instrument to use for the softening–up process, because it invariably irritates and prejudices public opinion.

"But I would say that the general strike, if one is to be called, should be the immediate prelude to the supreme act of violence itself, the seizure of political power, and if it is called prematurely, why, your Communist leadership, your Communist general staff, have just made a mistake, as I think they made in San Francisco."

Bridges's attorneys then asked Barrows another line of questions.

"Did you know a White Guard General named Semeonoff?"

"Yes," Barrows replied. "I met him in Mongolia, when he was organizing an anti-Bolshevik force."

"Are you aware that officers of the 27th U.S. Infantry, when they were in Siberia, sent in reports criticizing him for unnecessary brutality?"

"Well, yes," Barrows answered.

"And after the revolution, when Semeonoff was being kept out of the U.S. on the ground that he was an undesirable alien [he was not allowed in, and went to live in Japan], and the lawyer trying to get him in asked you for an estimate of his military behavior, what was your answer?"

"I stated that the war methods of Semeonoff were extremely rough," Barrows replied, "were repugnant, but they were no more repugnant than the war methods of almost any other military commander on either side engaged in the highly irregular warfare that went on in Siberia during the period that I was there."

The defense did not pursue this line of questioning, but one might hope that General Barrows erred in his estimate of Semeonoff's methods as typical. Major General William S. Graves, who commanded the American forces in Siberia, refers to Semeonoff in *America's Siberian Adventure* as "a murderer, robber, and a most dissolute scoundrel." Indeed, reading Graves, one gets the feeling that as he thought back over his experiences when he was writing the book in 1930, he was still choking with rage at the memory of having been on the same side with Semeonoff. Sprinkled through his account are a half–dozen grisly descriptions of atrocities carried out under the personal direction of the general. One was, "the almost unbelievable murder of an entire village by Semeonoff. When his troops reached the village, the inhabitants apparently tried to escape by flight from their homes, but the Semeonoff soldiers shot them down, men, women, and children, as if they were hunting rabbits, and left their bodies where they were killed. They shot, not one, but everyone in the village.

". . . four or five bodies of men were found who were evidently burned alive."

As the campaign against the Bolsheviks progressed, Graves reported, "Semeonoff established what were known as his 'killing stations' and . . . openly boasted that he could not sleep at night when he had not killed someone during the day."

Inevitably, Americans clashed with Semeonoff when his pursuit of Bolsheviks carried him into areas U.S. soldiers were responsible for. On one of these forays, he was so enraged when U. S. soldiers guarding a railroad depot refused to turn the station-master over to him that he ordered his men to shoot up their thirty–eight–man outpost in the middle of the night. Happily, his troops were less accurate against targets who could shoot back than against unarmed peasants. Semeonoff's raiders were repulsed with heavy losses, while the Americans suffered only two casualties, one killed and one wounded.

How Landis reacted to Barrows is impossible to tell. Having decided, when it came time to write this report, that the government had not proved Bridges was a member affiliated with the Party, he did not comment on Barrows's testimony nor on that of any of the other witnesses who testified on the question of whether or not Communists advocated overthrowing the government by force.

Toward the end of the morning on September 11th—almost two months to the day from when the hearing began—Landis observed that Doyle had wired that he was on his way to San Francisco, but it would be several days before he could get there.

"Inasmuch as it has become imperative for me to return to my business," Landis continued, ". . . I wish to put this on the record: that if it had not been for Mr. Doyle's complete disregard of the proprieties of the law this hearing would have been over prior to this time.

"But in the light of Mr. Doyle's record," Landis went on, his annoyance mounting, "a record, with my naive ideas about the importance of citizens observing the processes of the law in this country, I believe unpatriotic in the extreme, it is impossible for me to continue this hearing until such time as Mr. Doyle chooses to appear. . . ."

Landis then announced that John G. Clarkson, an old friend of his from the Securities and Exchange Commission would preside over the hearing when Doyle arrived. When Doyle testified, the hearing would be closed, even to the reporters who'd been covering it on Angel Island. Because Doyle's testimony would be part of the record, anyone interested could read it, Landis said, after his report was filed.

Landis reminded the attorneys that he had ruled out the usual summing–up by each side at the close of the hearing, but that they should submit briefs. He told them he especially wanted analyses of the meaning of "affiliation" as used in immigration law, and a complete collection of all the decisions in existence holding that the Communist Party advocated overthrowing the government by force and violence, and all those holding to the contrary.

"The briefs are to be submitted six weeks from today," he instructed the lawyers as he concluded the hearing. "I expect it will take me about a month after that to make my report."

Heading back to Harvard and the relative calm of the campus, Landis could look back with pride on his two months in San Francisco. He had presided over a hearing which in other hands could easily have degenerated into a kangaroo court, like the trials of Sacco and Vanzetti, Mooney and Billings, and the Wobblies. Instead, as a San Francisco newspaper said editorially after he left:

"Both the prosecution and the defense paid tribute to Dean James M. Landis for his conduct of the Harry Bridges deportation inquiry. They agreed that he gave a full and fair hearing. . . .

"A man of Supreme Court caliber, he brought to the hearings a rich philosophy of what American justice means, he held both sides to the issues and he was eminently fair."

The hearing took a one–day holiday after Landis left. Doyle had arrived in San Francisco, but he was tied up in court most of the day. In the morning, he went to the Hall of Justice to surrender and post bail in Municipal Court on a charge of assault and battery that had been hanging over him for more than a year, since an incident which occurred in April, 1938, when some anti–Nazis were picketing outside the German Consulate. Ernest Besig, secretary of the Northern California Branch of the American Civil Liberties Union, had been standing by with a camera in case anybody assaulted the pickets when Doyle, six–feet–four and heavily built, arrived on the scene with a police captain and proceeded to push the pickets toward a paddy wagon. Noticing that Besig was taking his picture, he rushed over, wrestled the camera away from Besig and opened it, spoiling the film. He then spied a *San Francisco News* photographer shooting his attack on Besig, so he knocked him down too.

From the Hall of Justice, Doyle went over to Federal Judge A. F. St. Sure's court where he spent several hours explaining why he had ignored the subpoena to appear at the hearing.

On the thirteenth of September, the sessions resumed in the Post Office Building in San Francisco, with Clarkson in the chair. Doyle was on hand with his lawyer, but he made it plain from the outset that he was going to be a prickly witness. For two and a half days, he kept the hearing in an uproar, refusing to take the stand until the defense, who had subpoenaed him, gave him a check covering his travel expenses and compensating him for the money he claimed he was losing by being kept away from his law practice.

He and Bridges's counsel weren't able to agree on the size of the check, and he vehemently refused to take the stand at their request. Finally, Clarkson turned to Shoemaker: "As long as Mr. Doyle is here, do you want to use him as a government witness?"

"No."

"Whereupon," the court reporter recorded, "at 4:30 p.m., the hearing in the above matter was concluded."

The nine–and–a–half–week hearing produced some impressive statistics. The government called thirty–two witnesses; the defense, twenty–nine (thirty, if you count Doyle). The government put in evidence 138 exhibits; the defense, 136. Interrogation of witnesses by Bridges's attorneys filled 4,324 pages of the 7,724–page transcript, interrogation by lawyers for the government another 2,900, and Landis's questions and comments took up the remaining five hundred.

How much all this cost the taxpayers is anybody's guess, but in November, Bridges's defense committee published the results of an audit of its books. "They may say that Harry Bridges is a Red," Estolv Ward, the committee chairman, remarked as he gave the story to the newspapers, "but his defense committee is in the black."

The committee had received $32,253.13 in contributions and spent $28,424.16, winding up with a surplus of $3,828.97, which it turned back to the longshoremen's locals. Legals costs were $16,322, publicity $6,476, administrative expenses $5,625. A lot of money, but peanuts compared to what Bridges's next three trials were to cost. And a bargain price for the quality of legal service he'd had.

When Landis had left San Francisco in September, he had estimated that he would file his report around November 20th. He was much too optimistic. It took him, not one month, but more than two, to finish it. And no wonder. When it was published by the government printing office in its final form, it was a medium–sized book of 152 pages. He sent it to Secretary of Labor Perkins on December 28th.

"The evidence" Landis concluded, "establishes neither that

Harry R. Bridges is a member of nor affiliated with the Communist Party of the United States of America."

NOTES

Kethenen v. *Reimer* is reported in 79 F 2d 315 (1935).

The description of the business and industrial membership of the Associated Farmers is in La Follette Committee, *Report, Part V*, p. 741.

Cox's speech to the San Francisco longshoremen's union, in which he compared himself with Christ, is in the *Proceedings* of the first convention of the ILWU (1938), pp. 149–152.

My description of the destruction of John Ferguson's career in the firemen's union is pieced together from Landis's *Final Report*; the September 17, 1937 *Waterfront Bulletin*, a CIO longshoremen's union paper published in San Francisco; and the December 8, 1938 *San Francisco Chronicle*.

The brief sketch of Morse's career is based upon Arthur R. Smith's biography of the Senator, *The Tiger in the Senate*.

7

A Bill of Pains and Penalties

The [Bridges] issue was one of those night-
mare contests between the government and an
individual that never seem to end.
FRANCIS BIDDLE, in
In Brief Authority

EARLY IN THE AFTERNOON of December 30, 1939, one of Bridges's friends called him from Washington to say that Landis had acquitted him. Bridges was delighted but not really surprised. Observing Landis during the hearing, he had become convinced the dean didn't believe the government's parade of witnesses. And then, when he had been on the stand and Landis had engaged him in those long philosophical discussions, he had become equally certain that the admiration he felt for Landis was mutual. Nonetheless, the verdict obviously called for a celebration, so Bridges rounded up a few friends from his office and set out for North Beach.

They were happily toasting his victory in a Broadway bistro when a reporter who had just picked up the news from one of the wire services burst in. "What are you going to do now?" he asked breathlessly.

"What I've been doing right along," Bridges replied. "I intend to do whatever I can to improve the conditions of the working class of this country, and I hope that now this red herring has been worn out by its frequent dragging across the trail."

But the red herring was still very much alive, as Byron Darnton, a *New York Times* reporter, discovered when he came out to San Francisco a few weeks later to do a story on Bridges. "Despite the Landis hearing, he is still being called a Communist," Darnton wrote on Feb. 25, 1940. "Mayor Rossi of San Francisco so labeled him recently in—of all places—a formal message on the subject of the municipal budget. Walk through a hotel lobby with him and you hear whispers of 'there's Harry Bridges,' and you see faces that look as though they were gazing at the devil."

But Bridges was less a devil than an enigma, Darnton concluded. Here is his description of him:

Harry Bridges talks at the rate of two hundred words a minute, has a lot of mannerisms reminiscent of Jimmy Walker [the elegant bon vivant who had been mayor of New York a few years earlier], drinks bourbon (but not too much of it), hates bosses, has a lively spring in his step and a belligerent hunch to his shoulders, punctuates his statements with a long finger, a soup spoon, a pencil or whatever else is handy, and says he believes that democracy is the way to social salvation.

Making a point, Bridges would wink an eye exaggeratedly and grin with one side of his face, in the Jimmy Walker manner. Or give a sudden hitch to one shoulder in unconscious imitation of the same model. His eyes are blue and fast moving, his thin nose rides his face like a figurehead on an old windjammer, he sits in a chair not as though he were resting but as though he were always about to spring instantly to his feet. . . .

Six years later, when he interviewed Bridges for *Inside USA*, John Gunther had the same reaction: "The person Harry Renton Bridges most reminded me of was Jimmy Walker, strange as that may seem. Lean, boyish, alert, with a hawklike humor and a touch of the dapper—also a touch of city streets—Bridges resembles in several respects the former mayor of New York. He is, however, not a playboy. He hasn't the time."

All in all, Darnton's picture of Bridges was highly flattering. Even so, his story was a good example of the pabulum the red herring fed on:

"The longshore leader," Darnton declared,

has a very warm spot in his heart for Russia. He has read Marx, Engels, Lenin, and the present Soviet Constitution. That constitution, he says, is a democratic document. To the argument that its democratic professions are observed in the breach, he replies that it still contains the promise of a better world.

"Along the waterfront," he says, "we've got guys that can sling any language. When the Soviet ships come over here, we see that they look clean. The seamen wear clothes that aren't very good, and their food isn't so hot, but our guys talk to them, and they're satisfied. They move about on shore freely, and they don't spread no tales of disaster at home."

When Darnton asked Bridges how he felt about the lack of civil liberties in Russia, Bridges's answer brought to mind a Roman Catholic who reels off repulsive facts of his church's history without hesitation because he distinguishes between the church militant, which is of this world and shares its imperfections, and the church triumphant, which is perfect, as we shall all see if we live long enough: "Look," Bridges said, "the Russian experiment is only twenty years old, and that isn't half an hour on the history clock."

It was remarks like that that helped produce reactions to the Landis decision ranging from shocked disbelief to suspicions that maybe Landis, himself, was a leftist. "I had thousands of letters on the decision," Landis said in his oral history, "maybe one in fifty complimenting me on it. The other forty–nine would be addressed to: 'You God-damned Communist,' 'You God-damned Jew,' 'You so-and-so,' etc. . . .

"Of course, the Congress thought it was terrible . . ."

So, it seems, did the White House. Before Angel Island, it had been rumored that Landis was headed for the Supreme Court. Afterward, doors in Washington that had been open to him quietly closed, and the appointment never came. He stayed on at Harvard until 1946, when President Truman asked him if he would come to Washington to head the Civil Aeronautics Board. Landis, delighted to get back into public service, accepted at once, but before a year was out, Truman unceremoniously fired him.

Landis then went to work for Joseph Kennedy, helping run the far–flung Kennedy business operations. It was a lucrative job, but it was a comedown for a New Deal crusader like Landis, for his new boss was something of a buccaneer. ("Joe Kennedy told me many years ago when he was chairman of the U. S. Maritime Commission, and we were kicking the gong around over some waterfront matter," Bridges has said, " 'One rule always to remember,' says Joe, 'is, don't get caught.' One thing about Joe Kennedy, he laid it straight out. No hypocritical double–talk there. I always admired him for it, too.")

Landis had been working for the Kennedy enterprises for fourteen years when John F. Kennedy, his boss's second son, entered the White House. Rumors had been circulating persistently that under Kennedy's predecessor, federal regulatory agencies had fallen into the hands of men more concerned with protecting the businesses they were supposed to regulate than they were with safeguarding the public interest, and the new President asked Landis to investigate them. Landis threw himself into the task with enthusiasm and produced a report uncompromisingly condemning the heads of a half–dozen agencies for engaging in unethical practices.

The beginning of the end came not long after, when Landis himself was accused by the Internal Revenue Service of an unethical practice—he had failed to pay income taxes on $360,000 he had received from 1956 through 1960. Victor Navasky has explained how it happened in *Kennedy Justice*:

> In the mid–Fifties James Landis' daughter and her husband both contracted polio. He brought them to New York and put them in the Rusk Institute for rehabilitation. He needed money, so he sold some stock which he had inherited from his mother in the 1920s. The total value of the stock was $3,700. When he went to file his return he found he didn't know the cost basis of the stock, so instead of making up a number or putting zero, he obtained a ninety–day extension and wrote to the Boston attorney who had represented his mother and who told him *she* had inherited it from his father—so Landis applied for a second extension.
>
> He got jammed up that summer and just didn't apply for the next extension. The following year he prepared a new return, but one of the questions on the return form is always: Did you file a return for last year? He wasn't going to say yes and he was afraid to say no. So he put the return aside and repeated the procedure every year through 1960, always computing how much it was going to be and putting the money aside in his checking account.

Hauled into court, Landis pleaded guilty, offering the explanation that he had been so engrossed in public affairs that he had forgotten to file the returns until the tax people called him. Then, he said, he had made a full settlement, paying $94,492, about one–fourth of which was penalties for late payment and interest charges. He was found guilty, nevertheless.

When Landis appeared in court a month later to be sentenced, the judge, visibly moved by the sight of Landis sitting at the defense table, frail and haggard, said he recognized that Landis was a sick man who needed medical attention rather than punishment.

"Passing sentence upon you is not a pleasant task," he went on. "But I can't let you go without the imposition of some small sentence. I must give you some time, not for punishment but to give you an opportunity to reflect and straighten yourself out." He gave him thirty days, to be spent in the Federal Public Health Service hospital on Staten Island, where he was to receive psychiatric treatment. Less than a year later, Landis was found dead in the swimming pool of his home in Westchester County, the victim, the coroner ruled after an autopsy, of accidental drowning.

While the White House's disapproval of Landis's decision was tacit, the House of Labor's was explicit. "The decision is not in accordance with the facts," AFL President William Green was quoted in the press as saying. "Everybody knows Harry Bridges is a Communist."

It was not surprising that the decision was unpopular in many places, considering the widespread propagation of the belief that Bridges was a Communist, and it was also to be expected that before long someone in Congress would propose a final solution to the Bridges question. It turned out to be A. Leonard Allen, an obscure congressman from Louisiana, who, on May 14, 1940 introduced a bill to send Bridges into exile. It consisted of exactly fifty words: "Be it enacted, etc., that the Secretary of Labor be, and is hereby authorized and directed to take into custody and deport to Australia, the country of which he is a citizen or subject, the alien, Harry Renton Bridges, in the manner provided by sections 155 and 156, title 8, United States Code."

The committee on immigration, to which the Allen Bill was referred decided that it was such an excellent way to dispose of Bridges that it wouldn't be necessary either to hold hearings on it or to allow Bridges to give the committee his side of the story. They discussed the bill briefly among themselves, then reported back to the House that it should pass. It came up for debate on June 13th.

Twenty–one congressmen spoke in favor of the bill, sixteen against. Vito Marcantonio of New York led the opposition, at one point reading a seven–page letter from Bridges rebutting the charges against him that had been falling like rain in Congress and in the newspapers. "Bridges was not given any hearing before the committee on immigration," Marcantonio explained as he asked to be allowed time to read it. "He was not permitted to appear before the rules committee. . . .

"We all know the real reason for this attempted deportation of

Bridges. Bridges organized the workers on the West Coast and made the labor exploiters pay decent wages. Now, taking advantage of the war hysteria, these same exploiters seek his deportation and use Congress for this foul job."

The House had been debating the bill for two hours when Congressman Van Zandt of Illinois, fearful that a Roosevelt–appointed Attorney General would find a loophole in the Allen Bill which would let Bridges stay in the country, offered an amendment. Strike out the words after the *Be it enacted, etc.,* he proposed, and put these in their place: "That notwithstanding any other provision of law, the Attorney General be, and is hereby, authorized and directed to take into custody forthwith and deport to Australia, the country of which he is a citizen or subject, the alien, Harry Renton Bridges, whose presence in this country the Congress deems hurtful."

As offensive to the Constitution as the Allen Bill was, there was never any doubt about the outcome. Speakers for it were loudly applauded, speakers against greeted with silence. After two hours of debate, the House voted 330 for to forty–two against. One of the yeas was cast by a congressman from Texas who in 1964 had Bridges's enthusiastic support for the Presidency. His name was Lyndon Baines Johnson.

June, 1940, was a bleak month for Bridges, in more ways than one. On June 13th, the day the House passed the Allen Bill, President Roosevelt ordered the Immigration Service taken out of Frances Perkins's hands and placed in the Justice Department so that control over aliens could be tightened. Two weeks later, on June 28th, Congress amended the deportation law by adding Section 23 to the Alien Registration Act of 1940, commonly known as the Smith Act. Before the vote, Sam Hobbs of Alabama, who sponsored Section 23, gave his colleagues the word on what it meant (his remarks are in the *Congressional Record*, volume 86, p. 9031):

It is my joy to announce that this bill will do, in a perfectly legal and constitutional manner, what the bill specifically aimed at the deportation of Harry Bridges seeks to accomplish. This bill changes the law so that the Department of Justice should now have little trouble in deporting Harry Bridges and all others of similar ilk. . . .

. . . after this bill becomes law, it will be perfectly clear that any alien who has ever been a member of such an organization before coming to this country cannot enter, or if at the time of

his entry or at any time thereafter he has been, even for one minute, a member of such an organization he shall be deported.

When Hobbs finished, there were a few cursory questions about
other sections of the bill. Only one Congressman, Marcantonio,
spoke against it. The House waited him out and then voted, 382 to
four, for its adoption.

Not long after Congress passed the Smith Act, Theodore Dreiser,
interviewing Bridges for an article in *Friday* magazine, asked him,
"What is the best you can say for America? Do you still like it?"
"Yes," Bridges replied.

It's pretty hard to find a country that's better. First of all, the
people in this country are generally very fair, generally very honest and decent; and we have proved that, despite many things.
Take my own case, for example: despite six years of pounding by
the organized press all over the nation, we are still alive and
going, and gaining ground as far as organizing is concerned,
which proves if you can get to the American people, and present
both sides to them, they will always decide right. . . .

The only reason the complaint against me of non–citizenship
gains any headway with the people at large is because my enemies use the inherent sense of fairness in the people in order to
deceive them. Their whole appeal to the American people is:
"He hasn't taken out citizenship papers—why hasn't he? The
least he could do if he cared to be an American would be to do
that!" It's put to the American people in an unfair light.

For really, the American people don't care about my nationality. But they do care about my seeming indifference to becoming
an American, solely because they are made to think it's an unfair
attitude on my part.

Passage of the Smith Act put the U.S. Attorney General, Robert
Jackson, in a quandary. Almost immediately, he began getting
pressure from the Congress to use Section 23 to get rid of Bridges,
but, like Frances Perkins, he was far from convinced he should act.
"This alien has been accused, investigated, and tried at great
length, and judgment has been rendered that he had been proved
not guilty of the charges against him," Jackson wrote the Senate
Committee on Immigration in August, 1940. But, the committee reminded him, that was under the old ground rules. The Smith Act
had changed all that. So, reluctantly, Jackson told J. Edgar Hoo-

ver, Director of the Federal Bureau of Investigation, to go ahead
with an investigation to see if Bridges was now deportable.

Hoover, whose interest in radicalism dated from World War I
when he was in charge of the Palmer Raids, had none of Jackson's
reluctance. Taking personal charge, on August 16, 1940, he flew out
to San Francisco for a week, inviting any one who had information
about Bridges to talk with him at his hotel:

"Our agents were put to work in Seattle, Portland, San Francisco, Los Angeles and San Diego a few minutes after we got the
order," he told reporters when he arrived.

"The investigation will seek to establish whether there is new or
additional evidence which would warrant the bringing or re-open-
ing of deportation charges against Bridges.

"This investigation is the first of its kind since 1919, when I was
in charge of the agents that investigated Emma Goldman. She was
deported."

The FBI spent three months on the investigation, and in December, 1940, Hoover sent the Attorney General his report. It was supposed to be highly confidential, but Hoover, always eager to exploit
the publicity value of an FBI achievement, couldn't resist leaking
its conclusion to the newspapers. "Our investigation shows beyond
a doubt," he told them, "that Bridges is a Red."

Under these circumstances, most men would have kept quiet
about controversial political matters. Not Bridges. In April, 1940,
in his address to the longshoremen's convention, he had attacked
the Roosevelt Administration on a variety of counts: FDR appointed William Leiserson to the NLRB, he charged, "to do a job
against the CIO . . ." The Justice Department was accusing unions of being monopolies and of violating the antitrust laws. The
Maritime Commission was by-passing ILWU longshore hiring
halls when its government-owned ships hired men to load cargoes
in West Coast ports. The President was even proposing that Congress cut back appropriations for relief. Worst of all, he declared,
Roosevelt was leading the country toward war, a war, Bridges asserted, "in which [America] can have no concern except the protection of investments of the large bankers and industrial interests
of the country." The CIO, Bridges concluded, was withholding support for a third term from FDR, and he urged the longshoremen to
wait and see what John L. Lewis was going to do before they endorsed anybody for the Presidency.

Then, a few days before the Presidential election, Bridges again attacked Roosevelt. He had just returned from Washington, where John L. Lewis, a major FDR supporter in 1936, had told him he had decided to endorse Wendell Wilkie, the Republican candidate, in 1940. Lewis had said that if CIO members voted for Roosevelt he would interpret that as a repudiation of his leadership, and he would resign from the CIO presidency.

"The most important job for labor," Bridges said to a CIO meeting when he got back to the Coast, "is to see that John L. Lewis remains as head of the CIO . . .

"A lot of people think the New Deal is a friend of mine, that it has kept me in this country. I've stayed in this country because of the trade union movement and John L. Lewis. The New Deal doesn't like me and wants to get rid of me—and soon will if I haven't got the support of organized labor and its leaders. If I haven't got that, I'm through. . . .

"Support of President Roosevelt," he concluded, "is one of the most foolish things a union man or woman can contemplate. I'm as positive as I can be that immediately after the election the blitzkrieg on labor will start."

From his first days as president of the union, Bridges's political pronouncements had provided his critics with plenty of ammunition to use against him. This was one of his most unpopular statements. Most of the locals in the union, despite Bridges's criticism of the President and the convention decision to wait and see what Lewis would do, had already endorsed FDR on their own. Several, including three of the largest on the Coast, hurriedly called special meetings to demand that Bridges resign.

"I'll stick to my belief that President Roosevelt and the New Deal administration have betrayed labor," he fired back.

"I didn't endorse Willkie. I took no public position on the election. I have stood, and I stand now, behind John L. Lewis. . . .

"The union constitution provides for a petition [signed by 15 percent of the membership] to recall the president, and I believe the question of my resignation or of being removed will be determined through that procedure."

The storm blew over as abruptly as it had come up when the union's national executive board, meeting at the height of the controversy, gave Bridges a vote of confidence. Presidential politics was not his major concern at the time, anyway, for he had been preoccupied with getting a new longshore agreement which was finally signed, after sixteen months of negotiations, on December 20, 1940.

Now, one might have thought, he could settle back and relax for a while.

He was able to, for about six weeks. Then, on February 12, 1941, Attorney General Jackson, acting on the FBI report and the new law, issued a warrant for his arrest and deportation. The grounds were essentially the same as those in the 1938 warrant, but this time, the government spread its net even wider than before. As before, there were four charges. The first two were identical with the first two in the earlier warrant. They charged that he had been a member of, or affiliated with, an organization that believes in, advises, advocates, or teaches the overthrow of the government; and that he had been a member of an organization that causes to be written and circulated printed matter advising the overthrow of the government.

What this meant, though the prosecution didn't tell him so until the hearing was underway, was that he was charged with having been a member of the Communist Party (it came out in the hearing that the government believed he joined in 1932 and was still a member in 1941), the Marine Workers' Industrial Union, the International Labor Defense, and the Trade Union Unity League.

The next two charges, which had not been brought against him in 1938, were designed to make his brief membership in the IWW a justification for banishing him. These were that he had been a member of an organization which advised, advocated, or taught the unlawful damage, injury or destruction of property and sabotage; and that he had been a member of an organization that caused to be written and circulated printed matter advocating those acts.

The hearing began on March 31, 1941, in the San Francisco Post Office Building. This time, it was open to the public. The hearing officer, again a man from outside the federal government, was Charles B. Sears. "All we could learn about Sears in advance was that he had been a conservative judge on the New York State appellate court," Aubrey Grossman said of him. "We found out in the hearing that he was a conservative, all right, technically as well as politically."

Bridges was represented by the same lawyers who had defended him on Angel Island: Carol King, Richard Gladstein and Aubrey Grossman. On the government side, the courtly, soft–spoken Shoemaker had been replaced by Albert Del Guercio, a Justice Department lawyer from Los Angeles, a man so dedicated to his task and so excitable that several times during his chronic wrangles with the defense he accused Gladstein of being a Communist.

He may have thought the hearing a two–and–a–half–month wrestling match with the devil; on the last day, when Judge Sears asked if he had anything more to say, he stood silent, his eyes shut. "Is something the matter, Mr. Del Guercio?" the judge asked. "I was just saying a prayer, your Honor."

Three Justice Department lawyers from Washington, D. C. took the places of Bonham, Norene and Phelan. And in place of the thirty–two witnesses who had testified on Angel Island, the government had found thirty–two brand new ones.

"You know," Landis said in his oral history, "in all these subsequent trials of Bridges, one amusing thing was, no witness for the government that was ever called before me eve. appeared again. The government never called them, just never dared call them."

As before, the identity of the witnesses was kept from the defense until the government put them on the stand, and so, once more, the trunk full of dossiers had to be carried in and out of the courtroom at the beginning and end of each session.

At the outset, the Sears hearing was drearily *déjà vu.* The presiding officer asked if Bridges were present, the prosecutor called him to the stand for some routine questions (Bridges's down–under accent proved too much for the court reporter, who spelled his mother's maiden name D–o–i–g–a–n), and Carol King made a long opening statement. But the similarity with Angel Island ended there.

This time, Miss King began by invoking *res judicata,* the legal principle that a matter once decided is not to be tried over again. "Is Mr. Bridges to be retried," she asked, "each time his enemies dig up some new witnesses against the CIO?" She got nowhere with *res judicata,* for Judge Sears ruled that this hearing was actually a different proceeding from the 1939 one, with a broader charge based on a new law, with new witnesses and new evidence.

By the same reasoning, he disposed of her contention that Bridges was being placed in double jeopardy: "No jeopardy at all is involved," he explained, "for that word has application only to prosecutions of a criminal nature. An order of deportation is but the revocation of a privilege, voluntarily granted." She was wrong, also, he added, in thinking that Section 23 of the Smith Act was an *ex post facto* law and therefore offensive to the Constitution. The constitutional bar against *ex post facto* laws applies only, he ruled, to criminal statutes.

Bridges's attorneys got no further with still another constitutional objection, that the broadened charge denied him equal protection of the laws. Since 1920, they pointed out, no one had been deported for being a Wobbly. Nor, since 1934, had membership in the Marine Workers Industrial Union, the International Labor Defense, or the Trade Union Unity League been grounds for deportation. To Judge Sears, the objection was irrelevant. What the Labor Department may have thought about these organizations, he ruled, would have no effect upon the hearing he was conducting.

The government thereupon called to the stand a succession of witnesses whose testimony about Bridges's Communist ties was reminiscent of Leech, Sapiro, Detrich, and the others the government had used on Angel Island. Judge Sears disregarded the testimony of all but two, either because it was irrelevant or hearsay, or because it was internally contradictory, bereft of credibility.

One whose story did impress the judge was James O'Neil, the government's seventeenth witness. A former marine fireman, he had been publicity director for the West Coast CIO in 1937, when Bridges was regional director. As soon as O'Neil was sworn in, Del Guercio announced that although O'Neil was being called by the prosecution, he was going to treat him as hostile, thereby making it possible, under courtroom rules, for the prosecutor to ask him leading questions. According to Del Guercio, O'Neil had first told the FBI he knew Bridges was a Communist, then had repudiated everything he had told them and refused to testify in the hearing. To get him on the stand, they had had to ask a federal judge to order him to appear.

The prosecutor took from the table a long statement he said O'Neil had made in the San Francisco FBI office in October, 1940, in the presence of two FBI men and a stenographer, who, he said, had taken it all down in shorthand. Reading a sentence of the statement at a time, Del Guercio paused after each one and asked O'Neil if he had told the FBI men what had just been read. No, O'Neil answered, sentence after sentence, for more than an hour.

According to the statement, O'Neil had admitted joining the Party in 1936. Then the prosecutor read a crucial paragraph:

". . . [in 1937] I walked into Bridges's office, it always being my privilege to do so after first having assured myself that he was alone, and on his desk was a new Party book . . . into which Bridges was putting assessment stamps. . . . I expressed amazement that he was doing this openly with the book in plain view on top of his desk; however, he nonchalantly continued to put the stamps in place and then returned the book to his pocket. I knew this was a Communist Party book because I had one myself and it was just like it. . . ."

"Did you tell the FBI agents that?" Del Guercio asked.

"No, I did not," O'Neil answered firmly.

The prosecutor took up another statement, which he said was an account of what O'Neil had said when he was called down to the FBI office a second time, a few days before he was called to testify in the hearing. As before, Del Guercio claimed a stenographer was on hand, as were himself and two men who had come out from Washington to make sure there weren't any slip–ups in the prosecution's case: Major Lemuel B. Schofield, who now headed the Immigration Service, and Hoover's number two man in the FBI, Assistant Director E. J. Connelley. Again, taking O'Neil through the statement sentence by sentence, Del Guercio told Sears that O'Neil had given the men from Washington the same story he had told local FBI agents several months earlier. And just as firmly as before, O'Neil denied having done so.

When Grossman cross–examined him, O'Neil said that FBI agents had several times come to his home and to the radio station where he worked as a newscaster, and that the station manager had asked who they were. "He made the remark that if I knew anything I should go down [to the FBI office] and I could become the biggest figure on the West Coast by 'turning in' Harry Bridges," O'Neil recalled. It was not long after that that he was called down to FBI headquarters for a second session. Before going, he told Bridges. "Harry laughed when I told him what had happened," he remembered. "He said, 'The only thing to do is to go down and tell them the truth. You have nothing to worry about.' " Bridges then asked him, he said, if he would like to go to work for the Bridges Defense Committee. He said no, thanks, he had a good job with the radio station.

At the FBI office, O'Neil said, he told Schofield, Connelley and Del Guercio that he had nothing to add to the government's case, so they wouldn't gain anything by having him testify in the hearing. Furthermore, merely going on the stand as a government witness would blacken his name in the labor movement. Therefore, he wasn't going to testify. The next day, he said, the manager of the radio station fired him with the remark, "We don't care to have in our employ a man who's been associated with Bridges."

After O'Neil's testimony, the government called two witnesses to

corroborate its version. First was Gertrude Segerstrom, the FBI stenographer, who read from her shorthand notes the October, 1940,
statement which she said O'Neil had dictated to her. "Was Mr.
O'Neil asked to sign your notes, or the statement after you typed
it?" Grossman asked when he cross–examined her. "I don't know,"
she answered. Next was Major Schofield, who testified that in the
session at the FBI office where he, Connelley and Del Guercio were
present, O'Neil had volunteered the assertion that he was the only
man who had visual evidence that Bridges was a Communist. "We
asked him what he meant by that," Schofield said, "and he said
that on one occasion he had actually seen Bridges pasting dues
stamps in Bridges's membership book in the Communist Party."
Then, Schofield recalled, when O'Neil said he wouldn't testify in
the hearing, they served a subpoena on him then and there.

What was Sears to believe? Had O'Neil been pressured by the
FBI into giving false statements in their office, which he then repudiated, under oath, on the stand? Or had he, as Segerstrom's and
Schofield's testimony suggested, freely told the FBI what he knew,
and then, for reasons of his own, decided to deny it all? And what
about Bridges's denial of the dues stamp scene, when Bridges testified later? Judge Sears decided to believe Segerstrom and
Schofield. "If their testimony is not true," he wrote in his report to
the Attorney General, "there has been a dastardly attempt to deceive me as Presiding Inspector, by false testimony . . . and if I
were to believe that O'Neil was 'framed', or his declarations fal-
sified, I should look with suspicion upon the entire case presented
by the Government."

The most significant testimony against Bridges was not the government's version of the O'Neil story but an incident recounted by
Bridges's enemy, Harry Lundeberg, who was produced by the government at the end of the long hearing, just two days before it adjourned. Lundeberg testified that in the summer of 1935, he was a
dinner guest at Bridges's house, the only time he was ever there, in
the company of Bridges's wife, stepson and daughter. Norma
Perry, then Bridges's secretary, and Sam Darcy were also there. At
one point when the three men were alone, Lundeberg said, Darcy
asked him to join the Communist Party, assuring him his membership could be kept secret if he wanted it that way. "I told him I
wasn't interested," Lundeberg testified, "and Bridges says, 'You
don't have to worry, because I am one too.' "

Under cross–examination, Lundeberg said that in 1939, while
the Angel Island hearing was going on, Shoemaker had come to his

office to ask him to testify. He had refused, telling the prosecutor he didn't have any information as to whether Bridges was a Communist or not. At the time, he wrote in his union's newspaper, the *West Coast Sailor*: "I never was and never intend to become involved in the Bridges deportation mess, nor to my knowledge do any of the people I work with in the union field.

"I also want to state for the record that so far as deporting Bridges is concerned, I am opposed to it. . . . Union labor . . . should not attempt to make a phony 'labor martyr' of him by holding pink tea government inquiries regarding him."

During J. Edgar Hoover's week in San Francisco, two FBI agents came to see Lundeberg, but he gave them the same answer he'd given Shoemaker. Then, after the present hearing had been underway for a month, he was called to the FBI office. When he arrived, waiting for him in the office were Del Guercio, Major Schofield, Connelley and an FBI man from the San Francisco office. They pressed him for information about Bridges but, for the third time, he denied knowing anything useful.

Nevertheless, they subpoenaed him to testify. He was out of the city for the next month, from mid–May to early in June. When he got back, he went to the FBI office on his own and told Del Guercio about the conversation with Darcy at Bridges's house. The prosecutor put him on the stand the following morning.

Lundeberg, like O'Neil, put Judge Sears on the horns of a dilemma. "He made no effort to conceal his enmity for Bridges," Sears noted in his report. "He expressed the view that Bridges's record as a labor leader 'stinks', and that the trade–union movement would be better off without him." Even so, Lundeberg struck Sears as a man whose bias would not cause him to lie about Bridges. On the other hand, Bridges stated on the stand that Darcy had never been in his home. But if Darcy hadn't been at his house, Sears said in his report, Bridges's lawyers could have called Agnes Bridges to corroborate his side of the story. Or his stepson or daughter. Or Norma Perry. Because they failed to do so, the judge decided Lundeberg must have been telling the truth.

"I reach the conclusion," he wrote, "that the conversation did take place substantially as testified by Lundeberg and that Bridges did there and then admit to Lundeberg that he was a member of the Communist Party."

As in the first hearing, most of Bridges's witnesses were called to show that witnesses for the prosecution had lied when they connected Bridges with the Communist Party. Some, like Henry Schmidt and Joe Curran, president of the National Maritime Union (the East Coast CIO counterpart of the AFL union Lundeberg headed on the West Coast), were impressive. But most of Bridges's witnesses carried no more weight with Sears than did most of the witnesses for the government.

The government was arguing that it was impossible for a man to be a Communist and a good labor leader at the same time, so the defense put on six character witnesses. One, a member of the California Personnel Management Association, testified that Bridges's reputation for truth and veracity among the members of that group was excellent. Henry Melnikow and Sam Kagel of the Pacific Coast Labor Bureau, a private consulting firm that represented unions in negotiations and arbitrations, said he was a good labor leader. Wayne Morse when he testified, agreed, adding, "I do not know of any conduct of Mr. Bridges in any of my relationships with him that would indicate to me that he is a Communist."

One day in mid-May, when Kagel was on the stand and the opposing lawyers were wrangling over what questions Bridges's lawyers could put to him, Judge Sears said wearily: "I notice that Dean Landis said there were very few objections in the other hearing, but we have gone to the other extreme, I think, in this one."

An even more striking difference between the two hearings was in the contrasting attitudes of Sears and Landis toward Bridges. Where Dean Landis had engaged him in long philosophical discussions, Judge Sears's questions, which he asked at the very end of the hearing, were confined to a few routine inquiries about when and where Bridges was born, where his family lived, what religion he was brought up in.

Judge Sears wound up the hearing by reading a warning to Bridges that any alien who is deported and then attempts to enter the United States without permission from the Attorney General is guilty of a felony and subject to two years in prison and/or a $1,000 fine. "Do you understand that?" Del Guercio asked sharply. Bridges ignored the prosecutor, whereupon Judge Sears asked quietly, "Do you understand that?" "Yes," Bridges replied. "That means after I have gone."

On that bleak note, the hearing ended, ten weeks after it began, at high noon on June 12, 1941.

The statistics of the second hearing closely paralleled those of the first. Each side called the same number of witnesses: the government, thirty–two; the defense, thirty. This time, Bridges was one of the thirty, having been called to testify on his own behalf. The government put in evidence 297 exhibits (on Angel Island, it had submitted 138), the defense sixty–two (as against 136 in the first hearing). The transcript came to 7,546 double–spaced typewritten pages, 268 less than the 7,724 in the first hearing. While the first hearing had lasted nine and a half weeks, this one lasted ten, from March 31st to June 12th.

The parallel between the hearings extended to the creation of a new Bridges defense committee operating across the nation with support from the CIO, even to a new folk song written by Woody Guthrie at the time of the second hearing and sung in union meetings and rallies, with a soloist doing the words and the crowd roaring out the chorus:

SONG OF BRIDGES

(I)

Let me tell you of a sailor, Harry Bridges is his name,
An honest union leader whom the bosses tried to frame,
He left home in Australia, to sail the seas around,
He sailed across the Ocean to land in Frisco town.

There was only a company union, the bosses had their way.
A worker had to stand in line for a lousy dollar a day.
When up spoke Harry Bridges, "Us workers got to get wise.
Our wives and kids will starve to death
   if we don't get organized."

Chorus

Oh, the F B I is worried, the bosses in a stew,
They can't deport six million men they know.
And we won't let them send Harry over-the-seas.
We'll fight for Harry Bridges and build the C I O.

(II)

They built a big bonfire by the Matson Line that night.
They threw their fink books in it
   and they said we're going to fight.
You've got to pay a living wage or we're going to take a walk.
They told it to the bosses but the bosses wouldn't talk.

They said there's only one way left to get that contract signed.
And all around the waterfront they threw their picket line.
They called it Bloody Thursday, the fifth day of July.
Four hundred men were wounded and two were left to die.

(Chorus)

(III)

Now that was seven years ago and in the time since then
Harry's organized thousands more and made them union men.
"We must try to bribe him," the shipping bosses said,
"And if he won't accept the bribe we'll say that he's a red."

The bosses brought a trial to deport him over the seas,
But the judge said he's an honest man, I got to set him free,
Then they brought another trial to frame him if they can.
But right by Harry Bridges stands every working man.

Judge Sears took back to New York 359 exhibits and forty–four
volumes of transcript (one for each day of the hearing) to pore over
and reach a verdict. He was about halfway through the two–and–
a–half month job when the Bridges case exploded again in the
headlines.

This time it was because a team of FBI agents who were tapping
his telephone bungled the job. Bridges spent most of July and August on the East Coast, staying at the Hotel Edison on West Forty-
seventh Street when he was in New York. On his first visit, the
hotel put him in room 1027, a large one with twin beds and a
locked door leading to an adjoining room. Then, when he was
given the same room when he stayed there a few weeks later, he
told the room clerk he didn't need that large a room. That was the
only one available, the clerk replied, and he could have it at a reduced rate. "I said that certainly was nice of the hotel," Bridges
said, "and I began to look around the lobby for the FBI men."

Bridges told some of his CIO friends in New York he was pretty
sure his room was bugged, and they in turn tipped off the liberal
newspaper *PM*. The result was a three–day series in *PM* on how
the FBI was tapping Bridges's telephone. In it, the paper named
the agents involved (one had carelessly left in the room next to
Bridges's a carbon of a report to FBI headquarters, with his name,
Evelle Younger, on it), and even produced an affidavit from a girl
friend of one of the agents, who had been invited up to their room
to see how the FBI operated.

The thought of a man living for a month in a hotel room knowing that FBI agents were occupying the room next to his, thinking
they were keeping him under surveillance when actually he was
spying on them intrigued St. Clair McKelway of the *New Yorker,*
who hurried over to Bridges's hotel for an interview. He published
it in the October 11, 1941 issue, under the title, "Some Fun With
the FBI."

"How do you manage to tell when you are being shadowed by
the FBI?" McKelway asked Bridges. Bridges answered by describing how, in other hotels he had stayed in, FBI men had taken
rooms next to his with a door between which had a space at the
bottom. "When you check into your room, you look under the door
and if the FBI men have their equipment in place, you can see a
tangle of wires and earphones on the floor. Then, too," he said,
"I've been followed by the FBI for so long that when I enter a hotel
lobby, I can usually spot one or two FBI men I've seen before." If
he didn't recognize any in the lobby, he looked in the mirrors for
men holding newspapers so that they came just to the bottom of
their eyes, and who sat there peeping over the top.

"Then," he went on, "if I suddenly start for the door and, just
as I'm about to go out, I stop and turn around quickly, one or
more of these fellows is likely to have just jumped up to his feet.
. . . If I want to be absolutely sure they are FBI men, of course, I
go out and lose anybody that might be following me and then go
back and stand in a doorway or something like that across the
street from the hotel, and when one of the men I've spotted
comes out of the hotel, I follow him down to the F.B.I. office
when he goes in to make his report on what I've been doing.
These F.B.I. men are nearly always tall guys, easy to follow in a
crowd, and they never seem to suspect that they are being followed."

The second time he stayed at the Edison, Bridges told McKelway, he used this procedure. By lunchtime, he was certain he had
three agents spotted. " 'Would it interest you to know how I remember the face of an F.B.I. man?' he asked. 'Yes, indeed.' "

" 'Well,' said Bridges, '. . . I look at him and get his face clearly
in my mind and then I try to think of somebody he reminds me of
—like a friend or a movie actor. . . . For instance, one of these
three guys I had spotted looked like a longshoreman on the Coast,
a very old friend of mine . . . The second of these three F.B.I. guys

reminded me of one of the C.I.O. attorneys on the Coast. The third one had a face very much like the face of Gary Cooper, the movie actor.' "

Bridges said that after spotting the agents, he went up to his room and called a friend at a C.I.O. office. " 'Look, I've got to see the big shot,' " he said into the phone. " 'This is the kind of talk that the F.B.I. men are always on the lookout for,' he confided to McKelway. 'They're sort of like college or high-school boys.' " His friend was mystified by the call, and Bridges shouted, " 'Do I have to tell you who I mean? The big shot! The Number One! Listen,' I said, 'meet me at the drugstore here on the corner in fifteen minutes and I'll explain.' "

He went down to the drugstore and had a milk shake to quiet his ulcer. Sure enough, in a few minutes the F.B.I. man who resembled the CIO attorney came in. He sat down at the soda fountain two stools away. When Bridges went out, the Gary Cooper one was standing in a doorway across the street. " 'I then called up the CIO office here in New York from a phone booth,' Bridges continued, 'and told my friend that my hotel wire was tapped for sure and that if any of them called me and wanted to say anything they didn't want the FBI to know to save it. The way things have been going, you see, we figure a union guy might as well tell a company labor spy all his plans for the union as to let the FBI know about it. . . .' "

For a few days Bridges and some of his friends watched the FBI men through field glasses from the roof garden of the Piccadilly Hotel, across the street from the Edison. Then he decided to rent a room there, so they could do their FBI–watching in comfort.

"Then I remembered," he told McKelway, "that one of the things the F.B.I. men always do is to get hold of any scraps of paper that are left in the room of a man they are shadowing. . . . Well, so we would tear up old letters and things and the next morning leave them in my room at the Edison, and then in the afternoon we'd see one of the F.B.I. men sitting at the table at the window in their room pasting little pieces of paper together. A couple of times I tore things up in the shape of six–pointed stars, or in the shape of a row of paper dolls—you know that trick of tearing paper, don't you? I used to do it for my kid. Then we'd see this F.B.I. guy holding up the stars and the rows of dolls next day at the window, studying them.

"We also left some well–used carbon paper in the wastebasket, so they could study that, too. The F.B.I. just loves carbon paper, you know. When they get hold of a piece of carbon paper that has been used for the writing of twenty or thirty letters, they really go to town—chemical processes, magnifying glasses, the whole works—and try to decipher what's been written on the carbon paper. I got a lawyer friend of mine to get me some from his office and another friend of mine got a stenographer he goes around with to bring me some from her office, which is a second-hand furniture concern. We left them five or six sheets to work on. . . ."

The FBI, understandably, refused to comment on *PM*'s exposé, so Bridges got in the last word. "The FBI," he explained, "is out to get me hook or crook because J. Edgar Hoover made a remark in Miami about a year and a half ago that he had enough on me to get me deported.

"Now," he added, winking characteristically, "they have to make that statement good."

Before a month was out, it looked as if Hoover had succeeded. On September 26, 1941, Judge Sears sent his 185-page report to the Attorney General. Bridges was guilty as charged, he ruled, and should be deported to Australia.

Judge Sears's recommendation, like Landis's, was only advisory. For Bridges to be deported, the Attorney General would have to agree with Sears's interpretation of the testimony. And now that Francis Biddle had succeeded Robert Jackson who had gone up to the Supreme Court in that office, there seemed a better than even chance that he wouldn't. Francis Biddle was a man of liberal credentials, uniquely equipped to understand the broad social and political aspects of the case and to see Bridges, as Frances Perkins had, as a labor martyr. A descendant of a patrician Philadelphia family, he had given up a lucrative law practice in the early years of FDR's administration to work in the New Deal. He had been chairman of the first National Labor Relations Board, had helped Senator Wagner write the National Labor Relations Act, and had been counsel to a Congressional committee which defended the T.V.A. in its infancy against assault by private power interests.

Biddle was also a member of long standing of the American Civil Liberties Union. But he was obsessed with Communism the way medieval Catholics were obsessed with heresy. He was convinced that Communists were in control of more than a few CIO unions, and he could not understand why neither the President nor Phil Murray, a devout Catholic, who followed Lewis as head of the CIO, were not equally concerned about it.

"When I was Solicitor General nearly a year before we entered the war," he said in his autobiography, "I had expressed my concern to Jackson of this situation, and suggested to him that we approach some of the union leaders—particularly in the CIO—to see if they would not quietly police the unions where there had been infiltration, avoiding publicity, and keeping known Communist leaders out of the key war industries."

Nothing had come of his scheme, and when the Nazis attacked Russia in June, 1941, Russia was transformed, for most Americans, from an ogre to an ally. "It was an example," Biddle reflects in *In Brief Authority*, "of the lack of realism behind so much American thinking in the war years, stemming from a flaccid optimism and innocent of the cumulative facts of Russian history." It followed for Biddle that if Bridges were in fact a Communist, he would have to order his deportation, no matter how unpopular that action might be with his liberal friends or what effect it might have on Soviet-American relations and the war effort.

The decision was, he has written, one of the most difficult he had to make in his four years (1941–1945) as Attorney General. He says in his chapter on Bridges that when the Sears decision was made public:

> Bob Jackson asked me to come to see him in Chambers. He was concerned, he said, about the Bridges case. He suggested that I bypass the Board of Immigration Appeals, and order that Sears' findings and the evidence supporting them be sent up directly to me for decision. He had the impression that the Board might be 'pro–Bridges', and would overrule Judge Sears' conclusions, so that, when the case came to me, I should find another obstacle to my sustaining Sears—that is, of course, if I agreed with him. The case was so important that it would not be out of line if I had it sent up to me directly. If I bypassed the board and simply sustained my own inspector, a former member of the highest court in New York, the case would eventually go to the Supreme Court in the best possible shape.
>
> The Board of Immigration Appeals was one of those convenient intermediary fact-finding departmental bodies, created not under any statute but by administrative order of the Secretary of Labor, for the purpose of taking the vast load of immigration de-

cisions off the Secretary's back. It had no power to put into effect warrants of deportation, and its findings were purely advisory. It was composed of five men whom I considered conscientious and fair. Ninety per cent of its decisions were affirmed without question by the Attorney General. Only occasionally I would send a case back involving a question of policy or statutory interpretation for reconsideration; but rarely overruled the board.

Thinking the suggestion over, I could not agree. I had no foregone conclusion. But if I bypassed my own board and then decided against Bridges, it would surely be said by those who supported him that I had already made up my mind. I could see no reason for not treating the case like any other, and deciding it in due course.

While the board was spending three months working its way through the hearing record, Bridges's friends and supporters were busy lobbying for him in Washington. Murray went to the White House to ask the President to stop the deportation, and delegations from national and local Bridges defense committees met with Biddle to urge him not to deport Bridges. They left Washington under the impression that the Attorney General was going to abide by whatever action the board recommended.

". . . we went to Washington and we told Mr. Biddle," the secretary of Bridges's Victory Committee told the longshoremen's 1943 convention,

> that the only concern of the CIO was to have the case decided on its merits, that we did not want any influence brought upon the members of the Board of Immigration Appeals, and Mr. Biddle assured us that no such pressure would be brought, but he did say that in the conduct of his office in such matters like the Bridges' case there were always tremendous influences being brought to bear upon him.

> He said that he had withstood them and he gave us a history of the members of the Board of Immigration Appeals, their qualifications as lawyers, and he told us that under his administration for the first time in the history of the Immigration Department the Board of Immigration Appeals had been established with real power, with real duties, with real responsibilities and with real authority.

> And he gave us to understand that our case would be fairly

judged and that when a decision was made, whatever it might be, that that decision would stand.

The board sent its decision to the Attorney General on January 3, 1942. The board concentrated, as Landis had, on two questions: had Bridges been affiliated with the Communist Party or the Marine Workers Industrial Union, and had he been a member of either or both? On the first, the board concluded that the government's case didn't amount to much. What it came down to was that, on occasion:

> . . . [Bridges] maintained friendly relations with some Communists, opposed "red-baiting", cooperated directly or indirectly with the M.W.I.U. or Communists in cases in which he states they were seeking specific ends which he and his union also sought for reasons legitimately connected with their own welfare, and expressed views thought to have similarity to some of those espoused by members of the M.W.I.U. and of the Communist Party. This presentation at best has but few elements not passed upon in the previous [Angel Island] proceeding. It is doubtful that, taken at their claimed value, those elements would justify departure from the result there reached. And, upon analysis, it becomes apparent that the elements of difference here present have no substantial tendency to worsen the Alien's position under existing law. But wholly apart from all such questions, we have concluded upon independent examination that the matters brought to our attention by the [Immigration] Service and relied on by the Presiding Inspector in his proposed findings, insofar as they find support in the record, do not warrant our holding that the Alien was affiliated to any proscribed organization within the meaning of the applicable statute.

The government's case as to membership was no better in the board's opinion, resting as it did on the testimony of Lundeberg and O'Neil. "James D. O'Neil," the board concluded at the end of a twenty-four-page analysis of his appearance on the stand, "was a most tantalizing witness. Speculation as to the ultimate motives for his testimony may fill many fascinating tomorrows. But on the record before us, decision on his testimony both on and off the stand is relatively simple. His testimony off the stand is not to be heard, and when heard his testimony on and off the stand cannot be believed."

Lundeberg's testimony also struck the board as unbelievable: "With considerable diffidence, we cannot accept the learned and experienced Presiding Inspector's statement that Lundeberg was impressive in his truthfulness. The record is clear—to the contrary."

By contrast, the board was impressed with Bridges, just as Landis had been. "In evaluating his denial [of Lundeberg's story of the dinner]," the board said, "we are concerned with the record here on Bridges as a witness. If self–interest led him to lie, to evade, to stretch the truth, the record should show it. Scrutinizing his testimony from end to end, we find no indication that self-interest so operated. Rather, he is impressive." The board also noted that when Bridges testified from memory about his personal records, he voluntarily corrected himself the next day after checking his memory against the records. "He frequently volunteers information which, in view of the approach of the Service in this case, might well have been thought dangerous on the issue of affiliation. For example, he did not in fact collaborate with William F. Dunne, a Communist, in writing 'The Great San Francisco Strike,' but he volunteers that he might have, if he had been asked."

"The evidence in this case," the board concluded, echoing Landis, "does not establish that Harry Bridges was at any time a member of or affiliated with any organization proscribed by statute . . . It is our unanimous opinion that the warrant must be cancelled."

Whether Bridges was to go or to stay was now up to Biddle. For several months, he agonized over what he should do, unable to make up his mind. At last, he tells us in *In Brief Authority*, he threw into a suitcase the record of the Sears hearing, Dean Landis's final report, and "some other documents bearing on the case," and went down to Florida, to study the records in private and to meditate on what he would do. It was the middle of May, five months after he got the case from the board, before he decided he would send Bridges back to Australia.

Biddle knew that Bridges's lawyers would appeal the decision to a federal district court and on up the judicial ladder to the Supreme Court. That would take two years, maybe three, for a final decision. Meanwhile, he thought to himself, Bridges would be out on bail, heading his union, and "now that Russia was in the war, performing" as Biddle put it sarcastically, "his patriotic duties along the waterfront." Whichever way the case went, the war would no doubt be over before it was finally disposed of.

Having reached a decision, Biddle wrote his analysis of the case, going over the points of disagreement between Sears and the appeal board one by one. One after another, he concluded that Sears had been right, the board wrong. He pointed out that the judge had seen and heard the witnesses while the board had only read the bare record. At the end, he reversed the board and upheld Sears.

Before making his decision public, Biddle went over to the White House to tell the President what he proposed to do.

". . . I did not ask his advice," he has recalled, "but spoke in some detail of the reasons for my action. He whistled, drew deeply on his cigarette, and for a moment was concentrated in thought. 'I'm sorry to hear that,' he said. Then his face cleared; he screwed the butt of his cigarette in the ash tray. 'I'll bet,' he said, 'that the Supreme Court will never let him be deported.' Then he said with a smile, 'And the decision is a long way off.' "

Biddle's decision was unpopular, even in some unexpected quarters. The *New York Herald Tribune*, then an influential Republican newspaper, rebuked him editorially. The *New York Daily News* carried a column which included the opinion: "Officials of the War and Navy Departments, the War Shipping Administration, and the War Production Board, today complained bitterly that Biddle's out—of—the—blue—sky—decree had handed them the war's No. 1 political headache." *Time* magazine, after first reassuring its readers that it was no friend of Bridges, accused Biddle of developing a sudden passion for the letter of the law. Wayne Morse was even more caustic: "Biddle's decision," he snorted, "appears to be pregnant with the twins of twisted logic and unsound public policy."

Reaction in labor circles was mixed. The AFL was pleased, as was John L. Lewis, who had broken with the CIO and the Left earlier in the year. The CIO, however, rallied to Bridges's support and raised $30,000 for legal expenses within a few months of Biddle's action. Phil Murray, President of the CIO, told the 1942 CIO convention that more was needed when he made a speech supporting a resolution urging the President to drop the deportation order, dismiss all charges against Bridges, and allow him to become a citizen.

"I have gone to federal agencies in defense of Bridges," Murray said.

I have called upon the Attorney General of the United States. I have talked to immigration authorities in the Department of Labor, before the Immigration Department was transferred from that department over to the Department of Justice. I have talked to almost everybody in government about the Bridges case, and I have asked them to present to me everything they may have in their possession regarding the so–called subversive activities of Harry Bridges—and I have never had a government official with whom I have been privileged to talk adduce a single, solitary little bit of evidence which would, in any way, prove that Bridges was associated with groups whose purposes and objectives ran to the overthrow of the Government of the United States of America.

The resolution was adopted unanimously when Murray finished.

The President got letters from all over the country urging him to use his emergency war powers to overrule Biddle and to drop the charges against Bridges. He even got a memorandum from his wife Eleanor, listing all the possible harmful effects Biddle's action might have on the war effort and concluding, "Please read and if you think worth passing on to the Attorney General, you may do so." A few days later, she got a terse reply from her husband: "About 90 per cent of this is just plain untrue. F.D.R." Her memo must have troubled him, even so, because four days later he sent her a second comment on it: "I have checked twelve statements in two pages which are questionable as to their correctness—and that is a pretty high average. F.D.R."

In view of Biddle's feelings about communism, it was probably inevitable that he would believe Sears rather than his appeals board. Dean Landis has suggested another reason. "I talked to him about it one day," he said in his oral history. "I met him on the train, going up from Washington to New York, and he sat down, had a drink. He had just upset the decision of the Board of Immigration Appeals. I asked him about it. . . . he thought it was the right thing to do, that there was enough in Sears's report to do it.

"He thought it was politically wise to do so. He was scared of the political consequences of the thing."

"To himself?" the interviewer asked.

"No," Landis replied. "To the administration as a whole, not to himself. I don't think Francis ever lacked any personal courage, as far as that goes."

Biddle tells us in his autobiography that the President thought he was making a mistake. But FDR had no time now for anything but the war. The White House let the letters and telegrams that poured in about Bridges pile up unanswered. Some were sent over to the Justice Department by Presidential aides and if the writer got a reply at all, it was a curt note from Biddle's office, accompanied by a printed copy of his decision. Meanwhile, as Biddle and the President had expected, the case was slowly working its way up through the courts.

At first, Bridges's chances of getting the deportation order reversed by the courts seemed hopeless. His lawyers, joined by Lee Pressman, general counsel of the CIO, reviewed all of their constitutional arguments—double jeopardy, *ex post facto, res judicata.* They were all wasted on the lower federal courts.

"It is well settled," the courts ruled, "that deportation, while it may be burdensome and severe for the alien, is not a punishment for a crime." Therefore, none of the Constitutional safeguards Bridges's lawyers pointed to was relevant. The lower courts also held that it was well settled in deportation cases that if there was any evidence to support the finding of the Attorney General, the courts should not second–guess his ruling. All that stood between Bridges and banishment now was the Supreme Court.

Typically, when cases are argued before the Supreme Court, the lawyer for each side is given a half–hour to present his arguments. If questions from the bench take up too much of his time, his half–hour is extended. Inevitably, that was the way it was in Bridges's case. The Chief Justice called it up for argument in mid-afternoon on April 2, 1945. Thus, although ample time had been allowed to hear both sides before adjourning for the day, it was well into the middle of the morning of the next day before it was over.

Pressman and Gladstein argued the case for Bridges. The Court also had before it three *amicus curiae* briefs—one from the American Civil Liberties Union and another from the American Committee for the Protection of the Foreign Born, both supporting Bridges, and a third from the American Legion, urging the Court to uphold his deportation.

Acting with uncommon speed, the Court handed down its decision two and a half months later, on June 18, 1945. As expected, the Court was divided, and the sharply–worded majority and minority opinions mirrored the skirmishes between the judicial activists and the apostles of judicial restraint that went on behind the locked door of the Court's conference room.

Stone, Frankfurter and Roberts thought the Court should uphold Biddle, for, as they said in a dissenting opinion, there was nothing novel about the Bridges case. It was merely one of a rapidly growing number of appeals from the action of a government official or some board or other (they cited the NLRB as an example), where the loser wanted the Court to overrule the administrator.

"Under our Constitution," Chief Justice Stone wrote, "Congress has its functions, the Attorney General has his, and the courts theirs in regard to the deportation of aliens. Our function is a very limited one . . ." And the limit was, as the two lower courts had said, that if there were even a scintilla of evidence to support Biddle, the courts had no authority to set aside his order. The question for the Court, then, was: was the testimony of O'Neil and Lundeberg that kind of evidence? Yes, Stone replied. It would not be proper for the Court to substitute its judgment as to the believability of O'Neil and Lundeberg for that of Judge Sears, who saw and heard them as they testified. Therefore, the dissent held, Bridges should be deported.

Justice Douglas wrote the majority opinion on behalf of himself and Justices Black, Reed, Rutledge and Murphy. He began by reviewing the eight–year effort to deport Bridges, from its beginnings after the '34 strike on up to Biddle's deportation order and its affirmance by the two lower federal courts. The order, he noted, rested on two grounds: *affiliation* and *membership* in the Communist Party. Neither, he concluded, had been proved. In order to find Bridges guilty of affiliation, Sears and Biddle had had to stretch its definition far beyond the one Landis used in finding him innocent. In doing so, Douglas wrote, they stretched it too far.

The majority opinion went on to say that the evidence as to Bridges's association with Communists showed only that he worked with them to achieve entirely legitimate objectives, like winning strikes and strengthening the longshoremen's union and the CIO. "Individuals, like nations," Douglas wrote, "may cooperate in a common cause over a period of months or years though their ultimate aims do not coincide. Alliances for limited objectives are well known. Certainly those who joined forces with Russia to defeat the Nazis may not be said to have made an alliance to spread the cause of Communism . . ."

The government's case as to membership, Douglas added, was no better. O'Neil's testimony should not have been admitted as evidence by Sears, for the Justice Department violated its own regulations when it took his statement in the FBI office without putting him under oath, and when it neglected to have him sign the typed copy of it. Nor was Lundeberg's testimony entitled to the weight

Sears and Biddle had given it. His hostility to Bridges was so obvious that it made his story unbelievable.

"Since Harry Bridges has been ordered deported," Douglas concluded, "on a misconstruction of the term 'affiliation' as used in the statute and by reason of an unfair hearing on the question of his membership in the Communist Party, his detention under the warrant is unlawful."

Bridges, at long last, was free to stay in the United States.

To students of the Court, the Bridges decision was a surprising departure from tradition. Ordinarily, when the Court can avoid a head–on collision with either the legislative or executive branch by deciding a case on a technical legal point, it does so. Bridges's lawyers had given the Court an ample supply of technical points—*res judicata,* double jeopardy, *ex post facto,* to do so. Instead, the Court chose to censure the government for the shameful way certain public officials had behaved toward Bridges. "The majority's ruling was legally indefensible," Aubrey Grossman said later. "But they were obviously so outraged by the government's continued persecution of Harry, they wanted to stop it once and for all."

As strong as Douglas's language was, it was still too mild for Murphy, who wrote a separate concurring opinion. Francis Biddle, who had been notified that the opinions in the Bridges case were going to be read that day, had come over to the Court to hear them. As it happened, his place at the government attorneys' table put him right in front of Murphy, up on the bench. Biddle says in his autobiography he was sure Murphy was speaking directly to him as he described the government's treatment of Bridges:

"The record in this case," Murphy began, "will stand forever as a monument to man's intolerance of man. Seldom if ever in the history of this nation has there been such a concentrated and relentless crusade to deport an individual because he dared to exercise the freedom that belongs to him as a human being and that is guaranteed to him by the Constitution . . .

"When the immutable freedoms guaranteed by the Bill of Rights have been so openly and concededly ignored," Murphy continued, "the full wrath of constitutional condemnation descends upon the action taken by the government."

"What a windbag he is," Biddle thought to himself.

Some of the majority went farther in their remarks in conference than Murphy himself. Black said he couldn't understand the mental processes of a man who could read O'Neil's and Lundeberg's testimony and believe them. What happened to Bridges, he said, was clear. Organized industry on the Coast started the campaign to deport him by tapping his phone and having him shadowed and then turned over what they had picked up to the government. "He is being deported," Black concluded, "because he is a labor union leader." Another told his colleagues that the way the case was handled ". . . offends my sense of how we shall approach a deportation."

Biddle would not have been happy either, with what Stone, Frankfurter and Roberts—who voted to uphold Biddle—said about his conduct of the case when they were discussing it in conference. Frankfurter said that even though he was going to vote to uphold the Attorney General, "I think Biddle is a damn fool in this action." Roberts said he would vote to deport Bridges "with the greatest reluctance," and only because he believed Congress had the authority to deport aliens for any reason it chose. Chief Justice Stone, after observing, "it was a rotten thing Congress did," said he would vote to uphold Biddle for fear that if he did not, Congress might retaliate by closing off immigration altogether which would inflict injustice on untold thousands of persons just to save Bridges.

Out in San Francisco, Bridges was jubilant but wary when he heard the news. He had other problems to worry about at this time, as *Time*, with obvious relish, pointed out on July 2, 1945 at the end of its story on the Supreme Court decision: "And again they lay in the courts. Seeking a divorce, his wife charged that he is the father of a New York dancer's illegitimate child. Harry denied it."

"Now that the Supreme Court has saved me from deportation," Bridges said at a press conference in his office, "my next battle will be to get my citizenship. It's already in the making that the same forces back of all this action against me will try to prevent or delay my citizenship. And," he added, "unless Justice Murphy's opinion is accepted as the attitude of the Court, there's nothing to prevent the government from starting another trial on the same evidence.

"As soon as the Attorney General's office dismisses the deportation warrant, I'll proceed at once to bring the whole issue to a close by applying for citizenship papers immediately."

His remarks intrigued one of the reporters, who perhaps thought that Bridges, like his boyhood idol, Charlie Chaplin, had become so embittered by the persecution he'd suffered that he'd spurn U.S. citizenship.

"You mean you're going to become a citizen?" the reporter asked.

"Naturally," Bridges retorted. "American citizenship is a prized possession. In fact, I made application a few days after Dean Landis found I wasn't guilty back in 1939. That's been held up all this time because of this proceeding."

Three months later—by coincidence, on the one–hundred–and–fifty–eighth anniversary of the adoption of the United States Constitution—Bridges, his daughter Betty beaming happily behind him, was in Judge Thomas C. Foley's court in San Francisco to take the oath and become a citizen.

For a moment, it looked as if he wouldn't make it. As the proceedings began, an immigration officer handed up a paper to the judge, saying, "I received this three days ago from Mr. Bridges's ex–wife." Bridges had been divorced three weeks earlier. It was an affidavit, alleging that Bridges had been a Communist under another name, and that he had kept his membership book hidden under the linoleum in their kitchen.

"Do you offer this as evidence?" the judge inquired.

"No, your Honor. Merely for what it is worth."

Turning to Bridges, the judge asked, "Do you care to make any statement?"

"As one who has tried for many years to obtain citizenship and been prevented by one thing and another," Bridges answered, "I perhaps realize more than most what a priceless privilege it is.

"If I am successful in becoming a citizen I will use the rights and freedoms that go with citizenship to preserve them and extend them to more people."

"You will make a fine citizen," Judge Foley observed. "Any man who has fought so long and so hard for citizenship as you have will certainly value and appreciate it.

"I know you'll understand that I'm required to ask you this," he added apologetically, "despite everything you've just been through. Are you now, or have you ever been a Communist?"

"No, your Honor," Bridges answered.

Judge Foley beckoned to Bridges's witnesses, Henry Schmidt and Bob Robertson—both long–time friends and officers of the union—asking each in turn, after he was sworn in, "To the best of your knowledge and belief, is Mr. Bridges now, or has he been, a member of the Communist Party?"

"No, sir," they answered.

NOTES

Quotes of testimony in the Sears hearing are from Case No. 55973/217, *In the Matter of Harry Bridges, Reporter's Transcript*. Sears's evaluation of witnesses' credibility is in his report: *Memorandum of Decision in the Matter of Harry Renton Bridges* (September 26, 1941).

The report of the board of immigration appeals is: *In re: HARRY RENTON BRIDGES*. (Case No. 55973/217) *Before the Board of Immigration Appeals in Deportation Hearings*, Mimeographed, (January 3, 1942).

Biddle's analysis of the case is: *In re: Harry Bridges, Before the Attorney General in Deportation Proceedings* (May 28, 1942).

FDR's exchange of memos with his wife is in Presidential File 1750, in the Roosevelt Memorial Library.

The source of what went on in the Supreme Court conference on the Bridges case is a six–page set of Murphy's handwritten notes, in Box 134 of the Frank Murphy Papers, in the Michigan Historical Collection, in Ann Arbor, Michigan.

8

Revolution in Paradise

There is now a street called Bridges Place in Honolulu, where, only a few years ago, the general feeling was that Harry Bridges' place was at the bottom of the sea.

HERB CAEN

EVER SINCE 1934, Harry Bridges had lived in an unrelieved atmosphere of crisis, but the spring and summer of 1941 were the worst so far. Early in the year, he spent four weeks in a National Labor Relations Board hearing trying to persuade the board not to allow the Northwest ports of Tacoma, Anacortes and Port Angeles to pull out of the coastwide bargaining unit West Coast longshoremen had fought for so many years to establish.

The hearing was no sooner over, although it would take the board several months to reach a decision, than Bridges plunged into a five–month–long contract arbitration before Dean Wayne Morse. The union submitted ninety–two changes in the working and dispatching rules, the employers, fifty–seven. Meanwhile, Bridges had to prepare for the union's fourth convention, scheduled to begin in Los Angeles on April 7th.

Hanging over his head, all this time, was the deportation hearing before Judge Sears. That was set to begin Monday, March 31st. So Bridges spent the first week of April in the U.S. Courthouse in San Francisco, and the second in Los Angeles chairing the convention (Sears recessed the hearing for a week to allow him to preside over it). He was a day late getting back to the courthouse, for the convention ran over to Monday night. Tuesday morning, he was back in Sears's courtroom in San Francisco, where he remained for the next two months.

When the Sears hearing came to an end on June 12th, it looked as if all Bridges had to worry about for the moment was the arbitration, which was still going on. But then from Washington came word that the NLRB had decided to hold representation elections in the Northwest ports. Harmless as the new ruling might seem—all told, there were only about three or four hundred longshoremen in the three ports—it was the most serious threat to the union's existence since '34. If the ports went ILA, Joe Ryan and the AFL would have an enclave on the West Coast from which, with the enthusiastic help of Dave Beck's teamsters and Lundeberg's sailors, they could send out raiding parties into other ILWU ports. Defection to the AFL would be a bonanza for the shipowners, too, for they would have liked nothing better than to see the longshoremen abandon Bridges's militant ILWU–CIO for Ryan's tractable ILA–AFL. Equally important, an AFL port or two on the Coast would give shipowners a handy place to divert cargoes to whenever the ILWU called a coastwide strike.

Bridges was working hard on the NLRB election and the arbitration when the news broke on June 22, 1941, that Hitler had sent his armies into Russia. Until then, Bridges had considered the war in Europe a struggle between rival imperialisms, one the U.S. should stay out of. The attack on Russia changed that; it became a people's war now and America should enlist to help defeat the Nazis. The turn of events confronted Bridges with a dilemma, for to speak out now could jeopardize the NLRB election in the three ports, where AFL supporters were already making much of the charges that he was a Communist and the ILWU un–American. (The AFL won in all three, as it turned out.) Even more important, to Bridges personally, was the effect that speaking out might have on Judge Sears, who had not yet handed down his decision. (He announced it on September 26th, 1941.)

Undeterred, Bridges went to the shipowners with a proposal. "We in the longshore industry," he told them, "can set an example of how to increase production by adding public members to our labor relations committees up and down the coast. Then, if our people and yours on the committees can't agree on how to settle some beef or other, the public members can mediate it. They can even arbitrate it if it comes to that."

The employers' reaction was chilly. "Why bring in outsiders," they asked, "when they aren't needed? We can do all that now, with our system of arbitrators in each port."

Bridges said no more about the plan for several months. Then, five days after Pearl Harbor, he brought it up again, this time proposing a tripartite board that would oversee longshore operations up and down the Pacific Coast. He pointed out that the union–employer–government council he was proposing could speed up cargo handling by finding ways to use more labor–saving machinery, providing central planning in each port to avoid congestion in loading the ships, making better use of small ports, studying the cost of longshore operations, insuring that enough reliable longshoremen would be constantly available, helping to settle disputes, and recommending the most econominical methods, even if that meant changes in working rules. He added that the council could also explore ways to work ships during blackouts and guard against accidents and deliberate sabotage.

At first, reaction in the press and among the shipowners was universally favorable. Even Bridges's archenemy, Frank Foisie, who had moved down from Seattle to head the coastwide shipowners' organization, had a good word for it. "We want to give Bridges every credit due him for his plan to secure maximum production on the docks," Foisie said on December 16, 1941. "He is entitled to it."

Within a few days, however, the employers' enthusiasm gave way to second thoughts. "The so–called Bridges Plan for joint control of Pacific Coast docks," Almon Roth, an employer spokesman, said in a speech at Stanford early in January, 1942, "is an example of the unions' strategy. What it means is that men who have no financial investment in or responsibilities for an enterprise and who in some cases have never worked in the industry are to join in the control of it." In any case, the shipowners contended that the plan was unnecessary. If Bridges and the union were sincere about wanting to increase efficiency, Roth said, all they would have to do is live up to the contract, which provided that if the union could show that productivity had gone up, the employers would consider raising the men's wages.

Meanwhile, Bridges, encouraged by an appeal from the chairman of the War Production Board in Washington asking industries engaged in war production to establish labor–management councils, was sending telegrams to Washington urging the government to put pressure on the shipowners to accept his plan. He didn't get any response. "Sam," he said to Sam Kagel one day late in February, "I'm going back there and force those people to talk to me. When I'm talking to them face–to–face, I know damn well I can get them to support us."

Kagel had a nightmarish picture of Washington bureaucrats re-
coiling in horror as this dangerous radical from the West Coast was
ushered into their offices. "Look, Harry," he promised, "I'll go
back and see what I can do about it. But for Godsakes, you stay
here. If you show up in Washington, you'll queer the whole thing."

Kagel was right, of course. The man who had veto power over
Bridges's plan was Admiral Emory S. Land, who headed the War
Shipping Board, and Land had no love for Bridges.

"Bridges never came to Washington in the nine years I was on
the Maritime Commission without insisting on having an appointment with me," Land said later (in an oral history at Columbia
University, in 1963).

> And it was always one of the most unhappy appointments I ever
> had. Naturally, we never agreed on a single thing. I won't say
> never, but very rarely. He always had a snarl on his upper lip.
> I've always said he had a crooked brain. He was an out–and–out
> Commie.
>
> And yet I had a letter from him, at the end of the war which I
> wouldn't care to publish, more or less saying that I was a pretty
> nice boy, and did a pretty fair job under the circumstances, and
> so on and so forth. He's a most unique character . . .
>
> He was always a thorn in my flesh, and I repeat it. He was al-
> ways fighting the seamen. He hated the best friend I had there,
> Harry Lundeberg . . .
>
> "Would you say that Bridges was patriotic enough in his atti-
> tude toward the war effort?" [Asked by interviewer.]
>
> He was patriotic enough in his attitude towards [himself] and
> his union, and that's as far as he ever saw. No, I wouldn't call
> him a patriot. I'd consider him a Communist. And everything
> that goes with that, directly or indirectly.
>
> Naturally, when Russia got into the war, his disturbing efforts
> were much less than they were before. But he was never satisfied
> with the way the Commission operated. He was never satisfied
> with me . . .

Bridges could scarcely have known how intensely Land distrusted him, but he did let Kagel talk him into staying in San Francisco for the time being, and Kagel set out alone. For two weeks he
made the rounds, trudging wearily from one war agency to another,
getting nowhere, when Bridges appeared in Washington, impatient
to take over. "Give me just a little more time, Harry," Kagel

pleaded, "and then if I haven't gotten anywhere, you try talking to these people. Meanwhile, I'll go to see Land one more time." "All right, Sam," Bridges conceded. "But only for a couple of days."

Kagel's next meeting with Land was on February 9, 1942. Land was listening noncommittally to his reasons why the government should endorse Bridges's proposal when a messenger broke in to hand the admiral a note. As Land read it tears began coursing down his cheeks. Silently, he handed the note to Kagel. Earlier in the day, it said, the mammoth French passenger ship "Normandie" had been gutted by fire, the work of a saboteur, as she lay at the dock in New York being converted into a troopship. By the time Kagel finished reading it, the admiral had recovered. "Where is your man Bridges?" he asked briskly. "I'll talk to him now about his production plan."

Within a month, the Bridges Plan, officially known as the Pacific Coast Maritime Industry Board, was in operation as an agency of the U.S. War Shipping Administration. Before another month was out, the longshoremen, highly praised by the Army and Navy, the shipowners and the local newspapers, were setting new records for loading the ships. The Bridges legend being what it was, there had to be a discordant note. It came from the tower of the *Chicago Tribune*, from which, on a nationwide radio hookup, Colonel Robert McCormick, the publisher, used to deliver weekly homilies on military history. On May 23, 1942, his topic was the war in the Pacific, where, he reported, we were suffering heavy losses, in part because our forces were under-manned and ill-equipped. Toward the end of this doleful analysis, he paused as if departing from his script to say with a sigh: "It is bitter for us to think in this crisis that American labor on the Pacific Coast has been corrupted by the Australian Communist Harry Bridges, who is still at large sabotaging our war effort."

If it was inevitable that Bridges's attitude toward the war would be changed by Russia's involvement, it was equally so that, once we were in, he would be intolerant of anything or anyone that seemed to stand in the way of victory. In his gallery of heroes and rogues, John L. Lewis and Roosevelt immediately changed places. "We are pledged to uphold the President, the Commander-in-Chief," Bridges told the union's convention after America entered the war, "and nobody in this convention or in this union has any right to complain about the actions of the President . . ."

With Lewis, it was the opposite: "John L. Lewis is a black disgrace to the laboring men and women of America," Bridges said when Lewis called the miners out on strike in 1943 for a long–delayed wage increase. "He has subverted his high post of office and the interests of his union members to his personal vindictiveness against our government and its Commander–in–Chief. He has become the single most effective agent of the fascist powers within the ranks of labor."

Bridges's impatience with Lewis was so intense, in fact, that when a resolution condemning the mineworkers' leader was introduced in the longshoremen's convention that year, he forgot his responsibility as president to protect the delegates' right to speak freely. "Now is the time," he said from the chair after the resolution was seconded, "for anyone who in any way believes or sympathizes with any part of John L. Lewis's policies or his leadership to stand up and say so because with the adoption of this resolution it will state the position of our union, reaffirm the position that he is a traitor to the nation and to labor, and there will be no room in our union for anybody who has any sympathy or support for him whatsoever."

No one spoke up in support of Lewis, but half a dozen delegates tried to outdo each other, in an unconscious imitation of the House of Representatives when it considered the bill to deport Bridges, in denouncing the miners' leader. When they subsided, the motion passed unanimously.

Bridges was not always so persuasive. Not long after the convention, he made a stirring speech to the San Francisco longshore local, urging the men to lift the one–year limit on their officers' terms of office. He pointed to the complexities of the jobs, the difficulties of dealing with the army and navy, and concluded by saying that passing the motion would help the war effort by making the union more efficient. When he finished, the membership, moved by the eloquence of his appeal, gave him a standing ovation.

Then, almost unanimously, they voted him down.

Los Angeles longshoremen were even more irreverent when he went to one of their meetings in mid–1942 to propose lifting the sling load limit for bags of cement. The meeting was in a boxing arena called the Wilmington Bowl. The officers and speakers sat in the ring surrounded by a sea of longshoremen.

"During the war, we loaded a tremendous amount of cement out of here," George Love, a Los Angeles longshoreman said in the 1960s.

We worked ten hours a day, seven days a week on. And man, that was work!

We had a sling limit of twenty–one one–hundred–pound bags. So Harry came down, and he told us, "Look, fellows, I talked with the general up in San Francisco. The army wants you to load thirty bags. And whether you like it or not, you're going to load thirty bags."

And then I saw this guy Mulligan coming down the aisle toward the ring. Hell, I'd never heard him speak before. I didn't know he could. But when he got up in the ring he started out by saying: "I never thought I'd hear Harry Bridges tell us to give up our conditions just because of a little old war.

"I remember when you came down here awhile back," he says, "and you wanted us to support your policy the Yanks aren't coming. I told you that was horse shit then. And I tell you this program is horse shit now. Just because your pal Joe Stalin is in trouble, don't expect us to give up our conditions to help him out.

"I'll tell you what to do, Harry. You go back up there to San Francisco and tell the employers, and that general up there, too, that if they want thirty sacks, they can come down here and load them.

"We sure as hell aren't going to!"

Everybody there was on his feet, all three thousand of them, stomping and clapping. Harry laughed, too.

And that was the last we heard about the thirty sacks.

Paradoxically, even as Bridges was waging his war to increase productivity, he was fighting off attacks on gains the union had labored hard to get. In 1942, President Roosevelt put the longshoremen's prized six–hour day in jeopardy when he issued Executive Order 924, prohibiting payment of overtime except after eight hours a day or forty hours a week. The order put Bridges in an interesting position. "If it becomes necessary to the war effort," he had told a *Christian Science Monitor* reporter a month earlier, in May, 1942, "I would favor a 48–hour week, with a ceiling on wages. I tell the men in the waterfront unions that they should not ask for more pay as long as they have enough to live on. Of course, in some other unions where a worker makes only $25 a week, say, the situation may be different because he may not be able to live on that amount. But on the waterfront, wages should be stabilized."

But Presidential Order 9240 was scarcely what he had in mind.

West Coast longshoremen were working ten hours a day, four of it at time and a half. The order would have meant a sharp cut in earnings, and prices were steadily going up. Bridges sent a strong protest to the President, pointing out that if the order stood, long-shoremen would have to give up the six–hour day they had won in the 1934 strike. A few days later, the President amended the order, allowing the longshoremen to keep their overtime.

When the contract came up for renewal in September, 1942, the shipowners proposed a list of changes by which they hoped to re-capture control of the hiring halls and discipline on the job. They seemed to have a fair chance of success. The longshoremen had withdrawn their objections to labor–saving machinery and had themselves proposed more efficient ways to handle cargo, and it seemed reasonable to believe that they might make further conces-sions to the employers in order to boost productivity.

It didn't turn out that way. To the longshoremen, the hiring halls stood for equality of earnings and protection against the indig-nities, the kickbacks, the brutality of the shape–up. They could no more allow tampering with the way they ran their hiring halls than they could allow the employers to tell them how to run their union. They felt the same way about the employers' demand for more control over the men on the job.

It was the kind of impasse which, given the heritage of conflict on the waterfront, would have led to a strike if it hadn't been for the war. But neither side was willing to stop the ships, so they asked the War Labor Board to settle the argument.

It took the board almost two years. The decision it finally reached in October, 1944, left the hiring halls and working condi-tions almost unchanged. It did award a five–cent an hour wage in-crease, retroactive to 1942. The board also, at the insistence of the union, added a clause to the contract prohibiting discrimination by the employers because of the usual reasons (union membership, race, creed, color, national origin, religion) and one that only one or two other unions in the U.S. have demanded: no discrimination because of political belief.

In mid-1944, five months before the War Labor Board ruling, Bridges and his fellow officers decided the time had come to send an organizer to Hawaii to help the restless sugar workers there get a union started. The results were breathtaking. In little more than a year, thirty–three of the Islands' thirty–five plantations were under contract with the ILWU, and by mid–1946, the pineapple industry had followed suit.

In a year and a half, thirty thousand new members were added, an exciting increase to a union that at the outset had a mainland membership of fifty thousand. More important, adding tens of thousands of plantation workers (and later, workers whose jobs ran the gamut from cowboys to gravediggers) saved the union from giving way to the parochialism that would have lain in wait for it if it had remained a craft union of longshoremen with a satellite of warehousemen. Even more significant, organizing the sugar and pineapple workers played an important part in transforming Hawaii from a feudal, racially–stratified plantation culture into a modern economy operating in a plural society.

As so often has happened in union history, even as brilliant an organizing campaign as this one might not have succeeded had it not been for earlier efforts it was able to build upon. In this case, the earlier effort was made by an organizer named Jack Hall, who is to Hawaii what Bridges is to the West Coast.

Like Bridges, Hall went to sea after finishing high school at sixteen. Three years later, he came down the gangplank in San Francisco with the battle sounds from Rincon Hill resounding in his ears. He stayed in San Francisco until the strike was over, picketing and doing strike chores for the sailors' union.

After the strike ended, Hall went back to sea for about a year. Then, one day in 1935, his ship dropped anchor in Honolulu. The sailors and marine firemen there had just opened hiring halls and were trying to organize the longshoremen. "The sailors' business agent asked me to help," Hall has recalled. "It looked like a good place to pitch in." One of the first steps, he decided, was to help a newspaper that had gotten started the same week he arrived in the Islands.

Called the *Voice of Labor*, it resembled the *Waterfront Worker*, sold for three cents, and castigated FDR and the New Deal for patching up a system that needed surgery. A special target was Joe Ryan, whom it accused of refusing to grant charters to the newly–formed longshoremen's locals in Hilo and Honolulu because he thought the Hawaiians too militant. The paper always spoke highly of Bridges, picturing him as "the best loved and respected man among the workers up and down the coast," and describing the methods by which he and the West Coast longshoremen had succeeded where earlier unions had failed. Hall wrote for the paper intermittently for a few years, then took over as editor early in 1938.

Before long, workers from all over the Islands were writing to Hall, telling him their stories and asking his advice. Then, in 1937, striking longshoremen on Kauai asked the sailors' union in Honolulu to send someone over to help them. The union sent Hall. "I was twenty–two, a tall, skinny haole in sailor moku pants and a T–shirt," Hall said later. "The old-timers—mostly first-generation Japanese—thought I was too young to give advice to men as mature as they were. But I knew what I was doing." He did. For the first time in the history of the Islands, a longshoremen's union came out of a strike with a contract. It was a weak one, but it was a contract.

When Honolulu longshoremen, encouraged by the Kauai victory, began to organize a union, Matson ignored the Wagner Act and promptly fired them. A *Voice of Labor* columnist who signed himself Paul O'Hashi, wrote in pidgin, and titled his column "This Day in Paradise," explained the significance of Matson's action:

> I see why Mr. Matson company trying to broke union, because if stevedore union win, this going to be step stone for all other hana–hana man of Hawaii. This, plantation boss and other boss no like and them too much kokua [help] to broke up stevedore union.
>
> Every stevedore hana-hana man attention to this. If you win this fight, it going to be victory not only for stevedore but for all hana–hana man Hawaii, so lili wake up and fight for you other brothers.

It would be almost impossible to invent a more tightly–controlled economy than the one O'Hashi was talking about. In her excellent two-part profile in the *New Yorker*, "The Sugar-Coated Fortress" (March 4 and 11, 1972), Francine du Plessix Gray described Hawaii this way:

> "There is a government in this territory which is centralized to an extent unknown in the United States, and probably as centralized as France was under Louis XIV," an Attorney General of Hawaii once said, referring to the islands' fabled Big Five firms. The Big Five—Castle & Cooke, Alexander & Baldwin, Theo. H. Davies, C. Brewer, and Amfac (which began as the German firm H. Hackfeld)—were organizations that became powerful as factors, or agencies, to serve the sugar plantations; they administered the shipment, distribution, and sale of the

crop. Felicitously isolated from the mainland's labor movement, these companies formed a cartel that totally controlled Hawaii's economic and political life until the Second World War . . .

The Big Five had their offices in stately, columned buildings of the Palm Beach Egyptian style standing within a couple of blocks of each other and just a few hundred yards from the Honolulu shipping docks, which they totally controlled . . .

The single most important reason why the unions, after Hall took over, were able effectively to challenge the Big Five was that for the first time, the new unions were multi–racial. Earlier unions had organized along racial lines: one union for Chinese, another for Japanese, another for Filipinos, and so on, and this made it easy for the employers to play one union off against the other. When one union struck, the others kept on working. The AFL wasn't much help, either, with its policy of excluding aliens and Orientals.

It was therefore not surprising that when Island longshoremen began talking about affiliating with longshoremen on the mainland, employers and Island newspapers warned the Islanders that if they joined a mainland union they would lose their jobs because of racial discrimination. And if they didn't lose them for that reason, they would be bumped off the job by longshoremen from the Coast who would come to Hawaii with more seniority.

"This Day in Paradise" had an answer to that. O'Hashi wrote:

This kind union they got no more race discrimination. Inside union, Pa–ke, Polokee, Kanaka, Haole,* Japanee, all they go hana–hana same kind job, all same time, and all–same pay. Anybody one time go Frisco and look–see how stevedore man hana–hana, they can believe this, but Hawaii man they only stay inside this kind small place and don't know nothing bout America, so they no can believe what union man tell them. This special for Japanee:

"Let me tell you, aikane, if Hawaii number two Japanee generation like live all same America citizen, they must work with all nationality all–same brother. They must think of nother man and fight for general interest all Japanee, or else number two generation going to walk same path their fathers—a path of bad wage, bad working condition . . ."

*Pa–ke = Chinese, Polokee = Portuguese, Kanaka = Hawaiian, Haole = Caucasian.

West Coast longshoremen had a good answer, too. They invited their new Island members to come to the Coast, paying their way where necessary. The Hawaiians worked on the docks, attended union meetings, took courses in a labor school, and wrote enthusiastic letters home extolling the union and the way things were done in West Coast ports.

The Hawaiian march inland began in 1937, when organizers from a CIO farm workers' union arrived in the islands. Within two months, Hall, aided by Kauai longshoremen who had relatives and friends on the plantations, had three thousand workers signed up. "For the first time in Hawaii's labor history," the *Voice of Labor* exulted, "plantation workers are united. Japanese and Filipinos, divided for years by a vicious caste system, have awakened to the fact that their interests are the same."

"We were really rolling just before the war," Hall said in 1960. "I asked Harry and Lou [Goldblatt] for CIO support, but they didn't think Hawaii was important. Not so long after, though, they recognized that if the union was to get at Matson effectively, they'd have to get at the Big Five. They figured the Big Five controlled Matson. But the war stopped organizing altogether because of martial law in the Islands.

"Now, wherever they have a buck, we hit 'em."

Hall's next campaign got him expelled from the sailors' union, and it changed the direction of his life. Asked in 1938 by the sailors from the inter–island fleet to help them organize, he signed them up in the CIO Inland Boatmen's Union instead of the AFL Sailors' Union of the Pacific. "We couldn't get them into the SUP," he recalled. "The SUP wouldn't take an alien in as a member. And naturally, most of the guys who worked those ships were aliens—first–generation Japanese. We had three guys vote for the SUP so Lundeberg wouldn't know for sure who voted for the IBU. That way, the SUP couldn't retaliate against the rank–and–filers.

"But they kicked me out—for ninety–nine years!"

Honolulu police were even rougher on him. The sailors had gone on strike in a hurry, without bothering to take their belongings off the ships. When they started back for them, police were at the foot of the gangplank, blocking their way. Somebody got to a phone and put in a call for Hall. He had barely set foot on the dock when the police closed in and seized him. They held him for fourteen hours, beat him severely, then released him. "He was about to talk to the strikers," the police chief explained. "And possibly about to incite them to illegal acts."

John Burns, Hawaii's governor in the 1960s and early seventies, was a policeman in Honolulu at the time. Asked in 1964 if he remembered the way his fellow–police had treated Hall back in 1938, he looked up at the ceiling for a moment before he answered:

"I agree that Harry Bridges deserves credit for having helped build a union that would have an appeal to workers in Hawaii," he began. "But the man who built this union is Jack Hall. And you know, it's a funny thing, but Jack wouldn't have stayed here, in my opinion, if it hadn't been for that beating he got from a cop named Taylor in 1938.

"That was when I first saw Jack. We had a line–up every morning and there he was in it. He was a tall, skinny kid in those days. And he was one helluva sight, bloody and battered."

When the strike ended after eighty–one days, inter–island sailors went back to work with higher pay, vacations with pay, overtime for holidays and Sundays, port arbitration committees. Once again, as Hall reminded his readers in the *Voice of Labor*, it was a victory for the new–found racial cooperation. In the next two years the union drive picked up speed, with longshoremen and plantation workers winning one NLRB election after another. At last, the stage was set for unionism to sweep across the Islands.

Pearl Harbor changed all that. From December 7, 1941 to October 24, 1944, labor was firmly supressed under martial law. On Oahu (the island where Honolulu and Pearl Harbor are located), where there were plenty of high–paying shipyard and other war–industry jobs, a private agreement between plantation managers and the military kept sugar and pineapple workers from leaving the plantations. Military HQ on Maui was more open: "It is ordered," said Regulation Number 56 on that island, "that no laborers, either skilled, semi–skilled, or unskilled, shall leave the Maui District without a permit." On Kauai, a worker had to get a formal release from his plantation manager before military authorities would let him move. Absenteeism, under General Order 32, could be punished by a fine of $200 and two months in jail.

The most telling blow to the union was the exclusion from the waterfront of the Japanese, its strongest supporters. This was, however, one of the relatively few restrictions placed upon Japanese–Americans in Hawaii, in contrast to the way they were herded into concentration camps on the West Coast. This may have been because persons of Japanese ancestry made up 40 per cent of Hawaii's population. It may also have been because while many Island Caucasians were fearful of what Hawaii's Japanese might do to help the enemy, influential community leaders kept their heads. One of these was the president of the Hawaiian Sugar Planters' Association. A retired major general, his military background gave his opinion extra weight, especially on a question of security. "Our whole country is made up from people of all races and one citizen is just as good as another as far as rights are concerned," he told the Roberts Commission in 1942 when it investigated the Pearl Harbor tragedy. "By rounding them up and putting them in a corner you can make them disloyal just as by pushing them in the face and showing that you suspect them."

Another influential figure at the time was the head of the local FBI office, Robert Shivers. He told the Roberts Commission that when he was assigned to Honolulu in 1939, "I made a tour of all the islands in Hawaii, asking the so–called haole populace—the businessmen, the plantation managers, the plantation owners—about the Japanese conditions and the Japanese situation. So far as I could learn the haole populace in Hawaii was not in a position to give any accurate information about the Japanese populace because there had been very little intercourse between the two." Did the Army and Navy have a list of suspicious persons, chairman Roberts asked Shivers. "The Army and Navy had such a list," Shivers replied, adding, "They had very little factual information to support such a list." One of the few who did know the Japanese, he added, was Jack Hall.

Military authorities helped out the Big Five in a variety of extralegal ways. In April 1942, MPs arrested the president of the Kauai longshore local for handing out copies of *The Pilot*, the newspaper of the CIO sailors' union. They held him incommunicado for a week, then brought him several times before a hearing board made up mostly of plantation managers. What they wanted to know, it developed, was what he thought of Harry Bridges and Communism. After four months of harassment, they let him go without bringing charges of any kind against him.

In this atmosphere, it was obvious that there was nothing a union organizer could do, so Hall took a job for the duration as a wage and hour inspector in the Territorial Department of Labor.

Even before the end of the war was in sight, the employers and the union began laying plans for the struggle they knew was coming. The employers moved first. Almon Roth, who had for a time headed the shipowners' association on the Coast, had been in Honolulu in 1941 and had urged Island management to profit from the San Francisco experience by preparing for unionization before it was upon them. Before they started, Pearl Harbor removed the urgency, but early in 1943, when military controls were partially lifted and plantation workers started talking union again, Island employers concluded that the time had come to act on Roth's advice and organized the Hawaiian Employers' Council.

They modeled it after its San Francisco counterpart and, to head it, brought over from San Francisco James Blaisdell, who for several years had bargained with Bridges as a negotiator for Bay Area warehouse employers. Blaisdell began by carrying Roth's advice a step farther. If Hawaiian employers showed right from the start that they were prepared to accept collective bargaining—which, Blaisdell reminded them, the law now required them to do—they stood a chance of avoiding the guerrilla warfare they'd heard so much about on the Coast. Breaking with their past, they took his advice.

The ILWU spent almost a year perfecting its organization before it approached the employers. In 1943, when military controls were first relaxed, sugar workers on the Big Island went to the longshoremen in Hilo for help. It was the moment Hall had been waiting for. He quit his job with the territorial government and, with $5,000 put up by the Honolulu longshoremen's local and with promises of help from Hilo dockworkers, set out to organize the sugar workers.

This time, as Blaisdell had told the employers, the union had the federal labor law on its side. Even so, there was plenty of room for argument as to which workers on the plantations the law applied to. The National Labor Relations Act excludes farm workers from protection and the NLRB had defined a farm worker as one who works in the fields. If he worked in agriculture but in a packing shed or in a warehouse—that is, if he had a roof over his head—he was involved in the distribution of the crop and entitled to the benefits of the law. Thus, the workers in the sugar mills were covered. If a worker drove a truck hauling crops or worked on a company railroad, he was covered too. When it came to a test, the board was expected to rule that about 15 to 20 percent of the workers on a sugar plantation would be eligible to vote in a union representation election.

As it turned out, both the union and the employers were in for a surprise. By March, 1944, the union had signed up majorities on five plantations and went to the managers to demand that they

start bargaining. The managers, convinced that the union was ex-
aggerating its strength, held out for NLRB elections in which the
owners hoped to convince the board that most of their employees
were farm workers, not eligible to vote.

"We could hardly believe it," an ILWU organizer, wrote back to
San Francisco. "Arnold Wills [the NLRB hearing officer] defined
the bargaining unit to include everybody from the sugar mill all the
way out to the end of the plantation railroad, where our people
load the cane into the cars. [By hand, in those days.] That means
that instead of 15 or 20 per cent, 50 to 60 per cent of the people are
covered!" In the elections, the union won overwhelmingly with majorities as high as 95 per cent.

In June 1944, the ILWU put Hall on the payroll as regional director for Hawaii. At the same time, it sent Frank Thompson, an
experienced organizer, out from the Coast to do the main organizing job in the field. "It isn't easy to get all the workers in one union
because of the racial question," Thompson wrote in one of his early
reports to San Francisco. "It is our job to break down the race barriers and we have some good people working on that. Jack Kawano
[a Honolulu longshore leader] and I had to go to Hawaii last week
because the Filipinos were going to declare war on the Japanese
that had been brought from one of the plantations to work on the
ships." Earlier he had written of Kawano: "He is under a handicap
at the present time, because he is of Japanese ancestry. Therefore,
it will be necessary to have a 'haole' (white, to you) to front for
him."

Hall's first move as regional director was to persuade several Hawaiian unions—four were AFL, two CIO, one unaffiliated—to
form a political action committee, which immediately set to work
registering voters in preparation for the 1944 elections. When the
results of the election were in, the committee had played a crucial
role in electing seventeen out of thirty–one members of the Territorial house of representatives and a substantial group of Territorial
senators.

In May 1945, the legislature passed a Territorial labor relations
law giving plantation workers the same rights to union activity the
federal law gives industrial workers. (As of 1972, Hawaii was still
the only state to have done so.) Politics paid off in patronage, too,
with union officials appointed to Territorial regulatory agencies.
When a vacancy came up on the Honolulu Police Commission in
1945, Governor Stainback, an FDR appointee, appointed Hall to
fill it. Hall laughed when he was asked in the 1960s if that implied

that Stainback was pro–labor. "Hell, no. He was a sonofabitch. We had good relations with Ickes [FDR's Secretary of the Interior], and he told Stainback to put some labor guys on some of the boards and commissions in the Territory." (In his new position, Hall should have been tempted to get back at Taylor, the policeman who, in 1937, beat him up in the backroom of the station house. When this was mentioned to Hall years afterward, his comment was that he held nothing against Taylor. "Hell," Hall said, "he had his orders.")

Within thirty–six months from the beginning of the campaign, the ILWU had working under contract all the longshoremen in the Territory, almost all the workers in sugar and pineapple, and was expanding into other fields as workers came to the union, asking to be admitted. By 1947, it had thirty thousand new members.

How could the union have carried off such a *tour de force?* The major factor seems to have been economic: "It is not hard to organize these workers," Frank Thompson wrote of the sugar mill workers soon after his arrival. "I find they are telling the organizers how important it is that they join. Many are skilled men such as electricians, plumbers, machinists, blacksmiths, etc."

"The workers on the plantations were ready," Phil Maxwell, then president of the Hawaiian employers' council, said in 1964. "They were frozen to their jobs on the plantations at low wages, and they'd seen people dredged up from the bottom of the barrel on the mainland and brought over here to work in defense industries at several times what they were getting. And those people who were brought over couldn't compare with them in skill."

Mechanization, which speeded up during the war, also played a part in the workers' eagerness to join. Fear of being displaced by the machine makes workers anywhere look to a union for protection, and in Hawaii, mechanization had yet another ugly face. Because of the new machines on the plantations, jobs in sugar and pineapple were becoming more desirable, and Orientals feared that when the war ended, their jobs would be turned over to white workers who had come down to the Islands to work in the war industries.

Education was a strong influence as well. As long as Japanese, Filipinos, and other ethnic groups were kept in segregated camps, uneducated and speaking only the language of the old country, the plantation owners' policy of divide and rule was easy to carry out. But when plantation workers' children went to school, language and cultural barriers began to break down. Moreover, in school the children learned about democracy and about the promise of American life. When they returned to the plantation, they came home to a feudal society and jobs from which there was no promotion, because the good jobs were reserved for haoles. The wartime influx of free-spending war workers and GIs exacerbated their resentment against the reality versus the promise.

And on the outer islands, racist behavior of U.S. Marines in the rest camps there also increased discontent. To many Marines, back from the fierce fighting in the Pacific with their trophies—samurai swords, flags, and the ears and other parts of the anatomy of Japanese soldiers pickled in bottles—anyone who looked Japanese was a "Jap", an enemy, to be treated accordingly.

The Marines' behavior was especially embittering because many of the Japanese–Americans the Marines were treating as enemies had husbands, sons and brothers fighting in Italy in Hawaii's 100th Infantry Battalion and 442nd Regimental Combat Team, the most decorated unit in World War II. Of the 7,500 men on its rolls, five thousand were awarded medals, 3,600 of them for battle wounds.

In this hostile atmosphere, one of the most attractive things about the ILWU was its promise of racial equality. "In 1944, I was working in the company store at the Lihue plantation," Takumi Akama, an ILWU official on Kauai, said in 1964.

and I decided we needed a union. I didn't know one union from another, but I had some friends who worked on the docks at Nawiliwili, so I got some union cards from them and began signing people up.

Then I read in the *Pacific Citizen* [a Japanese–American newspaper published on the West Coast] that Goldblatt, the Secretary–Treasurer of the California CIO and of a West Coast union, had testified that Japanese–Americans should be released from the camps they'd been put in after Pearl Harbor. I thought to myself, *"That's* the union for us."

A little while after that, an ILWU organizer came down from Honolulu. I told him about it and showed him the clippings. When he stopped laughing he told me: "That's *our* union!"

Akama would have been even more impressed had he known of Goldblatt's testimony before a Congressional committee that held hearings in the early months of 1942 on whether all 110,000 residents of Japanese ancestry should be removed from West Coast states and put in those concentration camps. "This entire episode of hysteria and mob chant against the native-born Japanese," Goldblatt told the committee, "will form a dark page of American history. It may well appear as one of the great victories won by the Axis powers."

After the war, the man who had been in charge of the camps wrote Goldblatt, "Your testimony stands out like a beacon light in an otherwise very dark picture. It is only too bad there were not more people with equal understanding and courage." It was not until 1959, however, that the Attorney General publicly asked forgiveness from the Japanese-Americans in a formal ceremony in Washington, D.C. "Americans must discipline themselves," he concluded, "to resist hysteria and emotional stress in times of alarms and danger in order that American ideals of justice may not yield, but be protected and successfully maintained." Goldblatt would no doubt have applauded that sentiment had he been at the ceremony. But he wasn't. He hadn't been invited.

Louis Goldblatt is a relative rarity in American labor history, an intellectual who deliberately chose to spend his life in the labor movement. About ten years younger than Bridges, he grew up in the Bronx, went to City College for a term, then moved out to California where he got a degree at the University of California in 1931. He stayed on for two more years of graduate work, then, in 1933, with only a thesis to go for a Ph.D., dropped out of academic life. He first went to Hollywood, where he spent a year trying to organize an industrial union in the motion picture industry.

In 1934, Goldblatt moved up to San Francisco where he got a job in a warehouse, joined the union, and plunged into organizing. He was fired from one job after another for union activity and in 1936 was elected chairman of the strike strategy committee. Not long after, he became vice-president of the warehousemen's local. In 1937, Bridges needed a man to head the CIO in Northern California, and Goldblatt got the job. A year later, at the founding convention of the state CIO, he was elected secretary. Four years after that, in 1942, he left the CIO to go back to the longshoremen's union as a staff member. In 1943, he was elected National Secretary-Treasurer of the ILWU, the number two position in the union, which he still holds.

The relationship between two men of such extraordinary talent as Bridges and Goldblatt was, almost from the beginning, a subject of unceasing speculation. The late Paul St. Sure, who, as the head of the waterfront employers in the fifties and sixties, knew both men well and got on well with both of them, suggested to a University of California oral history interviewer in the late 1950s that in Bridges the crusading spirit had ebbed, but in Goldblatt it was as strong as ever: "Goldblatt has the zeal. Bridges is a labor politician. . . . I think Bridges has changed as circumstances have changed. There's no exploitation to fight on the waterfront any more. Bridges accepts this . . .

"Goldblatt accepts it, too, but he wants a good deal more than that. He visualizes homes for workers, he visualizes a complete medical coverage for everybody . . . He has large social ideas . . . I think that Goldblatt's mind goes far beyond trade unionism . . ."

"Is there much truth to the common belief that Goldblatt is the real brains behind Bridges?" the interviewer asked.

"Oh, that is said," St. Sure replied.

I would doubt it. They've always had a strange relationship, as I've observed it. I've seen occasions when they apparently were miles apart, actually disagreeing with each other in the presence of an employer group. Next day they'd come in together, and usually Bridges would be the top guy. His side would prevail, or his policy would prevail.

I think Goldblatt is a good strategist. I think Bridges is a great opportunist. The combination is a very good one from their point of view. I don't think he dominates Bridges; I think that once in awhile he sells Bridges a bill of goods. Goldblatt has this faculty; he has a flair for the dramatic . . .

Most people who have known the two men would probably agree with that judgment.

St. Sure went on to tell another story about Goldblatt that reveals an additional facet of his personality. One day in the fifties, he and Goldblatt were talking about how violent the thirties had been, and how close the country had seemed to revolution.

"I remarked, I thought jestingly," St. Sure recalled,

that when the revolution came, I wasn't going to be concerned. I said I thought I was smart enough to be on the first committee of the workers.

He looked at me with a very cold eye and said: "No, when that time comes, they'll probably hang your kind." No smile. I think he meant it.

Nevertheless, over the many years I've dealt with Goldblatt, I think we respect each other intellectually. I don't think we try to fool each other. He will talk to me about many things, including philosophy and politics. He will discuss with me [the problem of legal] representation of some of their people who are in trouble with the Un-American Activities Committee.

He accepts me, apparently, as at least an intellectual equal, which I think is a compliment to me . . .

In 1944, not long after martial law was relaxed in Hawaii, the government began releasing Japanese-Americans from the concentration camps, and most of them returned to the Coast. When they came back home, they met stony hostility in most communities and in most unions they had belonged to before the evacuation. So it wasn't surprising that when some of the evacuees returned to Stockton, California, the ILWU warehouse local there told them they couldn't go back to their old jobs. So far as the local was concerned, they weren't members anymore. The Japanese–Americans turned to Bridges for help.

"We were watching that Stockton situation closely in Hawaii," a Hawaiian ILWU official told me. "If the union failed there, that would have been the end of the ILWU in Hawaii." Instead, what they saw delighted them. Bridges and Goldblatt called the Stockton members to a special meeting where they lectured them on the union's policy on race relations, suspended the local officers for violating the union constitution, and reinstated the Japanese–Americans.

By the summer of 1946, sugar workers in Hawaii were ready to start bargaining. With Goldblatt, who had come down from San Francisco to head the negotiating committee, in the chair, they decided to demand a 40 per cent wage increase (from forty–six–and–a–half cents an hour to sixty–five), a forty–hour week, and a union shop. On its face, a demand for a 40 per cent wage increase might have seemed exorbitant. In actuality, most of the increase represented the financial value of a union demand that plantations stop paying part of their wages in kind. Years earlier, when plantation managers had built camps for their workers to live in, "free," they had also decided to furnish them with water and fuel. Medical care was also provided.

How much these perquisites, as they were called, were worth as fringe benefits was anybody's guess. In 1939, when Washington ruled that the federal minimum wage of twenty–five cents an hour applied to the sugar mills, plantations were paying nineteen cents an hour. "The perquisites we provide for our workers cost us six cents an hour," plantation managers said then, "so we're actually paying the twenty–five cent minimum." During the war, when some of the skilled workers in the sugar mills were getting forty cents an hour, the War Manpower Commission ruled that it would not freeze a man in his job unless he was getting at least fifty–five. "That covers us," the industry said now. "We're only paying forty cents in cash, but the perquisites are worth fifteen. So that brings our wages to fifty–five cents." Thus, the union was demanding an end to the perquisites and a wage high enough to enable the workers to move out of the plantation camps and live where they chose, in their own homes.

The plantations offered fifteen cents an hour, so the union, unwilling to back down from eighteen and a half, prepared for a strike. It began by stockpiling canned milk, potatoes and rice. Union members were urged to plant vegetables on every patch of ground they could find, and committees were formed to hunt and fish for the common kitchens that would be set up in the camps. "A large supply of wild goats and pigs is available on the outside islands," the union told its members, "and we have received assurances from Territorial authorities that cooperation will be forthcoming in organizing mass hunts. The Territory has for several years been trying to exterminate these wild animals because of the damage they inflict on domestic food production."

In earlier strikes, plantation managers had evicted strikers from their camps, but this time they told the workers they could stay. Some plantations were even more cooperative. "The manager of the Ewa Plantation," Frank Thompson reported two weeks before the strike deadline, "has agreed to furnish two acres of ground to raise vegetables during the strike. He also agreed to furnish a tractor and plow. In addition, he has agreed to allow the strikers to use all recreational facilities, including the swimming pool."

It was a far cry from the days of throwing strikers and their families off the plantations, using the territorial anti–trespass law to keep union representatives out of the camps, police firing on strikers, mass arrests and conspiracy trials, as well as pitting one race against another. Even so, it was too much to expect that the sugar planters would be fully converted to accepting unionism as inevitable. In the past, a standard method of putting down strikes had been to import a new ethnic group to take the place of the strikers. This time, the planters dispatched recruiters to the Philippine

Islands with instructions to pick up six thousand men for work in Hawaii.

The new workers were to be hand–picked, without much education, and they shouldn't be able to speak English. That way, they wouldn't know they were being hired to break a strike, and the union would have a hard time getting its message to them. The scheme didn't work. A couple of Hawaiian longshoremen shipped out on the vessel going to pick up the Filipinos and, with the help of the ship's Filipino stewards who belonged to the CIO marine cooks' union, had most of the Filipinos signed up in the ILWU by the time the ship docked in Honolulu. As it turned out, when the strike ended, there was enough work to absorb the newcomers.

The strike ended after seventy-eight days, and while workers used up their wartime savings, there was a positive side. The community kitchens kept them from going hungry, the hunting and fishing committees had a grand time, and the workers were exhilarated by the new sense of solidarity, especially the blurring of racial lines. The strike ended when Washington announced an increase in the subsidy to domestic sugar producers. Plantation managers agreed to a twenty–cent wage increase (more than the union had originally asked), and conceded most of the union's other demands. It was to be twelve years before there would be another major strike in sugar.

Pineapple was different. In the sugar industry, the union was strong, with almost every sugar worker in the union. But in pineapple, it was weak. In sugar, where jobs were full–time the year around, the workers had been receptive, even enthusiastic, to unionism. In pineapple—especially in the canneries—only about 60 per cent of the workers were employed on a full–time, year–round basis. The others, students and housewives, came in during peak seasons. And only the year–around workers had joined the union.

The union had gotten its first industry–wide contract in pineapple in 1946, to run until February 1, 1947. As contracts go, it was a good one. Then, as the union began making plans for the new contract in 1947, pineapple workers were acutely aware of the twenty–cent increase it had negotiated for their brothers and sisters in sugar, and the thirty–cent increase on the docks. Wages became the major issue, with the union demanding thirty–five cents and the employers offering eight. As negotiations moved along, the union reduced its demand to twenty–three–and–a–half cents and the employers raised their offer to ten. February first came and went, with the contract extended week after week while negotiations continued.

They were still trying to reach a settlement in May, when the union had its first brush with Red-baiting. It was readying its strike machinery, taking votes on whether to strike, and on a $5.00 assessment for a strike fund, when pineapple managers, seeking to take advantage of the union's weakness, publicly proposed that the votes be supervised by an impartial agency. As they expected, the union refused. Then Robert Mookini, president of one of the locals, came out in favor of the employers' proposal, creating the impression that there was a split in the union although it turned out that he had no support. When he was suspended from office for his defection, he claimed it was really because he wouldn't follow Communist orders.

Taking a job with the teamsters, he called upon his members to follow him. Few did. Nevertheless, his defection gave Art Rutledge, the eccentric teamster leader in the Islands, a propaganda opening. "I'm going to take the pineapple workers into my union," he declared, "and give them a place to go from the Communist–dominated ILWU." Rutledge apparently never seriously intended to follow up his threat, and nothing came of it.

There were to be other, more serious attacks on the alleged Communism of ILWU leaders. One came not long after the Mookini–Rutledge affair, when Ichiro Izuka and Amos Ignacio, two leaders in the early days of sugar organizing, quit the ILWU in a blaze of publicity. Charging that the union was dominated by Communists, they started an independent union on the Big Island and on Kauai. It never took hold, but Izuka struck at Hall and the other officers in a thirty–one–page pamphlet entitled *The Truth About Communism in Hawaii*. Printed in English and Ilocano (a Filipino dialect), it was widely distributed in the Islands.

On its face, the pamphlet seemed extremely damaging, for Izuka identified himself as a former Communist who knew what he was talking about from the inside. On close reading, aside from asserting that perhaps a score of ILWU officials were Communists, what it contained was only Izuka's charge that the ILWU endorsement of Joseph Farrington, a Republican, for territorial delegate to Congress, was somehow a Communist plot. (Izuka supported William Borthwick, a Democrat.) The pamphlet inflamed much of the Island community, and it may have helped Izuka get a management job with the Honokaa Sugar Company, but it failed with ILWU members for several reasons.

Farrington had an extraordinary following among non–Caucasians, despite being a Republican, the party supported by the Big Five. When people in the Territory were polled on the question, "Who is the best person we could elect as delegate to Congress?", 70 per cent of the Japanese, 63 per cent of the Chinese, and 60 per cent of the Hawaiians answered, "Farrington." Moreover, Farrington's Honolulu newspaper, the *Star-Bulletin*, had been fair in reporting the sugar strikes.

At least as important was the ILWU's approach to politics, which was in the classic tradition of American labor: Reward your friends and punish your enemies, on a non–partisan basis. In accordance with that tradition, the union would support a conservative over a liberal if the liberal was too hard to pin down but the conservative was a man it could trust. And even as early as 1947, ILWU members had found that that tactic worked.

"Maybe what seems to be zany political behavior appeals to the rank–and–file," a Honolulu reporter said in 1964.

> They don't really give a goddam about politics. What has a politician done for them, they figure? One is as good or as bad as another. So when the union, which *has* done something for them, recommends a candidate, they may as well go along with it. And I think they like the way the union does the unexpected. It keeps the bosses off balance.
>
> The union pretends to have more political power than it has. But the bosses are never sure. They know one thing. If the union says it'll have four thousand guys out on the picket line, there'll be four thousand guys out on the picket line. They've seen that happen plenty of times.
>
> "So when the union says it has four thousand votes behind some candidate, who's to say it hasn't?"

The union's economic power and its ability to withstand Red–baiting were demonstrated dramatically in 1949, in a longshore strike that kept the Islands paralyzed for six months. It was a classic labor struggle that started out as an economic argument and was then transformed into a showdown, with the employers seeing the union as a threat to their survival and the workers seeing the employers as determined to destroy their union.

"You remember that strike," Governor Burns said in 1964. "It was over a fumdamental economic issue. Before the war longshoremen in Hawaii got ten cents an hour less than they did on the Coast. By 1949, there was a forty–two–cent differential!

"That was what the strike was about. Of course, the Big Five called it a political strike. They called it Communist. What else *could* they do? Their position was completely untenable."

For the first month, the strike was just another strike. In June, Alexander Budge, president of Castle and Cooke, explained the issues in a letter to President Truman. "The workers," he wrote, "are paid $1.40 now, and are demanding parity with the West Coast, where the pay is $1.82. We originally offered eight cents, later raised it to twelve. The union has asked for arbitration, but we're against it because arbitration will play into the hands of the union. The union," he added, "represents much more than just the dockworkers. It represents workers throughout the whole Island economy."

At about the time Budge was writing the White House, the *New York Times* West Coast correspondent was on his way out to Hawaii to cover the strike. It reminded him of Harlan County, Kentucky, in the thirties. "There are no neutrals here," he reported. "Every person accosted knows without doubt where he stands on the strike." Food supplies were running low. Businesses were cutting wages. Some were facing bankruptcy. He had even heard of a threat to tar–and–feather Bridges, who, people were daily reminded by Hawaiian newspapers, was under a federal indictment on a Communist charge.

The national paranoia about Communism was reflected in the same issue of the *Times* in three front–page stories—one about the tempestuous Smith Act trial in New York where the eleven national leaders of the Party were in the dock; another about Whittaker Chambers's testimony in the Alger Hiss case; and the third, about the army's rejection of TVA chairman Gordon Clapp for an assignment in the military government in Germany. According to the army, Clapp was a loyalty risk. On an inside page, a story on the Judith Coplon spy trial reported that Frederic March and his actress wife, Florence Eldridge, had been mentioned as members of the Communist Party in a report read by an FBI man on the witness stand. The Coplon story also said that Congresswoman Helen Gahagan Douglas, Pearl Buck, and Danny Kaye had been named as Communist sympathizers by the California Un–American Activities Committee.

As the strike continued, the temptation to use Communism as a stick to beat the union with proved irresistible to Hawaiian businessmen. On June 23rd, the fifty-fourth day of the strike, Lorrin Thurston, publisher of the *Honolulu Advertiser*, took a two-page ad in the *New York Times* to explain the strike to a mainland audience. It said in part:

> Because the business men of Hawaii have learned after fifteen years of experience that under this ILWU union and its leadership, there can NEVER be labor peace, they have as one man, big and small, through utter necessity, agreed to stand together and resist further demands, if it takes every dollar they have.
>
> . . . Like most American citizens, we are NOT in a position to prove this strike is Communist directed. But we do know that every move in the whole picture for fifteen years tallies exactly with the Communist manuals and their teachings—without any exceptions. We do know that every Communist list, as issued by the Un-American Activities Committee of the House of Representatives, contains as listed Communists the names of the men who are crucifying Hawaii.

The ad went on to say that Hawaii had been abandoned by Washington, which did nothing but send conciliators out to the Islands. It ended with an appeal to its readers for help. Twenty-five hundred of them responded, deluging the White House with telegrams and letters imploring President Truman to use the Taft-Hartley Act to force the workers back to work. "Don't arbitrate," was a common theme. "Stop Communism!"

The President decided against using Taft-Hartley, but Tom Clark, his Attorney General, joined the anti-Communist crusade in an effort to help the embattled employers. In a speech in Milwaukee early in June, 1949, when the strike was in its first month, Clark said, "Hawaii is the only spot at present where our domestic Communist problem is serious. We may have to take some drastic action there. But I think that the case against Bridges has already been of some help in the Hawaii situation. If we are successful in our prosecution of Bridges, as I am certain we will be, it may be that we can break the Hawaiian situation without any other intervention."

When the Attorney General spoke of breaking the Hawaiian situation, it was not clear whether he meant Communism, the strike, the union, or all three. The union was certain that he was talking about breaking the strike. His comments were further evidence, if anyone needed it, that the union was fighting for its life.

With businesses hard hit and empty shelves appearing in the stores, at the end of the second month Governor Stainback appointed a fact–finding board, asking it to recommend a solution. It wasn't much help. Where the employers were now offering twelve cents and the union demanding thirty–two, the board recommended fourteen. The longshoremen hooted it down.

Another month sent by. Then, early in August, a special session of the Territorial legislature enacted a law giving the Governor power to seize and operate the docks. "But that's unconstitutional!" Lou Goldblatt, who had come down to help out, objected. "Maybe so," the Territorial Attorney General retorted. "But it'll take two years to process it to the Supreme Court, and by that time it'll be moot, anyway." Bridges was arrested for picketing after the law went into effect, but when his case came up for trial the judge ruled that the First Amendment protected peaceful picketing, even when it was a protest against an act of the legislature.

If a bill like this had come up in the past, Bridges would have wired his friend CIO President Murray in Washington, Murray would have called his friend Harry Truman at the White House, Truman would have put in a call to Governor Stainback, his appointee in Honolulu, and the dock seizure bill would have been quietly scuttled. But these weren't ordinary times. By August, 1949, the Communist issue had so corroded relations between the longshoremen and the national CIO that Murray wasn't even acknowledging Bridges's telegrams. And even if Murray had called Truman, the President wouldn't have done anything to help Bridges. In the 1948 Presidential campaign, when Truman was fighting for his political life, Bridges had called him a strikebreaker for threatening to draft railroad strikers in 1946 and for using Taft–Hartley Act eighty–day injunctions against maritime strikers in 1948. "Any workingman who votes for Truman," Bridges asserted, "ought to have his head examined."

Desperate, Hall, supported by a rising young Democrat named Dan Inouye, turned to Jack Burns, an influential Island Democrat the union had supported when he ran unsuccessfully for Territorial Delegate against Farrington in 1948.

Burns has recalled:

They asked that I do whatever I could to keep the government from using Taft–Hartley, since they feared that President Truman might yield to the overwhelming pressure being put on him.

They also wanted, if at all possible, to get the active help of the Administration in assuring them a fair deal.

So I did. I took with me photostatic copies of the annual financial reports of the two stevedoring companies. I had a helluva time getting them but I got them. I also took three letters: one from Robert L. Shivers, head of the FBI in Hawaii in World War II, one from George Bicknell, Counter–Intelligence, U. S. Army, and one from General Kendall Fielder, G-2, U. S. Army, Pacific. Each commended my service as head of the Police Department Espionage Bureau from 1940 to 1945.

When Burns got to Washington, he frittered away his first week with people backing away from him, thinking he was an emissary of Communists. "Some of the people who gave me the most trouble," he said, "were my fellow fish–eaters." Then he remembered he had a cousin who was active in deanery work in Falls Church, Virginia. She got him an appointment with Fr. McGowan, a leading figure in the National Catholic Welfare Conference, who was close to Phil Murray and Secretary of Labor Maurice Tobin.

Father McGowan and Burns hit it off, Burns has recalled, when they found they had attended the same school in Atchison, Kansas, about some thirty years apart. "This established an opening, and I then gave him the Hawaii story briefly but fully in its socio–economic realities," Burns said. "I then asked for his help in the way of advice and counsel." McGowan responded by sending Burns to see Murray and Tobin.

When Burns arrived at Murray's office, James Carey, Secretary–Treasurer of the CIO, was with Murray. Burns was launching into an explanation of why he was there when Murray swung around to Carey. "Who sent this fellow to see us?" "Father McGowan," Carey replied. "Oh," Burns has recalled Murray answering, "if our 'organizer' sent him to see us we don't need to know anything more. Give him whatever help you can."

After listening to Burns's story of the dock strike in Hawaii as he saw it—a long overdue strike for justified economic demands— Carey's assistant, Harry Reid, suggested that Burns talk to Alex Campbell, in the Justice Department, and Frank Tavenner, chief counsel of the House Un–American Activities Committee. "Then," he concluded, "you'll have to see Tobin."

"I can see why I should see Tobin," Burns replied. "But why those first two?"

"Well, you've got to head off a HUAC hearing. I hear they're thinking about going out there."

"I said, 'Yes, I'm sure there's a lot of pressure for that from the Big Five'. That explains Tavenner. Why Campbell?"

"There's a lot of pressure on the Justice Department to call up Bridges's trial out on the Coast," Reid replied. "It would help if Campbell knows first hand what's behind the pressure he's getting. Otherwise, he might yield and push for trial now, while the strike is on."

Campbell was sympathetic, Burns has recalled, especially after Burns told him about the Big Five and their forty–seven years of Republican rule in the Islands. By the end of the conversation, Campbell acknowledged that an immediate trial was being demanded to prejudice the strike, and he promised to postpone it until late November or early December.

"Tavenner was understanding, too," Burns said. "We talked for about an hour and a half, going over the history of Hawaii and the strike." Tavenner agreed to hold off a hearing until the strike was over, but he asked Burns to send him a memo on what he had said about the allegations that ILWU leaders in the Islands were Communists or Communist sympathizers. "I had pointed out that because the economy and politics were so tightly controlled by Hawaii's socio–economic hegemony a man might accept any help to correct social and economic injustice," Burns said later.

Maurice Tobin, the Secretary of Labor, was next. "He was a fish–eater, too, you know," Burns recalled. "And the fact that McGowan had endorsed me naturally helped." Even so, Tobin's opening remark got the meeting off to a bad start.

"You'll have to admit that Bridges and the leadership of the ILWU on the West Coast and Hawaii are Communists," he challenged Burns.

"Sir, I'll not admit that what you say is true," Burns bristled. "But even if it were, it doesn't affect the merits of the strike."

"Will you look at these?" he asked, handing Tobin the letters he'd brought with him commending his service as head of the Honolulu police espionage bureau during World War II. "I'm not accusing you of being a Communist," Tobin replied. Burns then showed the Secretary the financial reports of the two stevedoring companies he'd brought along, explaining that they were really one company, in view of their interlocking directorships. The reports showed, moreover, that one company had declared a stock split two years earlier, followed by a 10 per cent dividend the year the strike began.

That convinced Tobin. "He agreed to drop the Taft–Hartley injunction, and he put me in touch with Cy Ching," Burns has said. "He was another grand old guy." (Ching, seventy–three, was the widely–admired head of the federal mediation and conciliation service.)

"Ching said to me, 'I can talk to Bridges, all right. He knows what he's doing and he'll negotiate, although he's tough. [Ching said in a *Newsweek* interview in September, 1967 that the two toughest bargainers he met in his forty years as a labor mediator were John L. Lewis and Harry Bridges.] But those employers you've got out there! They're completely out of their minds. Do you suppose they'd talk more sensibly if we got the negotiations out of Hawaii and met in New York, say?' "

As it happened, when Burns headed back for Hawaii, he found himself on the same plane with Tobin, Secretary of Agriculture Brannan, and Leon Keyserling, President Truman's chief economic adviser. The four talked about the strike for several hours, and when Tobin was met in San Francisco by reporters he issued a statement calling upon Hawaiian employers to accept the union's proposal for arbitration.

"Jack Hall told me the position taken by Secretary Tobin was the straw that broke the camel's back," Burns said later. "Anyway, we got the negotiations moved back to New York, and we got the strike settled."

It was a major victory for the union. By standing firm, it solidified its position in the longshoring industry, and, at least as important, in the Hawaiian economy. Moreover, the twenty–one–cent increase it obtained, being six cents more than West Coast longshoremen had settled for, assured that Hawaii would gradually come to parity with the Coast. It did so in 1959.

Early in 1950, the House Un–American Activities Committee swooped down on Hawaii, with its advance men and its scare stories about Communists holding the Islands in their iron grip. Sixty–six Island residents were called to explain why they had been named as Communists by HUAC's witnesses. Thirty–nine, most of them officers of the ILWU, refused to cooperate with the Committee by answering any questions. Following the standard practice of those days, they were charged with contempt of Congress, but a federal judge refused to sentence them to jail, ruling that the Constitution protected their right to remain silent.

They were cleared in the eyes of the law, but, as Dave Thompson, education director of the union in Hawaii, wrote in a letter to this author in 1972:

> After the hearings, the daily press and the establishment tried to make the thirty–nine and any who associated with them social and political untouchables. The '49 strike had split the community, and the split was maintained for ten years. *Star-Bulletin* editorials kept saying that "the long arm of the law" is reaching out for the guilty ones, implying that anything but hostility to any of the thirty–nine or their ills was dangerous for alien and citizen alike.
>
> There was a contradiction between the more extreme forms of this program and the practical considerations which led the employers to bargain with the union, and eventually the employers disclaimed any organized support for such outfits as IMUA. Imua is the Hawaiian word for forward. . . .

HUAC's pilgrimage to the Islands was to be expected, given the political capital a Congressman can acquire by exploiting reports of the Red menace. In the 1950s some members of Congress had the additional incentive of using the threat of Communism to block statehood for Hawaii. If, instead of having to admit that they were against annexing a state with a large Oriental population (and two more votes for civil rights in the Senate), opponents of statehood could claim that the Islands were in the grip of Harry Bridges and the Communists, their arguments against statehood would carry more weight.

After the Committee's visit, seven Island residents were arrested by the FBI and charged with being the top Communists in the territory, a violation of the Smith Act. Six were officials of the Party. The seventh was Jack Hall.

After Hall's arrest, two FBI agents appeared at the home of Dave Thompson, the union's education director, saying they wanted to talk with him about Hall and Bridges. Thompson asked them to come back that night, when he would have more time to talk. When they returned, they proposed that he persuade Hall to pull the union in Hawaii out of the ILWU in exchange for which the charges against him would be dropped. Thompson kept the agents there for more than an hour, talking about the pros and cons of the proposal. He didn't tell them that between their first and second visits he had planted a bug in his living room and that Bob McElrath, the union's public relations man, was recording the conversation down in the basement. It was published in the ILWU paper and for weeks afterward, McElrath played the recording on his weekly radio broadcast, which was carried throughout the Islands.

Before the trial began, Hall spoke to a Territory–wide meeting of the union, reminding the members that in each of the past two years he had filed a non–Communist affidavit with the National Labor Relations Board, as provided for in the Taft–Hartley Act. The penalty for filing a false statement, he pointed out, was ten years in jail. By contrast, the maximum jail sentence under the Smith Act was five. If the government actually had evidence that he was a Communist, he asked, why hadn't he been prosecuted under the heavier penalty?

"My seventeen years in Hawaii," he went on,

have been lived in a fishbowl. I am sure that I, more than any other individual, have had my activities watched, reported, documented, and distorted . . .

Bob Shivers told me in the closing days of 1941 that he had been asked to arrest me immediately after Pearl Harbor as a "subversive," as a person dangerous to the security of the country, by an executive of a Big Five firm who was then in charge of G–2 [military intelligence] under the civilian M–day setup. He told me that he had been supplied with a dossier on me nearly a foot high, which had not been collected by any government agency. In that whole voluminous file, he found nothing contrary to the best interests of this country in any of my activities, statements, or associations.

Hall was convicted, nevertheless, and along with the others, sentenced to five years in jail and fined $5,000. The Supreme Court reversed the convictions in January, 1958. "Indicting me under the Smith Act was phony," Hall later said scornfully. "The government knew damn well I hadn't been in the Party within the three years covered by the statute of limitations."

Hall's acquittal should presumably have laid the Communist bogy to rest, but fears of the Red menace died hard. "I can get in an argument in a bar anytime I mention I work for the union," Joe Kealalio, an ILWU officer, told me in the late sixties. "There's always some guy who'll pipe up, 'What're you doing, working for that Commie outfit?'

"What've *you* done lately for the working class, I ask the sonofabitch."

Those who, like Attorney General Clark, thought that cries of Communism would weaken the union were mistaken. Instead, just as the membership on the mainland rallied behind Bridges when he was attacked, these attacks united the union in the Islands behind its leaders.

Were the charges true? Were the Island union leaders Communists? The answer is that they probably were—in the 1940s. What led them to join? And what caused them to quit? Governor Burns, speaking from long experience in Hawaiian politics, looked at it this way when this author talked with him in the Iolani Palace in 1964:

What else could they do, in the situation they were in, in the early days? Where would they have gotten direction? Where would they have been able to learn about strike strategy, how to carry an organizing drive through to a contract, all those things, if it hadn't been for the Communist Party?

And you have to remember, they belonged to the American Communist Party. There wasn't anything illegal about that, then. Why hell, you could run for public office on the Communist ticket in California and other states, in those days.

Then there were two other reasons. It was tough being a union organizer in those days. I know. I was a cop then, you remember. We used to give them a rough time. And then, too, almost all the union leaders who weren't Communists got bought off by the Big Five or the plantation managers, one way or another.

Now, as to why they quit the Party in 1948. That was because the environment had changed. It was possible, in 1948, to work in the community as a union. And we had the two–party system in 1948, for the first time in the history of the Territory. Before 1948, Dillingham [Walter Dillingham, a classmate of FDR's at Harvard and one of the most powerful men in the Islands] was the Democratic Party in Hawaii. Nobody even got on the ticket unless he was all right with Dillingham. And that meant that the Big Five controlled the Democratic Party.

But when the organization of the sugar workers broke the dictatorial political control of the plantation managers as well as their economic control, then Jack Hall and the others associated with him could work through the two–party system. And they did.

In the 1950s, the union was a force to be reckoned with in the Islands. Economically, it was beyond dislodging, with its longshore members enjoying wages and working conditions equal to those on the West Coast, and its members out on the plantations getting wages undreamed of by farm workers on the mainland. On top of this, there were pensions, paid holidays, vacations, and employer–paid medical and dental care. And when plantation workers, displaced by the machines whose introduction was spurred on by their economic gains, moved out into other jobs, they carried their union with them. Before long, they were working under ILWU contracts in luxury hotels, grocery chains, auto sales agencies, garages, bakeries, manufacturing plants, cemeteries, newspapers, cattle ranches, lumber yards, laundries.

Politically, the union was a major force behind the Hawaiian legislature's impressive record of progressive social legislation in the fifties and sixties. "I've seen legislators who are lawyers for corporations, legislators who are small businessmen, legislators who are farmers, vote the way the ILWU wants them to," a Honolulu newspaperman told me. "And sometimes it's against their own interests. But they figure the ILWU has the votes."

Spectacular as were the union's economic and political achievements, its impact on the culture of the Islands was even more revolutionary. Before World War II, the popular conception of Hawaii as a paradise in which people of all races dwelt together in harmony and equality was, unfortunately, a myth.

Writing at the turn of the century, Ray Stannard Baker, in his *Wonderful Hawaii*, suggested an astonishing comparison:

> In the Old South, domination rested upon three essential advantages or privileges. First, upon the ownership of the best and most fertile cotton lands; second, upon the control of the indispensable machinery—the cotton gin; and third, upon the absolute domination of the labor supply—the Negro slaves. All these advantages gave the great planters wealth and political power, and by the use of wealth and power they were able to buy still more land, control still more machinery, and . . . acquire more slaves . . .

Now, the power of the corporation aristocracy of Hawaii, of

course, rests upon exactly the same fundamental advantages . . .

Control is made easier in Hawaii, as it was in the Old South, by the presence of a very large population of non–voting workmen. This not only includes that half of the population which is made up of Chinese and Japanese, but of thousands of ignorant Portuguese, Spanish, Russians, and others, who are not yet naturalized. Fully three–quarters of the population in Hawaii have no more say about the government under which they are living than the old slaves . . .

One is inclined to say in disbelief that even if Baker's description was accurate for the early 1900s, it couldn't have been that bad at the time of World War II. It wasn't, in Honolulu. But as Andrew Lind, dean of Hawaiian sociologists, has written in *Race Relations: Problems and Theory*:

"A wholly intrusive and unexpected element in the breakdown of racial barriers on the plantations since World War II is the sudden spread of unionization. Sometimes described as Hawaii's major revolution, surpassing in social significance the revolution of 1893 in which Queen Liliuokalani was dethroned, the establishment of the ILWU as the bargaining agent for workers in both the sugar and pineapple plantations brought about a degree of collaboration and fraternization across race lines which had never previously been thought possible."

Just how recent has been the acceptance of racial minorities in Hawaiian life was demonstrated in an apparently minor incident which occurred in the mid–sixties at an arbitration proceeding between several newspaper unions and staff members from the employers' council, who did the negotiating for the papers. Presided over by an urbane Japanese–Hawaiian (class of 1950, Yale Law School), the ethnic composition of the two sides of the table made an arresting contrast. On the union side was a Japanese, a Chinese, a part–Hawaiian, and one or two others who would be the despair of an ethnic taxonomist. The only Caucasian among them was Jack Hall, whom they had asked to be their chief spokesman. On the employer side sat a half–dozen Caucasians. When asked if the staff of the employers' council was exclusively Caucasian, an employer representative replied that just recently they had hired one or two Orientals.

When the meeting ended, the arbitrator remarked, "You know, there are three things that brought democracy to the Islands: pub-

lic school education, the 442nd Combat Team, and the ILWU."
That statement is made repeatedly in Hawaii. The arbitrator went
on to say, "Fifteen years ago, people representing the big owners
wouldn't have stayed in a meeting where the arbitrator was an
Island boy, and not a haole."

By the late sixties, how far the revolution had gone was demonstrated by an item in Herb Caen's column in the *San Francisco
Chronicle*: "There is now a street called Bridges Place in Honolulu,
where, only a few years ago, the general feeling was that Harry
Bridges's place was at the bottom of the sea."

NOTES

In this chapter I have drawn on Lawrence Fuchs's *Hawaii Pono*, Joyce
Matsumoto's *The 1947 Hawaiian Pineapple Strike*, and "Jack Hall Says
Aloha" in the *Honolulu Star Bulletin*, June 21, 1969. Frank Thompson's
1944 organizing reports to ILWU headquarters are in the ILWU library in
Honolulu.

Bridge's letter to President Truman is in Official File 407B, "Honolulu
Strike," in the Truman Presidential Library in Independence, Missouri.

9

The War Ends, the Battles Resume

*"If you criticize Truman when he acts inhu-
man, you're a Red, Red, Red, Red, Red . . ."*
PROGRESSIVE PARTY CAMPAIGN SONG, 1948

IT WAS PAINFULLY APPARENT to Bridges that when the war ended, it
was going to be back to guerrilla warfare on the waterfront unless
he could find a way to keep the peace. The shipowners were coop-
erating with the union as members of the Pacific Coast Maritime
Industry Board, but it was an uneasy partnership in which the employers nervously examined every union suggestion for a hidden
trick that would give the union an advantage when the war was
over.

In April, 1945 Bridges told the union convention it would have
to be prepared for a struggle on the docks when the war was over.
As he spoke, the battles in the Pacific were still raging with no end
in sight, yet, he reported, the shipowners were disdaining "every
union proposal that has as its sincere purpose increasing joint responsibility and effort toward the prosecution of the war."

Facing the union, also, as it looked beyond the war, was the un-
friendly climate of opinion in the nation, which in 1943 had shifted
to the position that unions had become too strong and that their
sense of responsibility had not kept pace. There were also two other
considerations that the union had to take into account: the role
America was going to play in rebuilding war-ravaged economies
around the world, and the unemployment that seemed inevitable
when the economy reconverted to peacetime production. If the resumption of a peacetime economy was held up by strikes and labor
disputes, unions would bear the brunt of the blame.

What was needed, Bridges decided, was a union proposal that
would keep strikes to a minimum and earn for the ILWU a reputa-

tion for being responsible and concerned, not just with the interests of the longshoremen, but with the welfare of the country as a whole. The solution he hit upon put him in the incongruous company of Phil Murray of the CIO, William Green of the AFL, Eric Johnston of the U.S. Chamber of Commerce, and the Communist Party. The first three had signed a charter for harmonious post–war labor–management relations. The Party was advocating that the wartime no–strike pledge be extended into the reconversion period.

The peace plan Bridges put forward was similar to the Party proposal, but with a difference in the form of a *quid pro quo:* if the shipowners would agree in writing to accept the union and stop trying to undermine it, the union would agree not to strike. But, he warned, "unreconstructed elements amongst employers who will seek to use the post–war period for an anti–union blitz will be met and fought effectivey with all the weapons at our command . . ." If a strike were unavoidable, he assured the union's 1945 convention, the union would win, "because lined up with us we will have large, important employer groups, and they [the unreconstructed employers] will not be able to organize all employers to fight us as they have been able to do in the past."

The shipowners wanted no part of Bridges's plan, and when the war ended in the fall of 1945, guerrilla warfare flamed up again on the docks. It was foreshadowed in the summer of that year, when negotiations began for a new contract (the old one expired in July). "In 1945," Bridges told the 1947 convention of the union, "employers' committees either ignored our demands or met just to pass the day."

The struggle went on for a year, until Bridges forged a new weapon, a latter–day Maritime Federation of the Pacific. It was called the Committee for Maritime Unity, and it included six CIO unions—longshoremen, East Coast sailors, marine cooks and stewards, marine engineers, ferryboatmen, and ships' radio operators—and the unaffiliated marine firemen. "One out, all out" was their motto, and they agreed no union would sign a new contract until they were all ready to sign. Heading the CMU were Bridges and Joe Curran, president of the National Maritime Union.

Curran, like Lundeberg, began his union career as a leftist and for years was accused of being either a Communist or a fellow–traveler. Like Lundeberg, he got his start in a protest against the corrupt leadership of the old AFL sailors' union. In 1936, he shipped out from New York on the intercoastal liner "California," the wages and working conditions of which had been set by a contract covering East Coast shipping. When the ship docked in San Pedro, the crew discovered that on the West Coast, wages, although negotiated by the West Coast branch of the same union, were higher than theirs. With Curran as their spokesman, they went on strike, refusing to sail the ship unless the owners matched the West Coast wage rates.

They agreed to go back to work at the request of Frances Perkins, who told them she would do what she could to get them the wage increase and to protect them against discrimination for having gone on strike. Instead, when the ship tied up in New York, Curran and two dozen others were docked six days' pay, fired, and their names put on the shipowners' blacklist. A charge of mutiny was lodged against them by the Justice Department, but it wasn't pressed. Not long after, Curran and eighteen others were expelled from the union, charged with being Communists. One thing led to another and in 1937, Curran and a group of rebels formed the National Maritime Union under the banner of the CIO.

The story of the NMU, and of Curran as its president, is a classic confirmation of Michels's iron law of oligarchy. At the beginning, the NMU was a model of participatory democracy, but over the years, control of the union was taken over by Curran and a small clique, in part by expelling a succession of men who had helped build the union from its infancy but who had become competitors with Curran for leadership of the union.

The take–over was foreshadowed, ironically, by the expulsion in 1937 of the members of the "Mariners' Club," an employer–supported group whose goal was to take the NMU back into the AFL sailors' union. Curran's move against them was enthusiastically supported by the Left in the union, as was his proposal to transfer decision–making power from the rank and file to the national executive board.

Curran's split with the Left began early in World War II, and showed itself first in policy disagreements with Blackie Myers, an executive board member and leader of the Left group in the union. In 1946, Curran made his first public and frontal attack on the Communist Party in an editorial in the NMU newspaper, *The Pilot*.

In December of that year he removed another Left critic, Joe Stack, from the union's vice–presidency, charging him with misfeasance and disruption. In the 1947 NMU convention, which lasted six weeks with much of that time taken up by Stack's appeal (he lost), Curran accused the Communists in the union of seeking to wreck the organization: "These guys are just like the Mariners. The bosses want 'em to do what they're doing."

In 1948, Curran got rid of several other Leftists who might have led an opposition: Ferdinand Smith, the union's secretary; Howard McKenzie, the vice–president responsible for contract negotiation; Paul Palazzi, chief union official in the Port of New York; and Dow Wilson, a non–ideological rank–and–filer whose goal was to re–establish democracy in the union.

For Curran, the purge was worthwhile. By the 1960s, he was being paid $80,000 a year, plus a generous expense account, to head the union which had 54,000 members. He did have to pay a price for his power, but it was nominal: the annoyance of having to fend off repeated charges that he rigged elections to keep himself in office. One election, in fact, was set aside by a federal court in 1969, on the ground that the NMU constitution limited the opportunity to run for office to only a tiny fraction of its members.

Despite all this, in the mid–sixties Curran was certified by the government as a labor statesman. The occasion was the dedication of his new $6.4 million union headquarters. On hand with Curran for the ceremony was his neighbor, Assistant Secretary of Commerce Franklin D. Roosevelt, Jr., who owned an adjoining farm near Beekman, New York and who had brought with him some trophies for Curran's new office. "You don't know how much red tape we had to cut to get these," Roosevelt beamed as he handed over the ship's wheel, the bell, and the nameplate from the "California."

Following the ritual for such occasions, photographers asked Curran and Roosevelt to pose holding the ship's wheel. An on-looker whispered, in a voice that carried up to the front of the room, "One will probably pull to starboard and the other to port." Roosevelt, overhearing, called out, "No sir, this is one wheel that's going to be steered right."

For Bridges and the longshoremen, the most tangible proof of the value of the CMU was the shock effect it had on the ship-owners. "Immediately after May 6, 1946 [the day the CMU was founded]," Bridges told the 1947 convention, "the employers began to give ground."

The CMU lived only six months as an effective force, but in that brief time it helped pull longshoremen's wages up by almost 40 per cent (from $1.15 an hour, when the CMU came on the scene in the middle of 1946, to $1.57 as of January, 1947). Even so, fissures in the united front began to show up within weeks of the CMU's birth. The first, and the most alarming, was when Curran, ignoring the vow of solidarity he took on May 6th, submitted to his membership for ratification an employer offer of a $12.50 a month increase. If the sailors had accepted it, Curran presumably would have defected from the CMU and signed a separate peace, but his members voted to turn the offer down. As it turned out, by sticking with the other unions, they got $17.50.

Although Bridges's peace plan never got off the ground and the CMU died in its infancy, the longshoremen's ability to fight on the economic front was not, as he had feared, seriously impaired in the post–war years. Instead, in one of history's ironies, the cold war, which Bridges opposed from the first, increased shipping out of West Coast ports, thereby increasing longshore work and, with it, the longshoremen's bargaining power.

The political front was another matter, for here Bridges was guilty of an unpardonable heresy. The CIO, forgetting Sam Gompers's counsel that labor should avoid an entangling alliance with one political party, was, with unalloyed enthusiasm, supporting President Truman and the Democrats. Bridges broke ranks early in 1947, calling Truman "a political accident, a back–room politician, a man without vision or courage . . . a strikebreaker." The last was a reference to Truman's threat in 1946 to use the army to break a railroad strike, and a similar threat he had made on the eve of a maritime strike later the same year.

Even worse, because of the suspicions it raised that he was following the Party Line, was Bridges's interpretation of America's role in the cold war. "In the international field," Bridges said in April, 1947, to the union convention,

the administration is well on its way to destroying the United Nations. The flagrant contempt for the machinery of peace manifested by interference in the affairs of the Greek people is but one example of our foreign policy. In spite of the fact that three commissions have been designated to conduct investigations in Greece, and although the machinery of the United Nations was ready and available to deal with any problems that might arise, this country is deliberately by–passing it to drive ahead with its imperialist adventures.

In this regard, it is important to remember that the United States delegates to the United Nations, together with the British, have successfully barred representation of world labor on the councils of the United Nations. The World Federation of Trade Unions, one of the greatest powers for securing world peace, has been forced to work on its own, even though it is equipped to make a great contribution to the functioning of world peace machinery.

The other side of the same policy is demonstrated in the support offered to Turkey by President Truman. Here is a country that prospered by its "neutrality" during the war, while offering a haven for fascists such as Von Papen, and which has suppressed every form of labor organization.

Under the guise of helping Turkey, American and British capital are seeking to assure for themselves continued control of the oil resources of the Near East. It becomes quite clear that the employers of this country are eagerly searching for allies in every corner of the world, including Franco, Peron, Chiang Kai–shek, and any other fascist who escaped the war criminal trials.

Strong language? Without doubt. Consistent with what the Communists were saying? Yes. But was he right? For twenty years, the conventional wisdom said "no." It took the Viet Nam war to force the United States to reexamine the origins of the cold war, but by the late sixties, Bridges's view was vindicated in the eyes of a growing body of Americans.

His opposition to the Marshall Plan was also interpreted by many as following orders from Moscow. In the beginning, Bridges and the ILWU executive board warmly endorsed General Marshall's formulation of the plan. Speaking at Harvard in June, 1947, Marshall urged a policy of generous U.S. economic aid to countries all around the globe. As he expressed it then, the program was non–ideological. "Our policy is not directed against any country or doctrine," Marshall explained, "but against hunger, poverty, desperation, and chaos. Its purpose should be the revival of a working economy in the world so as to permit the emergence of political and social conditions in which free institutions can exist."

In November, Bridges voted for a resolution in the CIO convention endorsing the spirit of the Marshall Plan, with the proviso that aid should go to hungry people in devastated countries throughout the world without interference in their economic, political and social affairs—except that labor's rights should be guaranteed. But by the time Congress adopted the plan in the spring of 1948, it was clear that aid was not going to go to countries within the Soviet

orbit. Indeed, Marshall's generous original concept had been transformed into a counter–offensive to the Soviet Union's moves in
Eastern Europe.

The Marshall Plan also appeared to be part of a cold war policy
of propping up unpopular governments, as long as they were anti–
Communist, whether labor in those countries had any rights or not.
For Bridges, it was a good idea gone wrong, and he had no alternative but to oppose it. It was, nevertheless, one of his more unpopular positions, even within his own union. For, as some longshoremen pointed out, if the ILWU opposed the Marshall Plan and then
struck on June 15, 1948, as seemed inescapable, the shipowners
would be able to claim that it was a political strike, designed to sabotage the Marshall Plan.

On the waterfront, 1947 was a quiet year. The longshore contract
came up for renewal in June, but both sides agreed to let it ride
while they waited to see what Congress was going to do with the
spate of anti–labor bills then before it. They got their answer late in
June, 1947 in the Taft–Hartley Act.

Two sections in particular seemed made to order for the Foisie–
Harrison wing of the employers' association. The first was a requirement that every union officer submit an affidavit annually to
the NLRB swearing that he was not a member of, or affiliated with,
the Communist Party, or a member of, or a believer in, or supporter of, any organization that teaches the overthrow of the
United States Government by force or illegal methods. If he fal-
sified the affidavit, he was subject to criminal prosecution, the maximum penalties being a $10,000 fine, ten years imprisonment, or
both. If, for whatever reason, Bridges refused to sign, that could be
used to weaken his influence in the industry.

The other was a section prohibiting the closed shop. During debate on it in the Senate, Senator Taft had made it clear that he had
in mind outlawing the hiring halls in the maritime industry. All the
employers had to do, it seemed, was argue that the longshore hiring
system was now illegal, and they could recapture control of hiring.

With all this as a backdrop, negotiations for a new contract
opened in an atmosphere of hostility unequaled since 1934. When
the deadline approached and it was apparent that a strike was
going to occur, President Truman set in motion the national emergency provisions of Taft–Hartley. The first step was the appointment of a board of inquiry, which went through the ritual of holding hearings (it concluded that control of the hiring hall was the

overriding issue) and predicted that a strike *was* going to occur, and that it would, indeed, create a national emergency. Accordingly, on July 2, 1948, the attorney general obtained the eighty–day injunction provided for in the law.

The notion behind the eighty–day injunction is that strikes often occur because negotiators get frantic as a strike deadline nears, consequently losing the composure they have to maintain in order to offer, and to accept, the compromises that will avoid a strike. If the status quo can be maintained for eighty days, the reasoning goes, they will have time to cool off and, in a more leisurely atmosphere, reach agreement. In practice, it hasn't worked that way very often, and it didn't in this one. "The employers were damn glad when the eighty days ended and the strike could begin," one ILWU official said after it was over. "The status quo was maintained but we slowed the work down so much it cost 'em plenty."

The last step in the national emergency procedure is for the NLRB to poll the workers on the question, "Do you accept the employers' last offer?" If a majority votes yes, the agreement is signed. If a majority votes no, the injunction is lifted, and the strike can go on. The last offer the shipowners put forward in this instance would almost certainly have been voted down, for it consisted of proposals that gave control of the hiring halls back to the employers. If there was any doubt, defeat was made certain when Foisie and Harrison, a few days before the NLRB vote, mailed to the home of each longshoreman a long summary of the issues in the dispute, ending with the charge: "Under its present leadership, the ILWU has been guided strictly by the Communist Party Line."

The longshoremen showed what they thought of that tactic and of the Taft–Hartley Act when the day came for the last–offer vote. When it was over, the NLRB reported the results:

Number of eligible employees	26,695
Ballots marked "yes"	0
Ballots marked "no"	0
Ballots challenged	0
Total ballots cast	0

With the injunction lifted, the strike began on September first. On the first day, the shipowners unveiled their strategy: "We're withdrawing all offers," they announced, "and we will not bargain further with a union whose officers have failed to sign the non–Communist affidavits." In most industries, the tactic probably would have worked. Union members, anxious to get back to work and to their paychecks, would have put pressure on their officers either to sign the affidavits or step aside.

But the shipowners weren't dealing with an ordinary union. They were dealing with a union whose leaders they, themselves, had reinforced by fourteen years of Red–baiting. Moreover, they had tried this same ploy without success in 1936, when they had locked out the longshoremen in San Francisco "until you get rid of Bridges . . ." And, although Foisie and Harrison seemed to have forgotten what happened on that occasion, even AFL conservatives had told Bridges then that he couldn't step aside and let the employers dictate who was, and who wasn't, qualified to represent his union.

The most effective way to answer the employers, Bridges decided, would be to put it up to a vote of the rank and file: "Do you want your officers to sign the non–Communist affidavits?" "No," they answered, ten to one, in a coastwide referendum. A year later, when ILWU warehouse locals were being raided by the teamsters' union and the ILWU needed the services of the NLRB, Bridges signed the affidavit. In his initial refusal to sign Bridges was, of course, on the side of the Constitution. It took seventeen years for history to catch up with him, but in 1965, in the Archie Brown case, the Supreme Court ruled the affidavit was a bill of attainder.

Why did the shipowners again attack Bridges in this way, if even an average student of politics could have told them that it would only cause the longshoremen to close ranks behind him? Paul St. Sure, who followed Foisie as head of the waterfront employers from the early Fifties until his death in 1966, explained it this way:

Of course, the '48 strike was based upon the public position taken by the maritime industry that it would no longer, or could no longer, do business with Communists, with Mr. Bridges. The records will show that the meeting at which this policy was voted was pretty much of a hoopla meeting. People got up and made speeches about "Don't let the old Flag touch the ground!", and "The time has come when we must stand up and be counted!" After somebody made such an impassioned speech on this subject, somebody else said, "Let's make that in the form of a resolution," whereupon they all voted on it and the strike was on on that issue.

Incongruous as that picture may seem, the stampede was possible because the shipowners' association was, in its own way, as good an example of the iron law of oligarchy as Curran's NMU. Included in its membership were 150 firms, many with conflicting interests: shipping companies in the passenger trade, others in intercoastal freight, some whose ships operated only along the Pacific Coast, still others whose vessels served the Far East and the entire Pacific basin. Then there were the foreign lines. Finally, there were the terminal operators and the stevedore companies. Although it might seem that companies with such divergent interests would vigorously participate in running the association, if only to protect themselves when policies binding them were laid down, in fact, they let Foisie and Harrison dominate their association and dictate its policy.

The Foisie–Harrison strategy would have prolonged the strike in any case, but in 1948 the employers had another reason to keep it going. If Thomas E. Dewey, the Republican candidate for the Presidency, won, the shipowners would, for the first time since 1932, have a friend in the White House. And Dewey seemed to have better than an even chance.

One reason was that President Truman's Greece and Turkey Doctrine had produced a rift in his party, causing many to bolt. Joining forces with others on the Left, they formed the Progressive Party, putting up former Vice President Henry Wallace, who had been speaking out against the cold war, as their candidate. Wallace was sure to draw votes away from Truman, and in the closing months of the campaign, Truman was almost the only man in the country who thought he had a prayer of being reelected.

Dewey would have been the shipowners' candidate anyway, merely by virtue of being a Republican, and as the campaign developed, he gave them a special reason to support him when he asserted that the Democratic administration had been coddling Communists in high places. Then, in the closing weeks of the campaign, Dewey raised the employers' hopes even higher. Truman had been attacking the Taft–Hartley Act as a Republican law, passed over his veto and over the unanimous protests of the unions. Dewey's response to that was that Truman's veto couldn't have been overridden if a large number of Democrats in both houses hadn't voted for it. Furthermore, he contended, Truman was being disingenuous in his condemnation of the Taft–Hartley Act.

"The Truman administration itself," the newspapers quoted Dewey as saying on October first, has used the emergency provisions of the law seven separate times. In all cases but one the dispute was settled before the emergency period ended. That one exception was a dispute involving the West Coast longshoremen's union headed by Harry Bridges.

The Attorney General of the United States flatly identifies Bridges as a Communist, and I assure you he is no red herring.

. . . I charge that the Taft–Hartley Act, which was passed by a majority of both parties, has been used by the Democratic Administration as an instrument for corralling votes rather than solving problems.

Under such administration of the law it is no wonder that Communists come to positions of power in some American unions and that is just one of the reasons why we need to get rid of this national administration.

A few days after Dewey's speech, Phil Murray and other top–level CIO officials, alarmed at the implications for the labor movement as a whole if the shipowners' strategy succeeded, approached the employers with a peace plan: "We'll guarantee that the longshoremen will live up to a contract you agree on if you'll drop your insistence that Bridges and the other ILWU officers sign the non–Communist affidavits." At the time, Murray himself, believing that the oath requirement was a gratuitous affront to union leaders as well as being unconstitutional, had not signed one.

Before the shipowners had time to respond to Murray, Bridges asked them if they would reopen talks (at this point, the union and the employers hadn't had a meeting in forty–four days) if he stepped aside and the union elected a new negotiating committee from the rank and file.

"No!" the shipowners shot back. "The composition of any negotiating committee which may be selected is not the key to our present impasse. The problem, as you well know, is the future administration and observances of any contract between ourselves and the ILWU, under its present leadership. Your fourteen year Party line record of irresponsibility and double dealing proves that any contract which you and your leadership are ultimately to administer, no matter how or by whom negotiated, is worthless."

Two weeks later, Truman narrowly defeated Dewey. Within a day or so, rebellious members of the waterfront employers' association seized control of the negotiating committee, pushed Foisie and Harrison into the background, and flew Dwight Steele up from Ha-

waii to serve as their spokesman. Steele immediately sought out
Bridges to reopen talks, privately assuring him that the shipowners
were ready to settle the strike.

The protagonist of the dissidents who finally challenged the
Foisie–Plant–Harrison strategy was Matson's Randolph Sevier,
who, like Steele, had come up to San Francisco from Honolulu,
where he was running the Hawaii end of the Matson operation, to
succeed Cushing, the aging president of the company. When Sevier
arrived, Cushing asked him to take his place in meetings of the
shipowners' strategy committee.

"After three days of those meetings," Sevier said in 1963,

I couldn't stomach any more. I just couldn't take the flag–waving
speeches Harrison was making.

You know what he and Foisie did one day? The longshoremen
were picketing the building where we were meeting up on the
eighth floor, and there was this big crowd down in the street.
Harrison and his people had some loudspeakers rigged up on the
outside of the building, and an enormous American flag was
rolled up just under our windows.

Harrison gave a signal, and they unfurled the flag so it
dropped down the side of the building. Then they turned up the
loudspeakers. They were playing "The Star–Spangled Banner"! I
guess they thought that would bring out the patriotism in the
longshoremen and they'd impeach Bridges!

When I got back to the office, I said to Cushing, "I'm not
going to any more of those meetings. Those people just don't
make any sense. Regardless of what we may think of Bridges and
his crowd, the law says we've got to do business with them. Why
don't we cut out the flag–waving and start doing so?"

Cushing, who went along with the hate–Bridges position,
thought awhile, and then he said to me, "You know, San Francisco has produced two great men so far this century. A. P. Gian-
nini [founder of the Bank of America] and Harry Bridges."

The strike had lasted ninety–five days and had turned into a
rout. All the employers suffered heavy losses. Some nearly went
bankrupt. And for what? Bridges was now more firmly entrenched
than ever, while they had impeached their leaders. The union was
still running the hiring halls, union members were still being given
preference for jobs, the employers had conceded a 10 per cent wage
increase, and—yielding to the union's parting shot at Gregory Har-

rison—they had agreed that they would no longer use lawyers as negotiators.

The defeat was a blow to their pride, and some were bitter. But to the pragmatists among them, substituting the new slogan, "We're going to get along with Bridges," for the old, "We won't do business with Communism," was good business. Once the shipowners began to view Bridges as a union leader rather than a member of a conspiracy, they found him to be a man of his word, and a man who, although an avowed anti–capitalist, was quite realistic about just how far the union could push an employer. Forty–eight may have been expensive in lost wages and profits, but it was worth it. Guerrilla warfare came to a stop, and from 1948 until 1971 the union didn't call a single major strike. At long last, employers and the longshoremen could settle back and enjoy the luxury of working without interruption.

But not Bridges. A few months after the strike ended, a federal grand jury was impanelled in San Francisco to look into the questions of whether Bridges perjured himself that day back in 1945 when he told the judge admitting him to citizenship that he wasn't a Communist, and whether his two witnesses, Bob Robertson, the union's vice president, and Henry Schmidt, conspired with him in that perjury. Two immigration officers, John Boyd and Bruce Barber, both long active in the campaign to deport Bridges, were seen going in and out of the jury room, and Jiggs Donohue, a prominent Washington lawyer and national figure in the Democratic Party, was in town to handle the government's case. (At about the same time, the Justice Department announced that on April 21, 1949, it had put the Citizens Committee for Harry Bridges on the Attorney General's list of subversive organizations, classified as a Communist front.)

One day in May, Morris Watson, editor of the ILWU newspaper, *The Dispatcher*, was tipped off by friends on the city's newspapers that an indictment was probably going to come down the next day. "Let's beat the government to the punch by getting out a news release on it," he suggested to Bridges. "Go ahead," Bridges replied.

"I've heard that the two key witnesses are going to be Schomaker and Rathborne," Watson went on. "Maybe we ought to say something about them." If Watson's tip was accurate, the two would be awesome witnesses. John Schomaker had been a hero of the '34 strike—in one of his exploits, he had pulled a mounted policeman off his horse—and a staunch ally of Bridges for several years after that. Mervyn Rathborne, once an important figure in the Maritime Federation of the Pacific, had long been a Bridges supporter.

Bridges refused, as he had in 1939, to believe his old comrades would turn against him. "Godamnit, Morris!" he yelled. "Lay off the bottle. Those guys wouldn't be stool pigeons."

He should have listened to Watson, for his editor was a man of unusual ability, with excellent contacts in newspaper circles. In 1933, when he was a reporter for the Associated Press, Watson and Heywood Broun founded the American Newspaper Guild, of which Broun became President and Watson, Vice–President. As Watson recalled later, at first he was timid about being active in the Guild.

"I had a moment of cowardice," he said. "I told the others I had a family to think of, and I felt sure I'd be fired. So I was excused.

"But on the way home, I said to myself, 'You cowardly bastard. We'll never have a union if you take this way out.'

"I went back and said I'd changed my mind. I said I'd probably be fired, but if it has to be it has to be."

As he expected, the AP fired him, so he went to the NLRB, which ordered the AP to put him back on the payroll. The AP refused, arguing that having to bargain with a union of reporters would violate freedom of the press. The Supreme Court, in a landmark decision in 1937, disagreed, holding that the Wagner Act was constitutional.

Watson went back to work for AP for a time, then left to create a federal theater project called "The Living Newspaper." In 1942, he founded the *Dispatcher*, and was its editor until he retired in 1966. He died of cancer in 1971.

When the indictment Watson had told Bridges about came down, it was front page news across the nation. Most newspapers applauded the indictment, depicting Bridges as a sinister Communist, who had been able to stay in the country only because he had slick lawyers and friends in high places in Washington. Some newspapers used Bridges as a stick to beat the Democrats with, though none was as sophisticated as the *Chicago Tribune*, which said on May 28:

It took the New Deal only a week after President Philip Murray of the CIO publicly declared his enmity to Harry Bridges [a reference to Murray's removal of Bridges as Northern California Regional Director of the CIO] to discover that the boss of the longshoremen's union is a Communist and an undesirable who ought to be deported to his native Australia. Everybody but the New Deal had recognized these facts for years, but the administration moved against Bridges, not because he offered affront to the American people or the lawful authority of the United States government, but because he now offends the puissant Mr. Murray.

Col. McCormick may not have been as wide of the mark as that editorial might seem. Murray and Bridges had fallen out over the cold war, which Murray and the CIO ardently supported. In fact, there were persistent rumors that Murray was collaborating with the Justice Department in working up the case against Bridges. The CIO, moreover, was publicly saying that in contrast to his earlier bouts with the government, there wasn't any civil liberties implication in this Bridges case and that consequently there were no reasons why unions should support his defense.

Bridges's own reaction to the indictment was that it was a monumental case of political spite. It was a frame–up and it indicated that the Truman Administration would go to any lengths to silence critics of its failure to meet its campaign promises. In 1964, when Truman was working on his memoirs in Independence, this author asked him about Bridges. He was impassive when I told him I was doing a book about Harry Bridges and remained so during the colloquy which followed.

"Mr. President, did you have any feelings about Bridges when you were President?"

"No, I didn't," Truman replied with his characteristic bluntness.

"I'm a little surprised to hear you say that, sir," I said, thinking of FDR's conversations with Perkins and Biddle. "He was an important CIO official, and he was put on trial while you were in the White House. I would have thought that in a matter of that much political importance you'd have been asked what you thought of it."

"No." Truman said. "Those matters don't come to the President's office. They're handled by the Attorney General and the Justice Department."

"That's very interesting, Mr. President," I persisted. "You remember the Progressive Party charged that after your Western campaign tour you instructed the Attorney General to bring the indictment because Bridges turned against you and supported Henry Wallace."

"That's wrong. A President can't be bothered with all the side issues. If he did, he wouldn't have time to do the big things the public elects him to do.

"I didn't know anything about it," he concluded, flashing the
broad Truman grin. "And didn't care."

When Bridges and his co–defendants, Bob Robertson and Henry
Schmidt, were arraigned early in June, the prosecutor put his finger
on the legal point the case ultimately turned on: "We expect our
entire case to be attacked on the ground that the statute of limitations has run out," Donohue said. "We hold that the statute of limitations is five years in immigration matters, not three. The Supreme Court has never ruled on the point and such a ruling may be
had in this case. If we do get an adverse ruling," he added complacently, "we shall proceed with the civil suit against Bridges." This
was a reference to a companion suit John Boyd, a West Coast immigration official, had filed the same day the grand jury handed
down the indictment, in which he had asked that Bridges be deported. "The Immigration Department has been investigating this
matter for two years," Boyd had said, adding, "and prominent
labor leaders have been very helpful."

The trial was held off for six months because of two requests for
postponement. The first came from the defense, which wanted to
wait until September when Gladstein would be back from New
York, where he was defending some of the leading U.S. Communists in a Smith Act trial. Then the government asked that the trial
be postponed until November 14th because the CIO was meeting
in October and was expected to expel the ILWU for being Communist–influenced. The CIO let the government down, however.
When it met, the convention decided to postpone expelling the
ILWU in order to avoid prejudicing Bridges's trial.

In September, the trial was assigned to Judge George Harris.
Harris suffered all the limitations of a man who fights his way up
from poverty into a self–conscious position in the upper middle
class. In the thirties, Harris had run for municipal court judge in
San Francisco on several occasions and seemingly undisturbed by
the shrill cries of Communist! being hurled at Bridges, had solicited
ILWU support. But in middle age, Harris married a rich Catholic
and was converted to Catholicism which may have brought on an
unreasoning fear and hatred of Communism. Just before the trial
began, Bridges's attorneys asked Harris to disqualify himself be-

cause of the bias he showed against the defendants in pre–trial proceedings, but he refused.

Judge Harris's feelings began to show through before the actual trial began. Bridges could not contend, he explained in a pre–trial conference, that he was being put in double jeopardy because he had not been tried before on a criminal charge. Nor was *res judicata* applicable. He had never before been subjected to a criminal prosecution under the statutes in the present indictment. Harris was equally unmoved by the plea that the Bridges case had become a cause célèbre, standing with the Salem witchcraft trials, the Alien and Sedition Act prosecutions, the Haymarket martyrs, Tom Mooney, and Sacco and Vanzetti. As such, Bridges's lawyers argued, it ought to be thrown out. Not so, replied the judge. "Historical and atmospheric background is no basis for dismissal."

To argue the statute of limitations question, the defense brought out from Washington James Fly, the prestigious former chairman of the Federal Communications Commission. What the government was doing, Fly argued, evaded the statute of limitations by broadening the charge. If the charge was that Bridges had made a false statement when he answered Judge Foley's question in 1945, the three–year limit would bar the trial, for the government had waited four years to bring the indictment.

By making the charge perjury and conspiracy to defraud the government, the prosecution was bringing the indictment under a wartime law never intended to apply to a case like this. During World War II, Congress had suspended the statute of limitations in cases involving war profiteers, so as to be able to try them when the war was over. But Fly's reasoning did not impress Judge Harris. "If these defendants are proved guilty," he snapped, "they would have perpetrated a greater fraud than absconding with thousands of dollars."

The defense suffered another setback in mid–October, when, with the opening of the trial just a month away, Judge Medina ruled in New York that Gladstein had been in contempt of court and would have to go to jail for six months. The Bridges trial was scheduled to begin on November 15th, at which time Gladstein would be serving the second day of his sentence. Bridges decided to look for a sharp criminal lawyer to replace him.

He found the man he was looking for in Vincent Hallinan, a successful San Francisco Attorney. Born in the Irish section of the city, Hallinan was the son of a gripman on the California Street cable cars, and he was a product of Catholic schools. He had been a football player and national boxing champion when he was in college, and he wasn't involved in politics. Hallinan has said in his autobiography, *A Lion in Court*, that he was surprisingly naive about politics, and especially about political trials.

After he agreed to take the case, he relates, he discussed it at length with Bridges, Robertson and Schmidt. They assured him that none of them had ever been a Communist, yet they fully expected to be found guilty. Hallinan was puzzled, so Bridges explained how, in the two deportation hearings, the government had used stool pigeons, spies, perjurers, and all kinds of dirty tricks to get him. And they got him, he said, in the Sears hearing. The Supreme Court saved him, but he was certain that this time, he'd end up in prison. "He's terrified of going to jail," Hallinan said later. "He told me during the trial, 'Vince, if I go to jail, I'll go insane.'"

Hallinan, seeking to reassure him, replied with unconscious irony:

> Hell, Harry, I've defended pimps, robbers, all kinds of criminals, who got sent to jail. And in almost every case, they were just as good when they came out as when they went in.
>
> Anyway, Harry, this time you're in a court and before a jury. The hearing officer in an immigration proceeding is part of the department which is trying to get you. That department can't use the Federal Courts in the same way they can use their own employees. The very fact that there have been so many previous attempts will warn the judge that there is some improper motive behind them.
>
> . . . If they try to use false witnesses, we should be able to show them up. The exposure of even one such witness is usually enough to finish off the prosecution's case. The jury feels that it is being imposed on and looks with suspicion on all the evidence.
>
> If the judge isn't fair, we'll take care of that. I've seen juries lean over backward to acquit because they thought the judge was helping the prosecution.

When Hallinan got around to reading the records of the Landis and Sears hearings, he found that every witness against Bridges had been impeached. "The trial," he said to himself, "will be a breeze." When it was over, he was a chastened man. Later, he wrote:

> In dealing with many agents of the U.S. Government, you must assume, until the contrary is completely established, that

these representatives might commit felonies, suborn perjury, conceal evidence, bribe witnesses, intimidate jurors, convey information to judges, and otherwise engage in practices which would be the cause for disbarment or imprisonment for a private attorney.

On the first day of the trial Hallinan and his young partner, James MacInnis who was representing Robertson and Schmidt, were still enjoying the illusion that it would be conducted in the courtroom atmosphere they were used to. They went up to the government lawyers who had come out from Washington, introduced themselves and offered their cooperation in anything that would facilitate the trial, even offered to help ensure their comfort and entertainment while they were in the city. When Judge Harris took the bench and smilingly greeted the participants, Hallinan smiled backed warmly.

Selection of the jury was accomplished smoothly, resulting in a panel of eight men and four women. Middle–aged or retired, most were middle class. One was a Chinese insurance broker, a graduate of the University of Florida. And, he testified, a member of the San Francisco branch of the Kuomintang Party. Leaving a member of the Kuomintang on a jury trying an alleged Communist seemed peculiar, in view of the recent defeat of Chiang Kai-shek's Kuomintang forces by mainland China Communists:

"Wasn't he a sure bet to vote against Harry?" Hallinan was asked after the trial.

"Hell, no," Hallinan replied. "The Chinese may pay lip service to Chiang Kai-shek, but they hate him.

"You know, the success of the Chinese on the mainland, and the fact that a Chinese army crossed the Yalu and beat the Americans back did more for the self–respect of the Chinese in this country than anything else in years and years.

"As a matter of fact, that Chinese, I found out later, was the last to vote against Harry. And he only did so after having severe diarrhea and vomiting. It almost finished him to do it."

The prosecution's opening statement was a familiar, if brief, replay of the government's case against Bridges in the first two hearings. With one difference. This time, the prosecutor said, the membership card in the Communist Party was going to be an important link in the chain of evidence the government was going to present.

When Hallinan rose to make his opening statement, it was apparent from the sheaf of notes he had with him that his was going to be much longer that the prosecutor's.

"It is my practice in criminal cases," Hallinan says in his autobiography,

> whenever the circumstances permit, to make an extensive opening statement on behalf of the defendant immediately after the prosecution has concluded its own. I consider this to be of vital importance. If the prosecution is permitted to conclude its evidence before any word from the defendant is heard, the jury will probably arrive at a judgment which must then be torn down and another constructed in its place. If the defense has already cast doubt on the prosecution's case, the jury will probably reserve judgment until it has a chance to hear from the other side.
>
> In the present instance it was absolutely necessary to get before the jury the history of the continued persecution of Bridges, the interests behind it, the corrupt and dishonest means to destroy him, and the fact that the present prosecution was but a continuation of the old campaign.

Hallinan had no doubt that he would be allowed to present such an opening statement. Before the trial began, he had met with Bridges, Gladstein, and Grossman to discuss his strategy. He had been confidently going on about how he was going to handle the case, and especially, how he was planning to develop its history at the outset. Grossman had listened quietly, but with mounting annoyance. Finally, he couldn't stand it any longer. "Vince, you don't know what you're up against," he burst out. "Hell, I'll bet you won't even get the 1945 [Supreme Court] decision before the jury without being held in contempt."

Hallinan had only been speaking for two minutes when Donohue was on his feet with his first objection. Hallinan was saying that this prosecution was part of an old story: ". . . this is the fifth inquiry into the subject." Donohue's protest was one of those distinctions–without–a–difference that only lawyers understand. Bridges *had* been tried and acquitted on a charge of being a Communist, he conceded. But this was the first time he had ever been charged with conspiring to obtain his citizenship by fraudulently saying he wasn't a Communist. Moreover, Donohue pointed out, Judge Harris had agreed with him when he rejected the defense claims of double jeopardy and *res judicata*. Therefore, Hallinan's review of previous prosecutions was irrelevant.

The judge upheld the prosecutor. And so it went, Hallinan persisting in telling his story to the jury, the prosecutor objecting, the judge upholding the objection, Hallinan plunging ahead anyway.

On the morning of the third day of this, Judge Harris called a recess and retired to his chambers. He returned after about an hour, and then, for almost two hours, read a statement he had written the night before. In it, he recited thirty–seven specific instances in which Hallinan had transgressed courtroom decorum and had flouted and disregarded his rulings. As Harris read, he occasionally interjected comments: "Here counsel rode unbridled through my rulings"; "Here counsel indulged in wholesale character assassination"; "Here counsel stabbed a witness in the back"; "Here tempers were wearing thin and I warned counsel." He finished by declaring: "I find you, Vincent Hallinan, in contempt of this court, and I sentence you to a term of six months in the federal penitentiary, and I further order that your name be stricken from the list of attorneys licensed to practice in this court." Motioning to the bailiff, he ordered, "Take him into custody."

Two marshals seized Hallinan by the arms and were hustling him, surprised and protesting, toward the door when MacInnis asked the judge at least to postpone sending Hallinan to jail until the trial ended because of the difficulty of finding a replacement. "Hold on a minute!" Harris called out to the marshals. Turning to Bridges, he asked if he thought he could get another attorney if the trial were postponed for two weeks.

"I have something to say—but what good would it do?" Bridges replied. "I've selected the counsel I want and now he's not available. I doubt that by December 6th, or for some time after that, I could find another lawyer in whom I have the confidence I have in Mr. Hallinan.

"I presume that if the court orders it, it will have to do. But if things go wrong, I'll never, never, think that it was a square deal."

Forgetting that Gladstein was in jail, Harris inquired of Bridges if he might not be able to take over the case. "He is not available," Hallinan interjected sadly. "He has met with a misfortune similar to mine." The judge withdrew to his chambers again. Fifteen minutes later, he came back to say: "We have given consideration to Mr. Bridges's request. The court will grant a stay of execution until the end of the trial."

The government put on the stand seventeen witnesses, eleven of them ex–Communists. Among the most formidable was, as expected, John Schomaker, who testified that he had been a Communist in the thirties and had been in Party meetings with Bridges. Even more damaging was his testimony that he, Bridges and Schmidt had regularly met with Sam Darcy during the '34 strike and that Darcy gave them orders on how to conduct the strike. In cross–examination, the defense brought out that Schomaker had earlier testified, also under oath, that Bridges was *not* a Party member.

Why, after holding out so long against government efforts to get him to testify against Bridges, did Schomaker do so now? Donohue put the question to Bridges this way: "Do you think John Schomaker would have any reason for coming here and testifying under oath falsely against you?"

"Why, of course," Bridges answered.

Let me tell you, Mr. Donohue, I have known Schomaker a long time . . . He didn't move along fast enough in the labor movement; he didn't make enough money out of it; it took too much hard work and sacrifice; his wife used to come to me and complain bitterly. She said, "I have served notice on John, he can choose between me and the union . . . There is no money in it," and so forth . . .

. . . That is all that happened to Schomaker. So he got bogged down in the country down there with his boarding house, and mortgages and so forth. His business to be a housebuilder didn't work out . . .

So the story of Schomaker is not a new story. It happens all the time, not only in labor unions but in governments, too, you know. Even members of the bench, you know, sometimes sell out . . ."

Bridges's analysis of Rathborne, who corroborated Schomaker's testimony, was equally withering:

One of the difficulties I had with Rathborne, while he was serving in the labor movement, he used to drink too much. He had a hankering for getting into big poker games. He used to play down on the Peninsula with a lot of people who was very wealthy. I have been down at the horse races with Rathborne and have saw him lose four or five hundred dollars. I knew what he was making. I would say, "How are you doing that, Merv?"

. . . He was a very, very heavy drinker, and time after time I tried to help him out . . . I said, "Look, you can't do these things and carry out an honest program in the labor movement . . ."

And when I told you the other day I know, Mr. Donohue, he has been getting a payoff for the past many, many months . . . You didn't have to pay him $25. I mean, you could get him for less . . .

It was truly no great surprise to me to hear that Rathborne had finally gotten down to the level that he did get. Another tragedy, another casualty in the labor movement, because people can become corrupted . . .

A shadow lay over Rathborne's testimony, in any case, because he too, had earlier refused to testify that Bridges was a Communist. Similar doubt enshrouded the next witness, a longshore foreman named Henry Schrimpf. Like Bridges, Schrimpf was a native of Australia who had come to the United States in 1920 and had gone to work on the San Francisco waterfront in 1923.

In '34, Schrimpf was a member of Albion Hall. He was secretly a Party member and worked closely with Sam Darcy to try to influence Bridges and the course of the strike. On the stand, he said that on one occasion, he met in a prune orchard near Palo Alto with Darcy, Henry Schmidt, Bridges, and Earl Browder, national chairman of the Party. This, he said, was a Communist meeting. After the strike, Schrimpf turned against Bridges. "It all started because of a woman Schrimpf was after," Darcy said in 1964, "but she went for Bridges."

Nevertheless, until 1949, Schrimpf refused to cooperate with the government. In 1937, he was taken by immigration agents to the Portland police station and grilled about Bridges. "They didn't get anything out of me," he told B. B. Jones, a fellow Communist and longshoreman, afterward, "Those sonsabitches!" After the trial, when Schrimpf went back to work on the front, some of the longshoremen refused to work with him, but it wasn't long before the only adverse reactions to his being on the job were muttered curses and dirty looks.

"We never felt much animosity against Schrimpf," one San Francisco longshoreman has recalled. "They had him by the balls. He could have been deported for joining the Party. And he would have done time first. They had him." When Schrimpf retired from the waterfront in 1962 and collected his $9,000 retirement pay—over and above his monthly pension—Sid Roger, assistant editor of the ILWU newspaper, asked Bridges what he thought about

Schrimpf cashing in on this benefit. "He's entitled to it," Bridges answered. "He worked for it. He deserves it."

A surprise witness whose appearance added poignancy to the trial was George Wilson, who from 1941 to 1945 had worked tirelessly as secretary of the Bridges Defense Committee. When Wilson was called to the stand, Schmidt nudged Bridges. "Look who's here." "Don't worry, Hank," Bridges whispered, "He isn't going to testify against us." But Wilson did, saying that he had joined the Party in 1940 or 1941, and had attended Communist meetings with the three defendants.

Wilson, who had never before given any sign that he was anything but Bridges's loyal friend, was palpably testifying against his will:

"He called them Harry, Henry and Bob," the *Chronicle* reported,

and his distress at what he had to do flowed from him in waves that lapped at the feelings of every man and woman in the courtroom.

It was like an acute, physical sickness; it caused him to figdet and move his hands aimlessly about and run his tongue around the inside of his mouth and swallow his words and give vent to odd contortions of the legs and shoulders.

By the time he had been on the stand a skimpy thirty minutes, his anguish was achieving such bizarre effects with his voice and his demeanor that Judge Harris gave it judicial notice. On his own motion, fully fifteen minutes before the customary time, he called for a recess.

Donohue's questions had been brief, and Hallinan had begun cross-examining Wilson just before the recess. During the break Hallinan asked several union staff members if he should go after Wilson when the court reconvened. "Hell, yes!" they exclaimed. Just then Bridges joined the group. "What do you think, Harry?" Hallinan asked. "No," Bridges said firmly. "His wife called me this morning. He's got a weak heart, and if you go after him too hard, it might be too much for him. After all, he's an old friend. There wasn't anything vicious in his testimony. He testified only because they had him on a spot and he had to."

One witness who made a deep impression upon the jury was a forty-one-year-old Black named Manning Johnson. He had joined the Party in the thirties, he testified, had become disillusioned and had decided to quit. The FBI, however, persuaded him to stay in the Party and act for them as an undercover agent. In the forties, he surfaced and spent his time going from one un–American activities hearing to another around the country, identifying labor leaders, teachers, etc., as Communists. When he died in 1964, the John Birch Society created the Manning Johnson Memorial Scholarship Fund to provide an annual $1,000 award to "a deserving Negro student." The announcement of the fund said it was named after "a great American patriot who tried to expose the Communist hands behind most of the 'civil rights' agitation now tearing our country apart."

Johnson testified that he was at the 1936 Party convention in New York, and that on June 28th he had seen Bridges there while it was being announced that he had been elected to the Party's national committee. Bridges couldn't have been seen by the people in the hall, Johnson said, because he was standing back in the wings. You had to be up at the front of the hall and way off to one side to see him. He saw him there at 4:30 in the afternoon, Johnson remembered, because immediately afterward the meeting adjourned.

"He's off the beam," Bridges whispered to Hallinan. "I was in Stockton on June 28th, giving a speech to our union there at 8:00 p.m. The minutes of the meeting will back me up. And I was there in the afternoon, and had dinner with some of our local officials."

Paul Crouch, the government's next ex–Communist, was, like Johnson, a professional witness. He corroborated Johnson, saying that he, too, had been at that 1936 convention and, at 4:30 p.m. on June 28th, he had seen Bridges off in the wings.

When the court opened the next day, Hallinan was ready. As soon as the jury was in the box, he laid on the clerk's desk the Stockton local's minutes and a copy of a Stockton newspaper reporting Bridges's speech. Turning to Judge Harris, he charged Johnson and Crouch with perjury.

The next day, a man came to Hallinan's office to tell him that he had read about the preceding day's activities in court and that he, too, had seen Bridges in Stockton on the evening of June 28th. His sister had been married on the 28th, he said, and there had been a wedding party at a local night club. A group of men at one of the tables had made remarks concerning the wedding party, after which one of them came over to the wedding table, introduced himself as Harry Bridges, and apologized for the misconduct of his companions. The man said that he was willing to testify, as were some of the other members of the wedding party. Hallinan put him and several others who had been in the night club on the stand to substantiate Bridges's presence in Stockton and then demanded that Johnson and Crouch be immediately taken into custody. The judge said he would have to have the district attorney look into the matter, but nothing came of it.

From that time on, the government's case was virtually identical to the government's case against Bridges in the two previous hearings. Oddly, once the trial was under way, the government said nothing about the Communist membership card which had figured so importantly in pre–trial publicity.

"Long afterward," Hallinan wrote in *A Lion in Court*,

> we found that the prosecution had pulled a trick on us which we had not discovered. A relative of Bridges [his former wife, Agnes, from whom by the time of the trial he was divorced] had furnished the Government with an affidavit, not admissible in court under California law, which stated that Harry Bridges was in fact a member of the Communist Party, that she had seen the card which had been issued to him under a fictitious name.
>
> . . . Donohue came forward with this document and asked to have introduced "for the purpose of identification." We assumed that he hoped the papers would print it and thus bring it to the attention of the jury, and we were insistent that the court prevent any such disclosure. Harris then instructed the clerk to keep the document locked in his desk and not to allow any person to read it.
>
> We wondered what use the prosecution intended to make of the affidavit. We supposed that some effort would be made to cross–examine Bridges concerning it, and thus bring to the jury's attention the fact that it existed. We were prepared to prevent this and to demand a mistrial if it were attempted.
>
> The case closed without any such effort having been made, and the document was forgotten. That is to say, it was forgotten by us. We did not know what the real purpose was until, as I have said, years later, when some of the jurors informed us that —during their deliberation—this affidavit had been smuggled into the jury room, had been read by all the jurors . . .

The defense produced thirty–seven witnesses, most of whom testified to Bridges's good character. This time, several employers appeared as character witnesses for Bridges. They were all scheduled to testify the same afternoon, and as they waited in an anteroom off the court, they discussed among themselves how best they could help Bridges in their testimony. The late Anne Rand, then the union's librarian, had also been called and was waiting with them. "I got to speculating in my own mind why they wanted to help Harry," she said later. "Two hypotheses, both obvious, I suppose, came to mind. One was that by testifying they hoped to keep the labor peace they got after the '48 strike. The other was that they knew the business about Harry being a Red was phony. They'd been in on the conspiracy, or on the edges of it. I decided it was probably the second when Oscar Pearson said to the rest of us, 'You know, we have to admit that whatever good has been done on the waterfront has been done by Bridges.' "

Pearson, who had been a sailor, a longshoreman and a stevedoring contractor before taking the presidency of the Pacific Maritime Association, the name adopted by the shipowners' association after '48, was the lead–off employer witness. He testified that Bridges's reputation for truth, honesty and integrity was very good, and that his own association with Bridges bore the reputation out. Two other members of the shipowners' negotiating committee were called and, in brief appearances, corroborated Pearson's testimony.

One of the most dramatic moments in the trial came during the questioning of another character witness, Father Paul Meinecke, a Franciscan priest who had been assistant pastor at St. Boniface's Church, across the street from ILWU headquarters, from 1937 to 1947. In those days there was a bar in the basement of the union building, and along toward the end of the day, Father Paul would saunter over to join Bridges for a drink. They became good friends. Bridges even asked his help in placing his daughter Betty in St. Brigid's, a Catholic school in San Francisco, Father Paul testified, and they had many long, philosophical conversations. The priest said, "In all of his associations with me personally as a priest, he not only was a truthful, honest, and upright man, he was more . . . The people who call Harry a Communist are all wrong. Harry is not a radical. He is a militant trade unionist, but he is not a Communist."

Donohue's cross–examination was especially interesting because he was a practicing Catholic. He went after Father Meinecke, ruthlessly seeking to show by the priest's own admission that he wouldn't know a Communist if he saw one. Then, at the end of his cross–examination, the prosecutor moved to strike the priest's testimony altogether because he was only giving his own personal opinion of Bridges rather than testifying about Bridges's reputation in the community.

Judge Harris didn't agree, and the questioning went on, with

Donohue asking if there was something peculiar about Father Paul's having been transferred, a year or so earlier, to a remote parish in Nevada. The priest answered that it was by his own choice. After an assignment as chaplain of a recreation camp in the high Sierras, he discovered he liked mountains and wide open spaces, and he requested the transfer. Judge Harris then asked him how much his memory had been refreshed by MacInnis, with whom he had had dinner the night before, and whether the priest had difficulty remembering things.

"In Nevada there are no clocks and no calendars," the priest answered. "We don't know one day from another, and it is easy for one to become careless about pegging dates, although I wasn't that way when I was here in San Francisco."

"In San Francisco, Father, you were perfectly conversant and well oriented, weren't you, with respect to dates and the like?" the judge asked. "Since you went to Nevada your orientation has become poor, has it?"

"No; the years have sort of run together," was the answer. "I say 'a couple of years ago,' and then I remember back, it was fifteen years ago."

MacInnis was becoming increasingly restive as he listened. Also a devout Catholic, Father Paul had officiated at his marriage. The next question brought him to his feet, knocking his chair over, choking with emotion. "Have you been recently subjected to medical treatment, Father?" Judge Harris asked. Before MacInnis could find his voice, Hallinan, who had also bounded to his feet, broke in breathlessly, "If the Court please, I am going to object to these questions." "Let me in!" MacInnis pleaded, but Hallinan kept on, "Your Honor has seen the Manning Johnsons, the Crouches, and everybody get on that stand and we asked whether they were insane or not. I object to your Honor's question . . . and I ask that the jury be instructed to ignore the implication of the question."

"There is no occasion for any admonition to the jury," the judge shot back.

"I never heard of such a question!" exclaimed MacInnis, finally getting a word in.

"I have the greatest respect for men of the cloth," Judge Harris protested, "as we all have."

"You are demonstrating it," MacInnis burst out.

"He asserted his present memory is not good," the judge said defensively. "I asked him whether or not his recollection was good while he was here years ago. He said yes, it was good years ago. I don't see any reason for the criticism."

"I think you should cite yourself for contempt," MacInnis said bitterly.

Judge Harris, instead, made a long speech to the jury about the risks of cross–examination any witness exposes himself to, even a priest. He repeated several times that he had great respect for men of the cloth and that the questions he and Donohue had asked the priest were dignified and proper. He denied Donohue's motion to strike the priest's testimony and then, turning to MacInnis, sentenced him to three months in jail for contempt, the jail term to begin at the conclusion of the trial.

Henry Schmidt was the first of the defendants to be called. Schmidt had helped Bridges start Albion Hall in 1933 and then remained loyal to him and the union until he retired in the late sixties. About the same age as Bridges, Schmidt was born in Germany and lived in Holland until he was twelve, when his family emigrated to America. He moved on to San Francisco in 1917 and went to work on the docks.

Like Bridges, Schmidt, whose father was a lithographer, had been exposed to trade union and socialist ideas as a child and had absorbed the anti–capitalist philosophy of the European working class Left. In 1938, he told a *San Francisco Chronicle* reporter doing a profile on him that foreign–born workers take more interest in unions than Americans do, "because they appreciate that conditions here are different from those abroad, and they are ready to fight for these conditions. Too, they are more familiar with capitalist exploitation."

Mild–mannered, soft–spoken, Schmidt looked and acted more like a professor than a union leader. The professorial impression was reinforced by a dry wit. At the end of the interview for the 1938 *Chronicle* profile, the reporter asked, "What do you do for recreation?" "Well," Schmidt answered, "on Sunday mornings I read Marxist literature, then in the afternoon I take the wife and kid for a ride in the union car."

Schmidt assumed the reporter would realize he was joking, but the writer solemnly took it down. A few days later, an indignant longshoreman got up in a union meeting to ask Schmidt, "Is that true what I read in the *Chronicle*? Do you use the union car to drive around on Sundays?" "Well, sometimes," Schmidt answered, "I use it for that." Shocked, the union members voted to sell the cars and give officials expense accounts in their place.

As a witness in his own defense, Schmidt was a defense counsel's dream: responsive to the questions put to him by MacInnis and later, in cross–examination by Donohue, never going beyond what was necessary to deal with the question. He denied being a Communist himself, and testified that he was confident Bridges wasn't a Communist, either. He unhesitatingly denied having been in Party meetings with the ex–Communists who had testified for the prosecution and disclaimed even knowing most of the Communists they said he had met with.

Schmidt flatly denied Schomaker's and Schrimpf's testimony that Darcy had called the shots in the '34 strike. His explanation, in response to a question from Donohue, as to why George Wilson had called him a Communist, was: "You people must have something on him . . . As far as I can recollect, he was the first witness who identified the three defendants by using only their first names. He said, 'Yes, there is Harry in the gray suit. Yes, there is Henry sitting next to him. And there is Bob sitting next to him.' And it was my impression that that man was talking to us three at that moment and he was in effect saying, 'Look, fellows, I can't help it. I don't like to do this but they have got something on me . . .' "

"If you believed that," the prosecutor queried, "why didn't you ask your lawyer to ask Wilson if he'd been forced to testify?" "I recall there was some discussion out in the hall," Schmidt replied. "Apparently the lawyers decided not to ask him any more questions, and they are running this little show, not I. Let me put it this way: If I had been handling my own affair, I would have interrogated him on that point."

At one point in the cross–examination, Donohue brought up Schmidt's endorsement of a Communist for supervisor in San Francisco. Hallinan then produced the entire slate Schmidt had endorsed: for Supervisor, Oleta O'Connor Yates, a Communist; for mayor and district attorney, two Democrats; for municipal judge, George Harris. Everyone in the courtroom exploded into laughter but Judge Harris. "The Court was not amused," the *San Francisco Chronicle* reported.

After the trial, Schmidt moved to a new home and went back to work on the waterfront. He called the telephone company to ask if his telephone could be moved to his new house, explaining that he was a longshoreman and needed the phone to find out whether the gang he was working in was being dispatched and where.

"Oh, I'm sorry, sir," the girl at the phone company replied, primly. "We have such a backlog of orders for new phones we can't install one in less than two months."

"Have you been reading about the Bridges–Robertson–Schmidt trial that just ended?" Schmidt asked her.

"Yes, sir, I have."

"Don't you recognize my name?" Schmidt asked.

"No sir, I don't."

"I'm one of the defendants of the Bridges–Robertson–Schmidt case. How can the FBI tap my phone if I don't have one?"

"I don't know," the girl replied haughtily, "if that would make any difference."

"I got a new phone the next day," Schmidt chuckled later.

Bob Robertson was called next. A big, rugged man, he looked much more like the type Central Casting would send to portray a worker than either of his co–defendants. Born in Texas in 1905 into a poverty–stricken farm family, he had left home in his early teens and worked as a harvest hand, lumberjack, and in other jobs a grade school dropout could get in those days. He even boxed for awhile under the name K. O. Rhodes, until he decided that splitting the $25 a fight fifty–fifty with his manager wasn't worth it.

He arrived in San Francisco in 1932, got a job in a warehouse and, in 1934, helped organize the warehouse division of the union. After that he became a district organizer and, in 1939, first vice-president of the national union. In 1938, when he was sent to New Orleans with two other organizers, the police of the city gave him his choice of leaving quietly or being beaten and run out of town. He insisted on staying. They beat him so ferociously they broke his back.

Robertson had, of course, known Bridges intimately for years before he appeared as his witness in Judge Foley's court, but he got involved in the case by a fluke. Bridges had made arrangements to have as his witnesses Henry Schmidt and Paul Schnurr, an old–timer in labor circles and, in 1945, president of the San Francisco CIO Council. Schnurr was, like Schmidt, a naturalized citizen and some technical question was raised as to whether he was eligible to serve as Bridges's witness. Robertson was out in the hall with a group of Bridges's well–wishers when, as he told the court, ". . . suddenly Dick Gladstein stuck his head out of the door and he looked over at the crowd and he saw me and he said, 'Come on, Robertson. You will be a witness for Bridges.' And, of course, I was proud of standing up for Bridges and being a character witness for him."

During the trial, the government lawyers decided they had no case against Robertson and privately told MacInnis they were willing to let him withdraw as a defendant. For most people, the news would have posed an agonizing dilemma. For Robertson, it was no problem at all:

"When our attorneys learned the government would accept a defense motion to dismiss all charges against me," he said in 1965, "we—the three defendants—talked about it. Harry left it up to me.

"But I had no choice. This union is my life, and it's been good to me. If I had deserted my two colleagues, I couldn't have called myself a man. I would have betrayed everything I've fought for and stood for all my life.

"I said, 'Gentlemen, we'll stand or fall together.'"

Even so, Robertson fully expected to pay a heavy price for his act of solidarity. The trial was held in the old Federal Building, and the courtroom had twelve fasces encrusted in the ceiling, and decorations used by American Indians that resembled swastikas were worked into the design. Running down the center of the pattern was a series of what looked suspiciously like KKKs but were probably thunderbirds.

"We were sure we were going to lose," Robertson said later. "And as I sat there for five months looking up at the ceiling at those swastikas and Fascist symbols, sometimes I wondered if I was in an American court."

On February 7, 1950, eighty–six days after the trial opened, Bridges was called to the stand. He was there for more than two weeks. Once again, he told the story of his early life in Australia, the influence on him of his uncle Renton, and his experiences as a sailor. At the outset he seemed nervous. One of the first questions Hallinan put to him was: "How many brothers and sisters do you have?" "Six," Bridges answered. He thought a moment. "No— four."

Once the questioning moved on to his experiences on the waterfront, he became his familiar, voluble self again. On his first day on the stand, he was describing the committees he had helped set up in the '34 strike when he remembered his first encounter with Hallinan. The defense committee, he said, was responsible for getting strikers out on bail. "There was a lot of trouble," he recalled, "because it was illegal to picket in those days. We had a picketing ordinance, and that reminds me, the lawyer we hired, if you recall, to try to get an injunction to stop the police from interfering with our picketing was a man named Hallinan, Vincent Hallinan."

"I was licked," Hallinan said.

"Yes, you were beaten. I can still recall," Bridges said, turning to the judge, "that the strike committee didn't want to hire him because he was a bourgeois capitalist lawyer; we didn't want to have anything to do with such characters."

"Maybe you would be better off," Hallinan muttered dejectedly, no doubt thinking of the six–month jail term awaiting him, "if you took their advice on this case."

Much of Bridges's testimony, when Hallinan was questioning him, was designed to rebut the statements of prosecution witnesses that Sam Darcy was the mastermind who directed the '34 strike. Characteristically, Bridges was long–winded, went off on tangents, was uninhibited in his comments about the government's witnesses and the case it was presenting against him. Just as inevitably, Donohue was on his feet again and again, objecting that Bridges's remarks were irrelevant and hearsay. Surprisingly, Judge Harris consistently overruled the prosecutor and let Bridges continue.

When Donohue got his turn, he led Bridges through a long review of the part played by Communists in the '34 strike, their role in the union afterward, Bridges's flip–flop, as the prosecutor referred to it, in World War II, his views on the Marshall Plan and the cold war, the CIO purge of left–wing unions, his version of the testimony that he'd been in closed Party meetings. This time, it was Hallinan's turn to object (he was overruled most of the time), and to insist that Donohue stop interrupting Bridges, who was even more discursive under cross–examination than he was earlier. "Let him finish!" Hallinan cried out at one point. "When he *is* finished," Donohue replied, adding, "And I sometimes doubt if he ever will be."

All the background material Hallinan had been rebuked for getting into the record in his opening statement was again put into the record in Bridges's testimony. During Donohue's cross–examination, he said it was clear to him that he wasn't on trial for being a Communist, because several witnesses for the prosecution were, like himself, naturalized citizens. Unlike him, they admitted having been Communists. Yet the government had not made any move to deport *them* or to put *them* on trial. It followed, then, that he was on trial because he was an effective union leader. In fact, the union itself was on trial:

It is one method of attack, Mr. Donohue. As long as I am up here—the three leading officers of the union are up here wasting our energy, our funds and everything, at the same time the Immigration people have got these characters running around in my union trying to sabotage things down below. All kinds of employer interests are at work, and rival unions are raiding our organization; we are being attacked right and left.

It is not because I am a Communist, as I have told you. We are an effective union that packs a certain amount of economic and political weight. We get in people's way. We stop people from putting over their phoney and crooked deals. Maybe we get into a lot of trouble because we put our nose into other people's business. We regard the trade union movement as our property. We are part of the trade union movement of the United States. What another union does is our business, and what we do we consider is someone else's business. As long as we are up here having to pay out tens of thousands of dollars to defend the officers of the union and we have to be in the courtroom, that cripples our union, that uses its funds, it ties up its energies, and it makes it more vulnerable to attack.

You have got another case. If this jury finds us not guilty in this case, you people know you have another civil suit pending against me; I have to go through another trial to defend my citizenship papers, notwithstanding what happens in this trial. You know that. And that means more money, more time spent, more months spent in court.

If Bridges had been nervous when he first took the stand, weeks earlier, he had fully regained his composure long before Donohue opened his cross–examination. "What discomfort accompanied the cross–questioning," Alvin Hyman wrote in the *San Francisco Chronicle*, "seemed to rest on the examiner rather than on the examined. Donohue was sometimes angry and sputtered. Bridges smiled and was deferential and at times almost patronizing.

"Early in the give–and–take, Donohue's attack lost its sharp edge and there was a querulous note in his protests to the court: 'I don't think the witness ought to be allowed to make a speech every time I ask a question.'

"Donohue . . . wore an unfamiliar mien as he jousted with Bridges. The suavity and urbanity which opposing attorneys have often and not unmaliciously remarked upon gave way to a determined waspishness."

Two days later, Bridges was going strong. "Bridges, for most of the day," Hyman reported, "exercised his durable and at times highly forensic powers with increasing strength; he crammed sixteen full minutes with one single answer to one short question—and didn't lose a single listener. Some jurors were sitting so far forward that they seemed in danger of toppling."

On February 21st, just two weeks after he took the witness stand, Bridges's testimony came to an end. All in all, it was a successful performance, but he hadn't quite carried it off with the élan he achieved on Angel Island. (On the other hand, it is doubtful that Donohue spoke for anyone but himself—and possibly Judge Harris—when he remarked as Bridges was leaving the stand, "I think everybody is tired of hearing Mr. Bridges talk. I know I am.")

The case went to the jury on March 31st, after two hours of instruction from Judge Harris. MacInnis filed sixty–seven objections to the judge's charge, while Donohue said the government was satisfied. Five days later, the jury filed back into the courtroom, heads down, lips tight. Henry Schmidt looked closely at the two jurors who, by some dubious telepathy, he had chosen as the chief advocates of acquittal. He turned to Robertson, then to Bridges. "It's going to be guilty."

The clerk, his voice trembling and his hands not entirely steady, read the verdict: "Guilty." Bridges turned ashen. He looked around at his wife, Nancy, seated in the front row. She pursed her lips and blew him a kiss. The blood surged back into his face and he resumed his familiar sardonic expression. Schmidt grimaced. Recovering quickly, he smiled at his teen–age daughter. She was crying. Robertson thrust out his jaw and glowered straight ahead.

"You have finally found the golden truth shimmering in the fiery crucible of this trial," the judge said to the jury, after complimenting them for their courage. Then, turning to the defense table, he sentenced Hallinan to six months in jail and MacInnis to three.

A week later the *Chronicle* interviewed the foreman of the jury. The witness who had the greatest influence on the jury was Schomaker, he said. Almost as important were Rathborne, Schrimpf, Wilson and a man named Hancock, who had testified that when he was a Communist functionary in San Diego he'd seen Bridges at Party meetings. It had taken four ballots to convict Bridges, the foreman said. On the first, there were six votes for conviction, two for acquittal, four abstentions. On the second, it was eight to convict, two to acquit, with two abstentions. On the third, only one was holding out for acquittal. It took five ballots to convict Schmidt, but only two to convict Robertson. The foreman was surprised when he was told the government thought its case against Robertson was weakest.

The jury went very carefully, the foreman said, into Bridges's Stockton alibi. After weighing it against the testimony of Manning Johnson and Paul Crouch, comparing air line schedules and so on, they decided to believe the government.

A week later, Judge Harris handed down the sentences: five years in jail for Bridges, two years each for Robertson and Schmidt. He set Bridges's bail at $25,000, Robertson's and Schmidt's at $10,000 each. I'm not imposing fines, he noted, even though I could fine each of these defendants $15,000. "I have reason to believe that such fines would be met through an assessment on the rank and file of the defendants' union, and I have no desire to impose any such penalty on those workingmen."

The next day, the prosecutor was back in court to ask the judge to revoke Bridges's citizenship. "If he wins his appeal," Harris asked, "will his citizenship be restored if I revoke it now?"

"Yes," Donohue replied.

"What would be the effect on the civil suit if I sign this order?"

"I doubt if it would be pressed."

10

Why Not Negotiate?

*Either you support your country or you're a
goddam traitor who ought to be locked up.*
A SAN FRANCISCO LONGSHOREMAN,
IN 1950.

WHILE BRIDGES'S APPEAL from the conviction was slowly making
its way up to the higher court, he was free on bail. Immediately
after the trial, he became embroiled in another defense action, this
time against the CIO move to expel the union. The CIO set the
hearing for May 17th. Arguing the case for expulsion would be
William Steinberg, president of the radio operators' union. Sitting
in judgment would be three vice–presidents of the CIO. After hearing the testimony, they would make a recommendation to the CIO
Executive Council, which had been authorized by the convention
to expel the union if the facts warranted it.

As Bridges and the fourteen–man delegation set out from San
Francisco for the hearing in Washington, the outlook was bleak.
Six left–wing unions had already been expelled, and similar charges
had been lodged against six others. The list, on which there were
several unions with fine records of making gains for their members,
included the American Communications Association, which had
about twenty thousand members; the Farm Equipment Workers,
with seventy–five thousand; the Food, Tobacco and Agricultural
Workers, with seventy thousand; the International Fishermen and
Allied Workers, a West Coast union of twenty–five thousand members; the International Fur and Leather Workers Union, a New
York City–based union with one hundred thousand members and
Ben Gold, the only admitted Communist union leader in the country, as its president; the ILWU, which had sixty–five thousand
members; the Marine Cooks and Stewards, whose six thousand

members shipped out of West Coast ports; the Mine, Mill and Smelter Workers, a hundred–thousand–member union which was once headed by Big Bill Haywood; the United Electrical, Radio and Machine Workers, with almost a half–million members and gifted leaders like Julius Emspak and James Matles; the United Furniture Workers, a fifty–thousand–member union; the United Office and Professional Workers, with fifty thousand members, many of whom worked in the offices of CIO unions across the country; and the United Public Workers, which did not disclose its membership. When the trials were over, all were expelled except one—the furniture workers, which jettisoned its officers who offended the CIO.

The longshoremen's major offense was their repeated criticism of America's cold war policies. This part of the prosecution's case was presented by Paul Jacobs, a member of the CIO research staff, who showed that on one foreign policy issue after another, the position of the Party and the ILWU were the same. Another charge was pressed by Mike Quill of the New York transport workers and Hedley Stone of the East Coast sailors' union, who testified that they had attended closed Party meetings with Bridges in which high Communist officials gave him orders. Neither, however, was willing to say under oath that Bridges was a Party member. Nor was either ever called by the government in any of its prosecutions of Bridges.

In view of the way the earlier CIO trials had gone, the expulsion of the ILWU on August 29, 1950 was a foregone conclusion. You could reasonably conclude, in fact, that the trials had the earmarks of a cold war kangaroo court.

Arthur Goldberg, then general counsel for the CIO and later, a Justice on the U.S. Supreme Court, saw it differently: "Our CIO boards," he told a *New Yorker* writer doing a profile on him in 1962, "operated in a very careful, judicial way. Both sides were heard—that is, if the other side wanted to be heard—and the cases were developed fully. For instance, we established in detail and beyond doubt that Harry Bridges steadily followed the Communist Line. We did this not through any evidence from informers but through the plain record of his statements and his publications, and we did a far more thorough job on Bridges than the government did."

Paul Jacobs, who prepared the case against the ILWU, has described the expulsion in *The State of the Unions*:

The CIO trial of the ILWU was held in May, 1950. I do not know whether it would have been possible to find impartial judges within the CIO but not much attempt to do so was made. The three–man trial committee was headed by O. A. Knight, president of the Oil Workers Union, my boss at the time. The other two members of the committee were comparative newcomers to the CIO and rather conservative in their politics. But it didn't really matter who they were, for Bridges and everyone else knew the verdict was decided before the trial was held. The committee's decision to recommend expulsion was so certain that I began to work on the writing of it while the trial was still in progress. . . .

Later in this book, there is a discussion of the general problem of whether or not the CIO's decision to expel the Communists was a wise one; now, I only want to raise the specific issue of whether or not the ILWU got a fair due–process shake from the CIO in 1950. I must admit, much as I hate to provide Bridges with ammunition to prove the assertions he made at the time, that there was very little due process in the trial that took place the three tense days of May 17, 18 and 19, 1950, in the boardroom of the old CIO headquarters on Jackson Place in Washington, D.C.

By the 1960s, only the ILWU and one other of the eleven expelled unions—the electrical workers—were still in existence. The other nine had gone under or had been absorbed by rival unions after first purging themselves, as the furniture workers had done, of the offending left–wingers in their leadership. Aside from giving ILWU members a disquieting sense of being out of the mainstream of American labor, the main disadvantage of expulsion was, for a few years, a weakening of the union's political influence. Another was its vulnerability to red–baiting by the unions.

As recently as the mid–Sixties, for example, the hotel workers' union used the tactic when it and the ILWU competed for the three hundred employees of Lawrence Rockefeller's posh Mauna Kea Hotel on the island of Hawaii. On the day of the election, the hotel workers passed out leaflets accusing the ILWU of supporting Castro and the Viet Cong, and urging admission of Red China to the U.N.

"One of these days," the leaflet admonished the workers, "you or a member of your family will want to get SECURITY CLEARANCE for a government job. Do you think that you or your family could get that clearance when you say that you belong to a union that favors the Moscow line and is against American policy?"

When the result came in, it was no union—159, ILWU—144, hotel workers—10. The NLRB held another election, warning the hotel workers not to repeat the Red-baiting tactic. This time, the ILWU won easily.

In late June, about a month after the CIO expulsion trial, fighting broke out along the 38th Parallel in Korea, the boundary line between North and South. Because the United States looked upon South Korea as an American outpost in our containment perimeter against China, on June 27, 1950, President Truman sent U.S. air and sea forces into battle in support of the South Koreans. At the same time, he ordered increased military assistance to the Philippines and to the French Foreign Legion fighting in Viet Nam to hold the French colony there. The President then called upon the U.N. Security Council to authorize a U.N. military force to go to the aid of South Korea. Overnight, the cold war was a shooting war.

As it happened, the regular meeting of the San Francisco longshoremen's local was scheduled for June 28th. As the members straggled in for the meeting, they were handed a resolution their local officers had prepared. It endorsed without reservation the President's action in Korea, and pledged that shipping would not be disrupted for the duration of the fighting.

Bridges, having learned during the day about the officers' resolution, came to the meeting with a substitute resolution which would have put the local on record supporting a United Nations order for a cease fire, with the combatants retiring to their respective sides of the 38th parallel while the U.N. settled the dispute through negotiations.

"Our country is at war!" one speaker after another shouted into the mikes set up around the hall. "Either you support your country or you're a goddam traitor who ought to be locked up!"

"Or deported!" one speaker bawled.

By the time Bridges got the floor, members were starting to drift out of the hall. "There's no need for the officers' resolution," he pleaded. "Nobody is impugning the loyalty or questioning the patriotism of the members of this union. Moreover, the blanket endorsement the officers are proposing would put this local on record endorsing intervention by the U.S. in any civil war or revolt against colonialism."

Even while Bridges was speaking, longshoremen continued moving toward the doors. Someone called for a vote on Bridges's motion, but it was obvious there was no longer a quorum, so the meeting adjourned.

That night, the wire services carried a story across the nation that Harry Bridges, "Red longshore leader and convicted felon," had opposed a union resolution endorsing the Korean war. Within a few days, newspapers all over the country were calling for his head. Some went so far as to assert that he had proposed that longshoremen refuse to load ships carrying supplies or troops to Korea.

San Francisco longshoremen met again on July 13th. "We will now take up the resolution on Korea proposed by the officers at our last meeting," the local president announced, as he called the session to order.

"Hold on there a minute!" Bridges called out. "My amendment takes precedence. It has to be voted on first."

"No," the president said. "Your motion was voted down at the last meeting."

"Then I appeal the ruling of the chair," Bridges replied. "My recollection is that we adjourned before the vote was completed."

The chair was sustained, overwhelmingly, but such an uproar ensued that the police were called and the meeting broke up without acting on either resolution. A week later, at a special meeting, the longshoremen adopted the officers' resolution.

All of a sudden, it seemed as if everybody was against Bridges. Longshoremen up and down the coast passed resolutions endorsing President Truman's intervention in Korea. In Washington, the Senate Judiciary Committee was called together by Senator Eastland to look into ways to revoke Bridges's bail and jail him at once. The Attorney General said the FBI was looking into the matter. The newspapers took up the cry that Bridges belonged in jail, and on July 20th, Jiggs Donohue was on his way back to San Francisco to see if he could persuade Judge Harris to cooperate.

The hearing began on August 2nd. To hear Donohue's description of the Korean war, you would have thought North Koreans were crawling up the beaches of San Francisco Bay. "We face a crisis," he told Judge Harris, "such as this nation has never faced before. There can be no minority opinion on this. We are fighting for survival."

Bridges took the stand on the third day, after long, heated arguments by opposing lawyers over whether putting him in jail would violate his First Amendment right of free speech and whether it was reasonable to think he would jump bail now that the Korean war had broken out.

"What do you think, Mr. Bridges," Judge Harris asked, "of the program for screening Communists off the waterfront?" The judge was referring to a voluntary screening scheme agreed upon in Washington a few weeks earlier by government officials and representatives of maritime unions and employers. In all unions but the ILWU, the men invited to the meeting were the unions' top elected officials. But the government, in selecting longshoremen from the West Coast, had by-passed Bridges and invited three little-known local officials, two from San Francisco and one from Seattle, who stood out from the rank and file only by their opposition to Bridges. Under the screening program they put their signatures to, a sailor or longshoreman suspected of Communist sympathies could be barred from the industry. There was no provision for an appeal, nor was the screened-off worker to be given reasons why he was screened off the waterfront.

"As president of my union," Bridges reminded the judge, "I am obligated to protect the rights of the union members, no matter what their political beliefs are. I wired the President and the Secretary of Labor—before this security program was established—that I favored security measures. But I meant security measures on a coastwide basis, with the union and employers working together on them, so that an employer couldn't take advantage of the program."

"Why not do it this way," he went on. "Classify certain areas of the waterfront, like the Navy and Army docks, as high security areas. For a man to work there, he'd have to have a pass. But in the rest of the port, where he'd be working passenger ships and commercial cargoes, he wouldn't have to have one. There's no need to screen anybody off the waterfront altogether. Moreover, anyone denied a pass ought to be able to appeal.

"We're not opposed to security," he concluded, "so long as steps are taken against discrimination. We don't want it to be a program employers can use to blacklist militant union members."

"Do you believe your obligation to your union is greater than your obligation to the United States?" the judge inquired.

"My obligations to both are not incompatible, your Honor."

"Would you refuse to obey any order given you by your country in connection with the war effort?" Hallinan asked. It was an interesting question, considering that Bridges had had his citizenship taken away a fortnight earlier.

"I would not," he replied. "I don't see how I could. I would be punished if I did not. But I thought I could have an opinion without engaging in acts of sabotage. I've spoken out against war before and I'll continue to do so. "If I haven't that right, I may as well go to jail."

Donohue then read a statement by President Truman that international communism was turning from internal subversion to armed aggression against innocent nations. "Do you believe that?" he asked.

"No. There's a question in my mind who started the war in Korea, whether an invasion has really taken place. For that matter, whether Koreans can invade Korea."

What was happening, Bridges continued, was an internal situation, complicated by the presence of the U.S. arming and directing the South Koreans, and the Russians doing the same in the north: "I am against both sides," he concluded.

Judge Harris then asked if Bridges thought the World Federation of Trade Unions was a Communist organization. Founded in 1944, in the halcyon period of East–West relations, the WFTU was to be the labor counterpart of the United Nations, with unions from Communist countries presumably playing an important part in it. The AFL, true to its isolationist and anti–Communist tradition, would have nothing to do with the WFTU from the start. The CIO was in at the founding, but pulled out in the late forties, complaining that unions from Communist countries now had a disproportionate influence in the WFTU, which as a result had become anti–American and was opposing the Marshall Plan. The longshoremen kept their affiliation, and just before his 1950 trial, Bridges was elected, in absentia, honorary president of the maritime unit of the World Federation.

"I suppose it might be considered Communist–dominated," Bridges answered. "But we still need the support of the WFTU during strikes." How much support the WFTU could actually give was anybody's guess.

"In the CMU days, Harry and I were in a meeting with Joe Curran and the CMU group," Bill Glazier has said.

There was a guy named Ed Traynor there, from the marine engineers. An old Wobbly, always with a pamphlet in his pocket on disarmament, birth control, or what not.

Harry gave a rousing speech, talking about the help we'd get all over the world if we struck. All we had to do was say the word, and they'd stop any ships that got through our blockade. It sounded great.

Then Traynor got up. "You know, Brother Bridges," he said, "your speech reminded me of what Hotspur said to Prince Hal." And he quoted from Henry V, where Prince Hal says he has ten thousand men, and he says " 'I can call upon the forces of the deep, from the nether regions . . .' And Hotspur says, 'You can call them. But will they come?' "

Harry was speechless. All he could do was mutter to me, "Those goddam Wobblies. They never change, the phonies."

The WFTU is against the Marshall Plan, Donohue persisted, and has proposed that maritime workers sabotage shipments of Marshall Plan cargoes. "What is your position on that?"

"We haven't received any sabotage orders from the WFTU," Bridges replied. "But even if we did, it wouldn't mean anything, because our union only takes orders from its members."

"Does your position as honorary president of the maritime unit of the WFTU carry any power?" Donohue asked.

"It's like an honorary degree from a university," Bridges answered. "Something you don't deserve, and something you couldn't get in any other way."

On August 5, 1950, with Senator Joseph McCarthy in the ascendancy and Americans in a shoot-out in Korea, to Judge Harris there was nothing amusing about Bridges's answer to that last question.

"Mr. Bridges," the judge said as he brought the hearing to an end,

is an agent dedicated to the execution of the Communist program nationally and internationally. I am led to believe from the proceedings before me that he probably is one of the most important figures in the Communist Party in America today.

Mr. Bridges's conduct since the inception of hostilities in Korea has been such as to justify this Court in concluding that when the welfare of this country is at stake, his loyalty is and must be with the Communists.

He has spearheaded, since his release on bail, a serious opposition to security measures designed to protect the people of San Francisco, this port and the welfare of our armed forces. This opposition was taken to protect the Communist Party and his Communist cohorts within his union—not for the benefit of the union.

Of equal significance is his refusal to disavow his affiliation with the World Federation of Trade Unionists, which he admits is controlled and dominated by the Communists. I say adherence to the program of the WFTU is traitorous!

The Army and Navy and the Marine Corps will hold the beachheads in Korea. Our duty at home is to protect the beachheads that involve internal security. Mr. Bridges instituted a delaying action regarding certain vital resolutions before his union.

I say he will continue this delaying action so long as this country is engaged in conflict with the Communists on the other side.

Accordingly, and for good cause, I revoke and vacate the order admitting Harry Bridges to bail.

Judge Harris then stood up, gathered his robes and strode from the court, accompanied by hissing from the spectators. Bridges rose, too. A marshal put a hand on his arm, but made no move to handcuff him. Another marshal, standing near Nancy, Bridges's second wife, patted her gently on the shoulder. Bridges turned to her: "No tears." Bridges and the two deputies, one on each side— still no handcuffs—moved off down the hall.

As the three men emerged from the building, a crowd assembled on the sidewalk cheered. "Did you expect this, Harry?" a reporter asked.

"Hell, yes! What else could you expect?" Then he stopped. "Change that. Take this instead. I believe that right now anybody who speaks his opinion on the current world situation is liable for jail."

A man ran up to Bridges out of the crowd, shouting, "You deserved this! You're a traitor!" Bridges's face flushed. He took a step toward the man as if to strike him, but he was pulled back by the marshals. At the booking desk in the county jail, Bridges thanked the marshals, wishing them "Good luck," as they left. "Well," he said to the reporters crowding around him as he awaited processing, "I'll get a little sleep at last. Nothing to do but sit around and read. Maybe I'll write my memoirs."

Most of the nation's press praised the judge's courage and applauded his jailing of Bridges. Some, by an eccentric logic, saw a similarity in the Bridges and Alger Hiss cases, in that they proved the worth of non–Communist oaths: "A Communist signs one, then we nail him with perjury." There were, of course, other voices. The American Civil Liberties Union announced that it would sup-

port Bridges's attorneys in the appeal with an *amicus curiae* brief.
"In addition to the infringement of freedom of speech," the ACLU
declared, "there is a question of law: whether Judge Harris has the
right to revoke bail.

"Supreme Court Justice William O. Douglas ruled in the *Tokyo
Rose* case that the defendant is entitled to bail as a matter of right,
if the defendant has lodged an appeal which raises serious federal
questions and is not frivolous in character."

The Federal Court of Appeals heard the appeal a few days later.
As the hearing progressed, its outcome seemed anything but promising. "I think," the chief judge said from the bench at one point,
"there is a perfectly good reason for regarding any member of the
Communist Party as an enemy alien at all times, not just when we
are at war; in peacetime, too."

The hearing over, Bridges was returned to his cell in the county
jail to await the decision. Herb Caen, the *San Francisco Chronicle*
columnist, visited him there in his second week. "He's reading a lot,
has gained fifteen pounds and feels good," Caen reported. "He says
Sheriff Dan Murphy runs a good jail."

Bridges had been put in a cell by himself, it turned out, and he
had plenty to read: eleven books, among them Warden Johnston's
Alcatraz: Island Prison, George McCune's *Korea Today*, Kyle
Crichton's *The Marx Brothers*, Owen Lattimore's *Ordeal by Slan-
der*, John Gunther's *Roosevelt in Retrospect*, Charles Jackson's *The
Sunnier Side*, Harold Laski's *The American Democracy*.

Laski, especially, impressed him. When he got out of jail, a reporter asked him, "Do you think revocation of your bail means
there are forces working for war in this country?"

"I think that government contracts, which are required by war,
are the only thing that stands between us and depression," Bridges
answered. "We would have millions of unemployed now if it
weren't for the war.

"Unemployment occurs because the big corporations of the
United States are determined not to spread the benefits and profits
among the majority of the American people.

"In case anyone is curious as to where I get my ideas, I got them
from a book by Harold Laski called *The American Democracy*. I re–
read it and I found out the main reasons why I was in jail."

The appeals court handed down its decision on Friday, August
24th, twenty days after Bridges was jailed, reversing Judge Harris
and ordering Bridges freed. But it still took a while for Bridges to
actually get out of jail. The decision was technically an order to the

district court below, instructing the lower court to send an order along to the sheriff telling him to release the prisoner. By the time Bridges's lawyers were able to get to the district court, it was late afternoon. When they handed the decision, which was fifteen pages long, to the presiding judge, he looked it over and told them to come back at ten o'clock the following morning. He needed time to read it, he said, and he wanted "to spread the mandate on the court records." Even to someone with a compulsion for respecting the formalities, leaving Bridges in jail for one more night must have seemed vindictive, for the last sentence of the decision was unequivocal: "The revocation order of [Judge Harris] is vacated and set aside, mandate to go down immediately."

It was a divided decision. Chief Judge Mathews, dissenting, thought Judge Harris had acted wisely and properly, in view of the conspiratorial nature of the Communist Party and the opportunities open to the longshoremen's union to sabotage Korea–bound shipments. (East Coast longshoremen, for one, agreed. On the day Bridges was let out of jail, they refused to unload two thousand Polish hams, believing that would be helping international communism.)

The majority opinion, written by Judge Healy and joined in by Judge Orr, was a compound of principle and pragmatism. The purpose of Bridges's resolution, they noted, was to support a United Nations order for a cease fire, for a return to the status quo, and for the U.N. to settle the dispute peacefully through discussions with all parties concerned, in order to avoid a worldwide atomic war: "There is no showing," Judge Healy pointed out,

> that Bridges has in the present juncture committed any recognizable crime, or that he has himself counseled or advocated sabotage, or sought to foment strikes or the establishment of picket lines on the waterfront, or to impede by other means the prompt loading and dispatch of ships to the Far East.
>
> The whole matter appears finally to boil down to the contention that Bridges is a proven Communist . . . and that the Korean crisis renders him per se a menace to the public security; hence the District Court was right in revoking his bail and ordering him confined.
>
> The conclusion, if we may say so, is as startling as it is novel.

Judge Healy and Orr were especially critical of the way Judge Harris had allowed his court to be used by the executive branch of the government. As they saw it, in his eagerness to accuse Bridges of subverting the war effort, Harris was himself a subversive: ". . . we say now, with all the emphasis that we are able to command, that however hard and disagreeable may be the task in times of passion and excitement, it is the duty of the courts to set their faces like flint against this erosive subversion of the judicial process."

Reactions around the country to the decision were reminiscent of the reactions to Dean Landis's decision, back in 1939. Very few newspapers commented favorably. The *Christian Science Monitor* was glad to see any doubts about dangers to individual freedom "resolved in the direction of the spirit of the Bill of Rights." But the *Portland Oregonian*, as Olympian on the West Coast as the *Times* is nationally, spoke for the majority of the press: "What distinction can or should be made in wartime between an alien who is a member of an international revolutionary party? In the last war, we even locked up American citizens of Japanese descent. A Communist is a Communist, whether he is a Korean, a Russian, an American or an Australian."

"God help America!" Jiggs Donohue exclaimed when he heard the news. "This is a tremendous shock to me. I'll turn in my resignation tomorrow. Then I can speak my mind as a private citizen." So far as can be determined, the extent of Donohue's speaking out was his return to California in November to help former Congresswoman Helen Gahagan Douglas run for the U.S. Senate. Her opponent was Richard Nixon, whose Red–baiting campaign against her in 1946 had won him her seat in the House. In her Senate campaign, Mrs. Douglas introduced Donohue as "the man who convicted Harry Bridges." Donohue reciprocated with a dubious tribute: "She has a better anti–Communist record than Mr. Nixon." It wasn't good enough. She lost.

There was also the usual wind on Capitol Hill. Senator Langer thought Judges Healy and Orr ought to be impeached. Senator Bricker went farther. He demanded that Congress investigate all federal judges who granted bail to Communists, suggesting as immediate targets the seven members of the court of appeals in San Francisco. This so outraged Judge William Denman, who had succeeded Judge Mathews as chief judge, that he wrote a blistering open letter to Bricker, challenging him to publish Judge Healy's opinion in the *Congressional Record*. It was a letter to gladden the hearts of Bridges supporters: "The opinion shows that Bridges was indicted more than three years after his alleged offense," Judge Denman said in part, "and that the statute continuing the jurisdiction to indict him has been held invalid by a court of appeals whose decision was upheld by the Supreme Court . . ."

The court of appeals heard the appeal from Bridges's conviction on March 18, 1952. On the bench this time were Judges Stephens, Bone and Pope. Judge Denman had disqualified himself because, he said, he had made critical remarks about "longshoremen's goon squads" during the '34 strike. Bridges's lawyers asked the court to reverse the conviction on several grounds: *res judicata*, double jeopardy, the statute of limitations, and Judge Harris's prejudicial conduct of the trial. The prosecutor conceded that the decision Judge Denman cited in his letter to Senator Bricker raised doubts about the validity of Bridges's conviction for perjury. But the conspiracy part of the conviction should be upheld, he contended, because the statute of limitations didn't apply to it. And he couldn't see anything prejudicial about the judge's handling of the trial.

Three weeks after the appeals court hearing, Hallinan, handcuffed to a dope peddler he had unsuccessfully represented, left San Francisco to begin his term in the federal prison on McNeil Island. MacInnis joined him there a week later. At the end of a month, MacInnis was feeling penitent: "My conduct," he wrote Judge Harris apologetically, "was due to the mounting stress and strain in the long, arduous and emotionally–charged trial." His wife, he added, had had to go to work when he went to prison but now she was sick and under a doctor's care. The judge, moved by the letter, commuted his sentence to time served. Hallinan was not so fortunate. He got out on good behavior in August, after serving four months of his six–month sentence. Three weeks after Hallinan got back to San Francisco, the court of appeals handed down its decision. It was unanimous, seventy pages long, and it upheld Bridges's conviction without reservation.

In Hawaii, 26,000 members of the union struck for twenty–four hours in protest. "You know," some of the Hawaiians said later, "those guys on the mainland were all set to dump Harry after that decision. We shamed 'em into supporting him."

When San Francisco longshoremen met for their regular meeting on September 8th, two days after the decision came down, somebody moved that they follow Hawaii's example. The president of the local looked out over the crowd. "We can't vote on that," he ruled. "We don't have a quorum." Two days later, at the insistence of Bridges supporters, local officers called a special meeting. This time, the longshoremen voted to stay off the job—except for handling military cargoes, mail, and passenger ships—for one day. During debate on the proposal, a member asked from the floor how the local officers felt about it. The chairman turned to Bridges as he answered: "We've always supported you in labor matters, Harry," he said. "But I consider this a political action, and I, personally, am opposed to this resolution."

Seven months later, on March 9, 1953, the Supreme Court announced that it would review the case. It would consider two major questions: did *res judicata* bar the trial, and did the statute of limitations apply?

Bridges, Robertson and Schmidt were in the audience on May 4, 1953, as Telford Taylor, a prestigious attorney who had been chief prosecutor at the Nuremberg war crimes trials, pleaded their case before the Supreme Court. Representing the government was an eminent constitutional lawyer, John F. Davis, especially appointed for the occasion. Davis had an ingenious answer to Taylor's argument that the Wartime Suspension Act applied only to cases directly connected with the war itself, and which involved things of monetary value. It's true, Davis conceded, that when Congress passed the Act, profiteering was what it was primarily concerned with. But it didn't intend to exclude other kinds of fraud. Anyway, the question is irrelevant, he told the Court. The government contends that American citizenship has a definite monetary value to Bridges. Therefore, we hold that the Act applies.

On the bench that day were only seven justices. Robert Jackson was ill, and Tom Clark had disqualified himself because, as Attorney General, he'd been in on the prosecution. It was a lively session, especially for Davis. He was just getting under way when Justice Frankfurter threw him off course with some pointed questions about the nature of fraud. Justice Black joined in with more sharp questions, and finally Frankfurter, after grilling Davis closely about the Wartime Suspension Act and how the Bridges case was brought under it, said to the lawyer: "You appear to be uneasy and embarrassed. Could it be the case that bothers you?"

A few weeks after the hearing before the Supreme Court, the Bridges–Robertson–Schmidt Defense Committee announced the state of its treasury. From March 1951, to March 1953, it had received $99,496. Donations from West Coast locals, it turned out,

had been modest, totaling $25,000. Hawaiian members had con-
tributed $18,000. $10,000 had come from a few left–wing unions.
The ILWU itself had advanced $45,000 as a loan, to cover the bail.
The rest had come in from individuals from all over the country.

Printing the transcript of the trial for the appeal to the higher
court came to $25,000, about equal to the lawyers' fees. Leaflets
and informational material the committee flooded the country with
cost another $15,000 or so. But neither the committee's financial
rectitude nor its origins (it was established by the international
union executive board) was sufficient to dissuade Herbert Brow-
nell, President Eisenhower's Attorney General, from listing the
committee as a Communist front on his Subversive List. Now,
there were two Bridges defense committees on the list.

Not to be outdone, the Internal Revenue Service a few years
later ruled that the contributions received by the committee were
personal income to the three defendants. That meant that each of
them owed the government income taxes on the money spent for
his legal expenses. They could, of course, have appealed the ruling.
There didn't seem to be a precedent for it, and the higher courts
might have ruled in their favor on the ground that the government
was being vindictive. But to carry the case on up through the appellate courts would have cost more in time and money than the income tax they allegedly owed. They eventually settled out of court
for a fraction of the amount the government originally claimed.

On June 15, 1953, newspapers across the nation carried two
major stories on their front pages. One was datelined Panmunjon,
Korea; "The United Nations command has decided to sign an ar-
mistice agreement with the Communists." The other came from
Washington: "The Supreme Court today, by a vote of four to three,
reversed the conviction of West Coast labor leader Harry Bridges."

The decision must have shocked the White House, despite President Truman's disclaimer of interest. Resurrecting the case was,
after all, an act of his administration, and he no doubt thought he
could count on the justices he had put on the bench to back him
up. Two, Chief Justice Vinson and Minton, did back him up, along
with Reed, a holdover from the FDR era. But Burton, another of
Truman's appointees, joined Black, Douglas and Frankfurter in reversing the conviction. Burton, moreover, not only voted to reverse.
He wrote the opinion.

Although the judges on the court of appeals hadn't been able to
find an unequivocal clue as to what Congress intended when it

adopted the Wartime Suspension Act, the majority of the Supreme Court had no trouble at all doing so. "The legislative history of this exception," the Court said, "emphasizes the propriety of its conservative interpretation. It indicates a purpose to suspend the general statute of limitations only as to war frauds of a pecuniary nature or of a nature concerning property. It nowhere suggests a purpose to swallow up the three–year limitation to the extent necessary to reach the offenses before us."

It was as simple as that. And because the majority held that the three–year limit barred the trial, it didn't go into the question of *res judicata*. The dissenting opinion boiled down to the view that because Bridges was convicted of *conspiracy* to obtain his citizenship by fraud, the Wartime Suspension Act applied.

For the second time, Bridges was reprieved by a one–man majority on the Supreme Court. This time, though, the government left no doubt that it wasn't giving up. A week after the Court's ruling, Warren Olney III, the Assistant Attorney General who headed the Justice Department's criminal division was in San Francisco for a meeting of the Bar Association. In one of the sessions he attended the panelists were congratulating themselves on the way the legal profession represents its clients in civil suits, when a lawyer in the group injected a mildly sobering note: "Among lawyers in America there is a higher standard for civil than for criminal cases, and more has been done to protect property rights in civil courts than to protect human rights in criminal courts.

"I realize," he went on, "that civil practice is more remunerative and more pleasant, but I wonder if winning any civil case affords a thrill commensurate with gaining the acquittal of a fellow citizen charged with a felony?"

Justice Jackson, who was on the panel, spoke up, saying he so heartily agreed that he had enlisted to do something about it. He then remarked that the San Francisco Bar had contributed two men to Washington who had made a deeply favorable impression. One was in the State Department. The other was Warren Olney III . . . "By the way, Olney," someone asked. "Are you fellows going to file a civil suit to denaturalize Harry Bridges?"

"We certainly are," Olney replied. "If the statute of limitations isn't a legal bar to denaturalizing him. And," he added silkily, "I don't think it is."

In January 1954, just six months after his Supreme Court reprieve, Bridges's second marriage ended in divorce. "He's married to the union, not to me," his wife said as she left for Reno. Within a year, to finance child support and accumulated debts, he had to sell his home to raise cash. It brought $9,601.

He lived alone for a couple of years, then decided to marry again, this time to Noriko (Nikki) Sawada, a petite and charming, San Francisco legal secretary twenty–five years his junior. The two set off for Reno, where they checked in at a hotel as Mr. and Mrs. Harry Bridges, then headed for the county clerk's office to get a marriage license. "But I can't issue you one," the flustered clerk told them. "Nevada law prohibits intermarriage between Caucasians and Orientals."

It was too late in the day to challenge the ruling, so they went back to the hotel, which chastely put them in separate rooms. The next day, Bridges was knocking on the door of the court, asking for an order to the clerk to issue the license. "The law was never questioned before," the bemused district attorney mumbled as Bridges left with the order.

"The law came as a complete surprise to Nikki and me," Bridges told reporters. But actually, at one time or another, thirty–eight states had such laws, and in the early thirties, when the Nazis were writing their anti–Semitic laws, they sent a mission to America to see what they could learn from our anti–miscegenation statutes. As recently as 1948, California was still enforcing its anti–miscegenation law when the State Supreme Court struck it down as unconstitutional. In 1966, the U.S. Supreme Court finally ruled that the anti–miscegenation laws still on the books of sixteen states were offensive to the Constitution.

Despite Bridges's Supreme Court diploma, as he called it, that he got in 1953, the civil suit asking for his denaturalization was still hanging over his head. In 1954, he asked the federal court in San Francisco to throw it out, arguing that the basis for it had been decided three times, always adversely to the government. In August, the court denied his motion and set the trial for June 1955.

Compared with Bridges's previous trials, this one was anticlimactic. This time, the trial was before Judge Irving Goodman, without a jury. Only the prestige of Bridges's lawyer—Telford Taylor, chief prosecutor at the Nuremberg war crimes trials—added excitement to the case. The government put on only seven witnesses, five of whom claimed to be ex–Communists; the defense put on four, three claiming to be former members of the Party.

They all made a poor impression on the judge: "The testimony of the 'former Communists,' " he wrote in his opinion, "was tinged and colored with discrepancies, animosities, vituperations, hates and above all, with lengthy speeches and declarations of viewpoints . . ."

He was ambivalent about Bridges's performance on the stand: "Respondent, himself, was not a good witness; he was perhaps the most voluble of all; he made misstatements and was at times evasive. His denial of party membership and avowal of loyalty to the United States were, however, articulate and emphatic . . ."

Summing up the case, Judge Goodman was even more caustic in his judgment of the government's witnesses than Landis had been after Angel Island. "The inherent infirmity of the government's case," the judge concluded, "lies in its own evidence and does not manifest itself out of any conflict between the opposing witnesses."

The final paragraphs of his decision brought to mind Justice Murphy's acid comments in the Supreme Court's 1945 reversal of the Sears decision. "Only a weak yielding to extra–judicial clamor," Judge Goodman wrote, "would excuse acceptance of the testimony of the witnesses in this case as proof of the allegations of the complaint.

"My conclusion is that the Government has failed to prove the allegations of its complaint as to respondent's alleged membership in the Communist Party by clear and convincing evidence."

Bridges had been pessimistic about the case. Sidney Roger, a San Francisco CIO news commentator who later became a ship clerk and then, editor of the ILWU *Dispatcher*, was watching him as the judge read his decision. When it was apparent that it was going to be acquittal, tears welled up in Bridges's eyes.

"When the judge finished reading the decision," Roger said,

I threw open the door and shouted "We've won! We've won!" to the crowd from the union who couldn't get in and were waiting in the hall. They looked back at me with that look of shock that you sometimes see when people see or hear something they can't believe. You know, eyes wide, mouths open.

And then, over in a corner, was a guy who could've been in the courtroom if he'd wanted to. I think he stayed outside because he knew in advance what the verdict was going to be.

It was Bruce Barber. You know, that sonofabitch from the Immigration Service. He looked like he'd been brought back from the grave.

In 1958, Bridges and Bill Glazier, his administrative assistant, took a month off and toured Europe, the Middle East and the Soviet Union.

"When we went to Europe together," Glazier has recalled,

I was struck with how he got on immediately with longshoremen wherever we went. He and they spoke the same language. There just wasn't any barrier between them, nationality, language, or whatever. And everywhere we went, we were with longshoremen. He'd look over the port, and he'd immediately think of how it could be made more productive . . .

But his reaction to Rome was what floored me. We stayed there for days, and he was constantly on the go. We walked until I was worn out [Glazier is twenty years Bridges's junior]. He had to soak himself in the history of the place. He'd read quite a lot about it before we got there. And he was insatiable. We went everywhere, the Vatican . . .

In Haifa, an Israeli told Bridges, "You'll see something here you won't see anywhere else in the world. We've got Ph.Ds working on the docks here."

"That's what's wrong with this country," Bridges retorted. But when he got back, he said that Haifa was the most efficient port on the trip, almost on a par with Honolulu. "Honolulu, no thanks to us, is the most efficient anywhere, not leaving out the socialist countries, either."

"Odessa was the strangest port on the trip," Glazier continued.

They had machines more efficient than any we saw anywhere else, more efficient than what we have here.

They had a machine, I remember, for picking up sacks. It was like something out of Chaplin's "Modern Times." All arms and fingers that moved down and encircled the sacks and picked 'em up. And right alongside they were unloading sacks into a wooden sled about three feet high, on metal runners. A horse pulled it along the wharf! And then, when the longshoremen went to unload it, they were straddling the sides of the sled, reaching awkwardly down to get the sacks out!

So after we saw the docks, we were sitting around a table with the people who ran the port. Harry took out a pack of cigarettes and laid them in a pattern on the table. Some were ships at the piers, some were warehouses, some represented staging areas where cargo could be held for a ship. And he went on for quite awhile, explaining how, by rearranging the port, they could increase efficiency.

Those guys didn't know what to make of him. They were low–echelon bureaucrats, used to carrying out orders. The farthest thing from their minds was to suggest the kind of sweeping reorganization Harry was proposing.

During their stay in the Soviet Union, Bridges was interviewed by a reporter for *Trud*, the trade union newspaper. "What do you think about our trade unions, Mr. Bridges?" Bridges's answer was characteristically good copy, both for the Russians and for his enemies at home. "I have studied the activities of the Russian All–Union Central Council of Trade Unions and twenty–three trade unions," he replied. "And I've come to the conclusion that the organization and system of elections in Soviet unions are democratic. In this respect, Soviet trade unions are more democratic than many American ones."

When Bridges got home he was immediately called up before the House Un–American Activities Committee. For the first time in all his bouts with the government he invoked the privilege against self–incrimination, the Fifth Amendment, when he was asked was he then, or had he been, a Communist. "I've answered that same question dozens of times under oath in a court of law," he explained. "But I'm not going to answer it for this committee." He was asked questions about Communist influence in unions, and especially in the ILWU. He answered those as he had many times before.

As he emerged from the hearing room, he found himself face to face with a woman wearing a fur piece and a flowered hat. On her dress was a blue ribbon that identified her as a delegate to a convention of the Daughters of the American Revolution, then being held in Washington. In her hand, held high, was a flash camera.

Bridges stopped, looked at her and grinned. "No, not the D.A.R.!" he exclaimed. "You'll be expelled for taking my picture."

The woman blushed, adjusted her glasses and stomped off without taking her snapshot.

"They've never really given up on Harry," Richard Gladstein said in 1967.

You remember they passed a section of Landrum–Griffin that made it a crime for a man to hold union office if he'd been a

Communist within the past five years. Archie Brown ran for the local executive board to test it, with Harry's support.

Before that, the Labor Department asked the union to report any officer who might be in violation. I advised against it. We found out later, from the *Wall Street Journal*, as a matter of fact, that the Justice Department agreed with us.

If the *Brown* case had gone against us, then they'd have gone against Harry. There's a sentence in that section, you know, that provides the same penalty for an officer of a union who . . . [He looked up the section and read it aloud:] *"No labor organization or officer thereof shall knowingly permit any person to assume or hold any office or paid position in violation of this section."*

In most U.S. labor unions the *Brown* case could not have come up, for their constitutions prohibit Communists from holding union office. The longshoremen's union, by contrast, makes union office open to any member, regardless of political affiliation.

Archie Brown, who had always been open about his membership in the Communist Party, had worked on the San Francisco waterfront since the mid–1930s, except for a couple of years in Spain, fighting with the International Brigade on the side of the Loyalists. An active member of the union, he had over the years been elected to a variety of offices in the San Francisco local.

Then, in 1959 Congress passed the Landrum–Griffin Act, Section 504 of which made it a crime for a person to hold union office if he had been a Communist or convicted of certain felonies within the preceding five years. In 1961, Brown, who was serving as a member of the local's thirty–five–member executive board, was convicted of violating Sec. 504 and sentenced to six months in jail. He appealed the decision to the federal court of appeals, supported by the ILWU and the American Civil Liberties Union.

An eight–judge panel heard the appeal, and in June, 1964, reversed the conviction, holding in a five to three decision that Sec. 504 was unconstitutional because it deprived Brown of freedom of speech and assembly guaranteed by the First Amendment. The government appealed the reversal to the U.S. Supreme Court, saying the issue was too important to be decided on a lower court level.

A year later, in June, 1965 the Supreme Court affirmed the decision of the court of appeals, but for a different reason. The lower court had overturned Brown's conviction because of the conflict between Sec. 504 and the First Amendment. The Supreme Court, in a five to four decision written by Chief Justice Warren, ruled that Section 504 was a bill of attainder, forbidden by Article I, Section 9 of the Constitution. The decision was an especial victory for Justice Black, who was for years the Court's most determined defender of the Bill of Rights. In 1950, when the Vinson Court upheld the constitutionality of Taft–Hartley's non–Communist affidavit, he had been the lone dissenter, and he had said then the affidavit requirement was a bill of attainder.

The *Brown* case was another five to four reprieve, in a way, for Bridges. In 1962, after Brown was convicted and while his appeal was pending, Bridges had opened the session by reading a letter he had received that morning from Washington. "Dear Mr. Bridges," the Attorney General's office had written, "we note that Archie Brown has been convicted of violating Section 504 of the Landrum–Griffin Act. We thought we'd call your attention to the fact that if he loses his appeal, you may be in violation of the Act. You knowingly supported him when he ran for that office . . ."

NOTES

The profile of former Justice Goldberg is by Robert Shaplen, and was published in the April 7, 1962 *New Yorker.*

The description of Bridges's appearance before Judge Harris when his bail was revoked was in a human interest story written by Pierre Salinger, who was then on the staff of the *San Francisco Chronicle.* It appeared on August 6, 1950.

The court of appeals decision releasing Bridges from jail (after his bail was revoked) is *Bridges* v. *United States,* 184 F 2d 881 (1950). The decision upholding his conviction is *Bridges* v. *United States,* 199 F 2d 811 (1952). The Supreme Court decision reversing the conviction is *Bridges* v. *United States,* 346 U.S. 209 (1953).

The Supreme Court decision reversing Brown's conviction is *United States* v. *Brown,* 381 U.S. 437 (1965).

1.

Labor Statesman

When the newspapers start to say good things about me, that's the time to get the recall machinery in motion.

HARRY BRIDGES, in the 1930s

"RIGHT AFTER THE WAR," a Los Angeles longshoreman said in 1967, "John L. Lewis was beginning to get pensions and welfare for his members. We'd gone for three years without a wage increase, and we'd just gotten a good one, after the '46 strike. So I said to Harry, 'Harry, when are you going to get some of those benefits?'

"And he said, 'Look George, what our union should do is get the wages up so you can pay your doctor, and I can pay my doctor. And let the government pay decent pensions. When this union goes after medical care paid for by the employers, and pensions, that's when this union goes downhill.' "

At that time, Bridges felt that when unions got these benefits they lost their fighting spirit and degenerated into social welfare agencies. But with Social Security failing to keep pace with rising prices and a rising standard of living, the rank and file insisted on industry–paid pensions. Reluctantly, in 1950, Bridges negotiated pensions which substantially supplemented Social Security for all longshoremen who had worked in the industry for twenty–five years and were at least sixty–seven years old.

Fifteen hundred longshoremen were eligible, many anxious to retire as soon as the pension fund could start the checks coming. Unfortunately, the pensions were negotiated just when the Korean War began, and the government, worried about costs and prices getting out of hand, had created a wage board to hold down inflation. Before the men could retire, the board had to decide whether or not the pension plan would be inflationary. For economists who

345

man such boards, a question like that can take months, even a year, to resolve.

After six months, the longshoremen, many of whom were in their late sixties and seventies, lost patience and began sending telegrams to the President. One local warned that if the board turned their pensions down it would probably cause a coastwide strike. The White House sent the wire to the office of John Steelman, the President's labor adviser, for a recommendation. Steelman passed it on to one of his labor experts who sent it back with a note: "This is Harry Bridges' union. The telegram should not be acknowledged."

A week later, another local, which had sent Truman a message of support when he committed American forces to the Korean War, sent a similar telegram and got the same treatment. The union finally won the skirmish after nine months, when the board decided to let the pensions go through.

Another struggle with the government was more prolonged. In August, 1950 Congress made screening of "security risks" off the docks and off the ships an official government operation, with the Coast Guard designated to enforce it. In the beginning, a man screened out of the industry found himself in a Kafkaesque world. He couldn't work at his job, and while the Coast Guard would give him a hearing, he couldn't find out why he had been screened out, and he couldn't find out who his accusers were. "You tell us why you think you've been classified a security risk," was all the Coast Guard would tell him.

The major problem was the FBI, which told the Coast Guard its informants would disappear if they had to risk being produced in a hearing. So it went for three years, until a federal court of appeals, in *Parker* v. *Lester,* ruled that while it could understand the FBI's position, the Constitutional right to due process was more important than protecting FBI sources. Meanwhile, the government adopted Bridges's suggestion that longshoremen screened out of the military area of a port be allowed to work civilian cargoes.

For Bridges and the ILWU, one of the best things that happened in the early fifties was the shipowners' selection of Paul St. Sure to head their organization. When St. Sure died in 1966 (he was exactly the same age as Bridges), Bridges said of him:

Our union and the whole organized labor movement has lost a courageous champion of its basic rights. Paul St. Sure never hesitated when it came to speaking for equal treatment for all men and women. He was a particularly eloquent defender of civil rights and a bitter critic of bigoted elements who sought to practice racial discrimination in any form. That he affirmed such beliefs—while at the same time he so ably and honorably represented large and powerful management interests—not only made him all the more effective in such matters but it served to give us all a true measure of the man. For myself, there is a profound feeling of sorrow at the loss of a staunch and trusted personal friend.

St. Sure was the son of A. F. St. Sure, the federal judge mentioned earlier. "He was very much on the conservative side," St. Sure said of his father. The younger St. Sure began practicing law in the twenties as an assistant to Earl Warren when Warren was District Attorney for Alameda County and in 1931, he went into private practice. The '34 strike gave him his start as a management lawyer. At the time, he hadn't had any labor law experience, but the Oakland Chamber of Commerce needed someone to act as liaison between public agencies and employers on both sides of the Bay and they chose St. Sure.

He handled his first labor case in 1937, when the Warehouse Division of the ILWU was trying to organize the Santa Cruz Fruit Packing Company, which he represented. The company was ignoring the Wagner Act and firing workers for union activity. The union filed an unfair labor practice charge with the NLRB, the first such charge in Northern California. "Despite the fact that the Supreme Court had decided that the Act was constitutional in the *Jones & Laughlin* case, we made no defense other than to challenge the constitutionality of the Act," St. Sure has said. The NLRB found the company guilty, and St. Sure appealed the ruling all the way to the Supreme Court, only to lose. After that, he quickly learned how to get along with unions, and before long was the number one management attorney in the Bay Area, representing almost every major industry on the Oakland side of the Bay.

In 1943, St. Sure was representing the hospital association when Shirley Titus, a former teacher of nursing in the Midwest, came to San Francisco to retire. She looked up some of her former students and discovered that their working conditions were deplorable. St. Sure's name was given to her as someone who might advise her about what could be done. When she approached him, he was so touched by her story that he decided to help her. He suggested that the nurses' association be used as the bargaining agent to negotiate contracts with the hospitals.

"We had to think up euphemisms for practically every collective bargaining term," he said in his oral history,

> like calling collective bargaining an "economic security program." I can recall the first time we were negotiating, or attempting to negotiate, the contract with the San Francisco hospitals. We met at the Employers' Council offices, and I arrived and met the negotiators for the doctors and the hospital administrators, all of whom I knew.
>
> We sat around and chatted for awhile, and I finally said, "When does the negotiation start?" And they said, "When is the nurses' representative going to be here?" And I said, "Here I am." Whereupon they got up and walked out.
>
> The idea of someone who was an "employer man" representing the nurses was something unheard of, and we had a rather difficult bargaining session following that. They felt that I was a traitor as well as a radical because I even dared discuss the matter of representing the nurses.

In the late forties and early fifties, St. Sure helped the American Nurses' Association develop a policy on strikes. The nurses reaffirmed their traditional opposition to strikes, and, at St. Sure's urging, said that as long as the hospitals were willing to accept the professional standards set by the nurses, the no–strike pledge would be kept. But if the hospitals disregarded the standards and exploited the nurses, then they would strike. "This was pretty strong stuff for the American Nurses' Association," St. Sure reflected, "but it really did go quite a ways down the road to at least fairness as a policy."

One reason St. Sure was able to establish rapport with Bridges was that he was an old-fashioned liberal who wasn't afraid to consort with radicals. In 1951, a bill was pending before the California legislature which would have required lawyers to sign a non–Communist oath. Barney Dreyfus, a lawyer St. Sure thought of as a left–winger, came to him to ask if he would serve on a committee to oppose the bill. The McCarthy repression was well under way by this time, and it was hard, Dreyfus told him, to get anyone to come out against the oath.

St. Sure thought about it overnight, then called Dreyfus and told him: "I would be glad to be a member of the committee, provided

it wasn't loaded; and I told him that I assumed they wanted me because I was a Republican, because I probably had the reputation of
not being a Communist, and because I had conservative political
connections, such as the Knowlands.

"He said, 'Yes, frankly, that's why we want you.'

"I said, 'In spite of that, and perhaps because of that, I'm still
willing to do it.' . . ."

They managed to get forty or fifty lawyers from up and down the
state to lend their names to the committee. "It was pretty heavily
weighted with the unpopular–cause guys," St. Sure remembered.

He appeared at the hearing in the state capitol as the spokesman
for the committee, following the principal speaker for the bill, a
member of the Sons of the American Revolution.

> He was a flag–waving gentleman who went around advocating
> anti–Communist oaths for a lot of people. I remember this par-
> ticularly because he was proud of his Revolutionary background,
> and my own position was that I wasn't a revolutionist, I was a
> Republican and a lawyer, and I frankly rang the changes on the
> fact that my father was an appointee of Calvin Coolidge and I
> was a member of the State Central Republican Committee. . . .
>
> I said that I had no objection to taking an oath of allegiance,
> which I had done many times. And I wasn't holding any brief for
> Communists, but I certainly *was* opposing any test oath for law-
> yers . . .
>
> It was a very fine argument, I'm sure. The committee promptly
> voted the bill out "do pass," and the Senate passed it. The As-
> sembly killed it later on.

It was just a year after the oath episode that the shipowners persuaded St. Sure to give up his law practice to head their organization. "The first two people I called," he said later, "were Harry
Lundeberg and Harry Bridges." He knew almost nothing about
them beyond what he had heard from the shipowners, who still believed that Lundeberg was a man they could work with, whereas
Bridges was dedicated to wrecking the industry. "Lundeberg came
over to see me, about the last time in three or four years that he
ever was in my office. After that, I could go to see him. He'd never
come over here. And I told him at that time one basic thing: we
wouldn't lie to each other and we could get along."

Lundeberg made that difficult. St. Sure had barely taken office
before the sailors struck to corner some jobs the shipowners had

decided were longshore work. Lundeberg, infuriated, wrote William Knowland, the conservative Republican Senator from California, "a typical Lundeberg diatribe," as St. Sure put it, "accusing not only me, but the shipowners, of being Communists, saying that the sailors' strike he had been forced into was caused by a combination of shipowners and St. Sure to give aid and comfort to Bridges, who was a Communist . . ."

The letter might have posed a problem for Senator Knowland, if he hadn't been so determined to be known as a leading anti–Communist in the Senate. St. Sure was an old friend and had been his campaign manager back in the days of his political debut. But Lundeberg was the only nationally prominent labor leader who had supported Knowland for the Senate. And Lundeberg wanted him to put the letter in the *Congressional Record*. "I doubt that he'd read it," St. Sure said hopefully, when he learned Knowland had done what Lundeberg asked.

Not long after that, the sailors were using a familiar union tactic, striking one member of the shipowners' association at a time. Lundeberg was in New York, so St. Sure went there to talk with him about it. "All I want of you," he said, "is that you not divide my group into two camps. If you're going to tie up some of the ships, some of the members, at least you should tie them all up. On the other hand, if you let some of them sail free, they should all sail free."

"Lundeberg said, 'I agree with you.'

"Right afterwards," St. Sure recalled ruefully, "he got on the phone to the head of one of the companies and told him I was back in New York trying to sabotage their operation."

In view of the prickly relationship the shipowners had had with Bridges in their first fourteen years of association, St. Sure decided he would go to Bridges's office for their first talk. "I wasn't sure he'd come to see me. I told him the same thing I'd told Lundeberg. The difference between the two men was that so far as Bridges and I are concerned, since the discussion we had on that first day, we haven't fought each other as individuals."

"I wonder if you have, and I'm using the word in quotes, 'corrupted' Bridges. You, personally, I mean?" St. Sure was asked.

"I wouldn't know," he answered, "I made his job easier, by the reason that you can't fight a guy if the other fellow doesn't want to fight."

Over the years, the relationship between Bridges and St. Sure became ideal for mature collective bargaining. They developed con-

fidence in each other's integrity and a healthy respect for the other's ability to put up a good fight if necessary. In the mid–sixties,
one of Bridges's critics charged him with being afraid of St. Sure.
"Sure I'm afraid of him," Bridges unhesitatingly conceded. "But
that doesn't mean we can't work with him. And if we keep our
fighting strength up as a union, we'll get what we want, no matter
who heads the PMA, whether it's St. Sure or somebody else."

In the mid–fifties, after it became clear the '48 strike and the
Bridges–St. Sure relationship had produced an enduring peace on
the waterfront, the conventional wisdom among Bridges's critics
shifted 180 degrees. Earlier, they had been writing articles predict-
ing that union members were going to jettison him because he was
too radical. Now, their stories appeared under titles like "The Twi-
light of Harry Bridges," or "Is Harry Bridges Mellowing?"

"In 1956 or thereabouts," St. Sure has recalled, "the *Christian
Science Monitor* had a longish piece on Harry. 'He's outlived his
time,' it said. 'He's leveled off. There's nowhere to go. He's a relic
of a bygone era.'

"I showed it to Harry. 'What do you think of it?' I asked him.

"He read it very carefully. Then he said thoughtfully, 'Maybe
they're right, Paul.' "

Bridges must have been feeling especially gloomy that day to answer St. Sure that way. For at that very moment he was marshaling
support within the union for a path–breaking answer to the classic
problem: How does an industry mechanize without throwing workers on the scrap heap? The union's answer, from 1934 to the mid–
fifties, had been hold back mechanization as long as you can, and if
you can't stop it, slow it down. "We did as good a job, maybe a better job, as any union in the country in holding back the effects of
mechanization," Bridges has said. "We had eight–man gangs when
maybe two or four men were needed."

He could have gone on to talk about four–on, four–off, a featherbedding system, where four of the eight men in a gang rested while
the other four worked. Usually, the four who were resting stayed
somewhere on the ship, playing cards or drinking coffee. But one
evening in the early fifties, after the union had promised the employers it would discourage four–on, four–off, the San Francisco
port arbitrator was called to a ship to adjust a safety grievance.
When he climbed down into the hold to watch the operation in action he found only four men. And they weren't working. They were
sitting there, drinking coffee. The arbitrator, himself a retired long-

shoreman, exclaimed, "Come on, you guys. You're supposed to have given up four–on, four–off.

"By the way, where's the other four members of your gang?"

"Oh," one of the coffee–drinkers said easily, "they don't come on till midnight. They're at the ball game."

By the mid–fifties, shippers, who had to pay in rising freight rates for this technological backwardness, began putting pressure on the shipowners and the union to reduce costs. Some shippers loaded their cartons or bags on pallet boards at the factory, strapped them in place with steel bands and shipped them as a unit. Shipowners, too, stepped up the use of machines that substituted for the costly longshoremen. "Mr. Bridges and I had many discussions about this," St. Sure has said, "and I can recall my saying to him at one time in the mid– or late fifties that, whether he or I, or the union, or the steamship operators, liked it or not, these pressures were going to continue to mount to the point where we were going to have a showdown battle . . ."

Avoiding that showdown battle wasn't easy for Bridges. To many members of the union, any retreat from opposition to machines was a sell–out. But Bridges came to realize that mechanization was unavoidable. "Those guys who think we can go on holding back mechanization are still back in the thirties, fighting the fight we won 'way back then," he contended. "Their trouble is they think we're still putting out the *Waterfront Worker*." With the union isolated from the official labor movement, its enemies waiting to pounce on it if its vulnerability were exposed, with the Administration in Washington hostile to him and to the union ("We don't even answer their letters," a high government official said in 1957.), a showdown with the employers would be disastrous. Early in 1957 with the contract up for renewal in 1958, Bridges began talking at a coastwide longshore meeting about the desirability of an about–face on mechanization. His listeners were startled, but eventually they instructed him and the other officers to study the problem and make a report to a special meeting to be held in October of that year.

The first ten pages of the report consisted of an impressive list of mechanized operations already in use despite the longshoremen's cherished belief that they were holding the line. The issue to be thrashed out was this: "Do we want to stick with our present policy of guerrilla resistance to the machine or do we want to adopt a more flexible policy in order to buy specific benefits in return?" The employers, the report pointed out, were willing to talk with the union about cutting the men in on some of the savings from mechanization.

Two alternatives, then, were open to the union: It could go on fighting the machine for a few more years before the showdown would come. On the other hand, if the union gave the employers a free hand to mechanize, it could insist that the employers share the savings with the longshoremen.

"Presently," the report concluded, "it seems possible for the union to negotiate a contract embracing the full use of labor–saving machinery with maximum protection for the welfare of the workers." The contract would have to ensure that they wouldn't be forced into a speed–up when a new machine was put into use, that machines would not create safety hazards, that dockworkers wouldn't be thrown out of the industry, that the workday would be cut while take–home pay stayed the same, that pensions and other benefits would be improved, and that if mechanization reduced the amount of available work, dockworkers would be guaranteed their weekly take–home pay nevertheless.

After a long debate, Bridges was authorized by the longshoremen to open talks with St. Sure on the proposals. "As you might imagine," St. Sure has said, "this wasn't an easy thing for the employers to accept. Many of them felt this was a form of bribing the men on the job to do the job they were hired to do in the first place."

It took three years to reach an agreement. Bridges and St. Sure, flanked by their respective committees and technicians, met every day during the final six months. In 1959, after the discussions had been going on for a year and a half, it was apparent that they would continue for perhaps another year or so. "To buy time," St. Sure has recalled, "I offered the union, on behalf of the employers, $1 million for another year's delay for discussion and experimentation. When I made the offer, Mr. Bridges asked, 'Where did you get the million?' I said, 'It's a nice round figure and I didn't want to insult you by offering you less than a nice round figure.'

"He came back the following day and said, 'The figure is $1,500,000.' So I said, 'Where did you get the million and a half?' He said, 'From the same place you got the million.' So we settled on that."

What does a union do with a windfall of a million and a half? The ILWU used it to help men displaced by new loading methods in one port to move to another where men were needed and to subsidize retirement at sixty–two instead of sixty–five.

The agreement was signed in the middle of October, 1960, to run for five and a half years, from January 1, 1961, to July 1, 1966. Because it encompassed modernization of work practices as well as mechanization, it was called the Mechanization and Modernization Agreement, M & M for short. It provided that the size of the gang on an operation would be whatever number was needed to do the job efficiently, safely, and without a speed-up. If an employer wanted to reduce the gang on a current operation by rearranging the work and the men, he began by talking to the union. If the union agreed, the reduction was made. If the union objected, a compromise would be attempted, and if one couldn't be worked out, the arbitrator would settle the disagreement. Where a new machine was to be introduced, the employer had the right to say how many men he would need on it. If the union disagreed and they couldn't reach a compromise, the arbitrator would settle that, too.

No one, naturally, could even begin to guess how many men would be displaced by these changes. To give older men an incentive to leave the industry, the agreement provided for early retirement and for a lump sum of $7,920, over and above their pensions, upon retirement at sixty-five. If they retired at sixty-two, they could draw on the $7,920 at the rate of $200 a month for three years. There were to be no lay-offs if mechanization moved ahead so fast that there wasn't enough work left for the remaining men. They would be guaranteed thirty-five hours of pay a week, even if there wasn't any work for them to do. To pay for all this, the employers agreed to put $5 million a year for five and a half years into the M & M fund.

The longshoremen's way of looking at all this was that $3 million a year was their share of the savings that would come from putting in the machines. That money could go into a fund to pay for the increased medical and pension benefits. The other $2 million a year, as they saw it, was being paid to them for their property rights in the featherbedding practices they were giving up. If necessary, the money that was to accumulate from this source could be used to pay out the thirty-five-hour pay guarantee.

A longshoreman now had a guaranteed wage for the life of the contract. Even more important, once he was registered as a regular longshoreman, he had a job for life. The only occupation that would equal his, as far as job security was concerned, would be a university professorship with tenure. But in fact, his job was more secure than a professor's. Professors get fired with depressing regularity because someone doesn't approve of their politics. But under the contract, a longshoreman could be a Communist, a fascist, a long–haired revolutionary, and he couldn't be fired for it.

Mechanization also meant that backbreaking, dangerous jobs could be eliminated. New and better jobs operating the machines would become available, and the employers agreed the new jobs would go to longshoremen who, if necessary, would be trained at employer expense to move up to them.

Under the new contract, longshoremen were now able to make $8,000 to $9,000 a year. Pensions—on top of the $7,920 lump sum M & M retirement payment—went up, medical and dental benefits, paid for by the employers, was increased.

If the workers benefitted handsomely, the employers came off even better. They were enabled to reassert their authority by getting rid of unneeded workers on a job, they could load a cargo sling to capacity rather than having to stop at the 2,100–pound limit the union had held them to since 1937, and they could put in labor-saving machines. When the contract's five–and–a–half years were up, they had paid $29 million for M & M, and they had saved $200 million.

Nevertheless, there were some on both sides who weren't happy with M & M. For one thing, when the shipowners agreed to pay the thirty–five–hour guarantee, they insisted that to be eligible for it, a longshoreman had to be available for work at the hiring hall at least 70 per cent of the time—an intrusion into the casual work habits of some longshoremen.

Moreover, the contract treated the whole coast as one labor market. If men were out of work in one port, it seemed logical to move them to another where work was available rather than pay them for not working. But men in the busy ports preferred overtime to having men coming in from outside, even if they were fellow union members. Furthermore, if men were to be permanently added to the labor force in the port, some longshoremen thought that first crack at a new job should be given their son or nephew, instead of some out–of–towner.

Then there were longshoremen who called M & M an old man's contract. They accused Bridges of paying off his friends who had been with him in the old days. Mostly young men, the critics complained that the old men got everything while they got practically nothing, and they couldn't even be certain that M & M would be renewed in 1966. For reasons such as these, 3,695 of the longshoremen voted against M & M. Six thousand, eight hundred and

eighty–two men voted for it. Of all the contracts Bridges had negotiated, this was the least popular.

Some objections were philosophical. "Working conditions are
like a park," one young longshoreman said. "You take 'em as you
find 'em. You use 'em, and you leave 'em when you're through the
way you found 'em."

Eric Hoffer, who was working on the waterfront when M & M
came in, had a similar objection: "This generation has no right to
give away, or sell for money, conditions that were handed on to us
by a previous generation."

Under M & M, sling loads got bigger, cargoes were piled higher.
A common complaint heard along the waterfront and scrawled on
the walls of pier warehouses was that because of the big loads—
they called them "Bridges loads"—the speed–up was back. "If you
guys weren't determined to keep the hook moving all the time,"
Bridges would say when they complained about the big loads, "you
could set a reasonable pace. If you work a big load at the same
speed as you would a small one, the hook is going to hang there.
Let the boss worry about that."

On its face, Bridges's response was reasonable. The flaw in it was
that all their lives the longshoremen had taken pride in moving
cargoes in and out of the hold at a speed that kept the booms and
the winches continuously moving. "The hook never stops," is the
mark of a good longshore gang. Try talking with a winch operator
when he's working on a ship and you'll see what that means. When
he lowers his cargo hook down into the hold, a sling load is ready
to be hooked on and lifted out. The hook literally doesn't stop.

The complaint about big loads came up so often that Bridges's
response to it became almost automatic: "You arbitrate it." He
must have been daydreaming one night at a meeting of the San
Francisco local when the big load beef was raised by a longshoreman who spoke with a Portuguese accent. He had been describing
the big loads he'd had to work around the front when he came to
the worst example of all:

"Now at the army dock, they're not satisfied with handling big
loads. They put one load on top of another! What are we supposed
to do about that?"

"I don't know," the local president replied. "Maybe Harry has
the answer. What about it, Harry?"

"I don't know," Bridges muttered.

"Well, goddamit!" the longshoreman exploded. "I don't know

what to do. I ask my partner. He says, 'I don't know. Ask the gang boss.'

"I ask the gang boss. He tells me, 'I don't know. Ask the steward.'

"So I ask the steward. 'What are we going to do about these double loads?' He tells me, 'I don't know. Ask the b.a.'

"I ask the b.a. He tells me, 'Ask the president.' He says—you heard him, 'I don't know. Maybe Harry has the answer.'

"So he asks you, and you—the big Captain—you tells us, *you* don't know!

"What the hell kind of a union," he yelled, "is this?"

Understandably, M & M was hailed in most of the news media —the *Wall Street Journal* called it "socialism"—as an example of labor statesmanship, which only exacerbated the negative feelings of some in the rank and file. "Brother Bridges," a member of the San Francisco local said in a meeting in 1963, "has been saying for years that when the newspapers begin saying good things about him, it's time to get the recall machinery in motion.

"Brothers!" he shouted, "that time has come!"

The local's executive board, shocked by this display of *lèse-majesté*, censured the speaker at their next meeting. ("Most militants are canonized after their death," one of Bridges's friends said in the late 1960s. "Harry's made it while he's still alive.") When the board reported the censure to the membership at the next meeting, they boisterously hooted it down.

Some longshoremen saw M & M as turning the poacher into the gamekeeper, perhaps because it made the union reluctant to jeopardize its good relations with the employers. Perhaps, too, because the increased regularity of longshore work under M & M and the good money the men were earning sapped their militant spirit. ("The capitalists cannot exterminate a real labor organization by fighting it," Vincent St. John, the IWW leader, once said, "they are only dangerous when they fraternize with it.")

"Sure," a longshoreman said in a union meeting in the mid–sixties,

we adopt resolutions saying we won't handle cargoes from Alabama, and South Africa. But what the hell does it mean? Harry talks about socialism. You heard him last night: "We ought to be running the ships." For Chrissake! We can't even tie up a South African ship when we have a policy that we'll boycott South African goods.

You remember. About two months ago we adopted that resolution. So a few days later a South African ship comes in. It was here five days. Did we refuse to work it? Hell, no!

And San Pedro. When the employers locked out the guys down there, did we refuse to work ships diverted from Pedro? Oh, no. We scabbed!

When the contract ran out in 1966, there was $13 million in the fund. The Vietnam war had provided so much work on West Coast docks, the wage guarantee hadn't been needed. Who owned the money, and what should be done with it? The employers conceded it belonged to the workers; if the money hadn't been paid into the fund, it could have gone into the men's paychecks. "You figure out what to do with it," they said as they handed it over to the union.

A coastwide meeting called by Bridges decided to divide it equally among the ten thousand or so full–time longshoremen on the Coast. They got their $1,200 bonuses a few days before Christmas. When M & M came up for renewal, Vietnam was going full blast with no end in sight, and the thirty–five–hour guarantee was dropped.

Union negotiators recommended a five–year extension of the contract, but how the dockworkers would vote on it was anybody's guess. Bridges toured the coast, explaining, answering questions, often facing hostile audiences in the union halls. Actually, the contract shouldn't have been so hard to defend for it substantially increased both wages and benefits. The basic wage went to $35 a day. The pension was set at $235 a month, and a man would be eligible at sixty–three after twenty–five years service. The M & M lump–sum retirement benefit went up from $7,920 to $13,000. Vacations, medical and dental care were improved. And the new contract required employers to use machines when feasible and practical, in order to make the work easier for the men.

The changes in cargo handling produced by M & M could have gotten the longshoremen into a bedlam of jurisdictional fights. Think of the arguments it could produce with the operating engineers' union over who would run the towering dockside cranes. Or with the sailors. Especially, with the teamsters. Take the development of ships designed to carry cargoes already loaded in the huge containers you see on railroad flat cars and on trailer trucks. Teamsters pull the containers onto the docks and into a staging area, unhook them from the tractor and leave them there until the containership comes in. So far, so good. But who should drive the tractor that pulls the container from the staging yard to alongside the ship when it's time to load it aboard? A teamster or a longshoreman, sent down from the hiring hall?

What happens when somebody hits upon the idea that shipping costs can be pared by setting up freight stations back from the waterfront? A shipper whose consignment isn't enough to fill up a container at his factory can send it to a freight station, where it will be put into a container along with other shipments until the container is filled. And the stuffing at the freight station can be done by men working at substantially less than a longshoreman's wages. Who would do that work? Teamster warehousemen or ILWU warehousemen? Or for that matter, suppose the freight station is just across the way from the piers? Would that make it longshoremen's work?

These problems of jurisdiction were real enough, but luck was with the longshoremen. The NLRB ruled that the employers had the right, under the Taft–Hartley Act, to give the crane jobs to longshoremen. That took care of the operating engineers. Lundeberg died in 1957, and his place was filled by Morris Weissberger, who had enough trouble holding the sailors' union together without wasting energy fighting the ILWU. That took care of the sailors. The threat from the teamsters vanished when a U.S. Senate committee sent Dave Beck to jail for taking money from the union treasury. His place was taken by Jimmy Hoffa, who had headed the teamsters in the Midwest. Hoffa, like Weissberger, had his hands full making a national union out of the collection of regions run by warlords that made up the teamsters' union. He had no interest in continuing Beck's battles with the longshoremen.

". . . for long numbers of years this international union thought it was popular to fight with local unions of the longshoremen who are called Communists," he told a teamsters' meeting in 1960.

When I came to this office I recognized the futility of trying to fight and pit one union against the other, and I traveled to the West Coast to sit down with Harry Bridges and his organization.

We worked out an understanding where we would stop the raiding, stop the fighting and the bitterness between our unions and negotiate jointly [he was referring to warehousemen] for the benefit of our rank and file. Out of the very first negotiations on the West Coast where we participated as a joint negotiating committee, we received 21¢ an hour, the greatest single increase they had received over the period of time we were organized.

A working partnership between longshoremen and teamsters clearly made sense, yet Bridges and Hoffa made strange partners. "Hoffa is a complex embodiment of a populist rebel, a robber baron, a job–oriented unionist in the tradition of business union- ism," William Gomberg, a labor economist at the Wharton School, said of him in the early sixties. "He is also in the best tradition of free enterprise." He was indeed, regarding his salary of $100,000 a year, with all expenses paid, as nothing more than his due. He was astonished when someone suggested it was questionable for him to own a fleet of trucks employing his own members. If he had money to invest, he asked, why shouldn't he put it into the industry he knew best?

In the 1961 teamster's convention that reelected Hoffa to a sec- ond term, several resolutions greatly expanded his power as presi- dent. Bridges was appalled. "You know, Jimmy," he said, "if I sug- gested in my union that my power as president should be increased to even a fraction of yours, I'd be impeached on the spot. How come you let the convention do that?"

"Oh, the boys don't have to worry about how I'll use the power," Hoffa replied complacently. "They know I'll take care of them."

A Hoffa–Bridges partnership could scarcely be equal because of the inequality of size and power of the two unions. And Hoffa was extremely aware of his power. "When Bridges and I were discuss- ing the M & M agreement," St. Sure said in 1965,

we arranged a meeting of the two of us with Hoffa, to avoid the jurisdictional problems we knew would come up.

We met in a suite at the Fairmont, and I got there first. Shortly afterward, Hoffa came swirling in with a half–dozen bodyguards. He made quite an entrance. After a bit, Bridges entered unob- trusively, all by himself.

At one point, Bridges and Hoffa got down on the floor and were manipulating ashtrays and glasses to show where the truck drivers' jurisdiction ended and the longshoremen's began. Then Hoffa got up and picked up his coat with the remark, "What the hell's the use of going on with this, Harry? I already know more about operations on the docks than you ever will."

I think that's the only time I ever saw Harry speechless.

Nevertheless, when Hoffa sounded a call in the late 1950s for a coalition of transportation unions called the Conference on Transportation Unity, Bridges responded at once. Nothing came of it, however, because the only other unions reacting favorably were Curran's East Coast sailors and the East Coast longshoremen. The airline pilots, West Coast sailors, and railway workers stayed away. "Such a group of unions," a railway union officer observed, "might be so powerful that it could result in destruction of the nation." Senator Eastland, who headed the Senate counterpart of the House Un-American Activities Committee, felt the same way. Within a few months of Hoffa's announcement, Eastland's committee was in print with a pamphlet awesomely titled, "An Alliance of Racketeer and Communist Dominated Unions in the Field of Transportation as a Threat to National Security."

To Bridges, Hoffa's proposal was the resurrection of the Maritime Federation of the Pacific. His absorption with this dream came out during his 1958 European tour when he was talking with British union leader Frank Cousins of the Transport and General Workers' Union. Bill Glazier, Bridges's traveling companion, was present:

"Listening to Harry and Frank Cousins talk was a fascinating experience," Glazier has said.

They understood each other immediately. Harry got to talking about the importance of transportation in an economy, how, if you wanted to advance the interests of the working class, controlling transportation from the docks through warehousing, then trucking and railroads, was the way to do it. Cousins, who headed the T & GWU [Transport and General Workers' Union], which has all those groups in it—it's a Conference on Transportation Unity in itself—readily agreed.

Harry and I'd been arguing a few years earlier about the same point. It had come up when we were talking about Hawaii. I'd argued that, sure, it's not hard to organize an economy like Hawaii once you control the docks, because it's an island economy. But Harry said no, the same held true of any economy, once you controlled *transportation,* by which he meant the docks, trucking and so on.

In the early sixties, just as Bridges was becoming adjusted to being treated in the news media as a labor statesman, he became a cause célèbre again. This time, instead of being called a Leftist, he was accused of selling out the working class and, incredibly, of being a racist. The new denouncements were the product of a combination of the Taft–Hartley Act, M & M, his insistence that Blacks be accepted on the waterfront and, his over–reaction to a rebellious newcomer to the waterfront named Stan Weir.

Before Taft–Hartley, there had been three categories of longshoremen on the waterfront: union members, who had first crack at jobs; men who had a permit from the union to work, who came next; and, finally, casuals. Taft–Hartley made it unlawful to give preference in employment to union members or to men chosen by the union (permit men), so in 1959 when the employers and the union opened up the job rolls for the first time in ten years, they renamed the categories.

Men who were registered for work in the port—they were all union members—were now classified as A–men, and they had first crack at jobs. Men newly added to the labor force—the old permit men—were called B–men. As had been true of their predecessors, B–men were dispatched after the A–men, and they did not become union members until they completed a probationary period and were promoted to A–status. Last to be dispatched, as in the old system, were the casuals.

To become a B–man, a man went before a joint union–employer committee. If they accepted him, his name was placed on a list of registered B–men in the port. Following tradition, dispatchers would assign him as a new man, to work in the hold. Everyone expected him to move up to A–status and union membership without much delay but in the meantime he would make good money as a B–man. If he got in enough hours, he qualified for vacations and medical benefits, and his time as a B–man counted toward retirement and pensions.

In 1959, under the new arrangement, 743 men, about 60 per cent of them Black, were taken on as B–men in San Francisco. There were ten thousand applicants. Six months later, M & M was signed. At that point the employers, to give themselves time to see how M & M was going to affect the number of men they would need on a permanent basis, proposed that B–men be left in their probationary status for the time being. That seemed reasonable, and the union agreed. But it was 1963, four years later, before they were ready to take the B–men in. By that time, in San Francisco, 561 of the original 743 were still working on the docks.

For the B–men, four years in limbo were frustrating enough. Many of the 561 were mavericks of one kind or another: refugees from reactionary unions, leftists, non–conformists. They'd been attracted to the waterfront at least partly because the ILWU would be a congenial home for them, and they were anxious to take an active part in its affairs. But now, just when they were within reach of A–status, an unexpected hurdle loomed up. A joint union–employer committee was going to evaluate their qualifications to become A–men.

The committee had an unenviable assignment, because its decisions had to be based on the assumption that there wasn't room for more than about five hundred new men in the A category. It decided to evaluate the B–men on four aspects of waterfront citizenship. Most important was a B–man's attitude toward the dispatching rules. These, an integral part of the longshore system, were designed to guarantee that every longshoreman who wants to work gets an equal share of it. It's a low–man–out system. At the beginning of each day, the longshoremen sign in at the hiring hall, each one putting down the number of hours he's worked in a given period. When the men are dispatched to the ships, those who have worked the lowest number of hours go out first. If a man puts down fewer hours than he has actually worked, he gets an unfair advantage over the others. It's an honor system, with union dispatchers and PMA record clerks making spot checks to catch offenders.

The committee checked B–men's work records for a period of six to eight weeks. If a man was guilty of ten or more hours of low-man-out violations, the committee disqualified him for A–status. Then there were cases of B–men for whom the waterfront was a place to moonlight. If a man had not been signing in for work, at least 70 per cent of the time in a 30–day period, the committee assumed he wasn't serious about being a longshoreman and dropped him.

The union was interested in a B–man's record of paying his pro rata share of hiring hall costs. It estimated that its half of the cost of running the hiring hall worked out to $6.00 a month per man. A–men and B–men alike were expected to pay their $6.00 at the union office in the hiring hall. A–men paid another $6.00 to $8.00 in union dues and assessments, as well. Some members had to be reminded over and over again that they were delinquent. The union took the position, therefore, that a B–man who was late in payment of his pro rata share eight or more times while he was a probationer would not be a desirable union member and should be dropped. The employers were interested in screening out men who had a record of being drunk on the job, disappearing in the middle of a shift, or refusing to work as directed.

When the committee finished its job, ninety–four men were scheduled for dismissal. After a recheck, it reversed itself on twelve. That left eighty–two. The committee notified them that they could appeal, before a committee of three employers and three union officials. Forty–four did so.

Some of those who didn't appeal may have been discouraged by the tone of the letter notifying them of their right to appeal. It was a form letter, bleakly reminiscent of the government's letters to Bridges in his deportation hearings. It didn't state what the charges were, only that "you have violated the applicable rules."

The hearing itself was no better. "We're not saints on the water-front," one longshoreman said in defense of the procedure. "Civil liberties are the property of middle class intellectuals. Workers never bought civil liberties." As each appellant entered the hearing room, he was told that he could not be represented by counsel, nor could he present witnesses on his behalf. If he had been dropped because of insubordination, drunkenness, failure to make himself available for work, or for some other reason the employers were concerned about, an employer member of the committee read the list of his violations. In almost all of these cases, the men admitted the charges and accepted the verdict.

If the man had been dropped because he was accused of chisel-ing on the low–man–out rule or of chronic late payments of pro rata, a union member of the committee read the charges. A few ap-pellants said they had put down fewer hours than they had actually worked only because they weren't good at arithmetic. "I didn't in-tend to chisel," they asserted, holding out to the committee the dog–eared notebook they kept their hours in. "You can see for yourselves where I made my mistakes."

Several men said, "The reason I was late with my pro rata was because I didn't actually have anything to do with it. I had a lot of debts pile up on me, see, and the man was gettin' on me to pay. Well, I couldn't pay, so I went to one of those loan places. You know, where a guy takes your check each month, pays some on this bill, some on that, a little bit here and a little bit there. And I guess he just put that pro rata down at the bottom . . ."

The appeal that produced the denouncements of Bridges came from a man who suffered neither from an inability to keep his hours straight nor to handle his money. He was a forty–one–year-old ex–sailor named Stan Weir, and his defect was that he had picked up a reputation as a troublemaker. In the 1940s, he had shared an apartment in Greenwich Village with James Baldwin, the author, which was enough to make Bridges distrust him as an intellectual. When Bridges heard that Weir was critical of him and of M & M, he wrote him off as a Trotskyite, a Red–baiting phony.

Weir was convinced, it is true, that the M & M agreement was a sell–out, a classic example of class collaboration, and that the union, under Bridges's leadership, had become bureaucratic and was acting as a disciplinary agent for the employers. "A gang made up of B–men does 30 to 80 per cent more work than a gang of A–men," Weir said in 1963. "You know why? Because B–men can be intimidated. The union doesn't protect them, the way it does the A–men." He also felt that the B–men had become hostile to Bridges: "They get the dirty jobs in the hold, and they've waited for four years, with one broken promise after another about when they'd be taken into the union."

Weir lived in Berkeley, where one of his neighbors was a young University of California professor. The two frequently talked about politics and the state of the unions. The professor was interested in Weir's life as a longshoreman, and Weir poured out to him his resentment about the treatment B–men were getting. One night at a party, the professor was introduced to a longshoreman from San Francisco who, he learned, was close to Bridges. "When are you guys going to take in the B–men?" the professor asked.

"What do you know about the B–men?" the longshoreman countered. "And who told you all this?"

Not long after that, the same longshoreman was at another party where a Stanford professor criticized the union's treatment of the B–men. As it happened, the two professors were friends, but to Bridges it looked as if Weir was going around the Bay Area lining up support from outside the union.

By 1963, Weir had emerged as the voice of aggrieved B–men. "I arranged a meeting of the B–men in 1963," he said, "for the purpose of presenting their grievances to the union. I was asked to do it by a representative of the international union, and the union made it compulsory.

"I presented the grievances. I think I alarmed Bridges and the international. It was the first time they'd heard an articulate, well–organized presentation of how the B–men felt about how they're treated.

"I think I was a threat in another way, too. If I were taken into the union, I'd come in with five hundred votes. Maybe Bridges saw me as another Kearney."

The reference was to Jim Kearney, who in 1940 had been the spokesman for a large group of permit men on the San Francisco waterfront. When they got in the union, they voted as a bloc for Kearney, who held one union office or another continuously until his death in 1972. He had an abrasive effect on Bridges, especially when he became the spokesman for the conservative wing of the San Francisco longshore local.

Of the forty–four B–men who appealed the decisions against them, only four were successful. Weir was not. A month later, the discharged B–men formed the Longshore Jobs Defense Committee, with Weir as chairman. They went first to the NLRB, but the board turned them away, finding no basis in the national labor law for hearing their complaint that they had been fired arbitrarily. They went next to a federal court, asking for reinstatement, damages of $600,000, and a ruling that the union contract was null and void. The lawyer who represented them, even after four appearances in court, was unable to explain to the judge precisely where in the law he saw a ground for the suit. "The complaint," the judge said, "is both redundant and ambiguous . . . defense lawyers could not safely determine issues of relevancy and judges could not safely decide them."

In the fall of 1964, the B–men went to the Workers Defense League in New York for help, charging that because half the B–men who were dropped were Black, Bridges and the union were guilty of racism. The result was a national committee which immediately began soliciting money and publicizing their plight. It was an imposing committee, its letterhead studded with names of men long known for their work in civil liberties and civil rights—Norman Thomas, Michael Harrington, Herbert Hill, Thomas Burbridge, Harvey Swados, Seymour Lipset, Bayard Rustin. Most of them, also, were cold warriors who for years had been opposed to Bridges on ideological grounds, and, it is highly probable, as Bridges believed, that the opportunity to attack him and the union on charges of racial discrimination was one they couldn't resist, even though, as their pronouncements show, they weren't really clear about what had happened out in San Francisco.

The irony of it all was that in San Francisco, largely due to Bridges's efforts during World War II and afterward, a majority of the longshoremen were Black. It was true, nevertheless, that despite the policy of the national union, reaffirmed in convention resolutions time after time since its founding, as recently as the sixties there were ports on the Coast where for days you could watch ships being loaded without once seeing a black longshoreman. In some, a remote lumber port up in the Northwest like Coos Bay, you might believe the explanation that the port was all–white because there weren't any Blacks in the community. But in others—Portland and Los Angeles, for example—the lily–white labor force was obviously the product of a policy of exclusion.

In convention after convention, when delegates from these ports were asked when they were going to get into line with the policy of the international, they would make speeches embarrassingly reminiscent of states' righters in the Congress dragging their feet on civil rights legislation. "It's our problem," they would declaim. "If you'll just give us more time, we'll handle it. But we have to do it our way. And don't you guys forget. This union was founded on the principle of local autonomy. Neither Harry Bridges nor nobody else in the international has any right under the ILWU Constitution to come into our local and tell us what to do!"

Listening to men from some of these ports, it was obvious they could never end discrimination without help from outside. "We checked back into the records of longshore employment as far as 1886," a seventy–two–year–old pensioner—he had been a foreman on the Portland docks for forty–one years—said in 1965. "We found that not a single Negro had worked on the waterfront as a longshoreman in all that time. So we figure that if they weren't willing to work with us when we were having our troubles, why should we let them come in now and get in on the gravy?"

The explanation offered by another Portland old–timer was on a par with the pensioner's. "A long time ago," he said, "the employers were going to bring in Negroes to break a strike. The Chamber of Commerce went to the shipowners and said, 'You can't do that.'

"Well, if Negroes aren't good enough for the Chamber of Commerce," he concluded in triumph, as if he'd hit on an unassailable explanation, "they're not good enough for us, either!"

As president of the union, it was Bridges's responsibility to enforce the union constitution, which forbade discrimination. But what sanctions would work? He could have recommended expelling offending locals. Or putting them in trusteeship and sending in temporary officers appointed by the national union executive board to run the local until it decided to abandon its unconstitutional policy.

But expulsion would only drive the local into the waiting arms of the AFL longshoremen's union and its West Coast allies, Dave Beck's teamsters and Lundeberg's sailors. And for trusteeship to work, the local membership would have to be willing to go along with the national union. Portland longshoremen had shown they were not willing to do so. In the late fifties, organizers set up from San Francisco by the international signed up a majority of the workers in a grain–handling operation on the Portland waterfront. The NLRB was all set to hold an election when Portland long-shoremen, having discovered that some of the grain handlers were Black, voted to tell the NLRB to call off the election. It was, and the grain handlers remained non–union. Bridges was convinced, moreover, that Portland longshoremen had the support of local wa-terfront employers and the police, who wanted to keep the port white.

In 1963, Bridges found a way to end the problem without a direct confrontation. Military shipments to Southeast Asia were making it necessary to hire three hundred more longshoremen in Portland. In the past, when more men were needed, the union and the em-ployers had taken ads in Portland's two major newspapers. Thou-sands of men would apply, but none would be Black for they had learned that they would never be hired. Bridges's first move took him to St. Sure, who, at Bridges's request, replaced two officers of the Portland branch of the employers' association who had been parties to the segregation policy.

Next, Bridges dispatched Louis Goldblatt to Portland, where he spent two weeks alerting CORE and the NAACP about the vacan-cies that were going to open up and urging them to get Blacks ready to apply. Goldblatt promised that, this time, Blacks would have a good chance of being accepted, pointing out that when let-ters asking for application forms came in, they would be numbered as they were received and processed in that order. If they could get about one thousand Blacks to write for applications, a substantial number of them would end up on the waterfront. All told, 2,600 men wrote for applications. Fifteen hundred filled them out. Five hundred were called in for interviews and physical exams. In the end, three hundred were hired. Between forty and fifty were Black. It was a modest start, but the door was open.

Nevertheless, the charges levelled by Weir and his national com-mittee were not entirely hollow. From the standpoint of due proc-ess, the appeal procedure was defective. And in a time when we are discovering that institutional requirements sometimes produce racist results even when uniformly applied, the appeals committee might have shown more compassion when they heard the explanations given by men fired for low–man–out violations and delinquency in their pro rata payments.

Then there was the troublesome matter of Stan Weir. "I think Harry's way off the beam on Weir," one of Bridges's friends told me regretfully. "I don't really believe there was enough evidence to pass him over for A–status. But I'm not going to fight Harry on it. I don't want to be on the same side with those phonies and right–wingers who don't care about Weir except as a stick to beat Harry with." One of Bridges's friends thought back over the years when Bridges was under attack from within the union almost as much as he was from outside and remarked, "If you had been in a position at the time to deregister some of the guys who were working to get Harry—Schrimpf and some of those guys—would you have deregistered them?"

There was an exquisite incongruity in Bridges's attacks on Weir for Bridges had successfully dedicated his life to building a union that would be a haven for heretics. A union where men who had been hounded from one job to another by the FBI would be safe because the union constitution and the contract with the employers prohibited discrimination based on a man's politics. Where a petition signed by 15 per cent of the membership could set recall machinery in motion. Where union officers, at every level, had to stand for election every two years. Where local unions met regularly every two weeks. Where every major policy of the union was submitted to the membership in a coastwide referendum vote. Where, when controversial decisions had to be made, special meetings were convened, at considerable expense, and stayed in session until consensus was reached—or the meeting recessed, to meet again later and reach a consensus. Where an elaborate committee system protected union members against arbitrary treatment, even if the accuser were Bridges himself.

Bridges's attack on Weir, moreover, was not in character. There had been other critics down through the years whom he had consistently ignored. "Don't worry," he had assured his supporters when they urged him to act against his attackers. "If they go too far, the rank and file will roll right over them." His reaction to Weir was especially paradoxical because he himself had pointed to the second–class citizenship of the holdmen which Weir was objecting to.

"We find everybody breaking their damn back to get out of that hold," Bridges said in 1956 before the B–men came in, when hold work was done mostly by casuals. "That is true in every port. And mostly your work in the hold today is being done by people who are not members of the union. They are not members of the industry. Nobody wants to go in the hold . . .

"To hell with this business of eight holdmen bucking a completely mechanized operation in the hold and all kinds of people standing around on the dock or running machines and the guys down below really taking a beating. That is not unionism."

Bridges's attitude toward Weir had a piquancy about it for another reason. Weir came to his attention just at the time the decimation of the older leaders by death and retirement was pushing Bridges to search for new leadership to take their places. "To meet the qualifications we'd set," Bridges told the executive board in 1962, "he'd have to be young. He'd have to be a man with a good grasp of economics and politics. But," he quickly added, "we don't want a man who's a union politician. He'd have to be a trained Marxist or a socialist. Or a combination of all of those."

He paused for a moment to let that sink in, then continued, "We thought we'd get a lot of experienced leadership by the local practice of limiting a term of office to two years. But it didn't work that way. We got politicians.

"The trouble is, our rank and file is too well satisfied. They won't even come to meetings. They don't have to. Hell, they won't even vote to ratify the contract . . ."

Goldblatt had an answer to that. "The trouble is," he suggested, "that there isn't the necessary scope for new leadership. There's no challenge. We've settled down to an organization that negotiates contracts without too much trouble and the officers administer them.

"But if we were taking up some of the challenges that we might, we'd find there's plenty of leadership in our ranks. To take one example, if we put on an organizing drive among agricultural workers in California as we did in the Islands, I think we'd find any number of good young men coming up to assume leadership roles."

Bridges did not respond. Even as early as the 1960s, some of his members were beginning to feel that he had lost his drive, that he had not kept up with the times. Hal Yanoff, then in his late thirties, an A–man of ten years standing, typified the feelings of many when he reflected one day in 1963 on what seemed to be happening to Bridges. "I used to live a block from Harry," he began.

I'd see him in the supermarket, comparing the big boxes with the little boxes to see which was the most for the money. Just like any other working guy, I thought, there's a big union president. You can't take that away from him.

I was in law school when the '49 trial came up. I was—what's the word—a millenialist. I thought, if they can do this, what's the use of going to law school? So I went to work fulltime for the BRS [Bridges–Robertson–Schmidt] Committee, and then I decided to work on the 'front. And now, now I think St. Sure has taken him in . . .

You know, if my own father sold me out, I don't think I'd feel worse than if Harry gets phony. I know he's a sonofabitch in his personal relations with people but goddamit, he's stood for something, and that's what I care about. Hell, I sold $500 worth of Bridges defense stamps when I was going to sea, and now, when I criticize the contract, he calls me a young punk, a Johnny–come–lately . . ."

There was no doubt that as Bridges moved into his sixties, it was increasingly difficult for him to appreciate the feelings and attitudes of contemporary rebels. During the Free Speech Movement at Berkeley, Lou Goldblatt, one of whose daughters sat–in in Sproul Hall, went with Wayne Horvitz, a young Matson executive, over to the campus to offer President Clark Kerr their help in mediating the dispute. (Kerr, a labor economist, had been a waterfront arbitrator for a year or so. He declined their help.) Bridges stayed in his office, writing off the campus rebels as a bunch of middle-class kooks. After the troubles were over, he happened to meet Mario Savio, the FSM leader and in a way as effective a speaker and tactician as Bridges himself had been in the '34 strike. "You know," Bridges mused afterward to Sid Roger, "That Savio isn't as goofy as the newspapers made him out to be."

Bridges was aware that the years must inexorably take their toll, even though he was unable to bring himself to yield the leadership of the union to someone else. "I'll tell you one thing," he said in 1966 to Harry Bernstein of the *Los Angeles Times*, "I'm not going to hang on like some of those labor fakers who keep their job for years after they should have stepped aside."

NOTES

Emarson's note to Steelman is in the Truman Presidential Library, in Official File 407B, "Maritime Strikes. The wire supporting President Truman's Korea policy was sent by the ILWU local in North Bend, Oregon. It is in President's Personal File 0-1321, "ILWU".

St. Sure described his early experiences as a management attorney in *Two Views of American Labor: Frances Perkins and J. Paul St. Sure,* Institute of Industrial Relations, UCLA.

Bridges's *Trial* interview was reported in the *New York Times,* February 13, 1959.

St. Sure's explanation of the talks leading up to M & M is in *Fairplay Shipping Journal,* May 13, 1965. For an excellent and thorough economic analysis of M & M, see Paul Hartman, *Collective Bargaining and Productivity.*

Bridges's remarks to Harry Bernstein are in "The Two Worlds of Harry Bridges," *Los Angeles Times,* May 1, 1966.

Old Soldiers Never Die

You guys are always talking about the generation gap, so I'm trying to do something about it.
HARRY BRIDGES, IN THE 1971 CONVENTION.

IN 1966, Bridges became eligible for retirement, and from time to time he would drop hints that at one of the biennial conventions coming up he—perhaps in 1969 or 1971—he would announce he was going to retire.

In the Sixties, he wasn't taken seriously, for he still had the brilliance of leadership, the energy, and the charisma he had always had. Watching him in union meetings, one could be reminded of a passage in Kingsley Martin's *New Statesman* obituary of Jawaharlal Nehru: "I remember standing by him at a vast public meeting and being amazed at the way they listened, though he was not being oratorical or even brilliant. He spoke simply and from his heart. Often he rambled. The reason was that he was determined to educate and to explain, to make sure that his rule really depended on the agreement of the masses . . ."

"You know, that could be a description of Harry," Bill Glazier, Bridges's old friend and union associate, said when he was shown the obituary of Nehru. He had been talking about the matter of Bridges's leadership qualities and why the men had such faith in him. "He thinks like a worker," Glazier went on,

he has a great many of the attitudes and quirks of a working class person, the reserve about his personal life, the wariness, the distrust of middle class intellectuals that workers have.

And because he thinks like a worker, they respond to him. He instinctively understands what they're thinking, even when they can't articulate it very clearly. A middle–class person wouldn't get their point. But he does. And they can feel it. And then he's able to express what they're trying to say, what they want, in a way that they want it said.

So many of the guys who helped organize and build the union were pretty stern, pretty disciplined guys. Rigid, with no visible weaknesses or flaws in their personalities or characters. Harry was flexible, able to see the humor or the ridiculous in a situation, able to laugh at himself.

And the guys could see that he had weaknesses. That he loved to gamble, to play the horses. That he liked to drink. That he liked women. And the fact that he had the same weaknesses they had made them feel a little better about themselves.

Harry enjoys associating with wealthy people, too, you know. He was a sucker for the glamorous Hollywood crowd that lionized him at one time. But he won't permit himself to live like that. When he travels, he stays in an inexpensive hotel, usually one of those wretched commercial places. He actually isn't very sophisticated about some things. There's no place in his life for music or art. Not that he disparages it. He just doesn't know about it. He still has some of the Wobbly qualities, even if he's critical of their tactics.

Some of the points which Glazier made were reiterated by other people who had been involved with Bridges and the ILWU. When asked why Bridges had become the spokesman for Albion Hall, B. B. Jones, a former Communist who had been an Albion Hall member with Bridges in 1934 and 1935, said "It was because Harry had a way of putting forward our program in a way we weren't able to. We Communists formulated our program and our tactics from what we'd learned about the Russian Revolution and from the Communist International. And then Harry would—and I know it's strange to say this, considering he came from Australia—he'd Americanize the proposals and make them acceptable to the longshoremen."

Sam Darcy provided a story which underlined Glazier's statement about Bridges's fondness for women and high living. During the '34 strike, Darcy said he had arranged to meet Bridges one morning, and Bridges showed up late, looking bleary–eyed.

"Where the hell have you been?" Darcy demanded.

"You won't believe it, Sam," Bridges grinned, "but I was at a stag party last night. You should have seen those naked girls. And you won't believe some of the things they did . . ."

"For Chrissakes, Harry! Do you mean to say that at a time like this, you went to a stag party? Don't you realize what would have happened if that place'd been raided?

"And I'm not talking about you. I'm talking about the strike, and the movement. And I'm talking about all the people who are depending on you. You're the leader of the whole thing. You can't afford to take chances like that."

"Ah, hell, Sam, there wasn't any danger of that place being raided. They had the cops paid off."

"Yes, Harry. But do you suppose that would have meant anything if somebody'd found out you were there?"

"Well," a chastened Bridges conceded, "maybe you're right, Sam."

One quality Bridges shares with the Wobblies, as Glazier mentioned, is a fiercely-held independence of mind. One day Linc Fairley, the union's former research director, was late joining a group of friends for lunch.

"What held you up?" he was asked.

"I made the mistake of stopping by Harry's office when he had something on his mind."

"What was it?"

"He wanted to talk about the China-India border war."

"What's his position on it?"

"That's the trouble. He can't figure out what his position is."

As the Sixties wore on, events in China—the cultural revolution, the Red Guards, the chaos—increasingly intrigued Bridges. In 1967, he decided to try to go there to see for himself what was going on. "He's got a great sense of self-confidence," Glazier has said. "He's perfectly capable of telling Mao he's way off the beam if he thinks Mao's policies of attacking the rest of the Communist world aren't good for the working class of the world."

1967 seemed a good time to go. He was going to be in Australia —his first visit home—as a guest of the Australian longshoremen's union, and he could go from there to Hong Kong, then into China. Tomitaro Kaneda, president of the Japanese longshoremen's union and a friend of Bridges, was to make the arrangements with Chinese labor leaders. Before leaving for Australia, Bridges dropped in on an old acquaintance, Secretary of State Dean Rusk, whom he had known when Rusk was the liberal president of Mills College in Oakland. Rusk assured him the U. S. government wouldn't stand in his way if he could make arrangements to get to the mainland.

"The main purpose of the proposal to visit China," Bridges wrote in the *Dispatcher*, "was not so much to observe conditions in that country as to ask the Chinese labor movement . . . to accept a delegation of rank and file workers from our union to go and live and work in China for six months and thereafter bring back a report to the ILWU membership."

The trip didn't come off. At the last minute, the Cultural Revolution was in full swing and the Chinese cancelled the invitation, notifying Bridges that the time was not convenient, and that the Chinese labor movement was temporarily not functioning. "The Chinese Republic now seems to be the only country in the world," Bridges said ruefully, "where a delegation of our members cannot visit and observe for themselves what is going on."

The incident confirmed in Bridges's mind an opinion he had reached about China. "Harry's been obsessed with the China–Russia fight," one of his staff said while Bridges was waiting for word from China about getting in. "He's convinced that China's mistaken. That's why he wants to go there, so he can tell them they're wrong."

As the sixties moved along, it became apparent that for the first time in his life Bridges wasn't moving with the times. He had no sympathy for the student movement, nor apparently any understanding of it. While he sympathized with the civil rights movement, he remained on the edge of it. And while he spoke out early against the Vietnam War, he remained aloof from the peace movement, refusing to participate in the massive marches and demonstrations against the war.

On the union front, too, he seemed content to consolidate the gains made under the M & M contract. When Goldblatt and, later, Jack Hall, who in the latter 1960s left Hawaii and came to San Francisco as vice president for organizing, urged that the ILWU move aggressively into organizing California farm workers, Bridges held back. It was an especially bitter pill for Hall, who had given up an enviable life in Hawaii to come to the Coast to get the union off dead center. Bridges's unwillingness to support him put a severe strain on their relationship, and Bridges and Hall seemed headed for the same kind of unhealthy partnership Bridges had with Goldblatt when Hall suddenly died in January, 1971.

But a sure way to infuriate Bridges was to suggest that he had mellowed, that he had given up his radicalism. "Look, some people talk about me getting more mellow, whatever the hell that means," he barked at Harry Bernstein, a *Los Angeles Times* columnist. "I don't think it is sound to say that I'm getting mellow. They mistake finding more effective ways of doing things for mellowness."

"Would you call a strike to protest what we're doing in Vietnam?" Bernstein asked.

"Sure I would, in a minute," Bridges snapped. Then he thought a moment. "I couldn't, though, even if I wanted to. My rank and file wouldn't let me."

To some of Bridges's critics, his reply seemed hypocritical. "If he really believes what we are doing in Vietnam is wrong," Bernstein quotes one as saying, "why doesn't he take a chance for a change and call a strike to block shipments of war materiel? If he gets tossed out of his job by his membership as a result, that's tough. He can't have it both ways. He's a fake radical."

If Bridges had gone in for quixotic gestures like that, he would never have lasted as a labor leader. After the eleven unions were expelled from the CIO, all of their top officers, with the exception of Bridges and Goldblatt of the ILWU, and Albert Fitzgerald and James Matles of UE, had sunk, together with their unions, into oblivion. Bridges had survived because, along with delivering the goods at contract time, he never got too far out ahead of his members on political issues. And with the new people in the union who had been attracted to longshoring by the enviable working conditions on the docks, getting ahead of the members was easy to do.

At the 1965 convention, for example, Bridges postponed action to the last on a resolution condemning the Viet Nam war, knowing the delegates were divided on it. "The guys don't favor war, you understand, but most of them figure you've got to support our country in this thing, even if we're wrong," he told Bernstein. Before the resolutions committee discussed the Viet Nam proposal, they heard Ernest Gruening, the respected senator from Alaska, address the convention with an eloquent speech against the war. Even so, the committee was almost equally divided, with the younger delegates supporting the war.

"We have to support the President, even if we think he's wrong," one kept repeating.

"Suppose we were on strike," an old–timer asked, "and the President says we should go back to work. Would you say we should go back just because the President says we should?"

"Well, no . . . But that's different!"

The committee voted, by a slim majority, for the resolution condemning the war. The convention itself voted for it overwhelmingly, thereby confounding economic determinists who preach that a union will support a war because it provides jobs. Some unions do, no doubt, but the longshoremen, working full–time at premium pay because they were handling military cargoes to Indochina, took the lead among U. S. unions in condemning the war. The resolution which, alas, was equally appropriate in 1972, was years ahead of its time in 1965:

> . . . We say, let the Vietnamese people decide. They have suffered war and foreign intervention too long already; first from France and now the U. S. Let them have the supervised free elections which they were promised by the Geneva Agreement of 1954 which ended their war with France. Those elections were prevented by the corrupt Diem regime which we supported.
> The Geneva Agreement promised freedom from foreign arms and interference. There would be no war today if the agreement had been lived up to. Our government violated it for years, calling our troops "advisors."
> "United States policy now follows the incredible path of "negotiation through escalation." This terrifying concept is but one step removed from escalation to a world holocaust!
> . . . we propose:
> 1. Cease fire.
> 2. Withdrawal of all foreign troops.
> 3. Negotiate.
> 4. Settlement and peace.

"You know," one of Bridges's friends said to this author one day, "when you write your book you should point out Harry's really had two lives. The first one was when he was a radical. That would be, say, from '33 to the fifties. The second was after he became a labor statesman. That would be from the middle 1950s on, especially after M & M."

The point was well taken. Once M & M was "coopered down", as Bridges liked to put it, he had more time on his hands than he'd had in years. He used some of it to ingratiate himself with City Hall and became a warm supporter of San Francisco Mayor Joseph Alioto (and, through him, of Hubert Humphrey), who rewarded Bridges's support with a variety of cushy jobs for ILWU members and friends. In 1970, Alioto bemused San Franciscans by appointing Bridges himself to the prestigious board that ran the port. The

Chronicle expressed the city's ambivalent reaction in an editorial on June 4, 1970:

Harry Bridges has been duly appointed to the San Francisco Port Authority and nobody has cried out that a fox is in charge of the henhouse.

This is remarkable, inasmuch as Harry Bridges is, or was, a flaming agitator, a red–hot radical, an activist labor leader who waged many a war against the very port he is now to preside over, and closed it down repeatedly with stoppages, dockside union meetings, and outright strikes, including one that escalated into a general strike and closed the entire town down. This is the Harry Bridges that the Federal Government tried on four occasions to deport as a member of the Communist Party, but couldn't make it stick.

Whether the appointee is the same Harry Bridges of the labor wars seems open to dispute. He says he is and refers to his demands of those days as "a few lousy parlor pink suggestions that damn near got me thrown out of the country." Some of his ILWU members think he has mellowed or worse. Politically, he has indisputably changed, having registered first as a Democrat, then as an Independent Progressive, and later as a Republican. The last shift, occurring in 1956, inspired Richard Nixon, the incumbent Vice President, to warn his party about "trojan horses" in its midst.

If Bridges is indeed immutable, his waterfront is not. Waterfront employers, once his mortal enemies, now regard his ILWU, which hasn't struck since 1948, as one of the more stabilizing elements of the Pacific maritime industry. It embraced rather than fought mechanization and acquired one of the coziest working agreements extant, including unprecedented bonuses and fringe benefits and pensions.

It is possible to say that Port Authority appointment clinches and affirms Harry Bridges's romance with The Establishment, but it would not be prudent to do so in his presence.

When Bridges didn't step down in 1969, it seemed almost certain that he would in 1971, and then, most people assumed, Louis Goldblatt, the union's brilliant and long–suffering secretary–treasurer, could take over. Then, they figured, the union would regain the militancy and the forward momentum it had lost in the 1960s.

But when the 1971 convention opened, it was apparent that

Bridges was not only not going to step down, he was going to do everything he could to prevent Goldblatt becoming president. The first clue, if one were needed, was the presence, in the front row, of Teddy Gleason, president of the ILA, with his entire executive board, looking stiff and out of place in their silk suits against the background of the ILWU delegates in their flowered Hawaiian shirts and their easy–going manner.

The appearance of the ILA officials, it soom came out, was a trial balloon for a proposal to merge the two unions. Bridges, in his introduction of the ILA delegation, and Gleason, in his response, talked about the desirability of a merger, but the delegates' response was icy, and the proposal never got off the ground. If it had, it would have been an incongruous marriage.

On the one side would have been the ILWU, with its tradition of a progressive leadership and its aware, articulate membership that participated democratically to the utmost in union operations. It was a union that had consistently provided leaders, money and marchers in peace and civil rights demonstrations, and had been an outspoken opponent of the Vietnam War and U. S. foreign policy from Presidents Truman to Nixon.

On the other would have been the ILA, with its long–standing record of corruption and lack of democracy, whose members, cheered on by Teddy Gleason, had bloodily assaulted peace marchers in New York City in the late 1960s. And no labor leader, not even George Meany, the hawkish president of the AFL–CIO, had been more vocal than Gleason in support of the Vietnam policies of Presidents Lyndon Johnson and Richard Nixon.

For all their differences, Bridges and Gleason, both of whom off the convention floor argued strongly for the merger, gave the same reason for supporting it: that it would strengthen the two unions in the contract negotiations that were looming ahead a few months after the convention.

Gleason's desire for the merger was clear enough. His union, with its 115,000 members, was twice the size of the 65,000–member ILWU, and, the ILWU would be coming home to the ILA and the AFL–CIO, as Gleason put it.

But why would Bridges want to submerge the union he helped found and helped make into a unique and important instrument for social, economic, and political justice? His own answer, that he had no choice, that the ILWU could no longer stand alone, failed to persuade the delegates. Another explanation, put forward by some of the delegates in private conversations, was that Bridges could not bear the thought of the ILWU continuing to live on, after he left office, as the fiercely independent union it had been under him. When I go, his actions seemed to be saying, the union I built goes under with me.

Bridges made it painfully apparent, moreover, that he did not want Louis Goldblatt to succeed him as president of the ILWU. If there were any doubts about that, they were dispelled when Bridges put forward a constitutional amendment that would deny union office after 1973 to anyone over sixty. "You guys are always talking about the generation gap," he said as he asked the convention to adopt the amendment, "so I'm trying to do something about it."

The remark was transparently disingenuous, for everyone knew it was aimed at Goldblatt, who would be sixty-one two months after the convention ended. During the debate, Bridges made his amendment's purpose even more clear when he declared the union should always be led by a longshoreman, for, he said, it was the economically strategic power of the ILWU's 14,000 longshoremen that gave the union its muscle.

If the merger with the ILA had gone through, the ILWU would once again have become merely a division of the ILA under Gleason who, whatever else he might be, was at least not a left-wing intellectual and a warehouseman, two of Goldblatt's qualities that seemingly disqualified him in Bridges's eyes.

The delegates, led by the warehouse division and the Hawaii contingent, overwhelmingly rejected the ILA merger and voted down the stop–Goldblatt amendment. Several months after the convention, Bridges went to Washington to talk about a merger with another conservative labor leader, Frank Fitzimmons of the Teamsters. If the ILA caper had seemed ideologically bizarre, this one was no less so.

The two–million–member teamsters' union had always been run from the top down, and had a record of corruption much like that of the ILA. Fitzimmons, moreover, was an ardent supporter of President Nixon's inflation and unemployment policies, which the rest of the labor movement was vociferously against, as well as of Nixon's Vietnam policy. Like Gleason before him, Fitzimmons welcomed a merger, notifying Bridges by letter that—unlike the ILWU, which could not merge unless a majority of the rank and file voted to do so in a unionwide referendum—the teamsters' executive board had full authority to accept the ILWU as an affiliate. (As of the time this was written (1972), action on a merger with the teamsters' union seemed at least a year off, and it seemed possible that at the 1973 convention the front row might be occupied, then, by Fitzimmons and his executive board in their silk suits.)

The convention over, Bridges began making preparations for the strike that now seemed unavoidable when the contract expired on June 30th. For one thing, the M & M agreement had become increasingly unpopular among the rank and file. Many of the older men, who benefitted so well from its retirement provisions, were now out of the industry, and the younger men were determined to get rid of M & M in favor of immediate increases in their paychecks.

For another, there was sentiment among the ranks that in the ten years of M & M, the union had been too cooperative with the employers, that it had done less than it could to protect them against loss of jobs due to the use of containers, and that it had allowed working conditions to deteriorate more than was necessary. Much of the blame, many felt, belonged on Bridges's shoulders for allowing his friendship with Paul St. Sure to blunt his old militancy as a negotiator and as a contract enforcer.

Bridges's reaction to these criticisms was to counterattack. For the first time, he was being assaulted from the Left within the union, and as the time to negotiate the new contract neared, he used his column in the *Dispatcher* to warn the membership against his critics, calling them "super–militants" and "hot shot radicals" who were advocating impossible demands to provoke an unnecessary strike.

Nevertheless, when the demands of the union were announced, M & M was abandoned. The union asked, instead, for a wage increase of $1.60 spread over two years; a forty–hour–a–week wage guarantee for A–men, with a thirty–two hour guarantee, for B–men; improvements in pensions and medical care; and protection against loss of work because of containers.

The restlessness of the rank and file put the employers in a position they hadn't been in for twenty years. "They couldn't put their best offer on the table at the start and avoid a strike the way they'd been able to in the past, because Harry couldn't persuade the membership to accept it," a dockworker explained. "The employers knew Harry didn't want a strike any more than they did, but it had to happen so their offer could unravel."

West Coast ports were shut down on July 1, 1971 after 96 per cent of the longshoremen voted to strike. From the outset, it was apparent that the strike was going to be a long one. The longshoremen had put aside savings to carry them through the strike, West

Coast merchants, in many cases, declared a moratorium on their debt payments and, as the strike progressed, the strikers supplemented their dwindling savings with food stamps.

Unlike previous strikes on the West Coast, there was a total absence of red–baiting, or even employer charges of union irresponsibility. For the first few days, the police were out in force, but when they saw how orderly it all was, they were reassigned to their regular duties. It reminded this author of a drive he took around the waterfront one day in the mid–sixties with a longshore business agent. The only convenient parking place was in front of a fire hydrant. Having been reading about the '34 strike, the author's mind was reeling with mental images of tear gas, police charges on picket lines and the Battle of Rincon Hill, and he said to the b.a., who was driving, "You're not going to park here, are you?"

"Why not?"

"That fire hydrant, there. Won't the cops give you a ticket?"

"Give me a ticket?" he retorted, as if the idea were outlandish. "Hell, no. The cops all know my car. They wouldn't give me a ticket."

It was also apparent that, so far as the union was concerned, not much progress toward a settlement was going to be made until September 30th, when East Coast longshoremen were expected to go on strike for their new contract. "How will it help us if they go out with us, Harry?" Bridges was asked from time to time by his members. "Won't a national strike bring the government down on us with a Taft–Hartley injunction? Maybe even special legislation barring longshore strikes altogether?"

Bridges's answers were vague, as if he either had an explanation he didn't want to talk about, or he didn't quite know for sure himself. "As long as I've been around Harry," a staff member mused after the strike, "I could never tell whether he was confused himself or whether he was confusing the others deliberately." The rank and file, however, had the old faith. "Sure, I don't understand Harry's thinking on this one," was a typical reaction on the picket line, "but look at how many times in the past we thought he was off the beam, and he turned out to be right all along."

Bridges had good reasons to think the government would not interfere with the strike, even if East Coast longshoremen joined the West Coast by striking after September 30th. The Labor Department had recently published a study of three longshore strikes that had been enjoined for eighty days under the Taft–Hartley Act. The study concluded that in each case, there actually hadn't been an emergency. Estimates of losses caused by the strikes had been grossly exaggerated, the Department concluded, and the government, when it obtained the injunctions, had acted unnecessarily. President Nixon had said repeatedly, moreover, that his administration intended to maintain a hands–off policy toward the economy, and that, presumably, included collective bargaining and strikes.

It was reasonable to assume, also, that the government would stay out of an East Coast strike, for three reasons: A strike there was so expected that shippers had stockpiled to beat the deadline, and it would be months before serious shortages would show up. Second, an East Coast dock strike would help the U. S. auto industry by keeping auto imports out of the American market. That, Washington was thinking, could make the auto industry the pump primer of economic recovery. Furthermore, the government was handling the ILA with delicacy, for fear the union, if provoked, would balk at loading grain shipments to Russia, which the Nixon administration had just negotiated as part of a detente with the Soviets.

Then, in August, 1971, when the West Coast strike was in its sixth week, the President did an about–face, announcing that the monetary measures he'd been relying on to stop inflation hadn't worked, and he was freezing wage and price increases. He let the strike go on, nevertheless, until October 6th, its one hundredth day, when he obtained an eighty–day injunction.

As in 1948, while the injunction got the men back to work, it failed to inspire the union and the employers to do any bargaining. As a result, when the longshoremen voted on December 14th and 15th on the employers' last offer, they were voting on an offer their negotiating committee had rejected in October: a 72¢ increase in the first year, from $4.28 to $5.00; an additional 40¢ twelve months after the contract was ratified; an increase in pension benefits; wage guarantees of thirty–six hours a week for A men, eighteen for B men; protection against loss of work because of containers; and improvements in family benefits under the dental plan.

The longshoremen, voting in NLRB balloting places in twenty–four ports, rejected the offer by a vote of 10,072 against, 746 in favor. Bridges gave his interpretation of the vote in a column headed, "What Next?" in the December 22nd *Dispatcher*, just three days before the injunction was to be lifted and the longshoremen would be free to strike again.

Was it a strike vote? Will it soften up the employers enough to offer us a contract we can accept? Not in my opinion.

Then let's get down to the nitty gritty and say what we should do.

We get together with the East and Gulf longshoremen and their union, the ILA, that's what. And when I say get together, as I have been urging for a long time, and I am asked do I mean affiliating our union with the ILA, therefore the AFL–CIO? I answer, "Hell, yes, if doing so means we secure our container jurisdiction and win this battle." And I know damn well that without the ILA threat we can forget getting more on containers than we have now, plus doing a job for Hawaii [where a new longshore contract was being negotiated]. And, finally, there is the matter of getting a contract approved by the Wage/Price Boards [which had put a ceiling of 5.5 per cent on negotiated wage increases]. Standing by ourselves, it's doubtful whether we could even have got an okay on the last offer contract.

If I am anywhere near right about the need for East Coast ties, then it's time for the rank and file, at least the longshore part of it, to take on those elements in our union who are always blasting away at the ILA, its leadership and policies, or at the AFL–CIO and its head, George Meany.

. . . So, to sum up: If we can have a few meetings with the PMA and talk them out of a good contract, fine. If that fails, the sooner we reach a firm understanding to get going all the way with the ILA the better. And such a program definitely does not leave out merger by any means.

To give himself time to go to New York to sound out the ILA again, Bridges postponed a resumption of the strike to mid–January, but on January 6th, Gleason torpedoed Bridges's hope that both coasts would be shut down together when he recommended to his ILA members that they accept the East Coast employers' offer for a new contract.

West Coast longshoremen were back on the picket lines on January 17th, mainly because they and the employers couldn't agree on how to protect the jobs being lost because of containers, or on how the employers should finance the work guarantees. This time, President Nixon reacted quickly. Calling the strike irresponsible, he asked Congress to enact a resolution that would end the strike immediately. Under it, the Secretary of Labor would appoint a three–member arbitration board that would hand down a decision within

forty days from the day Congress adopted the resolution. The resolution would also prohibit a strike for eighteen months after that.
President Nixon sent the message to Congress on Friday, January
21th, ending it with an appeal: "I earnestly implore the Congress to
have this resolution on my desk by the end of next week."

The Democratic–controlled Senate and House Labor Committees were in no hurry to act, knowing that the AFL–CIO and most
of the business community were solidly against compulsory arbitration, and that Nixon's proposal would be a precedent for other key
industries. The danger that Nixon's proposal would pass was real,
nevertheless, so early in February the union and the employers
went back to the bargaining table. This time they asked Sam Kagel
to sit in as a mediator, hoping that with his help they could reach
an agreement and head off the threatened government intervention.

A few days later they had succeeded, but the momentum behind
the President's request for emergency powers was such that the day
after the new contract was agreed upon, Congress passed the compulsory arbitration resolution. By the time it was ready for the
President's signature, Nixon was in Peking, where he signed it, as
he said, "as a symbolic gesture," in case the longshore agreement
broke down.

The contract, which ran for two years, provided for a pay increase of 72¢ an hour the first year, retroactive to December 25,
1971, and 40¢ an hour more on July 1, 1972. The employers agreed
to pay a $1.00 per ton royalty on any container loaded or unloaded
within a fifty–mile radius of a West Coast port. The money would
go into the fund from which the employers would pay the wage
guarantees of $180 a week to A–men and $90 to B–men. Pensions
were up from $235 to $350 a month, prescription drug coverage
was added, with a longshoreman paying only one dollar a prescription, and the prepaid dental care program for longshoremen and
their families was liberalized.

It was essentially the same contract the union had turned down
in October, 1971, and again in December as the employers' last
offer, but it was a good contract nonetheless. A longshoreman, an
A–man without any special skill (like those of a winch driver or a
crane operator) would have job security for life, a good pension
waiting for him at retirement, virtually complete prepaid medical
and dental care for himself and his family. And with the new wage
rate, if he worked fairly regularly, he would be making almost

$12,000 a year. That's not bad, considering he had qualified for the job without even a high school diploma.

There was one catch before this could become a reality. That was that the new wage had to be approved by the Pay Board. In the first year alone, with the fringe benefits added to the wage increase, it came to 25.9 per cent, almost five times the board's limit of 5.5 per cent. It was a crucial test for the board, already under fire for having made exceptions in several major settlements, and some of the board's business and public members immediately announced that they were going to vote to cut back the increase.

The board had to reckon, on the other side, with a rare display of militancy and solidarity the case stirred up on labor circles. Bridges led off with a threat that he would lead the longshoremen back out on strike "if the Pay Board cuts back our negotia ed increase by as much as 1¢." Next, full–page ads, paid for by the ILWU, the UAW, the Teamsters and, surprisingly, in view of the ideological gulf separating Bridges from Meany, by the AFL–CIO, in whose Washington offices the ad was prepared, appeared in major newspapers under the heading: "The Pacific Coast Longshore Agreement Deserves Approval by the U. S. Pay Board."

The ads claimed that productivity in West Coast ports had gone up 138 per cent from 1961 to 1971, that labor cost per ton of cargo handled had dropped 30 per cent, that by opening up new markets (for the lumber industry, for example, which was enabled to export logs and wood chips to Europe and the Far East) and expanding others (for farmers and producers of low–cost materials such as chemicals, coal, iron ore, potash, and coke), "the benefits of this rising efficiency streamed back into cities and towns all across America."

Two days later, the staff of the Pay Board made public a report it submitted to the board members. Productivity in West Coast longshoring had indeed, the report showed, gone up almost 140 per cent, while in the economy as a whole productivity had risen only 30 per cent. As a result, the report estimated, West Coast longshore employers saved $900 million in labor costs while they paid out $62 million in M & M benefits. "There are sufficient grounds," the staff suggested, "to consider an exception to the Board's 5.5 per cent ceiling."

On March 17th, the board voted eight to five to cut the wage increase and fringe benefit from 25.9 to 14.9 per cent. The five labor members, who voted as a bloc against the cut, calculated the wage cut would take $1,150 out of each longshoreman's paycheck over the next eighteen months and hand it over to the employers. "That," they concluded, "will be a windfall profit of $17 million for the employers."

The decision put Bridges in a difficult position. After 135 days on strike, not many longshoremen wanted to go out again. He had, however, threatened a strike if the board cut a penny off the increase, and the staff report's estimate of the $900 million saving for the employers, while the workers got $62 million, was powerful ammunition for his critics in the union who were accusing him of having lost his touch as a negotiator. The AFL–CIO, moreover, saw him as carrying the ball for all labor against the Pay Board's ceiling, and appeared ready to give him massive support if he called a strike. "And with that kind of backing," the press speculated, "the old warrior might just decide to go out in a blaze of glory."

In the end, Bridges backed down, and the only walkout in protest against the cut was by four labor members of the Pay Board, who, led by Meany, quit the board, leaving only Fitzimmons of the teamsters, who stayed behind, to help his President.

"In the old days, Harry'd never have let 'em call his bluff like that," one of his close associates said. "He never said he'd strike unless he knew the men were behind him. The employers and Uncle Sam knew he meant it, too."

The Harry of the old days surfaced again in June, 1972, when he helped sponsor a meeting in St. Louis, where 985 union officers and members met for two days to show by their presence and by the organization they were founding, Labor for Peace, that even if George Meany and the AFL–CIO supported the war in Vietnam, a large segment of U. S. unions and their members did not.

A teachers' delegate, carried away by the ambience of the gathering, made a motion that would have committed the new organization to a one–day strike against the war and wage controls. A show of hands revealed substantial support for the idea, until Bridges brought the meeting back to reality by reminding it that you don't win strikes unless you have the rank and file with you. "Before we call a strike," he admonished, "we'd better go back to our unions and see if we can sell our own membership on it. No body like this is going to tell our members to have a work stoppage."

"One found oneself wondering," Steve Murdock, a former San Francisco newspaper man, mused in the *Nation*, "as the distinctive voice of Harry Bridges . . . reached out through the . . . sophisticated amplifying system, how many of those present had ever heard him speak. The labor generation of the thirties, the forties and even the fifties is full of people who have heard Bridges speak. But not so many heard him in the sixties, and for the seventies it was a historic moment."

Looking back over the whole of Bridges's life he could, if it were not considered bad form to pass judgment on a man's place in U. S. labor history while he's still very much alive, be ranked with the labor giants: Eugene Debs, Big Bill Haywood, John L. Lewis, even, incongruous as it might at first seem, Sam Gompers.

But that judgment will probably have to be made by future historians who have the perspective of history at their command. It surely is not premature, however, to say that because of his leadership, West Coast longshoremen are better off economically than dockworkers anywhere in the world. Their union, moreover, is one few others can rival for internal democracy and for a sense of the role a union can play in the wider struggle for social justice.

Because it is that kind of union, the multi–racial underclass of waterfront and field workers in Hawaii turned to it, with the result that Hawaii was transformed from a semi–feudal plantation society into the most progressive state in the nation.

Nor would it be premature, even though Bridges is alive, and even though, as Gladstein said in the late 1960s, "the government has never given up on Harry," to pass judgment on his place in the history of civil liberties in this country. Surely Carol King was right when she placed him with the Scottsboro Boys, Sacco and Vanzetti, Mooney and Billings.

Yet there are two differences between them and Bridges. One is, of course, that he won. The other is that the Bridges case is not like any other in our history. Never before has our government hounded one man over so many years, putting him on trial again and again and again for the same "offense." And it is doubtful if any other one man's jousts with the government have done more than Bridges's to broaden and to strengthen the Constitutional rights of immigrants, political dissenters and racial minorities.

"I worry about how you'll wind up your book," an admirer of Bridges said in 1972. "You can't have Harry deteriorating at the end, presiding over a divided union or taking it into the ILA or the Teamsters, with a lot of our members giving mostly lip service to his earlier ideals."

But, that is not necessarily a problem. Bridges's accomplishments as a labor leader are not diminished because the affluence he gained for his members made some of them think and act like petty bourgeoisie. Nor should his record be marred because he stayed on in office longer, perhaps, than he should. Nor should it, when looked at it in historical perspective, be seriously flawed because he reached the verge of leaving office without preparing for an orderly succession.

His life remains what it is, with the flaws and frailties to which we are all vulnerable, still an ennobling example for generations to come. For he is a man who fought back against forces which, time after time, seemed overwhelming: the awesome power of a government determined to crush him; the employers and their allies bent on breaking him; the official labor movement, which tried to silence him by putting him beyond the pale; even, at times, his own members.

Fighting back against them all took its toll. Early in his life it took part of his stomach and gave him an ulcer, weakening his resistance to alcohol so much it took only a few beers to get the better of him. "I wonder how often Harry's gotten into trouble," one of his friends said in the Sixties, "because he shot off his mouth to a reporter after he had a few beers at Harrington's?" And after he moved into his sixties, his emphysema got so bad he had to take a Seventh Day Adventist cure to stop his chain smoking.

As he moved into his seventies, nevertheless, he kept on fighting back. And until the years have passed and some future historian looks over the record from the vantage point of history, who can say he wasn't still winning?

NOTES

For my description of the 1971 convention and the strike, in addition to union members, I am much indebted to Dick Meister, who loaned me transcripts of reports he did on the convention for radio stations KPFA and KQED, where he is labor editor; and Harry Bernstein, who covered the convention for his syndicated articles which originate in the *Los Angeles Times*.

My conversation with Bill Glazier was in New York in 1968, after he had left the ILWU. My conversation with B. B. Jones was in Mill Valley, California, in 1967.

The 1965 Vietnam War resolution is in the Proceedings of the union's sixteenth convention, held in Vancouver, Canada.

Index